D1569789

AMERICAN WRITERS AND THE APPROACH OF WORLD WAR II, 1935–1941

Ichiro Takayoshi's *American Writers and the Approach of World War II, 1935–1941: A Literary History* argues that the approach of World War II transformed American literary culture. From the mid-1930s to America's entry into World War II in 1941, preeminent writers and intellectuals responded to the turn of the public's attention from the economic depression at home to the menace of dictatorships abroad by producing novels, short stories, plays, poems, and cultural criticism in which they prophesied the coming of a second world war and explored how America could prepare for it. Their competing answers left a rich legacy of idioms, symbols, and standard arguments that were destined to license America's promotion of its values and interests around the world for the rest of the twentieth century. Ambitious in scope and addressing an enormous range of writers, thinkers, and artists, this book is the first to establish the outlines of American letters during this pivotal period.

ICHIRO TAKAYOSHI is Associate Professor of English at Tufts University. His articles on modern U.S. literature have appeared in academic journals such as *Post45* and *Representations*. Takayoshi has also translated into Japanese the works of Don DeLillo, David Mitchell, and Richard Powers.

AMERICAN WRITERS AND THE APPROACH OF WORLD WAR II, 1935–1941

A Literary History

ICHIRO TAKAYOSHI

Tufts University

CAMBRIDGE
UNIVERSITY PRESS

CAMBRIDGE
UNIVERSITY PRESS

32 Avenue of the Americas, New York, NY 10013-2473, USA

Cambridge University Press is part of the University of Cambridge.

It furthers the University's mission by disseminating knowledge in the pursuit of
education, learning, and research at the highest international levels of excellence.

www.cambridge.org
Information on this title: www.cambridge.org/9781107085268

© Ichiro Takayoshi 2015

First published 2015

Printed in Great Britain by Clays Ltd, St Ives plc

A catalog record for this publication is available from the British Library.

Library of Congress Cataloging in Publication Data
Takayoshi, Ichiro.
American writers and the approach of World War II, 1930-1941 : a literary
history / Ichiro Takayoshi, Tufts University.
pages   cm
Includes bibliographical references.
ISBN 978-1-107-08526-8 (Hardback)
1. World War, 1939-1945–United States–Literature and the war.   2. Authors, American–20th
century–Political and social views.   3. American literature–20th century–History and criticism.
4. War in literature.   I. Title.
PN56.W3T34 2015
809'.93358–dc23   2014035120

ISBN 978-1-107-08526-8 Hardback

Contents

Only the prophecies are true. The present is an opportunity to repent.

Wallace Stevens, "The Noble Rider and the Sound of Words" (1941)

Acknowledgments

I owe very warm thanks to people and institutions that helped me during the many years that went into this book. This work began as a dissertation at Columbia University, so I start with my dissertation committee members. To Rachel Adams, I am indebted for timely advice and infectious enthusiasm. To Bruce Robbins, I am grateful for many tough questions and good humor. I had the fortune to receive from Anders Stephanson expert guidance across the literatures on U.S. foreign policy. Alan Henrikson similarly schooled me in the art of diplomatic history. I incurred my heaviest intellectual debt to Ann Douglas, the chair of the committee. My efforts to emulate her perception, imagination, and methodological versatility eventually led me to the historical problem explored in this book. Anyone familiar with her scholarship will plainly see her influences in the following pages. These scholars' generosity with time and advice and their unswerving trust in the promise of my work were nothing short of astounding. I stand humbled and inspired. I hope that whatever flaws remain in this book will not screen from their view a great deal of learning they imparted to me.

A wider intellectual community in the Department of English and Comparative Literature at Columbia also extended to me the benefits of friendship and support. I thank the department and the Graduate School of Arts and Sciences for funding my research with various fellowships: the Nicholson Fellowship, the Graduate School of Arts and Sciences Summer Fellowships, and the Dissertation Fellowship. My research significantly benefited from valuable conversations I have had with Casey Blake, Amanda Claybaugh, David Damrosch, Andrew Delbanco, Carol Gluck, and Ezra Tawil.

Gregory Baggett, Benjamin Carp, Radiclani Clytus, Peter Conn, David Ekbladh, Gordon Hutner, David Palumbo-Liu, Casey Shoop, and Richard Jean So read chapters in their various iterations. I acknowledge with deep gratitude their advice and encouragement. I also had the opportunity to present earlier versions of several chapters at conferences: the annual meeting of the American Studies Association in 2006; the annual meetings of the Modern Language Association in 2006 and 2012; and the annual meeting of the American Political Science Association in 2010. My work greatly profited from thoughtful comments and keen questions from the audiences. Cambridge University Press secured two outside reports that can be the envy of any scholar seeking feedback: detailed and productive criticisms informed by a sympathetic understanding of the author's intentions.

Portions of Chapter 3 first appeared in *Representations* 116 (2011) as the article "The Wages of War: Liberal Gullibility, Soviet Intervention, and the End of the Popular Front." I thank University of California Press for permission to reprint it.

I owe a special debt to Tufts University, where I wrote much of this book. My colleagues, former and present, inside and outside the English Department – Linda Bamber, Drusilla Brown, Jay Cantor, Ryan Centner, Kevin Dunn, Lee Edelman, Carol Flynn, John Fyler, Jim Glaser, Judith Haber, Andrea Haslanger, Hosea Hirata, Sonia Hofkosh, Charles Inouye, Virginia Jackson, Joseph Litvak, John Lurz, Kris Manjapra, Malik Mufti, Jeanne Penvenne, Katie Peterson, Lecia Rosenthal, Jonathan Strong, Vickie Sullivan, Jonathan Wilson, and Nathan Wolff, among others – have immersed me in an atmosphere of utmost geniality and intellectual seriousness. My students also improved this work. I have marveled at the intelligence and passion of the many seniors and juniors who took my capstone seminar "War and American Values" since my arrival at Tufts in 2008. Our discussions of many of the issues covered in this book refreshed my thinking and helped me sharpen my language. I am also deeply obliged for the Neubauer Family Fellowship that covered a large portion of my research funds, and for the Junior Faculty Research Leave, which generously gave me much needed time to expand my research.

Like any historian, I am a grateful beneficiary of many able librarians and archivists. I am particularly thankful for the professionalism of staffs at the Manuscript Division at the Library of Congress; the National Archives in College Park, the Wisconsin Historical Society, the Beineke Library at Yale University, the Randolph-Macon College Library, the John F. Kennedy Library and Museum, the Franklin D. Roosevelt Library and Museum, Houghton Library, Littaur Library, and Pusey Library at Harvard University, Firestone Library and Mudd Library at Princeton University, the Rare Book and Manuscript Library at the University of Pennsylvania, Burke Library at Union Theological Seminary, and the Special Collections Research Center at the University of Chicago.

Throughout, Ray Ryan, my editor at Cambridge University Press, has amazed me with his focus, speed, and steadfastness. His work on this book, as well as our happy relationship, has meant a great deal to me.

This book is dedicated to my parents, Yasuo and Hiroko Takayoshi, for teaching me the importance of learning. Without the appreciation of the life of the mind that they instilled in me, I would not have chosen this vocation. This is also for my wife, Kathryn Takayoshi, the rock of my life.

Fun to Be Free

It was October 5, 1941. Madison Square Garden in New York City. The Fight for Freedom Committee staged a patriotic extravaganza, "Fun To Be Free." An intense publicity blitz preceded the event. The show would feature an all-star $150,000-a-week cast, ballyhooed the Committee's Stage, Screen, Radio and Arts Division, headed by Helen Hayes and Burgess Meredith. The tickets had been selling briskly. On the first night of the show, a capacity crowd of 17,000 packed the arena.

The action opened with a concert, with several soloists taking turns singing Irving Berlin's new song "Arms for the Love of America":

> On land and on the sea and in the air
> We've gotta be there, we've gotta be there
> America is sounding her alarm
> We've gotta have arms, we've gotta have arms

The main event of the "Fun To Be Free" night followed – a pageant written by Ben Hecht and Charles MacArthur with Kurt Veill's music. The narrator, played in turn by Tallulah Bankhead, Burgess Meredith, and Claude Rains, challenged the audience with a question: "What is America? What is the USA?" To answer these queries, a phalanx of American patriots, from Patrick Henry, Thomas Jefferson, Benjamin Franklin, George Washington, Andrew Jackson to Abraham Lincoln, was summoned from the nation's hallowed past onto the stage. Reflecting their historical circumstances, their definitions of the national genius differed. Yet the libretto also made it crystal-clear that all these heroes spoke directly to the latest emergency confronting the country: the approach of World War II. After Lincoln denounced Vallandigham and Copperheads, a thinly veiled stand-in for the latter-day isolationists, the narrator announced to the audience that Lincoln had been recently reincarnated – in the person of Franklin D. Roosevelt. On cue, the speech that Roosevelt delivered a few weeks prior blared from the loudspeakers. What the audience heard was a stark reminder of the impending crisis.

Dubbed the "shoot-on-sight" speech by the press, this radio address called for an undeclared war on Germany in the Atlantic. Roosevelt's call was supported by four arguments that must have been familiar to most of the audience in Madison Square Garden. First was the charge of conspiratorial designs for world domination. A series of recent attacks on U.S. vessels by German submarines, Roosevelt's sonorous voice explained, formed "part of a general plan." Those attacks constituted "one determined step toward creating a permanent world system based on force, on terror, and on murder." Second was the military vulnerability of the Western Hemisphere. The Germans had recently attempted to subvert the governments of Uruguay and Bolivia. Secret landing fields had just been discovered in Colombia, "within easy range of the Panama Canal." Third, the United States was taking a defensive, not offensive, action against aggressor nations. The Navy would not hesitate to shoot on sight to control "any waters which America deems vital to its defense." "The aggression is not ours," Roosevelt reassured the audience, "Ours is solely defense." And finally, Roosevelt criminalized war. The torpedo attacks on U.S. convoys were acts of "piracy" and "international lawlessness." The Germans were "international outlaws," an "enemy of all law, all liberty, all morality, all religion."[1] Someone – presumably the United States – must enforce the law of civilization globally.

Agitated voices reading a news flash then interrupted Roosevelt. The audience must have instantly recognized these urgent voices belonging to Raymond Gram Swing, H. V. Kaltenborn, and Elmer Davis, all famous anti-Nazi radio commentators. Reports were coming from south, east, and west, they told the audience. Enemy planes were sighted over Laredo, Texas, bomber formations from Dakar were flying over the Atlantic toward New England, the sky over the Pacific darkened with Japanese bombers heading for San Francisco and Los Angeles, and finally, just outside Madison Square Garden, an armada of German planes was swarming the sky over Manhattan and dropping paratroopers. All the lights went out thereupon. From the loudspeakers blasted sirens, the roar of diving bombers, and explosions. Myriad white crisscrossing shafts of searchlight began sweeping the balconies and the ceiling. And the audience gawked at thousands of Aryan and Asiatic paratroopers descending from the sky – until they discovered that the parachutes were made of cardboard, only five-inch tall.

The finale was a variety show featuring Eddie Cantor, Jack Benny, Ella Logan, Ethel Merman, Bill Robinson, and the Lindy Hoppers. It opened with a column of Nazi soldiers, clad in brown shirts and sporting steel helmets, meandering through the audience, with Hitler's coffin on their shoulders. When the funeral procession reached the stage, Robinson, aged sixty-three and in his usual regalia of an ermine coat and gold pants, leaped on the coffin, shuffled a few gingerly steps, and then really went to town. To a jolly rhythm that Bonjangle's split cog shoes tapped out on the lid of Hitler's casket, a chorus of sixteen black voices boomed Berlin's song, "When That Man Is Dead and Gone:"

> When that man is dead and gone
> When that man is dead and gone
> We'll go dancing down the street
> Kissing everyone we meet
> When that man is dead and gone

As the song neared its close, Whitey's Lindy Hoppers rushed the stage. A bedlam of hilarious acrobatics ensued. To the quick rhythm of swing jazz, the jitterbugs celebrated the end of war.[2]

The show was a roaring success. It would tour major cities across the country.

A small but luminous detail in this episode shines a bright light on the main premise of this book. The first stanza of "When That Man Is Dead and Gone" depicted the day when, following Hitler's death, ordinary citizens would go dancing down the street kissing everyone they meet. Berlin was recalling that all-too-familiar iconic scene of spontaneous street celebrations at the end of World War II, captured in the black-and-white pictures showing the jubilant crowds on V-E Day and V-J Day – only that he wasn't. For on that night America was not yet even at war with the Axis powers. Berlin was prophesying the coming, and even the ending, of a new world war before it started.

Berlin's premonitions were also evident in the forgotten opening verse of another song, "God Bless America." Usually omitted in later performances, the original lyric, as it received its radio premier by Kate Smith on Armistice Day in 1938 (its first official observance), explained why Americans were in dire need of God's blessing:

> While the storm clouds gather far across the sea,
> Let us swear allegiance to a land that's free,
> Let us all be grateful that we're far from there,
> As we raise our voices in a solemn prayer.

Berlin originally composed this song during the Great War. At Camp Upton in Yaphank, New York, Sergeant Berlin was asked to produce a revue to raise funds for a communal building in the army base. *Yip Yip Yaphank* (1918), performed by an all-soldier cast, was the result. But for some reason Berlin dropped "God Bless America," one of the many songs he wrote for the show. Now, precisely two decades since the original Armistice and a mere month after the Munich Crisis portended another great war in Europe, he updated it with this new introductory verse. With the sighting of a dark storm far across the sea that originally motivated the entire song forgotten today, it is worth remembering that what compelled Berlin to dust off this anthem was the rumors of war, the danger from without. What is today universally considered America's unofficial anthem was originally intended by Berlin as a "great peace song." It prayed for guidance from the Almighty for the "land that's free." Berlin saw the ship of state navigating the stormy waters toward the war clouds, still "far away" but ominous and threatening. Berlin, the first-generation immigrant from a war-torn Europe, wished that his adopted country would avert this storm, "grateful" as he was, along with countless pacifists and isolationists of his day, "that we're far from there." In three years, however, it struck America head-on. And, by that time, Berlin had altered this fainthearted line to "grateful for a land so fair." As this minor but revealing change and a number of martial songs he composed for "Fun to Be Free" attested, Berlin's transformation from a nervous pacifist to the minstrel of righteous war had been completed.[3]

Berlin's was not a rare and isolated case of artistic clairvoyance or political conversion. On the contrary, his was part of an epidemic of sorts. Roughly from 1935 to 1941, during the prolonged run-up to America's direct participation in the global conflict, countless artists, writers, critics, thinkers, and journalists were exercised by the war they saw coming in slow motion. These prewar Americans thought they saw a world war coming because starting in the mid-1930s, omens proliferated far across the sea (China, Ethiopia, Spain, Austria, Czechoslovakia, Poland, Finland, France, England). By the late 1930s, all these geopolitical bush fires spotted in distant lands had come together to threaten a global holocaust, which seemed increasingly likely to reach American shores. The alarm over this slow advent of war pervaded all departments of American letters, including song writing, fiction, theater, poetry, and criticism. These writers all nervously "look[ed] from an uncertain present toward a more uncertain future," Wallace Stevens remarked in 1936. The mirage of the coming world war on the horizon transfixed writers, artists, critics, and intellectuals. They brooded, puzzled, and quarreled over what the next war would mean to their country. And from their worries and perplexities resulted a vibrant body of fictional and nonfictional writings that foretold, much like Berlin's songs, America's role in the future war.

The gradual approach of the world war gripped the literary world tightly, so tightly as to cause Stevens to ponder publicly its hazards on several occasions. In his 1936 lecture, given when the new civil conflict in Spain transfixed literary circles, Stevens – an insurance company executive, wine connoisseur, and collector of exotic tea leaves – told his audience at Harvard that artists then lived under the "pressure of the contemporaneous." A "sense of upheaval," "constant and extreme," impinged on the artists. "The end of civilization" appeared not "merely possible but measurably probable." It had already ended in Germany and Russia. It was then under siege in Spain. Most certainly the United States would be the next. There was no escaping this pressure, the sense of doom, which covered the epoch as did an all-pervading weather. The only way open to the artists lay in "resistance." And the only way to resist was by artistically sublimating "the pressure of ominous and destructive circumstance," by converting it "into a different, an explicable, an amenable circumstance."[4] In another lecture, delivered four years later when another world war had already erupted across the Atlantic, Stevens aired the same concern. "The pressure of reality," which was "the determining factor in the artistic character of an era," had turned much of contemporary literary productions into poetized headlines. "[I]n speaking of the pressure of reality," Stevens clarified, "I am thinking of life in a state of violence, not physically violent, as yet, for us in America, but physically violent for millions of our friends and for still more millions of our enemies and spiritually violent, it may be said, for everyone else." This pressure was ruinous for imaginative writers because it killed the essence of literature, the imagination, to save reality. The writer must not only receive what reality gave. He also had to give of himself, so that the reader could receive something other than reality, an entity that the writer unfortunately only could give but never receive. One could not receive one's own donation; hence the "nobility" of genuine literature. The main task of writers was then to figure out ways to conserve this noble faculty of the mind, to "resist or evade" overpowering realities of the approaching war by pitting "a violence from within" against "a violence without."[5] Whether intended or not, Stevens's insistence on resistance gave evidence to the irresistible appeal of the immediate and the contemporaneous to writers in the shadow of the approaching war. While many of Stevens's peers combated what another modernist Archibald MacLeish called in 1939 the "tyranny of time," still more writers, including MacLeish himself, chose to serve as its handmaidens.[6]

Today we remember little of the phenomenon that worried Stevens. The imprint that the "pressure of the contemporaneous" left on American letters in the 1930s, especially during the decade's latter half, is very hard to see. This absence of prewar writings from our collective memory has several causes. The most obvious one is that works addressing the approach of war usually deviated from modernist aesthetics. They exemplified the kinds of art that writers of Stevens's sensibility execrated. There was much less freedom, it would have seemed, in their selection and treatment of the subject matter. They appeared to contain more violence from without and less violence from within than modernists cared to see. In short, too many knowns and too few intimations of the unknown. Critics have not been kind to this sort of writings. The more time has elapsed, the deeper these works fell into the abyss of oblivion and the higher the reputation of brave resistors and tormented escapists has climbed. The current reputations of the two poets just mentioned, Stevens and MacLeish, personify this pattern. Another reason has to do with the transitional character of the prewar literary culture. Enough history books to fill a small library are devoted to exploring American writers' complex and often contradictory responses to the Great Depression. Scholars and critics have also scrutinized with equal thoroughness the nation's social, cultural, and economic transformations during and after World War II. But bracketed by the heat of war and the turbulence of the depression, the pivotal period that bridged the depression to war has slipped out of most influential versions of what happened to the literary and intellectual community from the mid-1930s to the early 1940s.[7]

Thus nowadays we are oblivious to the problem at the heart of this book: how the tyranny of time, the sense that time was running out, at once terrified and exhilarated the literary and intellectual world during the protracted lead-up to World War II. If you want to see a fuller picture of the literary events of the era, you will agree with me that it is long overdue to jolt ourselves out of this state of amnesia. Looking back on the decade in 1939, Malcolm Cowley discerned three distinct literary currents. While two of those responded to domestic developments, namely the political and economic struggles and the maturation of monopoly capitalism, the third grew out of "the new position of the United States in world affairs." In the 1930s, isolation became a doctrine, subject to debate, no longer a fact. As a result, the chief literary editor of *The New Republic* for much of this eventful decade claimed, "Americans have begun to write with their eyes on the world overseas."[8] To date no critic has attempted a reasonably comprehensive reconstruction of this third current. The following pages will show that, born under the shadow of the international crisis, the prewar literary culture was much more alive, its participants much more numerous and various, than has been acknowledged. World War II changed the shape and course of American letters before it actually came.

Socially engaged, politically active writers turned their attention from the depression at home to wars abroad as their burgeoning interest in foreign affairs, particularly threats, perceived and real, from foreign dictatorships to the American way of life, counterpoised, and soon overwhelmed, their rage against socioeconomic suffering. That did not mean that prewar writers simply dropped domestic problems to grasp for an untapped source of inspiration beyond national borders. Most writers remained preoccupied with economic upheavals and political strife on the domestic front until their country officially committed itself to war in 1941. Some of the most celebrated works of social protest were published on the eve of World War II. John Steinbeck's *The Grapes of Wrath* came out in 1939, Richard Wright's *Native Son* in 1940, and James Agee and Walker Evans's *Let Us Now Praise Famous Men* in 1941. And yet, from around 1935–1936 (the Italian invasion of Ethiopia; the outbreak of the Spanish Civil War) or 1937 (the Japanese invasion of China), certainly from 1938 (the Munich Crisis) onward, most writers troubled by "violence without" began dividing attention between domestic and foreign issues. Matthew Josephson recalled later:

> During the early thirties it was our own domestic convulsions, economic and political, that absorbed our attention almost exclusively. By 1936 however I was convinced that we Americans would somehow "muddle through," but thereafter my most anxious thoughts turned to the world abroad, toward Europe. There the mounting aggressions of Germany and Italy and the agonizing of Republican Spain in civil war gave the clearest warning of world catastrophe.[9]

The "most anxious thoughts" of his cohort also began turning about the same time, in the same direction.

This incipient interest in foreign affairs grew into an obsession when the new European war, long anticipated, finally broke out in September 1939. From this point on, the depression conditions passed to the background in prewar writers' social conscience. Surging to the fore in their place were the menace of totalitarianism, the future viability of liberal democracy, and the national debate between isolationists and interventionists that lacerated the body politic with the same ferocity with which the earlier debate over the roadmap for economic recovery did. Thus, toward the end of the decade, while documenting the ruinous effects of racial alienation on the psyche of African Americans in the depression era, Wright was also clashing with the Communist Party over the party line on U.S. foreign policy.[10] While painting sympathetic pictures of the Okies in their jalopies and the migrant fruit pickers in California, Steinbeck was increasingly consumed by the impending war. By 1941, his activist energies were largely directed toward schemes related to mobilization and morale building, which ranged from a planned propaganda novel about resistance fighters in a Nazi-occupied country (in his initial draft, the scene was set in America) to pro-democracy campaigns in Central and South America. By Pearl Harbor, he will have joined, along with prominent novelists and dramatists such as Thornton Wilder and Stephen Vincent Bénet, the Foreign Information Service (part of the Office of Strategic Information, the precursor of the CIA) headed by Robert Sherwood.[11] Toward the end of the decade, the conflicts around the world, with mounting urgency, competed with domestic affairs for these writers' resources and commitment. Their collective turn to international themes resulted in vast volumes of fictional and nonfictional writings that intently pondered America's role in the world.

The dark forebodings of the impending war were not confined to lettered classes. Prewar writers' engagement with the escalating world anarchy occurred against the backdrop of a historic change in their country's sense of its sacrosanct ideals and core interests. Between 1935 and 1941, a breakthrough came in the way Americans understood their country's relation to the rest of the world. First among elite circles of academics, policy makers, and opinion leaders, and then soon among the public at large, the perception of a world coming under the rule of undemocratic and illiberal regimes gradually but irreparably discredited age-old assumptions about America's economic self-sufficiency, military invulnerability, and cultural superiority. The prewar years buried the smug and unilateral provincialism of yore once and for all, and in its stead a new internationalism arose that would license the projection of American power and vision beyond the edenic New World.[12] During and after the war, it would serve as the intellectual foundation for America's global leadership. At various points in its history, America had ratcheted up its international commitment, but these bursts of internationalism had usually been followed by a slippage backward. Not after the prewar years.[13] In the mid-1930s, the American people reluctantly began sloughing off their traditional parochialism. A half calendar decade and intellectual eons later, their nation entered a total war of unprecedented scale with confidence in its capabilities and goodness.

Because the anticipatory impact of World War II touched almost all facets of the American life, its history can take various forms. One plausible version may set the evolution of U.S. foreign policy during the prewar years at its center. Another version can revolve around the reorganization of America's political economy. For the present book, I decided to give center stage to cultural productions, especially those of a literary and critical nature, in order to signalize the surpassing importance of three factors to any treatments of the nation's response to the advent of war: media, symbols, and their highly trained manipulators.

First, media. The "democratic process" (a keyword that entered the popular lexicon in the late 1930s) of debate and bargaining over the war-ravaged world's meaning depended on mass media, that is, the channels of mass communication that transmitted values and motives packaged in popular symbols to all parts of the nation. In the first third of the twentieth century, U.S. mass media took on a life of their own, adding to social process a new dimension of connectivity that was national in coverage and democratic in accessibility. These commercial vehicles of mass persuasion, enlightenment, and entertainment comprised radio and motion picture, public relations and advertisement, photo magazines, newspapers, and national bestsellers all marketed by increasingly oligopolistic corporations. These institutions were to the national-popular culture of the depression decade what railroads, waterways, and canals were to the nationally integrated economy in the nineteenth century.[14]

The mass media, flexibly conceived as cheap ways to know and connect with things outside regions that one could directly experience, should also include advocacy groups – "Committees," "Bureaus," "Friends," and "Leagues" that pushed for vigorous public discussions of America's stake in the international crisis. Most of these were small outfits founded and managed by local groups including business associations, community chests, fraternity orders, churches, colleges, and other civic-minded groups. But quite a few attained nationwide reach, with substantial budgets, full-time staff, and headquarters in major cities like New York, Chicago, and Washington. Those that took a position more or less in favor of America's deeper and wider engagement with the world included the Committee to Defend America by Aiding the Allies, the Union for Democratic Action, the Council for Democracy, the Committee for National Morale, the United China Relief, the American Committee for Non-Participation in Japanese Aggression in China, Contemporary Historians Inc (Archibald MacLeish, Ernest Hemingway, John Dos Passos, and talents from Holly-wood), and many small relief organizations like Medical Bureau to Aid

Spanish Democracy. On the pacifist and isolationist side, the most influential was the America First Committee, but countless other lesser-known organizations were also active, including groups tracing their roots back to the pacifist movement in the 1910s, the Women's International League for Peace and Freedom, as well as Christian groups such as A. J. Muste's Fellowship of Reconciliation. Particularly important to any studies focusing on the literati and intelligentsia of this era are a passel of Communist front organizations, which changed sides several times, depending on the line passed down through the chain of command extending from Moscow, through the Comintern, to the Party cadres. The principals in the following chapters all worked with and often against these advocacy groups.

The Fight for Freedom Committee, the organizer of "Fun To Be Free," was just one such group. It was founded in April 1941, as a spin-off from the increasingly dovish Committee to Defend America, by journalists, academics, writers, retired military men, clergy, and stage and screen actors with a view to staking out the most radically interventionist position in the ongoing public debate on American aid to democracies under Axis assault. Intellectuals, writers, and entertainers who joined this hawkish committee included Tallulah Bankhead, Van Wyck Brooks, Moss Hart, Helen Hayes, George S. Kaufman, Freda Kirchwey, Max Lerner, Lewis Mumford, Reinhold Niebuhr, Eugene O'Neil, Robert Sherwood, Archibald MacLeish, and Alfred Lunt. As their event at Madison Square Garden illustrates so vividly, their contributions went well beyond the gestural politics of crowded letterheads, testimonial dinners, and benefit soirées.

Coursing throughout this nationwide network of informational conduits were emotionally potent symbols that controlled the nation's thinking. Men and women in America from the mid-1930s to the early 1940s saw the rapidly changing world as it was filtered through certain idioms. When civilians interested themselves in the vexing questions over America's world leadership, their mind had to cope with the novelty of these questions by adapting conventional ways of thinking about more familiar, more recognizable issues. And, as Kenneth Burke, arguably the most original cultural theorist of his generation (born in 1897), tenaciously explained throughout the 1930s, it was through the alchemy of symbolization that these old ways were reworked to answer new purposes. Nationally circulating symbols fused the elite vanguard (writers, intellectuals, opinion leaders, policy makers) and the crowd in the street into one nation, joined together not by consensus but by the inescapable problem and the common language.

In the highly partisan and competitive marketplace of ideas and images, these symbols had to meet one requirement: they had to sound and look good, that is, they had to be ingratiating and recognizable so that strikingly fresh ideas about America's relation to foreign wars in distant lands could be wheedled into the nation's preexisting belief systems. Given this requirement, it was inevitable that those initiated into the wizardry of symbolization – poets, dramatists, novelists, cultural critics, and intellectuals – ended up playing a signal role in the prewar culture.[15] In his essay "The American Writers and the New World," Archibald MacLeish, the canniest of all the authors who appear in the subsequent pages, announced that the entire world was undergoing a revolutionary change and called on writers and artists to forge a new mythos that could make the unfamiliar new world intelligible. "[N]o purposed human action is conceivable without an image of the world which is coherent and distinguishable," he wrote, and "the creation of such an image of the world, recognizable to the emotions as well as to the mind, is the work of which the artist moving in the forms and words of art is capable."[16] As is wont of writers envious of social influence, MacLeish overestimated the ability of words and images to call the new world into being. But his wishful thinking was not entirely divorced from reality either. In a national culture tensed under the anticipatory impact of World War II, "the artist moving in the forms and words of art" was the principal purveyor of the arresting language that brokered the masses' hopes and tapped their fears.

These experienced manipulators of symbols gathered around a common concern: Would the foreign wars raging oceans away become *their* war? The defining characteristic of the prewar culture was a sense of uncertainty, which made writers and their readers at once fearful of and longing for the unknown. If not a ruling idea or a unifying logic, this peculiar mixture of apprehension and anticipation was the dominant mood, which permeated the substance of the prewar culture and tinctured its language. For all their divergent attitudes, opinions, and aesthetic strategies, a few dozen writers featured in the following chapters all grappled with the same question: How to give recognizable and believable form to the "next war," an event out of the reach of direct observation? Or as Malcolm Cowley put it to MacLeish in 1941, how to "make people realize the terrible nearness of the crisis"?[17]

The ineffability of the future war sparked controversies. This book thus goes behind the monochromatic, all-pervading climate of uncertainty, to reveal how prewar writers clashed with one another over a host of explosive questions raised by the approach of war. What, for example, was America's mission in the world? How useful was the Popular Front strategy in shoring up faltering democracies around the world against the menace of global fascism? Were the Communists America's friends or foes? How would the next war compare to other wars in the nation's past? How could writers make their versions of the next war believable to a public wary of propaganda? How could they annihilate space through aesthetic sleights of hand and bring remote violence home to America? Was liberalism compatible with democracy? Could liberalism stand up against its ideological rivals abroad that openly derogated its basic tenets? Painting a collective portrait of a wide range of writers, their works as well as their personal and professional lives, I explain how these questions came to be emphasized and how the prewar writers stylized their answers.

The great multiplicity of questions that the approach of war raised dictated the texture and structure of the present work. In the final analysis, the subsequent chapters all coalesce around the book's central contention: the intellectual and cultural groundwork for America's emergence as a global power in the mid-twentieth century was laid during the prewar years by various participants in the fiery debates over their country's ideals and interests. Nevertheless, the book's real wager is on a counterpoint to this tidy narrative, namely on my finding that Americans of the time did not accept their country's world leadership as a promised destiny. Actually the path to the eventual consensus on the American Century was full of twists and turns, which continued to disorient the nation throughout the prewar years. It was my desire to reenact this sense of disorientation as it was experienced by the American people that motivated the book's elastic syncretism. To use an oft-abused pair of figures, *American Writers and the Approach of World War II, 1935–1941* was envisaged to be a fox, not a hedgehog.

The following nine chapters catch prewar writers hard at work. Chapter 1 fulfills several introductory purposes. It first offers a tour d'horizon of the geopolitical developments from the mid-1930s to the onset of war in 1941. A clear sense of the chronology of important events that shook the world should help you follow detailed analyses to ensue. Second, I sketch out two unbroken threads that run through the entire book: (1) the problem of learning or unlearning the lessons of the Great War and (2) the problem of writing into existence violent events occurring – temporally or spatially – at a distance.

The rest of the book unfolds in chronological order. My narrative is organized around pivotal moments in the evolution of the prewar culture, from the Italo-Ethiopian War (1935), through the Spanish Civil War

(1936), the Munich Crisis (1938), the outbreak of World War II in Europe (1939), the deepening crisis in China (1937–1941), and the Axis conquest of Europe (1940–41). Each chapter brings to center stage a writer or a close-knit group of collaborators at a time in order to probe into the artistry involved in their handling of various dilemmas.

As we will see, quite a few authors publicly ventured thoughts that would be today deemed completely outside mainstream and thus illegitimate as the stuff of public conversation. This book pays special attention to those ideas and strategies that lost the battle over the soul of the nation on the eve of war and thus enjoy little afterlife in our contemporary discussion of analogous questions. Meanwhile, winners – that is, those symbols and arguments that won the battle – today circulate in our national culture oblivious of their not so ancient pedigrees. This book shows that they originated in these critical years. In this double sense, our basic attitudes and feelings about America's leadership in the world descend directly from that dark time when the fear of the global catastrophe pressed earnest answers out of writers and thinkers. The following history of prewar culture is a tale of births and deaths in equal number, of how certain lines of thinking became unthinkable while other lines of thinking came to be canonized as the eternal verities of national purpose.

I

From Depression to War

Following the onset of the global depression in 1929, the international system gradually descended into chaos as three latecomer imperial powers – Germany, Italy, and Japan – went on the warpath. Japan established its puppet regime in Manchuria in 1931 and started invading China proper in 1937. Mussolini's Italy invaded Ethiopia in 1935 and fielded large numbers of troops on the Franco side in the civil war that began in Spain the next year. The most destabilizing to the status quo was the recrudescence of militant expansionism in Germany, under the rule of National Socialists after 1933. Through a succession of policies (the intervention in the Spanish Civil War, the *Anschluss*, the destruction of Czechoslovakia, the alliance with Italy and Japan), it made frighteningly clear its intention to reorganize the political economy of Central and Eastern Europe under the aegis of the German Reich. The long-smoldering crisis came to a head when Hitler's army invaded Poland in September 1939, igniting a second European war in a generation. At the eastern and western extremes of the vast Eurasian continent, two regional wars raged for the next twenty-seven months, until the United States finally came under direct attack. Pearl Harbor finally jointed the war in Asia and the war in Europe, creating a total war of truly planetary scope.

The geopolitical tremors of the 1930s reverberated through the American literati and intelligentsia, who followed the deteriorating world situation nervously. Insurgent black writers wrote analyses, poems, and novels about the plight of Abyssinia and explored its meaning for Afro-Americans. When Spain came under attack from conservatives and rightists armed by Fascist Italy and Nazi Germany in 1936, the literary and intellectual circles erupted with fulsome support for the Popular Front government in Madrid. Some prominent writers who paid attention to events across the Pacific began rousing public interest in the Japanese depredations in China as early as 1937. By the Western capitulation at Munich in the fall of 1938, a vocal minority of internationally minded writers had concluded that Germany's ambition went beyond mere revanchism. All along, the awareness that there was a pattern, indeed a diabolical design, to all these seemingly isolated events slowly gelled. The stark narrative of liberal democracies around the world beating total retreat in the face of autocratic revisionist powers (the conveniently simplifying term "totalitarianism" entered the national lexicon exactly at this juncture) was swiftly gaining traction.[1]

The German invasion of Poland on September 1, 1939, and the ensuing British and French declarations of war on Germany thrust the question over America's responsibility into the center of national debate. During the following twenty-seven months until Pearl Harbor, public opinion was split between interventionists and isolationists, who fought the "Great Debate" in Congress, on airwaves, and in the pages of newspapers and periodicals. The debate was ferocious. Its fury haunted Arthur Schlesinger, Jr. to the very close of his long career. The eruption of the new war in Europe, Schlesinger recalled, "ushered in the most savage national debate of my lifetime–more savage than the debate over communism in the late 1940s, more savage the debate over McCarthyism in the early 1950s, more savage than the debate over Vietnam in the 1960s. The debate between interventionists and isolationists in 1940–41 had an inner fury that tore apart families, friends, churches, universities, and political parties."[2] Although confusion led most citizens to occupy a middle ground, a tangle of options in no time crystallized into this question: Was aiding countries under Axis assault (Poland, Finland, the British Empire, France, Russia–the list of "democracies" grew longer as the conflict engulfed Europe) more vital to national interests than staying out of war?

Historians are united in the view that these prewar years were marked by the steady rise of "geopolitical mindedness" within highly educated segments of the nation.[3] Across the globe, one democracy after another suffered its sovereignty to be snuffed by the Axis, while the United States sat idly by. And as Alan Henrikson shows, in response to the tightening encirclement by antidemocratic powers, a "new global geostrategic image, a revised mental picture of the world and of the geographic and strategic interrelationships of its parts" emerged. Ultimately, it filtered through to relatively isolationist segments of the nation (women, the undereducated, the population in the Midwest, and so on).[4] On the eve of the Japanese raid on Hawaii in December 1941, this new "geopolitical mindedness" was poised to displace the traditional isolationism reposing on the economic self-sufficiency and geostrategic invulnerability of the Western Hemisphere.

For its part, the U.S. government continually if not programmatically escalated American involvement in foreign wars.[5] At Roosevelt's urging, Congress revised the Neutrality Act to allow "cash and carry" in October 1939 and legislated the first peacetime conscription in September 1940. In February 1941, the Lend-Lease bill devised by the administration became law, neutering the Neutrality Act. By the time "Fun To Be Free" opened in Madison Square Garden in October 1941, the U.S. Navy was waging an undeclared war on *Kriegsmarine* in the Atlantic, while Claire Chennault's Flying Tiger pilots were defending the Burma Road against Japanese bombers.[6] In terms of both the nation's general mindset and its foreign policy position, the United States was in a zone of geopolitical "indistinguishablity" by 1940–1941, simultaneously in and out of war.[7] This ambivalent state eventuated in nothing short of a radical reorientation in American thinking about geopolitical and legal categories. The traditional distinctions between territoriality and extraterritoriality, belligerency and neutrality, and war and peace were stretched to the breaking point.

The war of words and ideas that attended this development affected the thinking of numberless writers. In the end even the thinning rank of writers indifferent to foreign affairs got dragged into what Schlesinger called "the most savage debate of my lifetime." Almost all writers commenting on social issues perforce took sides. Unlike in the previous controversies over remedies for the depression, where the overwhelming majority rallied around or to the left of the New Deal, neither consensus nor a common enemy was in sight. Writers grew voluble and eloquent as if to compensate for the absence of physical danger. The shared problem–America's responsibility for foreign wars in faraway lands–and the luxury of peace united to generate a wealth of tropes and opinions. The prewar culture was born. Although this culture had many disparate parts to it, these parts all partook of the universal unease about two problems: the problem of history and the problem of geography.

The Lessons of the Last War

Few generations go through two major wars in their lifetimes. When they do, though, the second war is inevitably seen through the lens of the first. The coloration of this lens varies. The first war can signal an elating, frightening, or disillusioning experience. Whatever its emotional complexion, however, there is one sure rule: when the new war arrives, these emotions keyed to the last war are reactivated and turned into loaded idioms, and these idioms are in turn used to make sense of the second war in a generation. Ask a generation of Americans about the moral they draw from the last war. You will learn a lot about how they will react to a next war.

Lessons of the First World War shaped the various ways in which prewar writers reacted to the prospect of a second world war. According to the conventional view, so far as literary veterans were concerned, these lessons were chiefly of a disillusioning kind. This is not wholly false. While on the front line, most writers swung back and forth, between exaltation and regret. In a letter, John Dos Passos exulted, "I constantly feel the need of the drunken excitement of a good bombardment. ... [T]hrough it all I feel more alive than ever before." In another letter, he expostulated, "There is nothing beautiful about modern war. ... It is nothing but an enormous, tragic digression in people's lives."[8] Yet no sooner did the sordid reality of European politics dash their innocent hope at Versailles than bitter disillusionment and impotent rage displaced ambivalence, especially among those who intellectualized the war and took Wilsonian promises ("to save civilization," "to make the world safe for democracy," "to end all war") on faith. Their psychic wound was deep and festering, a sort of syndrome debilitating the entire generation of youths born in the last decades of the nineteenth century.[9] Nothing was more clearly symptomatic of the persistence of this psychological scar than the first *New Republic* editorial after the German invasion of Poland, titled, with knowing disgust, "1914 Repeats Itself." This erstwhile organ of progressive internationalism now exhorted the nation to remember the Palmer Raids, the Creel Committee, Versailles, and the Red Scare, and to stay out of Europe's demented repeat performance.[10]

Not surprisingly, however, this legend of the "lost" generation only outlines their disillusion. What did its visceral details look like? By far the most shocking, and hence enduring, lesson writers and intellectuals learned was that they must not trust what politicians said to the public in times of war. These disillusioned and angry writers directed much of their fury at what many of them called "rhetoric," the manner of speech by which politicians, decrepit, stupid, and malevolent, misused language to persuade their callow audience, instead of calling things exactly and accurately by their proper names. With a characteristic mixture of nihilism, sangfroid, and pragmatism, Hemingway's hero in *A Farewell to Arms* (1929) reflects that "[a]bstract words such as glory, honor, courage, or hallow were obscene beside the concrete names of villages, the numbers of roads, the names of rivers, the numbers of regiments and the dates." The "expression in vain" physically sickens another fictional veteran in

"Soldier's Home" (1925), more naïve and vulnerable than Frederic Henry: "Krebs acquired the nausea in regard to experience that is the result of untruth or exaggeration."[11] It was also the nauseating obscenity of "old men's lies" that revolted one of Hemingway's acquaintances in postwar Paris, Ezra Pound, who welcomed U.S. entry into the war in 1917.[12] The opening of Canto XIV (1925):

> Io venni in luogo d'ogni luce muto;
> The stench of wet coal, politicians
> ....e and .....n, their wrists bound to their ankles,
> Standing bare bum,
> Faces smeared on their rumps,
>   wide eye on flat buttock,
> Bush hanging for beard,
>   Addressing crowds through their arse-holes,
> Addressing the multitudes in the ooze, newtz, water-slugs, water-maggots ...

When manipulated by the "betrayers of language" and "perverters of language" like Lloyd George (".........e") and Wilson (".....n"), words turned into something fetid and toxic: "the sh-t."[13] In order to modernize literature, Pound wanted "direct treatment of the thing."[14] That would also help propagate knowledge, which in Pound's neo-Platonic symbolism was associated with light. All these dreams, however, demanded purity and exactitude of language. This necessary condition could not obtain in a world where politicians, usurers, and their lackeys in the press ("liars in public places") easily nullified efforts of a small vanguard of linguistic hygienists. There was no newness. Nor was there knowledge or light. The world was mute of all light ("d'ogni luce muto"). Pound titled the section at the beginning of which this stanza appeared the "Hell Cantos."

Another lesson that pursued American writers to these circles of Hell may well be called the lesson of Randolph Bourne in recognition of its most eloquent teacher. The acerbic attack on Wilson's war that Bourne kept up throughout much of 1917 exposed how phony realism and phony idealism colluded in pro-war writers' thinking. Writers and intellectuals pled American entry into the Great War on the strength of their purported "realism." They claimed that American involvement was inevitable. War would come to the United States no matter what. America was under duress. War was a necessity, not a choice. Given the inevitability of war, they further argued, it was delusional, unrealistic, and irresponsible for Americans to think and act as though their thought and action could have prevented the coming of war. This realism, however, was specious, Bourne wrote, because it asked Americans to pretend that a possibility in the future was an accomplished fact at hand, that what was uncertain was already certain and actual. These self-important realists were not observing reality. They were trying to fulfill their wish. Having convinced themselves that what was possible was what was inevitable, pro-war writers then had to hitch the machinery of this conjectured war to an ideal, in this case the primitive, almost Puritanical goal of teaching autocratic nations in the Old World the art of self-rule, of making the world safe for democracy. This sort of idealism was no less phony than the pro-war realism because it was an ex post idealization of a fait accompli: "Thought becomes an easy rationalization of what is actually going on or what is to happen inevitably tomorrow."[15] In the mental life of writers who wanted to stampede their country into a European imperial squabble, a wish masqueraded as a fact, thereby giving the lie to their realism, and an alibi masqueraded as a transcendent ideal, thereby calling into question their intention.

Already at this point, Bourne's analysis was thorough enough to haunt a generation of writers and intellectuals for the next two decades, but he gave his analytic dagger another twist with this question: Why did Wilson's cheerleaders choose to pretend that war was inevitable? After all, since a future possibility was at contention, they could have chosen to pretend that peace, not war, was inevitable. In other words, they made a choice, and some forces, conscious or unconscious, must have guided their choice. Bourne's answer was not cognitive or moral. It was physiological. Their choice, he discovered, was not a result of cognitive error (misrecognizing facts). Nor did it result from not knowing right from wrong. The real fault lay in these interventionists' lack of mental stamina, namely their inability to act creatively while living in intellectual suspense. War was preferable to peace because the latter made liberals think harder than the former. In war, the nation would be mobilized to achieve a simple and popular goal: defeat of the enemy. The writers' task would be straightforward: to rationalize this crude military objective in idealized terms. In peace, by sharp contrast, there would be no consensus, due to class antagonism and racism, on the goals and means of democratic reform at home, which would force liberal writers to be more inventive. In 1917, Bourne concluded, American intellectuals told themselves that war was inevitable and necessary because they were mentally lazy. Most likely, many objects of Bourne's attack did not fathom the full depth of his insight, but his most basic lesson was plain enough to learn. Virtues of irony, self-contradiction, irresolution, and indecision were made very much of in literary and intellectual circles when the nation faced the "next" war two decades later. At any rate, the main antagonist Bourne was most keen to persuade finally saw the light, as is evident in his antiwar stance that he maintained to the bitter end. Right after the German destruction of Czechoslovakia, John Dewey said in a speech:

> [T]he very persons who a few years ago were sure that they would not allow themselves to favor our entering another great war, and that we had been deceived by propaganda in entering the last one, are now thinking and talking as if it were inevitable that we should again go in. This attitude is a precursor of an event that is in no way necessary. If we but make up our minds that it is not inevitable, and if we now set ourselves deliberately to seeing that no matter what happens we stay out, we shall save this country from the greatest social catastrophe that could overtake us, the destruction of all the foundations upon which to erect a socialized democracy.[16]

Dewey, at the age of eighty, publicly conceded the victory he did not deserve to win two decades ago.

While many struggled through the 1930s to unlearn these lessons with little success, a significant number of postwar writers overcame their psychological block and convinced themselves that the next war would be unlike the last. The lives and works of the founding members of the Playwrights Company offer a good example. In the summer of 1938, fed up with interference from producers and eager to control every production detail of their own scripts, five of the busiest dramatists on Broadway – Elmer Rice (b.1892), Maxwell Anderson (b.1888), S. N. Behrman (b.1893), Robert Sherwood (b.1896), and Sidney Howard (b.1891) – formed this producing collective. On domestic social issues, their politics spread evenly along the political spectrum, from reformist Rice on the left to libertarian, rugged individualist Anderson on the right. On the threat posed by foreign dictatorships to democracy, however, there was a happy concord: they all abhorred totalitarianism, whether headquartered in Berlin, Rome, Moscow, or Tokyo. International themes defined the majority of their productions between 1938 and 1941: *Abe Lincoln in Illinois* (1938), *Key Largo* (1939), *No Time for Comedy* (1939), *There Shall Be No Night* (1940), *American Landscape* (1940), *Journey to Jerusalem* (1940), *Candle in the Wind* (1941), and *Flight to the West* (1941). These plays explored the social responsibility of a comedy writer living in serious times, rang the tocsin against dictatorships, advertised the bravery of democratic nations stemming the tides of global fascism, and sensationalized deviltries of Nazi thugs and tribulations of European refugees.

The drama of the European crisis did not become all the rage on Broadway overnight. The National Socialists' ascension to power in 1933 had already spawned a bevy of anti-Nazi dramas: Richard Maibaum's

Birthright (1933), Leslie Reade's *The Shatter'd Lamp* (1934), S. N. Behrman's *Rain from Heaven* (1934), Elmer Rice's *Judgment Day* (1934), Clifford Odets's *Till the Day I Die* (1935), and Sinclair Lewis's *It Can't Happen Here* (1935). A war with the Third Reich did not yet seem probable, even possible, to these dramatists. The histrionics of mass politics and the theatrics of ideologues chiefly absorbed them. Blond beasts in brown shirts and their devoted followers conduced to good theater. A fear unrelated to war also cast a shadow on these early antifascist plays. A similar mass movement, led by a charismatic leader, may exploit weak points in the democratic process and seize power in America.

As the decade drew to a close, domestic putsches became less likely while the dictatorships abroad grew more bellicose. Concurrently, in the American perception, totalitarianism evolved from the dangerous role model for domestic demagogues like Huey Long and Father Coughlin to a super-military power and an alternative ideological system with sinister designs on American interests and values. The Playwrights Company's plays produced between 1938 and 1941 punctually answered to this shift by casting the authoritarian regimes as a potential enemy America may battle soon. These often stridently interventionist plays have to be weaved back into a larger constellation of militantly antitotalitarian, prodemocratic dramas that became popular on Broadway toward the end of the decade. In plays like Sidney Howard's *The Ghost of Yankee Doodle* (1937), Robert Adrey's *Thunder Rock* (1939), Clare Boothe's *Margin for Error* (1939), Ernest Hemingway's *Fifth Column* (1940), and Lillian Hellman's *Watch on the Rhine* (1941), the autocracies sowing mayhem on the other side of the Atlantic stopped inspiring their American sympathizers. The next world war threatened, and Nazis, Fascists, and Communists emerged as chief instigators of this brewing crisis that may engulf America as well.

The Company's prewar plays did no show those playwrights to be scared by the future. Far from it, they appeared to long for a relief of suspense, for a clear, hard, final clash with their country's implacable enemies. Their path to this serene resolve had been anything but undeviating. The Great War of twenty years past was a formative experience for Howard, Anderson, Behrman, Sherwood, and Rice, who were all at the time in their early or mid-twenties. The war shook three of them, Howard, Sherwood, and Anderson, with particular force. In a rush of youthful patriotism and fired up by his Anglophilia, Sherwood was itching to jump in the trenches during America's prolonged neutrality. When the declaration of war finally came in 1917, Sherwood, a junior at Harvard, was ready to enlist, but the Army and the Navy both rejected him for his unusual physiology (he was a giant, at six feet and seven inches, dwarfing other recruits). No matter. He wasted no time, taking a train to Montreal to enlist in the Canadian Expeditionary Force. His anticipated prize – the thrill of winning the war to end all wars – was not to be had at the front, however. It was an illusion, Sherwood soon found out, and after the war, as with many other literary veterans, the soured illusion, rancid and corrosive, led him to a sort of pacifism that was necessitated more by nihilism than by an optimistic vision of love, peace, and justice – an outlook he did not outgrow until 1938. War, by the way, earned Sherwood's mistrust fair and square. The poison gas he inhaled at Vimy damaged his heart permanently.[17]

Retrospectively, *Idiot's Delight* (1936), for which Sherwood won his first Pulitzer Prize, reads as the epitaph to his hard-bitten mistrust of the war fought for noble abstractions. Sherwood's was a grotesque farce for the end times. All the follies and frivolities of the interwar years stood condemned before the God of War. The play is set in a resort hotel on the Austrian-Italian border, where a motley group of tourists are trapped. Rumors of an imminent world war are abroad and the trains would not cross the border. Familiar observations on America's naïve idealism, the munitions industry, febrile chauvinism in European powers, the Communists' slogan of antifascist international solidarity, Germany's incurable irredentism, and Britain's erratic continental policy are aired through characters representing all nations and all political stripes: a German doctor, a British couple on their honeymoon trip, a French Communist, a merchant of death, a Russian countess (Lynn Fontanne), and Harry (Alfred Lunt), an American vaudeville impresario on tour in Europe with a troupe of leggy blonde chorines. The play climaxes with an Italian air strike against Paris. France retaliates forthwith, and bombs begin to shower on all major European capitals. Lights go out all over Europe, again. The curtain falls on an Armageddon, a world "backsliding to that dark and tortured age."[18] Onstage the lights dim, and the darkened theater fills with the crackles and flashes of explosions as Harry, at a piano, leads his dancers with "Onward Christian Soldiers."

Five years Sherwood's senior, Howard trod a similar path.[19] He was finishing a Master's degree at Harvard, where he enrolled in George Pierce Baker's English 47 (one of his classmates was Behrman), when the guns of August began roaring in Europe. Like Sherwood, Howard was euphoric. He quickly joined the platoons of American ambulance drivers and roamed the Balkan front for two years, before enlisting in a fledging air force following America's official entry. He would rise to the rank of lieutenant, twice cited for gallantry in action and awarded the Silver Star. A young idealistic Wilsonian, Howard had vast but vague hopes, like many of his cohort, for miracles that the war promised to work. And so the ensuing string of unpleasant surprises (the wartime suppression of domestic dissent, the Versailles treaty, and the return of the same old European realpolitik) proved all the more upsetting. During the 1920s, he refashioned himself as a radical journalist, a defender of minorities, socialists, and organized labor, and a supporter of the newly established American Civil Liberties Union, a by-product of the wartime suppression of civil liberties. From his acerbic pen issued forth clever but sincere philippics against all forms of narrow-minded Americanism. A series of articles he published in *The New Republic* in 1924, "Our Professional Patriots," skewered war profiteers who had multiplied like "guinea pigs" during the war and after Armistice showed no signs of retiring to their old obscure lairs. "Some diseases – measles, for example – leave behind them inconvenient after-effects that have to be watched to prevent serious damage to eyes, ears and heart," Howard explained, and "War enthusiasm isn't unlike that. We haven't quite got the war poison out of our systems, and that's the truth of it."[20]

In 1939, Howard was killed in a freakish accident on his farm (a tractor he was repairing crushed him against a wall), and so we will never know if he would have unlearned the lesson of the Great War when the German conquest of Europe and the fall of the British Empire appeared inevitable without another American intervention. But if his plays serve as any reliable guide, he maintained a conflicted attitude toward another world war he saw looming. His *The Ghost of Yankee Doodle* (1937) picked up where Sherwood's *Idiot's Delight* left off just a year prior. Europe is already eighteen months into the next world war. The lineup of the belligerents accurately foretells the actual world war to come in three years: Germany, Italy, and Japan are fighting England, France, and Russia, while the United States remains neutral. The Garrison family serves as the microcosm of a hesitant nation. John Garrison runs a factory that manufactures tools and machines. This family business subsidizes Robert's (John's brother) unprofitable liberal newspaper. A third brother, Paul, died in the Great War, but his widow, Sara Garrison, manages the Garrisons' mansion. The family business is suffering as orders are cancelled due to war. Robert's liberal and pacifist newspaper also teeters on the brink of insolvency. The family thus has to decide whether to sell their mansion to the Italian government to save the factory and the newspaper. Into this financial crisis created by the new world war and American neutrality steps James Clevenger, a newspaper magnate and Sara's admirer in her youth. Moved by his rekindled love for Sara and his conviction that America must not stay neutral any longer, he unleashes an interventionist campaign with major newspapers under his control. Ironically, as American entry into the war impends, new orders start flooding the family's factory, thereby saving the Garrisons' mansion and Robert's liberal newspaper that takes a pacifist and isolationist position.[21]

Sherwood's and Howard's plays surely moralized. But a stark, zoroastrian vision of the next war that enlisted all Americans on the side of light and order against darkness and chaos had not yet crystallized in these two prescient dramas. The moral distinction drawn there was not, as it would in a few years, between democracy and dictatorship, the two abstractions facing off in another war to end all wars. Rather, the moral was that war always muddied such a bright-line distinction between infernal villains and righteous innocents. War was hell. Morality did not cut through it. It stopped at war's edge. Formulated otherwise, these two plays warned of the next war instead of the next enemy. Rather than rousing the nation for the coming battle, they missed the passing peace without blaming anyone, which amounted to blaming everyone. A "complete exposure of pacifist delusions of three years ago," Walter Lippmann would remark after he saw *Idiot's Delight* in a London tense with the approach of the Munich Crisis.[22]

The "theatre is a religious institution." Theatergoers may not realize this, "but they sit in church nevertheless." The playwright officiates "a communal religious service." Maxwell Anderson wrote these words in 1941 for an address delivered at Rutgers University. Brooks Atkins, chief theater critic of *The New York Times*, respected as much for his independence of judgment as for the powerful pulpit he held, happened to be in the audience. He promptly had his paper print the whole essay. Next Sunday, hundreds of thousands of New Yorkers were served with their morning coffee a crushingly intense 4,000-word treatise on tragedy, religion, and theater, right in the pages of their most favored daily. As they read on, they found out that Broadway, known mostly for its garish commercialism, was actually an apparatus of moral divination and transcendental judgment. Set on the stage an issue or a character whose morality was in contention, its good or evil would be decided with precision, so asseverated Anderson with his habitual solemnity. For the audience would never fail to be repelled if it saw evil onstage and it would never fail to be pleasured if it saw good: "Set Hitler on the stage and loathing will arise from every seat in the house." "Excellence on stage is," Anderson wrote, "always moral excellence." Morally dubious persons, such as Anne Morrow Lindbergh, the author of *The Wave of the Future* (1941), her husband, and Senator

Wheeler (influential isolationist), were ordered to stay away from this communal church on pain of having their despicable character pilloried to the public: "[T]hat which is considered despicable on the stage will be held despicable in real life – not only evil, but those who will not fight evil are hated on the stage."[23]

Essentially, Anderson defined success of a play as a function of its ability to condemn the sinful and commend the just. Thus defined, theater by nature "denies the doctrine of the Nineteen Twenties emphatically." Which was also to say, set under the blazing spotlight in the Lord's house that was Broadway, Anderson's younger self stood condemned as a shallow sham. During the Great War, Anderson the pacifist ran opposite the martial romanticism Howard and Sherwood embraced. He was fired from Whittier College for his comments critical of war efforts (technically a criminal offense under the newly legislated Sedition Act), joining hundreds of other college professors purged for their un-Americanism. He would remain unbent. Furiously unrepentant, in fact. The realities and achievements of America's massive intervention in a European imperial feud compelled no reconsideration of his position. He was at the forefront of the postwar boom of literature of disenchantment, coauthoring with Laurence Stallings (who lost a leg in the war) *What Price the Glory* (1924), a rather freakishly vulgar antiwar comedy and his first critical and commercial success. But during the 1930s, he placed his self and his art onstage, subjected them to the floodlight of divine judgment, and found them moral failures.[24] The doctrine of the Jazz Age gainsaid the absolute difference between good and evil. That same doctrine also lured writers, including himself, into a belief that "the war had been a mistake, that no war was worth fighting … that good and evil came in unavoidable waves, that good would inevitably turn into evil and evil into good." Furthermore, that doctrine also betook the Lost Generation writers ("bruised and decimated from this Victorian war," as F. Scott Fitzgerald's Amory Blaine phrased it) to the discovery of irreverent cynicism. And so its rejection by Anderson and his associates on Broadway was their *mea maxima culpa*, their first step in a journey of penance back to the pre–Great War moralism. The last war disclosed to them the perennial discrepancy between morality and reality. Many were their lessons: baseness and selfishness often defeated a noble cause, the righteous did not always win, the sinful often triumphed at the expense of the innocent, liberal intentions could have illiberal consequences. Twenty years later, with the next war looming larger and larger with each passing month, these playwrights, now in the early forties, decided that the theater was not a laboratory of frustration but a basilica of vindication and thus was not answerable to the demands of realism.[25]

During the prewar years, if a writer or an artist wanted to promote American involvement in the approaching war, he or she had to accept at least one of the following lines of argument. The next war would be unlike the last war, and hence the latter was an inappropriate prism through which to divine the meaning of another world war. The last war taught them lessons, no doubt, but it was just that those hard-earned lessons were irrelevant to understanding the next war, which, despite its deceptive resemblance, was a different kind of war altogether. Alternatively or concurrently, they could tell themselves that the American involvement in the last European war was not a mistake in itself. Where America erred was in handling the postwar settlement, that is, in withdrawing from the world stage in a bout of traditional unilateralism – a tremendous wastage of opportunities and an unforgivable abnegation of its global leadership. Most pro-war writers in the late 1930s accepted both of these rationalizations, or at least said so when explaining their change of heart to the public.

By contrast, antiwar writers disbelieved, to the final months of the prewar period, that the next war would differ from the last war in any meaningful ways. For these bitter-enders, like Dalton Trumbo, Theodore Dreiser, or John Dewey, the Great War offered a compelling rationale for their position and served as an extremely effective rhetorical weapon with which to club more sanguine writers.[26] Trumbo, for instance, published two novels during this period, *Johnny Got His Gun* in 1939 and *Remarkable Andrew* in 1941. The harrowing story centering on a quadruple amputee, the former is today firmly part of the canon of modern pacifist literature. Since its initial publication this novel has had a way of slipping back into print to galvanize new generations of antiwar activists each time the United States mired itself in a costly military adventure overseas. The novel's enduring popularity as a timeless piece of pacifist literature, however, has obscured the original timeliness of the novel. Published soon after the outbreak of the new European war, the novel presented to its initial readers the mutilated body of Joe Bonham, the veteran of the Great War, as a personification of the apparently inarguable parallel between the "last war" and the "next war."

Trumbo followed this gruesome novel with *Remarkable Andrew*, a frolicsome satire on the mobilization hysteria that was rearing its ugly head again by 1941, thereby vindicating the prophetic analogy that *Johnny Got His Gun* drew just two years before. By the time *Remarkable Andrew* appeared, many Americans had accepted that their direct involvement in the wars across the Atlantic and the Pacific was a matter of time. At the same time it dawned on them that the nation, riven by internal dissension, was not prepared morally and militarily. That sparked all stripes of scare, red or brown. The Inquisition was on, in what pacifists and isolationists viewed as a complete reprise of vigilantism during the Great War. A swarm of "professional patriots" Sidney Howard lampooned in the previous decade came out of the woodwork. The first step in national mobilization, they demanded, was to purge the body politic of heretics, ranging from Bundists, Communists, pacifists, and syndicalists to children of the Jehovah's Witnesses who refused to salute the flag in public schools.[27] The Communists were systematically removed from ballots during the 1940 elections. Both at federal and state levels, statutes restricting freedom of speech flew onto the books. In sixteen states, it was now a crime to express opposition to war. Thirty states had a law against public display of red flags and other insignia.[28] The Sedition Act was repealed in 1920, but now it was back, as a clause buried deep in the innocuous-sounding Alien Registration Act of 1940 (the first peacetime sedition act in the nation's history).

Andrew Long is Trumbo's victim of the prewar mass hysteria. Hailing from a small town in the Midwest, like Joe Bonham, he is young, innocent, and wholesome. An upright accountant responsible for the city's book, he discovers one day an irregularity and reports it to his superiors. His unsuspecting conscientiousness costs him dearly. Fearful of exposure, a gang of peculators in the city hall scapegoat Long. A public outrage ensues, and it quickly spirals out of control. Egged on by a demagogic district attorney, local newspapers make wild accusations: Long is a pacifist, a Communist, a saboteur, a fifth columnist. At this point, a ghost of his namesake Andrew Jackson comes to Long's rescue, accompanied by a brigade of other patriots: George Washington, Benjamin Franklin, John Marshall, and Thomas Jefferson. Thanks to damning evidence obtained by these apparitions, Andrew Long is finally exonerated, receives a promotion, and marries his winsome sweetheart. Sharply contrasting with *Johnny*, *The Remarkable Andrew* was a light-hearted slapstick, complete with stock characters, fantastic devices, and a picture-perfect happy ending – essentially, a novelized Hollywood comedy (it was adapted for the screen in 1942). But they were both patterned after the same archetype: corrupting adults exploiting youthful naïveté. Trumbo drove this point through John Marshall (his apparition), who says: "The chief internal enemies of any state are not spies nor saboteurs nor the paid agents of foreign governments. They are, on the contrary, those myriads of public officials who betray the trust imposed upon them by the people."[29] In the novel, Andrew Long and his fresh-faced girlfriend alone are able to see the ghosts; the rest of the town thinks they are touched. The moral of this national allegory requires that having deviated from the nation's mission and core values, adults be incapable of seeing those founding fathers. Meanwhile, the characters representing the future of the nation form a deep fraternity of patriotism with the nation's oldest – that is, youngest – past.

It was all natural that, facing the military conflicts proliferating across the globe, Americans during the years leading up to World War II scoured the nation's past for hints and clues. The situation, seemingly unprecedented and unintelligible, became recognizable and manageable when viewed as an iteration of familiar events in the past. So far as something was to recur in the coming war, Americans could prepare for the future by revamping old habits and maxims. The story of how prewar writers interpreted, ignored, or revised the lessons of the Great War was thus part of the broader collective ransacking of the national past for usable symbols. The Great War was not just one of many wars the nation had fought in the past. It had the distinction of being the "last." Thanks to this proximity, it was to the Great War that the general public most intently turned for lessons. So vivid and raw its memory still was that the last war could serve as the most accessible frame of reference. In theory, of course, other wars in the nation's past could also be profitably referenced to shed light on the shape of things to come, and in fact the American people did use them to make sense of their potentially unprecedented situation. Because the appeal to the last war showed the next war in an unfavorable light, those desiring of a more vigorous exercise of American power had a particularly strong incentive to find more flattering wars to compare the next world war to. As we will see in Chapter 4, many thought that the Civil War was one such usable war.

These wars in the past were not inert and asleep. They did not idly wait for their lessons to be retrieved and applied to the contemporary situation. If prewar writers explained and their readers understood the meaning of the growing crisis in terms of the past wars, it was equally true that they interpreted the meaning of those past wars in terms of the contemporary crisis unfolding before their eye. If a writer thought that American participation in the next war would be a senseless blunder and those spewing lofty ideals in their advocacy for aid to sister democracies were treasonous fanatics lacking any regard for true national interests, that writer was likely to see in the Civil War a needless war, a war of choice, imposed on the Union by zealots and lunatics who put their noble principle – abolitionism – ahead of the nation's common interest. If a writer believed that, in the ongoing war of ideologies in world politics, democracies followed the first rule of propaganda and cloaked their parochial interests in false universals, that belief probably tempted this writer to see in the American Revolution a precursor of modern propaganda warfare. Sam Adams, as the title of a distinguished history book put it in 1936, was a "pioneer in propaganda." All that hot air about England's conspiratorial designs to "enslave" the colonists was a deceptive rhetoric to jolt public opinion against the monarchists.[30]

In an attempt to prescribe America's mandate in the future war by reference to the lessons of the past, the prewar culture also rewrote the nation's history, particularly the legacy of all the wars the country had waged since its founding. The past and the present interfere with each other. History always informs discussions of current affairs. The prewar culture confirmed, in the most dramatic fashion possible, these commonplaces.

The Theater of Remote Violence

The prewar culture also dramatized another truism, that geography was amenable to symbolic manipulation. Foreign wars, America's mission, democracy, freedom, tyranny – these words were not abstractions suspended in a metaphysical vacuum. Their meanings changed because they were dependent on the context, which was in turn determined as much by accidents of geography as by the weight of history. Was America responsible for the survival of democracy in general? How about the survival of democracy in China? Or democracy in Europe, in Africa, or in Latin America? If democracy were to be defended under the aspect of eternity, these geographical qualifications must not influence how to answer these questions. But national debates during the prewar years gave color to the cliché that normative questions of this sort, when posed in relation to an actual region and to America's capabilities that were constrained by geographical and technological limitations, could be answered only by taking into account location, distance, and other accidentals, such as race and culture, that went with them.

Distance, embodied in the two vast expanses of water insulating the New World from carnage overseas, comforted those who wanted to believe that their country could afford to leave the rest of the hapless world to its own devices. But to other Americans who thought that democracies in far-off lands were fighting America's fight and who wanted to recruit an indifferent public to their point of view, the obstinate fact of distance was a problem to be creatively circumvented. Thus prewar poets, playwrights, and fiction writers who were inspired by violence in remote lands stocked their arsenal with rhetorical weapons specially designed to explode the American myth of geographical separation. One of the most widely used devices to offset the estranging effect of distance was the romantic plot. There were many variants, but in most, the American protagonist visits faraway war zones and falls in love with a local character. The resulting tension between the romantic tie and the distance between the United States and the locale generate guilt-triggering messages about how peace and economic recovery in America were made possible by the accident of its geographical isolation. This was a banal and crude device, but its banality and crudity made it useful for diverse genres of writing. And consequently war-themed works published during this time period were littered with international romances, both tragic marriages and torrid one-night stands, all ruined by war. Perhaps the most notorious case in point was Hemingway's *For Whom the Bell Tolls* (1941). As many contemporary and later readers thought, the romantic subplot involving an affair between the flinty American antifascist and Maria, a Spanish girl gang-raped by fascists, was the one blot that marred the novel's otherwise well-considered design.

Like Hemingway, whom she married in 1941, Martha Gellhorn also mixed journalism and fiction writing and alchemized into fictions things she saw as a pioneering female foreign correspondent. Also like Hemingway, she often used romantic ties between American characters and local characters to highlight the morally compromised nature of American isolation. Unlike Hemingway, however, for Gellhorn, icily dissecting the moral complexity of an American embedded in a foreign war was almost second nature. Her stories, thus, often emphasized how foreign crises she covered in fictions and dispatches were inaccessible not only to her readers back home but also to the journalists themselves who were temporarily entangled in the situations they reported on. A case in point is Mary, the journalist-protagonist of her novel on the crisis in Czechoslovakia, *A Stricken Field* (1940). She is clear-headed about her job's limits and, by extension, how little isolationist America could do to alleviate the plights of Europeans. Mary thinks of herself as a "rich brainless American." She self-flagellates, telling herself, "You get an eyeful and it gives you the horrors and you leave; you just buy a ticket and take a plane and leave." When Germany occupies Czechoslovakia, she exercises her American prerogative, namely the privilege of a neutral visitor, forsakes the local sources she has cultivated and grown attached to, and decamps for

Paris. Mary is conscious of the moral shabbiness of her action, but she also knows that her just being aware of it does not absolve her of guilt. At the airport in Prague, "Mary gave the customs inspector her passport first. It was always wise to establish yourself as an American. Americans travel all the time, blindly and cheerfully."[31] Less complicated correspondents like Dorothy Thompson would have blurted out that "Americans *should not* travel all the time, blindly and cheerfully," and that it is not "wise" but cowardly to shield oneself behind one's American passport. But Mary cannot say what she means, or cannot think what she wants to think, because she cannot stand the idea that her sincere thoughts change nothing about America's relation to a stricken field that was Europe. Therefore, she chooses to assume the voice of the cheerfully blind isolationist American, a choice that gives her a soupçon of consolation in her superior awareness of irony. When Gellhorn actually tried to ensnare her freewheeling American adventurer, and by proxy her readers, in the destinies of the locals through more explicitly romantic connections, the moral of her stories became altogether indecipherable. Her short story "Portrait of a Lady," for example, narrated a battlefield fling. Maynard – a bored, jaded, and hedonistic American correspondent covering the Winter War – meets Lahti, a lusty Finish ace pilot, and develops for some inexplicable reasons an intense crush on him. Possessive and predatory, she sleeps with the pilot the night before an important sortie. Deprived of sleep, crucial for pilots who need hair-trigger reflexes, Lahti is shot down next morning, and the story ends with Maynard staring dejectedly at his severely charred body retrieved from the crash site.[32]

In Maxwell Anderson's maudlin drama *Candle in the Wind* (directed by Alfred Lunt), the traveling American takes the form of an earnest American actress in France, Madeline (played by Helen Hayes), who falls in love with a French soldier, Raoul. The play was brazenly propagandistic, a failure both artistically and commercially, but Anderson didn't mind. He was so frustrated by American callousness to the predicament of European democracies that for once he volunteered to turn himself into a propaganda hack, fully aware that he was jeopardizing his reputation as a master craftsman of verse play. He admitted as much to Atkinson, who, along with most other reviewers, penned a mildly hostile review: "I didn't even try for it [a great play]. I tried for propaganda against Hitler. Maybe not very effectively, but that's what was in mind. And I still haven't given up hope that I'll write that great play."[33] The press release by the Playwrights Company all but dropped the pretension that it was a play or a piece of entertainment: "'Candle in the Wind' represents the crystallization of Anderson's thought concerning the present international situation. Seclusion in New York City does not to him mean isolation. Far from turning his home into an ivory tower, he has used it as a sanctuary wherein to clarify for himself, and possibly for others, the values at stake in today's conflict."[34] Putting into practice his theory that the theater clarified the audience's value system, Anderson's play served up a melodramatic picture of the global conflict in black and white, completely stripped of moral shadings in between, for the audience's approbation and damnation. The play pitted the angels, the French-American couple, against Satan, the Nazi occupiers. Raoul goes to Dunkirk to help the British Expeditionary Forces evacuate. Afterward, he wants to go back to Versailles to be reunited with Madeline as they previously planned, but the Nazis arrest and imprison him in a concentration camp in a Paris suburb. The Nazi goons come after Madeline, too, but predictably her American passport turns out to be an almighty talisman that awes all the warring governments in Europe. Instead of evacuating, Madeline stays in Paris and devises a scheme to bribe the prison guards and rescue Raoul. The heartless guards string the desperate American actress along. They take her ransom money but always break their word at the last minute – except for one good German, Schone, an assistant to the prison head, who is moved by Madeline and helps her. Raoul finally escapes, and the two lovers promise to reunite in England as the curtain falls.

International romance also triumphed over distance and American neutrality in Alice Miller's narrative poem *The White Cliffs*, which was published in late 1940. Of all the poems dealing with the new European war, it was without any doubt the most widely read. As a matter of fact, Miller's verse story proved to be the biggest commercial success for this prolific novelist, essayist, and dramatist. It sold more than 200,000 copies in the United States and 100,000 copies in England in two years.[35] Miller took it out on a nationwide reading tour. Lynn Fontanne read it on the radio and recorded it. In May 1941, *Life* featured a condensed version, which instantly reached additional millions.[36] The timing was opportune. After three months of congressional wrangling, the Lend-Lease was just signed into law. America was officially and legally the "arsenal of democracy." Miller's long poem, which span fifty-two rhythmical stanzas, sought to tighten the spiritual and racial tie between the two English-speaking nations with a story about a Yankee woman from Rhode Island, Susan Dunne, who marries into an old English family in Devon. Narrated by Susan, the poem tells a simple story. She falls in love with a British lad while visiting England as a tourist, marries him, conceives a son before her husband dies in the trenches during the Great War, and twenty years later, with England, her adopted country, again at war against Germany, agonizes how to respond to her son's question if England is worth fighting, and possibly dying, for. The poem ends thus:

> I am American bred,
> I have seen much to hate here – much to forgive,
> But in a world where England is finished and dead,
> I do not wish to live.

Miller's diction was supremely glib, perfectly attuned to the ear of the millions of middlebrow lovers of well-made verse. The poem as a whole did not follow any rigid pattern, but stanzas unspooled spontaneously on and on, thanks to a format vaguely reminiscent of a traditional ballad, with randomly rhymed trimeter and tetrameter alternating with each other. The main conceit was again transatlantic romance, in this case, the American woman's marriage to a man from a country now under Axis attack. The poem did not just sing an uncomplicated encomium for the British Empire. Miller preemptively addressed the most common sources of the public's mistrust of England: the bad blood running between the two countries (the war of independence and the war of 1812), Britain's class hierarchy that was offensive to American populism, and injustice it had historically done to the Irish. In the poem, Susan's father, a proud New Englander, serves as the main mouthpiece for anti-British sentiments. A letter he writers to his daughter during the Great War drips with the popular misgivings about British machination: "The English are clever as sin,/ Silently, subtly they inspire/ Most of youth with a holy fire; To shed their blood for the British Empire."[37] Toward the end of the poem, however, all these suspicions and reservations are swept aside by a ringing appeal to "our forefathers" who were English. Miller's unapologetic pandering to Anglophilia and her fawning compliments to British mannerisms and physiognomy that embroider the whole verse story must have been music to many pro-British Americans, although they certainly drove distraught a sizable segment of the public, the Irish Americans and other Anglophobes, who objected to America's global leadership precisely because they saw it as a pretext for aid to perfidious Albion.

Prewar writers also fanned the fear of airborne invasions in order to neutralize the remoteness of violence. Roosevelt set the example. Certainly, distance was a function of speed. It followed that new transportation technologies had to change America's distance from the world, he explained in his many fireside chats and public addresses. Roosevelt's almost childlike obsession with maps and his mastery of geography were widely known among insiders. Looking back on the "arsenal of democracy" speech, which introduced the Lend-Lease bill on the floor of Congress, Samuel Rosenman later wrote that "no one could equal the President in making geography clear, and in this speech he showed how the Nazis could step from base to base right up to our borders. He always dictated such passages himself, and we used to marvel that he was usually able to do it without even looking at a map."[38] Another bravura performance was his May 16, 1940, message to Congress. Following the German invasion of the Low Countries, Roosevelt asked Congress speedily to appropriate another $1.18 million for national defense. Just so that all the members of the Senate and the House present at this special joint session would know what calamitous consequences would follow a failure to act on his request, Roosevelt conjured up a vivid motion picture of a hypothetical German invasion of the Western Hemisphere step by step: "The islands off the west coast of Africa are only 1,500 miles from Brazil. Modern planes starting from the Cape Verde Islands can be over Brazil in seven hours. And Para, Brazil, near the mouth of the Amazon River, is but four flying-hours to Caracas, Venezuela; and Venezuela is but two and one-half hours to Cuba and the Canal Zone; and Cuba and the Canal Zone are two and one-quarter hours to Tampico, Mexico." It was proper and fitting that the final destination of this simulated German offensive was the symbolic heartland of America: "and Tampico is two and one-quarter hours to St. Louis, Kansas City and Omaha."[39]

In these graphic messages, Roosevelt was using gimmicks and formulas perfected by poets like Archibald MacLeish, who started helping him with his speeches once he assumed the position of Librarian of Congress in 1939. MacLeish's radio play *Air Raid* was broadcast on October 27, 1938. This particular date is of historical significance. It came fast on the heel of the Munich Crisis and only three days before Orson Welles's *War of the Worlds* sparked panics among listeners who mistook fantasy for fact. Musing on the mass hysteria provoked by Welles's *War of the Worlds* (though it was not as widespread as portrayed by the print media nervous about the radio's growing popularity and influence), cultural critic Lewis Mumford remarked that "[t]he terror that gripped a multitude of radio listeners in the United States at the dramatic broadcast of an invasion of the country – an invasion by imaginary creatures from Mars – demonstrates the pathological state into which fascism's brutalities have thrown the world. Our isolationism is gone. New York is actually nearer to Berlin today than it was to Philadelphia in Washington's time."[40] MacLeish's *Air Raid* preyed on this "pathological state."

The play opens with the unnamed announcer directly addressing the listeners as "you": "You have only one thought tonight and only one: Will there be war? Has war come? Is Europe burning from the Tiber to the Somme?" The announcer's role is more hypnotic than informative. Instead of communicating information to the listeners, he tells the listeners what thoughts to think, what sights to see, and what questions to ask. An unnamed aggressor nation has issued an ultimatum. If a small nation in a mountainous region does not surrender by sunrise, the aggressor nation vows to launch massive air strikes. The announcer's mesmeric voice not only eases the listeners into a particular mental state, the apprehension of air strikes; it also binds the radio listeners to the announcer. His voice flows into the listeners' most private space, their mind. He speaks now and the listeners hear now. This shared "now" creates the illusion of proximity, or even immediacy, despite the physical distance that separates the studio from millions of drawing rooms. Having primed the listeners with the fear of air strikes and merged his being with that of his listeners, the announcer next turns himself into a vehicle, presumably an airplane, when he promises to the listeners that "we'll try to take you through." "The visibility is perfect," and the announcer, like a pilot pointing passengers to sights down below, depicts the vast panorama of the European continent. "The sun is up on the whole curve of that continent" and the "whole continent lolls in summer sunlight." As the airplane approaches the destination, an idyllic village in a mountainous region, the announcer's descriptions grow more detailed: "across the merchant's villa with the vine above the porch, across the laborer's city with the flames above the forges, across the drover's plain, the planter's valley …," until the listeners are told "you are there." The Americans listening to their radios at night "are out the other side of the night." Alongside the announcer, the listeners turn up, so to speak, among villagers. Mostly they are women and children, as men have gone out to work in fields at dawn and won't return until evening. Not so subtly MacLeish compares these villagers to the American people oblivious of how the nature of war has changed due to the advent of airplanes: the traditional distinction between the front and the rear, between combatants and civilians, was no longer valid. War will not come, the village women chitchat with each other as they take care of their daily chores and children run about. Even if it comes, they assure one another, it would kill only soldiers and generals. "We are women. No one's making war on women," and they can be so confident because war "never harmed us!" All the while, the announcer anxiously keeps scanning the sky for signs of approaching bombers and encourages his listeners to do the same. First they hear the sound. Next they see squadron after squadron of bombers in fighting formation. Women ignore the order to hide in the vaults. Hoping that the pilots won't attack if they see they are only women, they run out to the plaza, only to be massacred by the nose-diving planes.[41]

As in MacLeish's previous radio play *Fall of the City* (April 1937) that similarly warned of foreign invasions, three elements–the listener, the announcer, and villagers–co-inhabit the fictional space overseas in *Air Raid*.[42] And the slightly differing relations among these three elements more or less determine its didactic effect. The listener is most identified with the announcer. There is a sense of reciprocity here, in the sense that the listener sees the announcer as much as the latter sees the former. They also join in their shared sense of separation from the villagers. The listener and the announcer see, hear, and think about (but never listen to) the villagers, but the latter cannot look back at the listener and the announcer, despite the illusion that they all occupy the same fictional space. Despite their witnessing the scene, the position of the announcer and the listener is essentially spectatorial or even voyeuristic. They are with but not of the village. There is also an infinitesimal gap between the listener and the announcer. While the announcer's direct address forms the illusion of the unified "we" between the addresser and the addressed, the listener relies on the announcer for the means of transportation and the prompts for what the listener should see and hear (the village women are pathetic-ally misinformed, the dive bombers won't discriminate, and so forth). The announcer is a reliable narrator, and the listener's sense of dependence may be forgotten momentarily but never disappears altogether. In short, the listener never becomes the announcer any more than the latter becomes the former. These relationships combine to narrow a gamut of the listen-er's responses. The listener cannot quite bring himself to pity this foreign country. Although he is present at its brutal destruction, he does not feel its suffering vicariously enough to feel sorry. The play does not induce in the listener an urge to help and participate. He is a passive spectator, busily comparing the announcer's correct running commentary with the villagers' errors. Nor does the play stir up in the listener a burning rage against the "unusual enemy." The enemy's representation is too impersonal to harden the listener's emotion. The only emotional state that remains for the listener is that of alarm, the feeling of being spooked out, which may give rise to the resolve to apply the village's lesson to his own situation.

Another Pulitzer Prize–winning poet Stephen Vincent Bénet also traf-ficked in the fear of air raids. After the outbreak of war in Europe, the author of the national epic *John Brown's Body* (1928) and former cryptographer for the State Department during the last war (fearing the Army would reject him for his poor eyesight, Bénet memorized an eye exam chart and managed to be sworn in, but the military soon discovered his severe myopia and discharged him) lent his patriotic credential to several propaganda campaigns. As *Luftwaffe* stepped up air raids on British cities in the fall of 1940, Bénet wrote a long poem *Nightmare at Noon*, to be disseminated by the Council for Democracy, a pro-Allies advocacy group run by East Coast interventionists working at the nexus of the academy and the publishing.[43] By juxtaposing a peaceful park in an American city on a sunny day with London, Paris, and Rotterdam under the threat of indiscriminate bombing, the poem at once mocked American complacency and warned of an imminent airborne invasion. The ending leaves the speaker terror-stricken by his "nightmare," listening for the distant hum of German bombers: "I shall not sleep tonight when I hear the plane."[44]

Incidentally, Bénet complemented, as MacLeish did, his versified attacks on pacifism with his spread-eagle oratories about the virility of American democratic tradition. On the evening of November 6, 1940, as the heat and clamor of the presidential election slowly subsided, actor Raymond Massey, who played the title character in Robert Sherwood's *Abe Lincoln in Illinois*, went on the air with a call for post-election national unity. Its text was prepared by Bénet. On July 4, 1941, his verse drama, "Listen to the People," was broadcast through a nationwide hookup, each part read by popular actors, airtime paid for by the Council of Democracy. The play was reprinted entirely in *Life* magazine, part of Henry Luce's media empire where C. D. Jackson, president of the Council for Democracy and later Eisenhower's chief of psychological warfare, was a vice president.[45] Bénet's collaboration with various propaganda outfits, within the government and without, would continue well into wartime, until his untimely death in 1943.

Edna St. Vincent Millay, very much politically engaged by the late 1930s, also used a hypothetical air raid on American mainland in her numerous anti-Axis poems. Notwithstanding her public image as the reigning poetess of the Jazz Age, a promiscuous "new woman," pale, willowy, and fey, burning her candle at both ends in a garret in Greenwich Village, Millay had never been an entirely apolitical writer, as attested by her most celebrated political poem that commemorated the executions of Sacco and Vanzetti, "Justice Denied in Massachusetts" (1927). Modernists and purists were not fooled by her racy lifestyle that defied the genteel tradition. They knew, however vaguely, that bisexuality and open marriage did not necessarily make the avant-garde art. In 1938, Allen Tate wrote in "Tension in Poetry," his manifesto for formalism, that "Mass language is the medium of 'communication,' and its users are less interested in bringing to formal order what is sometimes called the 'affective state' than in arousing that state."[46] To explain how "mass language" operated in poetry, he went on to let loose the smooth-running machine of New Criticism on a stanza from Millay's "Justice Denied." While it is debatable whether the communicative and agitational use of language was the definitive trait of Millay's poetry, her interest in communication rather than expression and her adeptness at "arousing" a desired "affective state" became more and more pronounced as her obsession with the plight of European democracies (and her addiction to morphine) grew in the late 1930s. The fact that her husband's family and relatives lived in a Nazi-occupied Holland also added to her impatience with her country's cautious foreign policy.[47] Her October 1939 radio speech, for example, gave expression to her impatience with America's dishonest pretension to neutrality. Just a month ago, Roosevelt said in his first radio address after the German invasion of Poland that Americans must remain neutral technically but in their heart they could not help wishing victory for the Allies. Millay agreed: "Why, then, should we be so afraid to say that as regards the war between a Germany whose political philosophy is repugnant to us and an allied Britain and France whose concepts of civilized living are so closely akin to our own that we hope with all our hearts that Great Britain and France may win this war and Germany lose?"[48] Her hope that American aid would effectively prop up European democracies was dashed by France's terrifyingly swift collapse in the early summer of 1940. On the day that Paris declared itself open city before the advancing Germany columns, Millay's "Lines Written in Passion and in Deep Concern for England, France and My Own Country" appeared in major New York dailies. The poem was soon reprinted by Harper in booklet form under the new title, "There Are No Islands, Any More." The poem opened with a mocking salutation to insular Americans:

> Dear Isolationist, you are
> So very, very insular!
> Surely you do not take offense? –
> The word's well used in such sense.
> 'Tis you, not I, sir, who insist
> You are Isolationist.

And it closed with a breathless exhortation to "the arsenal of democracy":

> Oh, build, assemble, transport, give,
> That England, France and we may live,

Before tonight, before too late,
To those who hold our country's fate
In desperate fingers, reaching out
For weapons we confer about...

Lest French and British fighters, deep
In battle, needing guns and sleep,
For lack of aid be overthrown,
And we be left to fight alone.[49]

Millay's prosodic virtuosity backfires. Since her breakout poem "Renascence" (1917), rhymed iambic tetrameter was one of her most sharply honed techniques, but its sing-song quality here detracts from the gravity of the occasion.

A premonition of surprise air strike against America shadowed "Four Sonnets," a cluster of poems Millay published in the fall of 1940, about the same time Bénet's *Nightmare at Noon* appeared. Poems and accompanying images were carefully arranged on the page of *The New York Times*. The four sonnets on war appeared in the middle as so many columns. Above this middle band of poetry was a large photograph of buildings in European cities reduced to rubble by air raids. Below was a photograph of the Statue of Liberty, silhouetted by a rising sun beyond. Lest this montage should allow scope for divergent interpretations, the first sonnet specified the poem's political message:

We are so sound asleep, how can we know
What thirst and want surround our sunny dream?
Men wide-awake, men well-equipped,
On certainty, attack the slumbering towns:

Following Bénet's example, Millay may well have titled this first sonnet *Nightmare at Sunrise*. The picture above visualized what could happen to the Statue of Liberty pictured below, at any moment in the age of air war. The technical riddle these poets had to solve at the height of the Battle over Britain was basically the same: how to annihilate distance, both temporal and geographical, between future and present, war and peace, Europe and America. For it was this distance that created uncertainty and hope, which misled Americans to presume that their country could stay out.

Radio, the new technology of mass communications that, along with air travel, determined how depression-era Americans understood distance, also transformed the meaning of threats and crises that originated in far-off lands. Diaries, letters, and memoirs of prewar writers are strewn with testimonies to the radio's ubiquity in their day-to-day lives. It was apparently by their radio more than anything else that they learned of most critical foreign events. In tense times of crisis, their waking hours were all spent in the radio's vicinity. The following letter by Martha Gellhorn describing her life with Hemingway in the spring 1940 captures well the atmosphere:

> We have a new radio. We got one new radio two days ago so that we could get our disaster fresh on the hour instead of waiting for the mail boat. It was a very puky [sic] radio and was just like having a damned soul in the house. So another radio came out today, with an old typical Cuban loony in charge, one of those who knows everything and immediately burns out all the fuses in the house. I am not a partisan of the radio normally but now that we are waiting to hear of England being invaded I am glad to have it. Ernest on the other hand is a fiend for the radio and cannot leave this one alone. It is very handsome and complicated and a round green light goes on and wavers about, and if the circle of light is closed that shows you have everything perfect. Ernest is busy with the radio all the time, and even in the middle of dinner will rush out to adjust it. So this evening he shouted to me, "I've got Delhi." "Have you," I said, "What are they saying?" "They say mahatma Gandhi's a bum," he said. What with the radio and the maps we are very busy. I think on the whole it would be quicker just to go to the war and see for ourselves.[50]

Unsurprisingly, the radio became an indispensable prop for prewar dramatists casting about for effective ways to circumvent distance and bring foreign wars home to the domestic audience. A massive and ornate radio console (this was the time when the radio was supposed to look like furniture) dominates the stage set (a German consulate in an unnamed American city) of Clare Boothe's *Margin for Error* (1939), an anti-Nazi play by Henry Luce's wife. In the scene where the Nazi consul is mysteriously murdered, Hitler's Reichstag speech, supposedly broadcast live from Berlin, floods the stage for two minutes. "THE VOICE" engulfs the entire theater and transforms the play into a dumb act. The stage direction reads: "*And now the Awful, Awful Voice of Hitler, the man who talked a nation and perhaps a civilization to its doom begins, hysterical, guttural, hideously sure and hard and loud.*"[51] The radio's unnerving capability to carry the deranged voice of the enemy instantly across the Atlantic elicited the fear that mere geographical distance may not guarantee national security.

Robert Adrey's *Thunder Rock* (1939) used the radio to a similar effect. The story was set on a tiny island in Lake Michigan, a rather literalistic substitute for an insular America. The play follows a conversion plot of sorts, which centers on Charleston, a veteran of the International Brigade in Spain and now a lighthouse guard. He has sequestered himself from

world events, nursing his idealism that has been mortally wounded by
Franco's victory in Spain. Even so, world politics manages to stalk him to
his sanctuary through the radio set he brings with him. The radio foreign
news bulletin – "From Warsaw: Frontier reports say that Polish soil has
been invaded by German motorized units" – catalyzes Charleston's
reawakening to internationalism, his calm resolution to brave the world
at large again.[52]

The main objective of these antifascist plays and radio plays was
essentially to "destroy" the "most obstinate of all the superstitions against
which poetry and all the arts have fought for centuries," the "superstition
of distance and of time." MacLeish articulated these thoughts at a party
honoring Edward Murrow:

> [Addressing to Murrow in the audience] You destroyed in the minds of
> many men and women of this country the superstition that what is done
> across three thousand miles of water is not really done at all; the ignorant
> superstition that violence and lies and murder on another continent are not
> violence and lies and murder here; the cowardly and brutal superstition that
> the enslavement of mankind in a country where the sun rises at midnight
> by our clocks is not enslavement by the time we live by; the black and
> stifling superstition that what we cannot see and hear and touch can have
> no meaning for us. ...
>
>   Sometimes you said you were speaking from a roof in London looking at
> the London sky. Sometimes you said you spoke from underground beneath
> that city. But it was not in London really that you spoke. It was in the back
> kitchens and the front living rooms and the moving automobiles and the
> hotdog stands and the observation cars of another country that your voice was
> truly speaking. And what you did was this: You made real and urgent and
> present to the men and women of those comfortable rooms, those safe
> enclosures, what these men and women had not known was present there
> or real. You burned the city of London in our houses and we felt the flames
> that burned it. You laid the dead of London at our doors and we know the
> dead were our dead – were all men's dead – were mankind's dead – and ours.[53]

Five days after this black-tie event, the Japanese bombers descended on
Pearl Harbor. And with this attack, the obstinacy of distance as superstition was broken, for good.

Not all dramatists adopted the radio as a convenient stage prop to
destroy the superstition of distance. Some actually used it to elongate it
in order to advocate American commitment to distant wars *despite* their
remoteness. A case in point was Robert Sherwood's play *There Shall Be No
Night* (among its working titles was *Come in, Helsinki*). Like *Thunder Rock*
and Sherwood's own *Abe Lincoln in Illinois* (1938), this play is patterned

after the conversion narrative: Finnish scientist Dr. Valkonen's (played by Alfred Lunt) conversion from peace-loving one-worldism to vigorous antitotalitarianism. Around this main storyline the play spins a web of analogies and connections between the United States and Finland, which is, as one character puts it, "a really free country" that "has made democracy work."[54] In Scene VI, Dr. Valkonen (who is married to an American woman from Minnesota, played by Lynn Fontanne) compares the Kalevala, the Finnish epic poem, to the Declaration of Independence: "Every Finnish child learns about the Kalevala – just as Americans learn those words about Life, Liberty and the Pursuit of Happiness."[55] Sherwood used these parallels to good effect, to shame America for abandoning its little sister republic in Scandinavia.[56] As a wealth of favorable reviews attests, Sherwood's message was blunt and ringing. Finns were just surrogates fighting America's war against the Red Army.

While his fellow dramatists impressed on the audience the need to ally with small democracies around the world by hypnotically annihilating distance with an enactment of life-like slaughters, Sherwood performed the same task by elongating distance. The action onstage obviously created the illusion of immediacy. The theater destroyed the distance separating the United States from the Winter War by magically transporting the audience from Broadway to Helsinki and to the Mannerheim Line. The audience was able to witness, safely reposed behind the proverbial fourth wall, another democracy in Europe laid waste by marauding totalitarians. And yet, this illusion of presence was interrupted by radio-broadcasting scenes interspersed throughout the play. Sherwood's scenario featured a CBS war correspondent David Corween (drawn from a real CBS correspondent in Helsinki, Bill White, William Allen White's son). Onstage, the audience saw him filing dispatches over radio from Helsinki. These radio-broadcasting scenes were simply a reenactment of what any radio audience would imagine was happening with war correspondents in the world's geopolitical hot spots. But at the same time, to the audience members in the theater, these scenes held up a mirror in which they saw themselves transformed into the absent American public, the distant audience the war correspondent in Europe wants to reach via airwaves. No sooner did the life-like actions onstage transport an American audience slumbering in the cocoon of geographical isolation to the front line than the transported audience was compelled to recognize itself as an invisible bystander removed from the battlefield. By this whip-sawing, Sherwood was able to create a believable theatrical metaphor for an isolationist America, that is, the spectator of remote violence.

If anything, thus, the radio in *There Shall Be No Night* stretched, not destroyed, the distance between America and Finland. The radio speech in Boothe's *Margin for Error* plunged the German threat right in the heart of the American audience. It signaled that the debate over neutrality was moot because the war was already "here." MacLeish's *Air Raid* hypnotized the audience and transported it to a foreign battlefield. By contrast, the transatlantic radio broadcasts in *There Shall Be No Night* shuttled the audience in the theater back and forth between America, where they actually resided, and the battlefield. This constant relocation back and forth should have had an effect of dramatizing, not hypnotically diminishing, the distance that the audience traveled while taking in the drama onstage. As Sherwood and his friends at the Playwrights Company left no doubt, *There Shall Be No Night* was designed to mobilize the audience for U.S. intervention on behalf of Finland against European dictatorships, but its persuasiveness did not depend on the magically or analogically evoked proximity to the conflict. On the contrary, the play insisted on a much more radical obligation – to defend democracy everywhere in the world regardless of distance.

From 1935 to 1941, these two problems – one of history and the other of geography – anchored the succession of eclectic, helter-skelter, and centrifugal debates over America's role in the world. The prewar culture raised a variety of questions, but most of them could be, and were actually, translated into the terms set by these two problems. In that regard, one could say that the problem of time and the problem of space imparted a sense of continuity to the series of episodes, that confronted America with their own distinct problems. Beginning in the next chapter, I retrace these episodes chronologically. I document a multitude of differentiated forms that the two problems of history and geography adopted, discuss other more distinctive dilemmas that each of these episodes posed, and explain how what came before overdetermined the perception of what came later.

2

ETHIOPIA, Lift Your Night-Dark Face

ETHIOPIA,
Lift your night-dark face
      Abyssinian
      Son of Sheba's race!
      Your Palm trees tall
      And your mountains high
      Are shade and shelter
      To men who die
      For freedom's sake
      But in the wake of your sacrifice
      May all Africa rise
      With blazing eyes and night-dark face
      In answer to the call of Sheba's race:
Ethiopia's free
Be like me
All of Africa
Arise and be free
All you black peoples
Be Free! Be Free!

                  Langston Hughes (1935)

European imperial powers had fully divided up Africa by the turn of the century. Three decades later, as the oppressive pall of economic depression began enveloping the entire world, the most basic fact about Africa's geopolitical condition remained unchanged: colonialism in Africa was at saturation point. No further colonial conquest could occur without disturbing the modus vivendi among the European occupiers.

The exception to this status quo was the ancient Kingdom of Abyssinia, alluded to three times in *Iliad* as ETHIOPIA, the Land of Burnt Faces. Unfortunately for Ethiopians, when Mussolini's Italy embarked on empire-building across the Mediterranean by consolidating Libya, Eritrea, and Italian Somaliland, this latecomer colonial power found a perfectly located prize in this kingdom. Around late 1934, skirmishing between Italy and Ethiopia over a border village began to escalate. Ethiopia appealed to the League of Nations, in vain. Just as during the Japanese invasion of Manchuria three years previously, Geneva showed itself inept and powerless. With the French and the British abetting the Italian invasion with nods and winks for fear that their resistance might drive a piqued Mussolini into Hitler's embrace, both Italy and Ethiopia steadily mobilized their armed forces over the next ten months. In October 1935, hostilities officially commenced with the Italian invasion across the Eritrean border.[1]

"In 1935, Italian troops invaded Ethiopia," notes a later historian, "and, in the eyes of black observers the world over, inaugurated World War II."[2] With the outbreak of the new African conflict, American prewar writers, most notably those of African descent, began producing works that explored the meaning of the world crisis to their country with an altogether unprecedented degree of urgency and seriousness. To put this all rather dramatically, the Fascist invasion of the oldest sovereign nation in the horn of Africa gave birth to the prewar literary culture.

12,000,000

With the nation's isolationist temper peaking around the same time, the U.S. government's response to Ethiopia's plea for succor was measured to the point of timorous. The administration invoked the Neutrality Act, which was just passed a few days before the onset of the war.[3] The policy of strict neutrality was enforced to the furthest peripheries of the federal government. When apprised that the first production, titled *Ethiopia*, of Living Newspaper–one of the innumerable units within the New York regional unit of the Federal Theatre Project–might offend Il Duce, the State Department swiftly pressured the Works Progress Administration to scrap it. Protesting against government censorship, Elmer Rice, director of the New York regional program, huffily resigned.[4]

Outside the realm of diplomacy, most ordinary white Americans barely heeded neo-Roman imperialism's rampage through the Ethiopian highlands, 7,000 miles away. If they evinced any interest, its sundry expressions were usually marked by a lack of urgency, outrage, or fear. Granted, not so negligible numbers of white citizens formed strong opinions and expressed them forcefully. Notable among them were many Italian Americans and Catholics who expressed their proud support for Il Duce's civilizing mission in East Africa.[5] Some in the press also disseminated similar apologies for Fascist colonialism, including the papers under Hearst's control. Their editorials, citing various Ethiopian customs like domestic "slavery" and inhumane criminal punishments like mutilation, argued that the Italians had a mandate to tutor the benighted subjects of Emperor Haile Selassie in the ways of civilization, humanism, and modernity.[6] All the same, what little negative coverage the Ethiopian cause suffered failed to sway an indifferent public one way or another. The great masses of white Americans simply did not interpret the Italian aggression in terms that directly bore on America's vital interests and core ideals.

The interests and ideals of the twelve million African Americans, however, were altogether different. Understandably, their reactions were molded by their peculiar living conditions that separated them from the white mainstream. Bigger Thomas, Richard Wright's avatar of black fury in *Native Son* (1940), affords us an intimate glimpse into the black people's worldview at the time. This slayer of a white maiden is imprisoned in a world of nebulous feelings and inchoate fantasies:

> Of late he had liked to hear of men who could rule others, for in actions such as these he felt that there was a way to escape from this tight morass of fear and shame that sapped at the base of his life. He liked to hear of how Japan was conquering China; of how Hitler was running the Jews to the ground; of how Mussolini was invading Spain. He was not concerned with whether these acts were right or wrong; they simply appealed to him as possible avenues of escape. He felt that some day there would be a black man who would whip the black people into a tight band and together they would act and end fear and shame.[7]

The most revealing detail is the hero's substitution of Spain for Ethiopia. The substitution betrayed the hero's effort to suppress the "morass of fear and shame" to which the Ethiopian defeat had already added. Thanks to this substitution, moreover, the resurgent ethnocentric nationalism could inspire the hero to destructive black fascism, a sort that was more aggressive than could have been envisioned if Wright had used Ethiopia's defensive and doomed battle as the occasion for the hero's dream of race chauvinism. Bigger Thomas was of course a fictional character, whose relation to his creator was at best tenuous and tortuous. But his fears and dreams clearly indicate that, unarticulated or unvoiced as they usually were, similar reactions to the world crisis were available to great numbers of blacks, who, James Baldwin thought, all had their private Bigger Thomas living in their skulls.[8]

Bigger Thomas's yearning for an "escape" in race war and his hankering for a black *Führer* should surprise no one tolerably acquainted with the deathly powerlessness of blacks in 1930s America. Despite the ongoing great migration north, the overwhelming majority (78.7 percent, according to the 1930 census) of blacks still resided in the Deep South (where Wright himself grew up before he joined the black exodus north, to Chicago). In states like Georgia, Alabama, Mississippi, and Texas, blacks arguably had fewer civil rights than did Jews in Germany, if not after the launch of officially sanctioned pogroms there in 1938. Seventy years after the Emancipation, an elaborate web of artfully designed legal trickeries and extralegal violence still ensnared blacks in disfranchisement. Lynching even increased during this time, the number jumping from seven in 1929 to twenty-one in 1930, 1931, and 1932, and twenty-eight in 1933.[9]

Meanwhile, in northern industrial centers like Chicago, Cleveland, Detroit, Cincinnati, and Pittsburgh, blacks' struggle to better their conditions made little headway against informal segregation, race prejudice, and lack of economic opportunities. In 1933, when nationwide unemployment stood just under 25 percent, unemployment among blacks in some cities exceeded a staggering 50 percent.[10] Their hardship was so relentless and their antagonists so openly hostile, black life came to resemble a daily warfare. Richard Wright certainly had in mind the ongoing war between European "democracies" and the Axis powers when he compared the inner-city life to war. "Again we say," the choric voice of *12 Million Black Voices* (1941) ululated, "that life of us is daily warfare and that we live hard, like soldiers" fighting "this slow death on the city pavements." Continuing with the figure, the collective voice of black folk told: "We are set apart from the civilian population; our kitchenettes comprise our barracks; the color of our skins constitutes our uniforms; the streets of our cities are our trenches; a job is a pill-box to be captured and held. ... We are always in battle, but the tidings of victory are few." White Americans had their attention riveted on headlines about Chungking, Guernica, Warsaw, Rotterdam, and London subjected to indiscriminate air raids, but, Wright reminded them, "[e]ven in times of peace some of the neighborhoods in which we live look as though they had been subjected to an intensive and prolonged aerial bombardment."[11] An accompanying photograph showed a lone waif, a black girl in a checkered short skirt and knee-high socks roaming a desolate ghetto landscape, bestrewn with debris, bricks, and trash – the detritus of the urban race war.

We will never know how many ordinary blacks buckling under the historically unprecedented level of economic strains regarded foreign wars and their significance to America through the lens of race war, but many surely did, as most clearly illustrated by their reaction to the Ethiopian war.

Fascist Italy's assault on the land of the sons of Sheba's race galvanized countless black communities across the country. The broad-based mobilization of black masses that ensued marked a watershed in the history of colored America's engagement with foreign affairs. Up to that moment, compared to white ethnics such as Irish Americans, American Czechs, and American Jews, blacks had been historically cagey about promoting African interests. One reason for this mixture of diffidence and indifference stemmed from the Victorian aspirations to civilization, gentility, sexual restraint, temperance, and respectability. These ideals influenced the way race leaders as well as the black bourgeoisie understood their relation to their continent of ancestry. They were certainly troubled by European powers' imperial deviltries, but until the 1920s or thereabout Africa remained to them a land of primitives and heathens awaiting guidance from their more civilized brethren in America.[12] Another reason had to do with African Americans' uniqueness in an increasingly multiethnic America, the sheer savagery of discrimination and oppression that separated them from other minorities. Their hold on what little political gains they had earned was very much precarious compared to that of other ethnic and racial groups. Black people could ill afford the appearance of disloyalty or divided allegiance.[13] Moreover, their ability to influence those in the position of political power was almost wholly tied up in initiatives connected with domestic issues (antilynching bills, anti-Jim Crow bills, causes célèbres like the Scottsboro Youths and Angelo Herndon). Blacks had little capital, political or financial, to spare for distant causes.

Even so, by the outbreak of the Italo-Ethiopian War, these unfavorable conditions had undergone significant modification, for the better. Now more than ever concentrated in overcrowded cities, key black institutions – black colleges, black churches, the black press, and the advocacy groups like the NAACP, the National Urban League, and the Brotherhood of Sleeping Car Porters – were more advantageously positioned to focalize their political energy. Speaking of Harlem, Duke Ellington could remark in 1931 that "we have what is practically our own city; we have our own newspapers and social service, and … we have almost achieved our own civilization."[14] A month after the Italian forces marched into Addis Ababa, W. E. B. Du Bois also remarked on the same paradox of segregation: "And yet, out of race segregation and compulsory degradation, arose a new loyalty, a new confidence, a new determination, which has welded the black people of the United States into a nation within a nation."[15] Segregation, whether de facto or de jure, had an ironical effect of inner ideological enrichment for blacks. It had compressed their energy into "a new confidence, a new determination." And their new assertiveness in turn helped enlarge the ambit of their political curiosity beyond domestic problems.

The Race War Fantasy

By the mid-1930s, a theory had long begun to dawn on a coterie of black intellectuals and activists who possessed limited influence but apparently unlimited shrewdness that European domination of the dark-skinned peoples of the world and white supremacy in America were both part of the same global conspiracy – that is, Jim Crow in America and colonialism in what later came to be called the Third World explained each other.[16] Just a few weeks before the fall of Addis Ababa, Du Bois reiterated his cherished belief: "I do not believe it is possible to settle the Negro problem in America until the color problems of the world are well on the way toward settlement." His grandfather Alexander, a mixed-race son of a French-American man and his slave mistress, used "strongly and bitterly" to insist: "He was not a Negro. He had nothing to do with Africa." But having outgrown such "race provincialism," his grandson now determined on the shared destiny of the African diaspora:

> [T]he descendants of Africans are [not] going to be received as American citizens so long as the peoples of Africa are kept by white civilization in semi-slavery, serfdom and economic exploitation. I may be wrong in this belief, but it is bolstered, in my opinion, by every fact and occurrence which has come forward in the last twenty-five years: the seizure of Haiti, the perilous present position of Liberia, the imminent conquest of Ethiopia, the pending disfranchisement of black South Africans, the continuation of lynching and segregation in America. All these are pieces of one cloth, evidences of one social pattern.[17]

The Italo-Ethiopian War only reinforced this line of thinking that linked colonialism abroad with the endless daily race war in America.

Given this growth of black internationalism in the 1920s and 1930s, it was natural that, unlike white antifascist writers, their black peers did not take the battle between Fascist Italy and Ethiopia to emblematize a worldwide confrontation between pacific democracies in one corner and aggressive dictatorships in the opposite corner. Ethiopia stood in for neither side. Rather it represented a third force, or the prize for which the next world war would be fought between two camps of white imperialists. George Padmore favored this kind of racial interpretation in "Ethiopia and World Politics," a dense and urgent exposition of geopolitical dynamics that appeared in the

Crisis in May 1935. A native of Trinidad and a graduate of Howard University, Padmore had recently broken with the Communists, relocated from Moscow to London, and was becoming a driving force, along with C. L. R. James and other black activist-thinkers there, in the International African Friends of Abyssinia. The new crisis in Africa, he held, signaled that the imperial rivalry between the "have" powers satiated with vast colonies and the revisionist "have-not" powers was bound to intensify, culminating inexorably in a squaring of accounts among the white empires on a scale even more colossal than the last world war.[18]

One merit of Padmore's analysis was that it explained why the white majority in America viewed the Italo-Ethiopian War the way it did. Because accusing Italy of imperial depredation would also implicate America's allies, Britain and France, white Americans had to frame Mussolini's behavior as a threat to the international peace system. To most African Americans, however, Fascism did not look like a new aberrant political force at war against the civilized international order. Ralph Bunche, still a young political science assistant professor at Howard developing a Marxist analysis of race and international political economy, drew a parallel between Fascist colonialism in East Africa and British and French imperialism in West Africa: "The doctrine of Fascism ... has given a new and greater impetus to the policy of world imperialism which has already conquered and subjected to systematic and ruthless exploitation virtually all of the darker populations of the earth."[19] A month after Bunche's address, Du Bois wrote in a lengthy essay, which appeared in *Foreign Affairs*, that "Economic exploitation based on the excuse of race prejudice is the program of the white world. Italy states it openly and plainly." According to his "negro view," the "program of the white world" was colonialism, the worldwide conspiracy to enslave and exploit "the Africas, which may be said to include the British West Indies and the Negroes of the United States."[20] Fascism was a direct outgrowth of this "program of the white world," the frankest expression of its essence.

Like Richard Wright, Langston Hughes likened black urban life to warfare in "Air Raid Over Harlem" (1935). Unlike Wright, he made his innuendo broader, by explicitly figuring the urban racial warfare in America and the Italo-Ethiopian War as just two flash points along the globe-girthing battle line between whites and the colored:

> Sure, I know
> The Ethiopian war broke out last night:
> BOMBS OVER HARLEM
> Cops on every corner

> Most of 'em white
> COPS IN HARLEM
> Guns and billy-clubs
> Double duty in Harlem
> Walking in pairs
> Under every light
> Their faces
> WHITE[21]

As discussed in Chapter 1, white prewar writers also often talked of air raid, for it was an effective device to talk about war over there while being here. Yet the crucial difference here was that while for his white peers aerial bombardment symbolized the threat just beyond the horizon of time and space, for Hughes air raids by Italian Fascists mirrored the white terror against black people that was already happening at home. Through parallelism, Hughes highlighted the color line that pitted white cops against dark-skinned denizens of ghettoes, the poorly equipped Ethiopian soldiers against Italian invaders, in order to awaken his readers to the existence of allies abroad and enemies at home, to a community of interest between Africa and Afro-America.

The thriving black press simplified and amplified these analyses and sentiments, broadcasting them to increasingly literate black masses. Facile and acidulous writers gifted with a knack for balancing sensationalism with social analysis, such as George Schuyler at the Pittsburgh *Courier*, Dan Burley at the Chicago *Defender*, Roi Ottley for the New York *Amsterdam*, Ralph Matthews for the Baltimore *Afro-American*, and Padmore, regularly contributing dispatches to the *Crisis*, the *Defender*, and the *Courier*, gave prominent play to the war in the far-off African kingdom, calling for unity of all dark-skinned peoples of the world and refuting all sorts of calumnies that the white press hurled at their "fatherland." Black workers, sharecroppers, tenants, or youths on street corners who thought they were fighting a war of attrition daily against cops, landowners, slumlords, white-only unions, and other exploiters of black powerlessness had little difficulty in romanticizing the Abyssinian imperial army as their comrades-in-arms. While they did not have Ph.Ds like Bunche or Du Bois, black plebeians still intuited the war's special meaning. Letters of inquiry to the State Department, the White House, and other government agencies from ordinary black citizens indicate clearly that a new Pan-African consciousness, if not an organized social movement, that connected colonial brigandage in Africa with racism in America quickly spread nationwide. Many of those who wrote letters asking about restrictions on travel to Ethiopia were the inhabitants of black metropolises like New York City and Chicago, but a considerable number also wrote from small towns and cities in the South and the Midwest. These people heard about the coming war in East Africa, through word of mouth and through black newspapers lying about in places like barbershops, Jim Crow cars, poolrooms, churches, and drawing rooms. They wished, their letters explained, to make a 7,000-mile journey to the Ethiopian highlands to render their services as soldiers or as workers skilled in useful trades like bricklaying and welding. It is realistic to suppose that mixed motives compelled many of these would-be volunteers. The lack of opportunities and high unemployment partially caused many to seek new lives and adventures in the East African kingdom. But at the same time at least as many were not blind to the physical dangers involved in confronting the modern Italian armies. These letter writers usually referred to Ethiopia as their "fatherland" and "mother land," called Ethiopians their "brother[s]" and "our people," because they thought blacks in America and Ethiopians both belonged to the "African race." Some kind of idealism indubitably pulled these volunteers toward the conflict in the faraway land.

The tone of these letters was often defiant and censorious. Some writers even told the officials that the second-class citizenship treatment by their own putatively democratic government made it all but impossible not to join the Ethiopian armies. One writer suspected that the official policy of neutrality, the refusal to censure Italy for its violation of the Kellogg–Briand Pact, and the federal government's slighting of the political rights and economic welfare of the black people arose from the same source, namely racism. The Roosevelt administration, one inquirer charged, "will not help Ethiopia because she is black. She won't do no more for Ethiopia than she will do to stop mob rule in the south." Responding to a flood of requests for a legal ruling on the American citizen's enlistment in foreign militaries, the State Department issued a statement in 1935 that construed certain clauses in the U.S. code and ruled that were African Americans to travel to the Horn of Africa and fight under the command of "Conquering Lion of Judah," they would be stripped of their citizenship. This predictably did not go down well with the black second-class citizens who were more outraged than bemused by the presumption that they had citizenship to be stripped of. One inquirer lectured: "As for losing our citizenship of this country, we don't give a nick about that. This citizenship is of no value to us. ... If your country can not protect us when we are citizens and living here, why should we worry about it?" Another letter writer expressed a similarly low estimate of the reputed benefits of "citizenship" for blacks:

"We are lynched, mobbed without an investigation, barred from millions of places and refused millions of jobs, regardless of our educational ability. If this is what citizenship means, where is the loss?"[22]

Fortifying this ensemble of apprehension, rage, and hope was a century – old tradition often referred to as Ethiopianism. In the strict sense, it was a designation for independent church movements in South Africa in the late nineteenth century. As critics and historians have shown, however, it also makes sense to talk of Ethiopianism more loosely, as shorthand for a medley of mutually entangling prophetic stories about the past and the future of the African diaspora.[23] These stories were first expounded by Afro-Atlantic evangelicals (black missionaries and emigrationists and their African collaborators) in the mid-nineteenth century. Then, slowly unloosened from their religious origins, they filtered into the collective dream world of black America by the first decades of the new century, influencing younger and secular Pan-Africanists like Marcus Garvey and Du Bois, who, ironically, hated each other. At the center of Ethiopianism was a prophesy about the imminent revival of Africa, which was inventively teased out of an inspirational passage in the Bible: "Envoys will come out of Egypt; Ethiopia will soon stretch out her hands to God" (Psalm 68:31). Ethiopianism also owed its popularity to revenge fantasy. The foretold redemption of the Dark Continent was believed to occur in tandem with the decline of the West. Finally, Ethiopianism evinced a revisionist impulse to imagine ancient Africa as a righteous empire of majestic civilization and military might. The recent ascent of Europe was a fluke. In the long run, Africa would reclaim its antediluvian glory. These intertwined dreams attracted Americans of African descent in the age of Jim Crow. The obviousness of its appeal is hard to overstate. Like Israelis in exile from their homeland and living in fear of godless empires, African Americans could derive from the Ethiopianist tradition hope, pride, escape, and a coping mechanism to deal with the hopeless, dehumanizing, and stressful world.

By the 1930s, Ethiopianism had lost much of its motivating power that used to make this bundle of nebulous wishes an actionable blueprint for classic nationalists such as Martin Delany, Henry Highland Garnet, Alexander Crummel, Edward Blyden, and Henry Turner. Yet still, its attenuated life survived in widely circulating mythic clichés and symbols. In 1931, a life-long mocker of Pan-Africanism, George Schuyler burlesqued it in a speech that Dr. Shakespeare Agamemnon Beard (Du Bois's caricature) gives in *Black No More*: "I want to tell you that our destiny lies in the stars. Ethiopia's fate is in the balance. The goddess of the Nile weeps bitter tears at the feet of the Great Sphinx. The lowering clouds gather over the Congo and the lightening flashes o'er Togoland. To your tents, O Israel! The hour is at hand."[24] Ethiopia, stars, the Nile, the Congo, the Sphinx – these are employed here for their symbolic values, namely at once becalming and stirring intimations of antiquity, stability, perdurance, majesty, and intelligence. Through the Jazz Age, the New Negroes, all urban sophisticates fascinated by frenetic pageants of modernity, came to assume a condescending and bemused attitude toward this sort of otherworldly Africanist homily, just as their white peers rolled their eyes at the Victorian sanctimoniousness of their parents. But these young moderns themselves were not beyond availing themselves of these symbols. Claude McKay was mainly known for his scandalous affirmation of the real and edgy but cheap and repetitive pleasure of living America's modernity, and yet he would also often yearn for the unreal but eternal solace that the fiction of Ethiopian glory alone could bring in poems like "Invocation" (1917) and "Exhortation: Summer, 1919." Bigger Thomas's yearning for a black *Führer* in *Native Son* was a thinly disguised variation on the Ethiopian legend of the Black Christ. When in "Call of Ethiopia" Hughes's speaker identified himself with Ethiopia and called on all of Africa to arise and be free "like me," his empathy was much more coherent and real to the poem's original readers than it appears to later generations. The abstract, august, and austere images of Ethiopianism and their corresponding moods retained even greater traction with the respectable black middle class as well as hardworking and churchgoing folks, subconsciously acting on the way they understood their destiny. For black America, whether genteel or modern, the anti-fascist, anticolonial resistance of the ancient dynasty of Ethiopia lent color and credibility to this half-forgotten mythic tradition.

"Boon To Darker Races"

Of all race thinkers and activists commenting on the Italo-Ethiopian War, the most vocal and influential was George Schuyler, chief columnist for the *Pittsburgh Courier*. As the Italians amassed their troops along the Ethiopian border throughout 1935, Schuyler turned his weekly columns for the then most widely read black weekly into a hugely effective megaphone through which to project his analyses to small hamlets in the South as well as congested black ghettoes in the North. Concurrently, he wrote, under his real name and pseudonyms, several novellas inspired by the war, all serialized in the *Courier*. His output was vast. His pen was unfailingly sharp. The breadth of formats he employed was matchless.

His new role as the spokesman for race pride and pan-African solidarity was rather out of character. Anyone who knew Schuyler's career must have doubted that he was wholly unaware of this. Like most of the notable prewar writers, he was born in the closing decade of the previous century. When he was still a small boy, his family moved from Providence, Rhode Island, to Syracuse, New York, where he attended racially mixed public schools. At the age of seventeen, he decided to join the Army (his mother agreed to sign papers that falsified his age). Wanderlust peculiar to adolescence was one reason. Another, more self-conscious motive sprung from his realization that, even in that town with the storied tradition of antebellum abolitionism, only dead-end menial jobs were open to the black youth. Schuyler found his strenuous life in the military rewarding. Its emphasis on order and discipline was congenial to his conservatism. Yet in 1918, after six years of service at a series of camps in Des Moines, Seattle, and Honolulu, following a dramatic incident, he quietly went AWOL. Soon after, fearing arrest, he decided to turn himself in, but he was sentenced to five years in prison. Eventually, the sentence was reduced to a year, and he served nine months at Castle Williams on Governor's Island in New York as a model inmate. His decision to join the military and his experience as a soldier in strictly segregated forces are the master key to the enigma of his complex personality, at once conservative and radical. On the one hand, his enlistment points to his deeply ingrained patriotism and his enduring faith in basic institutions of American democracy to provide determined and disciplined black citizens with opportunities for upward mobility. On the other, the six years of living a paradoxical existence – serving to defend a nation that treated his patriotism as second-class – radicalized his thinking on segregation in the military. This experience carried him to positions to the left of the black opinion elite when it came to the issues of war and democracy, exactly those issues that became increasingly contentious during the prewar years. It is telling that Schuyler's desertion was occasioned by a humiliating episode in a train station in Philadelphia: a Greek immigrant at a boot-black stand refused to shine the putties of a twenty-three-year-old first lieutenant Schuyler. Civilians in white skin could always pull rank on black soldiers in uniform.[25]

After the Great War, Schuyler put the literary talent he had honed writing for Army newspapers to creative use. In no time he wrote his way into the highly competitive Harlem literary scene as an at once incredibly funny and wickedly caustic commentator on race questions. Like his Harlem Renaissance colleagues, he was capable of prodigious productivity.

His hands – "as long and graceful as the wing of a raven," his white wife, a rebellious daughter of a Texas banker, described – pounded out reams of copy on a typewriter, first for A. Phillip Randolph's *Messenger* and then for Robert Vann's *Courier* and for Henry Mencken's *American Mercury* (no writers, black or white, published more articles than Schuyler in *Mercury*). While his combative essays and columns mainly skewered hypocrisy and prejudice of white Americans, his rapier-like wits were even more piercing when applied to foibles and follies of black people. As his sendup of Du Bois's misty-eyed Ethiopianism indicates, for him no icons, no ideas were too sacred to burlesque. He was a compulsive contrarian, an irreverent provocateur. With zest and glee, he mocked all sage counsels of black solons, all snobbish solemnities that awed the black booboisie, all utopian schemes and fads that mesmerized gullible black hoi polloi. He rejoiced to offend, to scandalize. And in the mid-1930s, Afro-Atlantic antifascism presented itself as a perfect idol for Schuyler's ready mockery. With its race chauvinism that was long on enthusiasm and short on practicalities, this new cause célèbre practically begged for Schuyler's ridicule.

The sage of Sugar Hill championed it.

And he did so with his characteristic brio. Reflecting the sentiments of the hundreds of thousands of his readers, Schuyler did not see the latest manifestation of Fascist expansionism as the leading-edge of a sinister global conspiracy against democracies. A race war was on. "It would be a major catastrophe for the darker peoples of the world," he wrote two months after the eruption of war, "if Ethiopia should be defeated and subjugated by the Italians. …There is not a red-blooded Negro, Mongolian or Malay in the world who does not want to see Ethiopia emerge from this present crisis with glory and victory and with sovereignty unimpaired."[26] The dark races around the world could not count on "democracies" like England, France, and the United States to stop the Italian aggression. Because these "democracies" were not militarily prepared to confront their more reckless competitors, they were only glad to maintain false comity at the sacrifice of a small African kingdom. Unusually for a writer, Schuyler had a healthy disdain for words, slogans, and exhortations ("I feel less than reverence for the written word," he wrote in his autobiography).[27] And so he did not even for an instant take seriously all the lip service that the self-styled "antifascist" nations paid to "world peace" and "nonaggression." Their deeds spoke louder than their high-minded words, and, he thought, any black gulls who bought into those fraudulent words reflected poorly on his race. The League of Nations' sanctions were just transparently insincere gestures (to add insult to injury, Ethiopia had the foresight to join the League and sign onto Article X, which forbade aggression among member states). And these half-measures were further eviscerated by France and Britain's deviousness and their general unseriousness about the Ethiopian claim to sovereignty. The white world's collusion against Ethiopia had direct bearing on African Americans. They were not just freedom-loving Americans but also members of the globe-girthing black belt, which ranged from the American South, through Latin America, Africa, India, and South East Asia, to the thousand islands in the South Sea. "If Ethiopia loses and is enslaved the cause of white imperialism will be immeasurably advanced and the cause of black liberalism will be hopelessly retarded," he wrote.[28]

Schuyler's views were squarely in the mainstream of the black press. The editorial pages of major black newspapers and periodicals all carried opinions and points of view consonant with Schuyler's. His analysis being rather a commonplace, his chief contribution came from his rhetoric, a style that was zany but acidic with a subtle hint of calculated meanness. Throughout his long career, he exhibited an almost congenital cynicism toward corny baronies and high-minded bromides, those holly words that no one privately feared or revered but that still in public cowered everyone into pious submission or knowing acquiescence because everyone was too scared, too credulous, or too complacent to call the bluff. An obsessive and compulsive caller of bluff, Schuyler would with relish deflate what many secretly despised as sanctimonious nonsense. His instinct for devastating turns of phrase was almost native. His sobriquet "Black Mencken" was as complimentary to that legendary iconoclast as to Schuyler himself.

His default mode of critique was *ad hominem*. Opinions, when held by certain people with an established record of inanities and idiocies, were automatically discreditable, meriting the vilest of ridicule. When Arthur Brisbane justified the Italian aggression as a civilizing mission in his widely syndicated columns, Schuyler aimed his venomous darts and shafts straight at this influential Hearst columnist. His open letter, which the *Courier* printed on the front page, began:

> My dear Mr. Brisbane: Among the few certainties of human life is your consistent and persistent Negrophobism. For two generations you have rung the changes on alleged white superiority, perpetuating race bias through your widely read column "Today." With crooked logic, distorted facts, pseudo-science and all the tricks of bogus scholarship beloved everywhere by journalistic charlatans you prostitute a proud profession to tickle the infantile mentalities of morons.[29]

With equal scurrilousness he also berated his black peers when he concluded that their ideas were ill-advised or soft-headed. If anything, his tone, which was indignant when railing against white prejudice, became supercilious due to his conviction – and wish – that blacks should know better. In 1940, a group of notable black academics launched a fundraising drive for France teetering on the brink of extinction in the face of German onslaught. Schuyler was incredulous that the genteel black intelligentsia was so dense as to think France was a friend of the dark-skinned peoples. "What is there so noble about France from the point of view of an intelligent Negro not befuddled by blondes, cognac or absinthe frappe?" he japed.[30] By that time, the reigning narrative in America cast the imminent world war as another war to make the world safe for democracy and enlisted Americans, white or black, in the fight for noble abstractions like liberty, peace, and fraternity. And that was exactly the kind of nauseatingly brazen lie circulating in broad daylight under the cover of its very brazenness, a cruel joke on millions of black innocents, that Schuyler could not pass up the opportunity to lance with an absolute maximum of sarcasm.

While Schuyler was angry and sad about Ethiopia's dim prospect, another world war portended by this crisis cheered him up. In the spring of 1935, the buildup of Italian forces was under way in Eritrea and Somaliland, and Schuyler sensed that "another World War is just minutes off us." That was good news to all but white Europeans, that is, to the majority of the world population living in Africa and Asia. Another world war would only further liberate black Americans and colonials. War "has been kind to" them in the past. Continued peace only meant a preservation of the status quo: "The countries that stand to gain the most from another World War are the colonies now ruled by the Big Powers or bulldozed and dominated by them: Ethiopia, Java, the Congo, Nigeria, China, Liberia, etc. World peace means to them only a continuation of their servile status."[31] The first European attempt at collective suicide – the Great War of two decades before – was unfortunately abortive. Even so, given the recent advancement in weaponry, white imperialists would surely do a more thorough job next time, he ratiocinated.

Three years later, as Hitler's demand for Sudetenland forced another crisis on Europe, Schuyler reiterated his longing for another world war in a long essay entitled "The Rise of the Black Internationale," which appeared in the *Crisis* where he was business manager. His essay was a breathtakingly stringent conspectus of the West's imperial expansion. With remarkable cogency Schuyler stitched together seemingly disparate developments around the world into a compelling story. The same logic, he explained, drove the European division of Africa since the Berlin Conference in 1885, the collapse of Reconstruction, the rollback of black civil rights, and the radicalization of pseudoscientific racism in the United States since 1875. Black life in America hit its nadir in the first decade of the century, and at about the same time, Western domination over nonwhite populations of the world reached its zenith. Was that a coincidence? "No" was Schuyler's emphatic answer. Like Padmore, Bunche, Du Bois, and Hughes, he thought that colonialism abroad and Jim Crowism at home were just two subplots composing the main plot, the White Internationale's systematic war against non-Europeans. The whole racket was premised on honor among thieves. And the last war raised the doubt if this premise would be sustainable. Ever since, the white powers had grown more cautious, aware of dire consequences that another imperialist war would precipitate. The "fear of losing the colonial peoples and their resources is all that prevents another World War." Thus, although another white-on-white world war could have happened any time, "democracies" had cannily postponed the inevitable falling-out by offering concessions bit by bit to Germans and Italians. Given this cautiousness, the most logical course of action for nonwhites was to form the "Black Internationale" and goad the reluctant Europeans and Americans to a final holocaust. Without the faintest display of embarrassment, Schuyler concluded his analysis by reviving the figure of the "New Negro" that he lambasted ten years previous. Race pride now served, to his thinking, as a useful rallying point for all dark-skinned subjects of the world. The New Negro, this combative, confident, ruthless, and disciplined insurgent, "welcomes a community of interest of all colored peoples. No longer ignorant, terrorized or lacking confidence, he awaits, and schemes and plans. He is the Damoclean sword dangling over the white world."[32]

A year after this essay appeared, Germany invaded Poland. At long last the White Internationale obliged. Jubilation hardly described Schuyler's exulted reaction. He could not even wait until the British and French declaration of war. Just a day after the Panzer corps breached the Polish border, a headline "War Will Be Boon to Darker Races, Schuyler Says" blared from the front page of the *Courier*. "When thieves fall out, honest men get their due," which was nothing less than the long-prophesied redemption of Africa and the decline of the West. "A new World War," he anticipated, "will destroy the enslaver and thus emancipate the enslaved."[33] In the fall of 1940, a year into the second imperialist war, the French Empire was no more, and British cities were under daily bombing. Schuyler was euphoric over the West's benumbed inability to step back from the precipice of self-annihilation. The ongoing carnage, however, left some room to be desired. White people were not dying in enough numbers yet, enough to bankrupt white supremacy and enough for whites to mobilize their colonial subjects and put in their dark hands coveted modern arms, which would be quickly turned against their white masters. "It is the hope of this commentator," he wrote, "that the war will continue as long as is required to impoverish Europe and arm all the dark peoples." Particularly unfortunate was the fact that, protected by the two wide oceans, the United States had yet to be directly threatened by the general conflagration in Asia and Europe – an unsatisfactory state of affairs for its black citizens. Only a national emergency would compel white Americans to sue for black cooperation. If America was directly involved in the world war, African Americans could take national security hostage and refuse to fight until offered substantial concessions. As long as blacks lacked full rights, whatever menaced the nation was good for them. Another world war meant a leverage, an opportunity: "If the Dorniers and Messerschmitts drop a few bombs on our Atlantic Coast we shall see Negroes again casting their ballots in elections in the American Congo [the Southern states], observe colored craftsmen working in defense industries in skilled categories, and see dark pilots in training at Randolph Field." He signed off with this exclamation:

"War, it's wonderful!"[34]

The Black Empire

In May 1936, the war had just ended in Italian victory. The last pocket of black resistance was finally wiped out. And the new world war was still three years in coming. But a-coming surely and ineluctably it did seem, to George Schuyler. And he blended his foresight and his revenge fantasy in a piece of pulp fiction, "The Black Internationale: A Story of Black Genius Against the World," one of several novellas he wrote during and after the Italo-Ethiopian War under various names, his own and some pseudonyms (this particular one was published under a Samuel I. Brooks). The story is told by Carl Slater, a newspaperman in Harlem, who serves as a pure point-of-view device, a passive witness to Dr. Belsidus's plot against all the white nations the world over. Slater's chance encounter with Belsidus in Harlem creates a series of complications, at the end of which Dr. Belsidus's henchmen drug the newspaperman and spirit him away to the lair of a

worldwide underground organization that calls itself the Black Internationale. Its sinister mastermind Belsidus commands Slater to work for him as
his personal secretary, or else. Under the spell of the doctor's mesmeric
personality, Slater goes along without much protest and joins this terroristic organization. From this point on to the end, the reader sees, through
Slater's oddly trusting eye, Dr. Belsidus execute step by step his elaborate
scheme of empire-building in Africa.

As its name proudly announces, Belsidus's network is global in scope.
On its executive committee serve the delegates from all major colonies,
black, brown, and yellow. Their modus operandi is a comic facsimile of
European plunderers and despoilers. His organization builds across the
world "temples" where unsuspecting congregations are indoctrinated in
the new religion of black power, a counter-religion to displace white
Christianity that has poisoned the minds of darker races and swindled
them into voluntary bondage. Another trick that the Black Internationale
borrows from the white man's playbook is investment in scientific research
and cutting-edge technologies. "We are using," Dr. Belsidus brags, "the
weapons and knowledge of the white man against him. ... It is the skilled
technician, the scientist, who wins modern wars, and we are mobilizing the
black scientists of the world."[35] These black terrorists exhibit a boyish
fascination with futuristic gadgets, just as did contemporary genre fictions
like science fiction and spy novels that were enjoying their golden age in
the mid-1930s. This clandestine organization owns and operates a chain of
farms and factories that harness newest scientific breakthroughs to production of everything from foodstuffs to wondrous weapons systems like
"death ray." The goal is the black world's complete economic autonomy,
technological supremacy, and military preponderance. The airplane, still a
novelty overlaid with symbolic connotations of freedom, progress, and
mobility, figures prominently. Their armadas of bombers and fighters (led
by a black aviatrix, an object of Slater's romantic adoration), not some
poorly equipped earth-crawling infantries, spearhead their first strike
against European imperialists.

The story was published in thirty-three installments in the *Courier* from
November 1936 to July 1937. This circumstance considerably shaped its
basic structure: a succession of technophilic set pieces meant to titillate the
black readership, all loosely strung together by cliffhangers and abrupt
transitions. This creates a problem for latter-day readers who encounter the
story in book form, but the choppy, discontinuous progression most likely
helped the novel with its original readers, for each installment was basically
a self-contained spectacle depicting an amazing technological achievement

of the black dictator. Nor do these episodes entirely lack motivation. They all eventually add up to the climax: the transatlantic expeditionary forces led by Dr. Belsidus invade Liberia, depose a corrupt black regime there, and use that country as a launching pad for surprise attacks on European military outposts across Africa. Belsidus's strategy of divide and conquer (another method turned against white imperialists) also creates something of plot interest and excitement, if not suspense. In the United States, Belsidus fans a strife between Catholics and Protestants by staging bogus attacks on each and engineers a white-on-white war, which gives a cover to the Black Internationale's massive mobilization. On the European front, a brigade of special operatives firebomb embassies and manufacture false claims of responsibility by nonexistent organizations. A mayhem ensues. A second world war the Black Internationale thus brings about finally completes the job that the Great War took up. The narrator observes, "War had been terrible in 1914–1918. It was nothing compared to what the world witnessed now. Europe's numerous thickly populated cities were blown to bits as swarms of opposing airplanes dropped their deadly wares. Tanks rumbled to meet tanks and the thunder of big guns made night and day horrible. Nothing like this swift, ruthless, unremitting bloodshed had ever been conceived." Belsidus's armies launch a war of extermination against white troops and white settlers all over the vast African continent, but the European metropoles are too preoccupied to divert their forces against the black invasion of Africa. To Dr. Belsidus, who awaits in the war room with a colossal map of Africa, come reports from his troops "slaughter[ing] white men, women and children with great ferocity": "All whites killed"; "No white person is alive."[36]

It is fairly plain where some of the themes originated and what their intended purposes were. One detail of the story, that the black empire owes its conquest of Africa and extermination of white colonists to its investment in science and technology, obviously served as a pretext for taking out shiny gadgets for a parade, which Schuyler knew pleased the black masses clamoring for cheap and satisfying entertainment in news-papers. Most papers sold for as little as two cents (by way of comparison: a movie ticket averaged about 25 cents). New technologies, especially airplane, also made the plot of "international intrigue" manageable. They allowed principal characters to move from one corner of the world to another with ease, without slowing down the tempo or straining the plausibility. Predictably, thus, airplane also figured prominently in Schuyler's other novellas inspired by the crisis in Africa. The novella entitled "Revolt in Ethiopia: A Tale of Black Insurrection Against Italian

Imperialism," written under a pseudonym Rachel Call and published in twenty-eight installments from July 1938 to January 1939, for instance, centered around a young black man on a cruise ship, who falls in with the Ethiopian princess seeking a hidden treasure needed to finance Ethiopia's war against Italian invaders. The true protagonist of the story, however, is the airplane, which enables the characters to move speedily over a vast space from the Mediterranean to the Red Sea. Another story, "The Ethiopian Murder Mystery: A Story of Love and International Intrigue" (serialized from October 1935 to February 1936), involved a team of Ethiopian assassins, whose mission is to murder an Ethiopian prince in America suspected of handing over vital information on "death ray" to Italians. As in "The Black Internationale," what makes this daring operation (the quick and secret insertion and extraction of Ethiopian commandos in Manhattan) is the airplane. "Come Sadja, we mustn't miss our plane," said by an Ethiopian agent to another as they leave America with their mission accomplished, is the last line of this formulaic pulp fiction.[37]

The format of science fiction was not just solely chosen out of commercial considerations. While pandering to his readers, Schuyler was also giving vent to his faith in development and modernization, his admiration for the main engine powering the West's global supremacy, that is, science and capitalism. His uncharacteristically sentimental attachment to business, machine, and technology was one salient theme that ran through his voluminous social commentaries. Wondering where the power gap between blacks and whites originated, Schuyler would often venture that race prejudice was less to blame than blacks' technological lag and their lack of savings available for investment. In one of his countless articles excoriating his bête noire, Marcus Garvey, Schuyler faulted the Garveyite variant of Pan-Africanism for neglecting to study the secret of white supremacy: "I did not then and do not now approve of the loud-mouthed, ignorant, inefficient manner in which Garvey went about the business. ... If Negroes are to develop Africa they will have to indulge in less wild talk and wilder mass meetings and go about the business in a businesslike way as do the white men they criticize. Africa can only be developed by brains plus capital."[38] Blacks and science; blacks and capitalism. These appositions may still have caused cognitive dissonance in his contemporary audience, but, Schuyler insisted, there was nothing foredoomed. The rising Asiatic empire of Japan was beating white imperialists at their own game. Further, new generations of black businessmen and black scientists in the United States stood as proof that modernization, fueled by the spirit of business and science, was color-blind. Schuyler sublimated his long-held developmentalist fantasy into the platoon of black warriors equipped with high-tech weapons whose development and production was bankrolled by the underground black economy. In actuality, as Schuyler must have been painfully conscious, capital and science did discriminate by skin color. While development and modernization presented a wide and logical avenue to the final victory over racism, the latter at the same time blocked a black quest for the ultimate instruments of empowerment: capital and science. The ridiculously excessive technological savvy of black spies, commandos, and aviators in Schuyler's novellas probably betrayed how frustrated he was with the excruciatingly sluggish modernization of the Dark Continent, for which he faulted black obduracy and white sabotage equally.

Other seemingly gratuitous conceits will make sense if they are compared with key tenets and imageries of Ethiopianism. The rise and unification of Africa, the fall of Europe, revenge fantasy, the establishment of the independent black church ("Temple of Love"), African Americans' leadership in the liberation of Africa – these dreams had already sustained black millennialism since almost a century back. Schuyler's Ethiopia stories modernized these hoary tales to make them refreshing and relatable for 1930s African Americans, whose tie with the continent of their ancestry was growing increasingly phantasmal. Accounting for these Ethiopianist sources of Schuyler's fiction, however, raises a further question: how did Schuyler feel about them?. Two supplementary forces drove Ethiopianism. One was the will to believe, in the face of the manifest diversity of so-called Africans in and out of the vast continent, that there was such a thing as African identity, a soul of black folk. The other was the idea that, partaking in this mystical soulfulness, black people exiled in America formed, in Du Bois's phrase, "a nation within a nation." Their distinctiveness was their strength. They should cultivate it. Because Schuyler consistently lambasted these two components of Ethiopianism (or "nationalism" as it became known by the prewar years), his relation to a miscellany of Ethiopianist themes in his novellas does not seem to be one of straightforward advocacy.

Since when the New Negro was in vogue, Schuyler had been a consistent critic of "nationalism." That was a solitary and toxic position during the Jazz Age, which earned him few friends and many vociferous enemies, but he stuck by it into the depression decade. Even during the Ethiopian crisis, a brief period of intellectual and political confusion, when he would often hitch the destiny of black liberation in America to Ethiopia's defensive war, Schuyler could write: "I have always seen people as they are, as individuals, not artificially as stereotypes representing a race or a nation. Some of the more racially chauvinistic of my Negro friends have occasionally charged that I am not a 'Race Man.' This is quite true. I have no concern for anything as abstract as a race, whatever a race may be."[39] Just a year after the Italian conquest of Ethiopia, Schuyler was back to his old antinationalist number, writing in his weekly column that "The worst enemies of the Negro race in America today are those Negroes who preach race chauvinism, segregation and ultimate isolation under the euphemism of group economy. If we are to survive, we must in every sense become a part of, must merge with the nation."[40]

Two days before this column appeared, Schuyler and Claude McKay had gone on air to debate the question "Shall Negroes Organize As a Racial Group?" Progressive Manhattanites who happened to tune in to WEVD (a popular Yiddish radio station run by Jewish socialists) heard McKay defend the position that the racially exclusive organizing would add to black prestige in the United States. A good example to follow was, McKay tipped his hat to the audience, the American Jews. Schuyler meanwhile launched his rebuttal on several fronts. Separatism was impracticable in a modern, interdependent world. Separatism may invite "white reprisals" that blacks were not ready to meet. And lastly, American society had been anyway making significant progress in racial integration.[41] The two debaters left the studio in a jovial mood, but when five months later McKay's admiring essay on the don't-buy-where-you-can't-work campaigns appeared in *The Nation*, Schuyler would not let that go unanswered. He called these separatist efforts to "save the Race by segregation; to build up a 'group economy'; to foster isolation" the "most suicidal policy." In applauding the hustlers, chiselers, and racketeers promoting these schemes, McKay was merely "wallowing in the black fascist trough along with the 49th Staters, the Garveyites, the Self-Determination-for-the-Black-Belters and the more recent distinguished converts to the infantile paralysis of 'voluntary segregation.'"[42]

Interracial equality was a goal never attractive or ambitious enough for Schuyler. Equal but separate simply meant to him "segregation de luxe."[43] For him, the ultimate emancipation would come to the twelve million blacks when racial distinctions dissolved into an undifferentiated nation and consequently the very notion of racial equality lost all its relevance. Some, of course, advocated separatism for the sake of separation, but many proponents of "voluntary segregation" made a realistic calculation that some sort of nationalistic rhetoric and practice could be justified as a means to rid the world of racial divisions. They were aware of the many downsides of outright integration. One of "the more recent distinguished converts," Du Bois wrote that the "process of thought and of action which scatters them [blacks] among people who do not want them, and which reduces their force and efficiency, and which tends to make them lose the peculiar gifts they may bring to culture is not only wrong and wasteful, but fatal."[44] First, the inward development of the "peculiar gifts" of black folk. And then, integration. Conservative *and* radical, Schuyler would have none of that, for he feared that the means could be easily turned into the goal. The fantasy of black nationalism and race war, to which Schuyler gave free rein in his columns and stories during the Ethiopian war, stood in direct contradiction with the political positions he publicly staked out for much of his career.

No less problematic than the "black" part of the Black Empire was the international solidarity "empire" connoted. As evident in his *Crisis* essay, "The Rise of the Black Internationale," Schuyler occasionally showed himself to be amenable to some versions of Afro-Atlantic anticolonial alliance espoused by the writers he genuinely respected, such as Du Bois and Padmore. For much of his life, however, his default position remained that Africans and African Americans faced different enemies, pursued different goals, and hence needed strategies not always complementary. One obvious source of his resistance against Afro-Atlantic solidarity was again his American exceptionalism. "To be sure," he would later write, "it is not easy being a black man in the United States but it is easier than anywhere else I know for him to get the best schooling, the best living conditions, the best economic advantages, the best security, the greatest mobility and the best health."[45] However striking the parallels among the various iniquitous ways in which the United States and the European powers treated their dark-skinned subjects, Schuyler more often than not settled, commingling some hard thinking with wishful thinking, for the conclusion that the destiny of African Americans veered from that of Africans and led to a happier, more just destination.

Schuyler's distrust of any international schemes to help his racial brethren abroad also dovetailed with his virulent opposition to Communism, his long-standing conviction that "the Negro had difficulties enough being black without becoming Red."[46] Schuyler had a number of reasons for execrating Communists: their shifty policy (the Party was always "flipping and flopping about like a walrus with epilepsy"), white working-class racism, or their maltreatment of his friends like Padmore.[47] But at the root of his burning animus against Communism was his realization that such an obviously foreign ideology meant only liability for African

Americans who were already saddled with so many other burdens. Black people were daily struggling to solidify what little progress they could make against the strong headwind of deep-seated race prejudice and crippling legacies of slavery. And therefore, while it was vital to press forward tirelessly, blacks also had to learn how to trim their sail craftily whenever advantageous, by distancing themselves from controversial goals that risked provoking a backlash from white racists without promising any concrete, near-term payoffs. This reasoning extended beyond Communism, to other comparable cases of distant idealism whose connection to "what I considered the Aframerican's best interest" seemed flimsy to him.[48] There is even the ghost of a suggestion in his reactions to race agitations in the Deep South (the Scottsboro Youths, Angelo Herndon, the civil rights movement) that, at his most conservative, Schuyler did not consider the struggle of blacks in Mississippi or Alabama connected robustly and beneficially enough to the lives of blacks in the North.[49] He would often hesitate or flatly refuse to express solidarity with his fellow African Americans bearing the full brunt of Jim Crowism only a thousand miles south of Harlem, mostly out of the fear that their quite understandable militancy may inflame public sentiment in the North, or because of his condescending view that the living conditions of the Southern blacks were not as grievous as they loudly declaimed. It should surprise no one then that the plight of dark races in underdeveloped colonies oceans away did not usually seem to Schuyler to warrant support, moral or material, from the blacks in America.

So, except during the Ethiopian crisis, Schuyler abused both race chauvinism and anticolonial international solidarity in his columns and articles, while his fantastic novellas peddled these escapist dreams to the black masses. What to make of this contradiction? One sensible and unavoidable inference from all the paper trail left by this prolific writer is that Schuyler's own testimony should be taken at face value when he acknowledged later that his Ethiopian serials were "hokum."[50] Evidently, he wrote them with his tongue lodged ever so mischievously in cheek, guying globe-trotting, airplane-operating black subversives, the black *Führer* (the sort Bigger Thomas daydreams about), lethal weapon systems, and the genocidal war against white races. These Ethiopian stories typecast characters, exaggerated bright contrasts rather than investigated obscure nuances, and pitted against one another extreme emotions abetted by firm convictions free from self-doubt. In other words, Schuyler's formulaic devices stimulated the most dogmatic regions of the readers' moral imagination. And if there was any constant in his career that was an unbroken series of intellectual somersaults, that had to be Schuyler's principle of going after whatever principles ossified into conventional wisdom among whites and blacks, his insistence on his right to take whatever happened to be a minority position.

The vagaries of journalism partially dictated his decision to think and write like this, including the need to write quickly to meet tight deadlines and the economic imperative of producing as much copy as possible (at the *Courier*, he would usually write unsigned official editorials in addition to his signed columns). And yet, Schuyler was also caused to be so consistently inconsistent by his recognition that there was a certain essential connection between, on the one hand, the pseudoscientific racism and the hierarchical arrangement of social institutions it justified, and on the other the melodramatic and sentimental imagination, all forms of dogmatism, black and white, that fed on idées fixes, naïve convictions, and self-righteousness.[51] It is not entirely clear whether he was aware of the dangers inherent in being a contrarian by principle. By reflexively debunking any consensus as "hokum," the debunker could end up on the wrong side of history, because conventional wisdom, however conventional, can still be a correct position to take. A case in point is Schuyler's attack on Martin Luther King, Jr. That notorious episode is today universally regarded as a plain mistake made by a self-indulgent, directionless jester estranged completely from the main current of history. Additionally, brave nonconformism could easily degrade into a rhetorical weapon wielded insincerely by a debater trying to score some cheap polemical points. Schuyler was fond of styling himself an army of one, his rants and invectives the lone keening of a prophet in the wilderness, while inflating the popularity of the views he opposed. But these posturings often amounted to a disingenuous sleight of hand. Often, dogmas he ridiculed were not as dogmatic as he pretended. Conventional categories he deconstructed were not as conventional. Social movements he disparaged were not supported by as large a constituency. The popular race leaders he slandered were not as popular. In short, the ugly truths he told were not as ugly as his self-serving rhetoric of debunking made them out to be. Likewise, heresies he preached were often orthodoxies clothed in a minoritarian language, serving the interests of those with power, influence, and prestige. Schuyler's fearsome iconoclasm only partially confirmed his intrepidity. Let us not forget that his views and reviews made him controversial, and popular.

Nonetheless, this reduction of motives behind Schuyler's freethinking to lowly calculations must be counterbalanced by a proper appreciation of what he got right about race relations in America. George Schuyler understood that the ardent protest against and the frontal attack on one kind of race prejudice could give issue to another kind of race prejudice. A correct answer to a particular social problem often turned into its negative, another social problem to be solved, when it absolutized itself, that is, when it took itself too seriously. Seriousness undermined efforts to enlighten society. Taking himself too seriously would not help the holder of a particular social truth disabuse his antagonist of false solutions and unserviceable categories. Actually, his seriousness could backfire insofar as it could embolden his opponents – racists, lynchers, segregationists – to take *their* ill-informed notions even more seriously. And that no doubt would sharpen the existing polarization, harden the existing fixed categories, and make the problem even more intractable. Schuyler was convinced, at least most of the time if not continuously, that the most important task devolved upon him was a negative one, that is, to keep reminding his readers that serious people, when too serious, turned into fools. Every social insight, when taken too seriously, transmuted into blindness.

This conviction explains why one technique that enabled defiance and rejection without risking seriousness, burlesque (and its related modes, satire and caricature), became the most potent weapon in Schuyler's rhetorical arsenal. He perfected its use. Its effects were often devastating, not to mention entertaining. But burlesque's potency contained within itself some imponderables, and his treatments of the Black Empire revealed them. As Schuyler's contemporary (two years younger) theorist Kenneth Burke observed in 1937, burlesque is a purely external approach that focuses on observable behavior to the exclusion of the depth of psychology. Its main aim is then to drive these externals to their "logical conclusion" and through exaggeration point out their absurdity. The burlesquer, Burke wrote, "converts every 'perhaps' into a 'positively,'" and that was exactly the formula Schuyler consistently followed in his serials.[52] Nothing the Black Internationale does is extenuated. Every feature, event, emotion, and action is immoderate. Dr. Belsidus never fails to be ruthless. Nothing in his plan goes wrong. White racists and imperialists are inept, stupid, and evil without fail. Belsidus's attack swiftly annihilates them. Slater's love for the black aviatrix is amply requited. The wondrous dream of the Black Empire is thus pushed to its logical conclusion without any check from reality, its absurdity wholly exposed, except that a great many contemporary readers, all exercised by the Italian assault on their symbolic fatherland, neither saw nor laughed at this absurdity. True, the artist's miscalculation of audience response is a common happening in mass communications and so should not surprise Schuyler or later critics. But this failure to elicit laughter raises a question about the burlesquer's relation to the victim at whom his ridicule was directed.

Would it be to overestimate Schuyler's savvy to suppose that his mockery was directed not only at the groundswell of black antifascism, the fantastic claim of pan-African solidarity, and the millions of readers who bought into such hokum but also at himself? Would it be to give too much credence to Schuyler's self-knowledge to conjecture that the author of the Ethiopian stories was not entirely certain if the fantasies of revenge, race pride, and international solidarity deserved the vial of withering vitriol he poured over them? Is it unrealistic to suspect that Schuyler was sincere in spite of himself? Not only did he show, through his red-blooded editorials and essays that he wrote during the crisis, that he was capable of desiring race chauvinism, black separatism, white extermination, and anticolonial internationalism. The wide popularity of his pulp fiction with his contemporary readers also indicates that he was capable of empathizing deeply and accurately with daydreams, wishful thinking, and vain but real longings of the twelve million American citizens of African descent. And if his empathy produced literary confections so delightful to the nameless masses of the black press consumers, that empathy must have been visceral enough to confound Schuyler from time to time whether he was bur-lesquing or enjoying his own stories.

The impact of the Ethiopian crisis on the prewar culture and its contribu-tion to the subsequent rise of a new American globalism were ambiguous and contradictory. The African-American writers, who played a signal role in the birth of the prewar culture, viewed the Italian aggression as another instantiation of white imperialism rather than as a threat to the inter-national order or an indirect assault on America. With the benefit of hindsight, during and after World War II, Americans would recall the Italo-Ethiopian conflict as its clear harbinger. But the way this conflict actually expanded the nation's sense of its global commitments was much less straightforward than is suggested by this retrospective interpretation. Italy's unprovoked aggression supplied a piece of evidence that would be woven five years later into the American consensus that the Axis' ultimate goal was world domination. Yet, the race war interpretation of the crisis propagated by African-American writers simultaneously complicated the gradual emergence and subsequent triumph of that consensus, because the forecast that the next world war would be a final showdown among white imperialist powers undermined the more simplistic definition of World War II as a war to make the world safe for democracy. And in a further twist, this complication, in a way unintended by anyone during this brief conflict in East Africa, ended up helping construct a more robust conception of America's global leadership than would have been possible without it. For caving to the pressures generated by the African Americans' anti-fascist and anticolonial activities, the actual war aims in the name of which America would mobilize the entire nation during the world war had to remedy the inconsistency of fighting against foreign dictatorships while tolerating European colonialism abroad and racism at home. Even if the Ethiopian war had never happened, anticolonialism and the conciliatory attitude toward the black outcry for civil rights would have been incorporated into wartime U.S. policy in one way or another, but their capacity to influence the blueprint for the postwar world should have been severely diminished.

3

Americans in Spain

Aptly enough, the next conflict broke out in Spain, "that arid square, that fragment nipped off from hot Africa, soldered so crudely to inventive Europe."[1] Initially the global depression had a liberalizing influence there, and the monarchy fell in 1931. But this backward country was not ready for constitutional democracy. Disagreements among interest groups, divided regionally, economically, and religiously, proved intractable. When in 1936 the Popular Front coalition of center-left and far-left parties won a large majority of seats in the parliament, the rightists refused to consider the election legitimate. In July, a group of right-wing generals mounted a coup. The ensuing civil war captured the public imagination in the United States. The fact that Germany and Italy supported the rebels deepend the suspicion that the dictatorships were putting the "program" into operation. Kenneth Fearing prophesied the future with surprising accuracy in his poem "The Program":

> ACT ONE, Barcelona, Time, the present
> ACT TWO, Paris in springtime, during the siege
> ACT THREE, London, Bank Holiday, after an air raid
> ACT FOUR, a short time later in the U.S.A.[2]

The nascent sense that America soon must take sides in a world polarizing between democracy and authoritarianism grew in strength.

Like the Italo-Ethiopian War, however, the Spanish conflict ultimately failed to cement once and for all a national agreement on how the Untied States should respond. Despite the public's willingness to believe that the Spanish Republic was fighting America's war against antidemocratic powers, a crosscutting characterization of this civil conflict as a proxy fight between Communism and bourgeois democracy fatally hurt this conflict's ability to galvanize Americans against foreign dictatorships. One of the major obstacles on America's road to Word War II was the fact that, except for a brief interlude between September 1939 and June 1941, the Soviet

Union was the militarily most formidable and ideologically most implacable antagonist of the Axis Powers. During the Spanish conflict, the Soviets kept their antifascist promises and aided the Republic militarily. In the U.S. context all this meant that writers who warned of the Axis threat had to explain away creatively their position's uneasy resemblance to what the Soviets – by no means a friendly figure to most Americans – said about the same enemy. Meantime, those who doubted "the program" could use the Soviets' fierce hostility to Germany, Italy, and Japan as an argument in favor of appeasement. Their argument boiled down to this crude but effective message: if Bolsheviks detested and feared Nazis and Fascists so much, there must have been something good about the latter.

The American writers' response to the Spanish Civil War offers a perfect site to study how the Soviet-led antifascism at once helped and impeded the trend to view a series of regional conflicts as part of an escalating global confrontation between democracy and tyranny. As in the case of the Italo-Ethiopian War, the role the Spanish Civil War fulfilled in the prewar culture was ambivalent. On the one hand, the rhetoric of international antifascist solidarity that arose out of the civil war was never able to overcome Americans' isolationist disposition, which was given additional boost by anti-Communism. To this extent, this episode marked another setback in the growth of a new globalism. On the other hand, when four years later the United States actually began fighting alongside the USSR against the Axis, the rhetoric of the Soviet-U.S. antifascist solidary touted during the Spanish conflict was reactivated to gloss over the fear that America might be in league with one dictatorship in a fight against another. In hindsight, then, it becomes clear that the Spanish Civil War tested on the public the idea that their country might share its anti-Axis leadership with the Soviets. The test returned negative results then, but it also prepared the public, in a way unanticipated by anyone, for the wartime cooperation with the Soviet Russia. A restoration of this mixture of failure and (unintended) success will be the main burden of the present chapter.

The Birth of the Popular Front

Like during the Ethiopian crisis, the U.S. government's response to the Spanish request for help was predictably timid. Fearing that the conflict would turn into a general European war, France and Britain chose to appease Franco's backers and withheld aid from the Spanish Republic. Roosevelt went along without much protest.[3] Unlike the Ethiopian crisis, however, the Spanish cause was much more widely recognized and much more popular in the United States. Various polls showed that the general public consistently favored the Republican side throughout the conflict.[4] The coalition government in Madrid had a support of a majority of popular votes, and the 1936 election seemed legitimate enough to those Americans who cared about elections in foreign countries. A junta-led coup d'état was clearly offensive to American sensibilities. Granted, the sympathy for the new Spanish republic was far from universal. Millions of Catholics, for example, who had to listen to local ecclesiastics visiting withering calumnies on atheists, anarchists, and Bolsheviks in the Spanish government, took seriously the Franco propaganda about the Communist infiltration of the Spanish government, the plundering of churches, the expropriation of church estates, the raped nuns, and the massacred priests. But it was also true that just as many simply dismissed this as propaganda. At conscious and unconscious levels, most Americans were struck by the resemblance the civil war in Spain bore to the battle at home between the haves and have-nots. Just four months after the army barracks across Spain rose up in arms, the 1936 elections, the most lopsided in American history, returned a Democratic majority to Congress and a triumphant Roosevelt to the White House. A loose confederacy of reactionary Spaniards (land-owners, monarchists, clerics, and generals) obviously did not cut a terribly sympathetic figure to the America moving leftward.

The reaction of writers and intellectuals mirrored and magnified the public's vague but nonetheless solid friendliness toward the Spanish Republic. For not a few writers, the war in Spain even became an overmastering passion, a source of mystical experience that fused them with world history. Looking back on the middle years of the depression decade, Alfred Kazin wrote:

> History was going our way, and in our need was the very life-blood of history. Everything in the outside world seemed to be moving toward some final decision, for by now the Spanish Civil War had begun, and every day felt choked with struggle. It was as if the planet had locked in combat. In the same way that unrest and unemployment, the political struggles inside the New Deal, suddenly became part of the single pattern of struggle in Europe against Franco and his allies Hitler and Mussolini, so I sensed that I could become a writer without giving up my people. The unmistakable and surging march of history might yet pass through me. There seemed to be no division between my effort at personal liberation and the apparent effort of humanity to deliver itself.[5]

The experience depicted here is intensely subjective ("seemed," "as if," "sensed"). It is also religious. The Spanish Civil War triggered an epiphany, disclosing the oneness underneath worldly divisions. Abroad, two sides, Fascism and Democracy, were locked in battle. At home, New Dealers and anti–New Dealers were locked in battle. And these two combats joined each other in world history. Nothing was local. Everything, even the American destiny, was part of the world. And with this realization, Kazin felt the last and the most obstinate division, the wall between the writer's whim and the law of world history, topple. Art (artist) was no longer alienated from truth (my people). The two merged in the one and same process: struggle.

Kazin's operatic bombast makes it look as though this sort of experience was rare and special, but Spain occasioned similar moments of epiphany for many writers, certainly much more writers than Ethiopia did. A few factors help explain Spain's advantage. First, as Kazin's passage indicates, the view of the Popular Front government in Spain as a sort of Spanish New Deal made the civil conflict relatable for the writers whose politics had been already radicalized in the early years of the depression decade. The analogy served as a convenient frame of reference. The Spanish rebels and their foreign abettors corresponded to the reactionaries in America, those "economic royalists" Roosevelt denounced in the Democratic National Convention just a month before the eruption of the civil war. Geography also helped. The latest conflict broke out in Europe, not in East Africa or Manchuria. On the whole, America's mental picture of the world was not much of an improvement on the old atlas from the great age of exploration. Nebulae of blankness, Africa and Asia, floated around the minutely surveyed North Atlantic world. At a visceral level, even writers and intellectuals often found it difficult to believe that the Japanese depredations in China or the Italian assault on Ethiopia directly bore on the interests and ideals of their country. Spain, meanwhile, was a different kettle of fish altogether.

Another facilitating factor, more important than any others, was that the Popular Front furnished for the prewar writers a catchy narrative. By the middle of the 1930s the Soviets faced a two-pronged thrust from the two latecomer imperial powers: Japan in Northeastern China, just below the Siberian border, and a resurgent Germany beyond Poland. To the chagrin of dialecticians in Kremlin, a prophesied second imperialist war among capitalist nations had not come to pass, and now Russia had to pull off a rhetorical tour de force: to explain in all seriousness to Western liberal democracies how and why it was in their national interest to build a "collective security" regime against those fascist powers threatening the Soviet borders. This imperative dictated a number of tactical decisions that constituted the broad strategic reorientation christened "the Popular Front." These tactical decisions ranged widely (for instance, the sidelining of colonial issues was one corollary), but the most crucial was the Communists' replacement of sectarianism with a new majoritarian strategy to forge a united front with the erstwhile liberal enemies. The ultimate goal was to form antifascist governments in the West with a broad national basis. In the 1936 election, Spaniards on the left adopted this strategy. It worked. But that was soon followed by civil war.

In the propaganda war that ensued in the court of world opinion, the Popular Front was vital. The Spanish reality on the ground was chaotic, particularly so to distant observers on the other side of the Atlantic. The rebels formed a loose alliance of convenience, absorbing conservatives, reactionaries, monarchists, and nationalists driven by mingled agendas and partially contradictory ideologies. The only faction that had an unmistakably fascist orientation was the Spanish Falange. The Republican side was equally fractured, an unstable conglomerate of liberals, socialists, Moscow-led Communists, Catalan nationalists, and anarchists. These confusing details had to be synthesized. Synthesis called for a simple narrative. And the Communist-led Popular Front purveyed that. The Popular Front line was stark and hence effective: the Spanish Civil War was a proxy battle between global fascism and world democracy. Spain was a besieged outpost of liberal democracy, the civil war a local skirmish of critical importance in the broader confrontation between totalitarian powers and constitutional democracies.[6]

We can see this process of verbal synthesis at work in a circular letter sent out to hundreds of writers by the League of American Writers, one of the Popular Front organizations that were mushrooming at that time. The letter from Donald Ogden Stewart (the League's first president) asked:

> We know how fascist countries everywhere destroy civil liberties within their borders and ignore international law beyond them. Today the struggle rages east of us and west of us. Tomorrow it may be in our midst. It is constantly drawing nearer. ... Are you for, or are you against Franco and fascism? Are you for, or are you against the legal government and the people of Republican Spain? Your verdict has world importance.

The letter gave prominence to an assortment of values dear to liberals, such as civil liberties, international law, the legality of election, basically all those fictions of "bourgeois legalism" that Communists used to ridicule as the soporific lullaby the capitalists sang to the restive proletariat. Tactfully omitted from the letter was the economic aspect of the conflict. The war was as much about expropriation and property rights as about liberal constitutionalism. The message that resulted from this combination of emphasis and de-emphasis was clear and attractive to the widest possible audience: fascists hated freedom and democracy, and that was why Franco's rebels, armed with Italian tanks and German dive bombers, wanted to crush the Spanish Republic. Because fascists were motivated by their profound hostility to constitution and democracy, not by the fear of Communism, social revolution, and anti-clericalism, it stood to reason to expect that if the republic in Spain was allowed to be overrun by the rebels and invaders, those enemies of freedom would next prey on other democracies.

Stewart's letter garnered more than 400 replies. 98 percent supported the Republican government.[7] Writers like Marianne Moore, who cautiously drew a line between politics and literature throughout the 1930s (and stayed on the literature side), apparently found the war important enough to make an exception. Best-selling middlebrow women writers like Pearl Buck, Edna Ferber, Kathleen Norris, and Dorothy Canfield Fisher were not squeamish about having their names prominently displayed alongside known Communist writers. The Popular Front line was apparently quite convincing to Norris, who wrote: "The issue is not between Christian ideals and the red rule of Russia. It is between dictatorships and democracies." John Steinbeck drew a direct parallel between Spanish peons and agricultural laborers in California, between the terroristic reactionaries in Spain and the goons and thugs in the employ of rapacious capitalists, between indiscriminate air raids like the one that reduced Guernica to rubble and the extralegal suppression of labor unions: "Just returned from a little tour in the agricultural fields of California. We have our own fascist groups out here. They haven't bombed open towns yet but in Salinas last year tear gas was thrown in a Union Hall and through the windows of workingmen's houses. That's rather close, isn't it?" Even Faulkner, undeterred by a southerner's mistrust of liberal optimism, cared enough to send in a letter of support: "I most sincerely wish to go on record as being unalterably opposed to Franco and fascism, to all violations of the legal government and outrages against the people of Republican Spain." Letters from Communist writers and fellow travelers like Dashiell Hammett and Theodore Dreiser basically copied party communiqués verbatim. Richard Wright thus wrote:

> Speaking as a Negro Communist writer, I am wholeheartedly and militantly pro-Loyalist and for the national freedom of the people of Spain. As an aid to this process, I believe that we Americans should urge the repeal of

the Neutrality Act so as to allow arms to be sent to the Spanish people. Liberty-loving people of all countries will find that the struggle for collective security will have been strengthened by the entry into their ranks of a free, courageous, and gallant Spain.[8]

To the architects of the Popular Front, the fact that more than 400 writers across the political spectrum took the trouble to publicize their pro-republican, antifascist stance itself demonstrated the soundness of its strategy and the appeal of its rhetoric.

Most of those 400 or so writers and artists cheered from the sidelines. Moreover, their cheers were of no more than symbolic value. But during the war, some prominent figures such as Langston Hughes, Dorothy Parker, Paul Robeson, Lillian Hellman, John Dos Passos, and Upton Sinclair visited Spain on the Republican side in a show of solidarity. American literati and intelligentsia were also duly represented at the Second International Congress for the Defense of Culture, held in Valencia and Madrid in 1938, by Malcolm Cowley, Louis Fischer, and Anna Louise Strong, a somewhat lackluster show of force in the company of literary giants like Alejo Carpentier, Octavio Paz, Pablo Neruda, André Malraux, Julien Benda, Tristan Tzara, W. H. Auden, and Ilya Ehrenburg.[9] Outside of the narrow literary circles, upward of 4,000 idealistic Americans, many of them affiliated with the Communist Party, enlisted in the International Brigade and made the difficult journey across the Atlantic and the Pyrenees to man the trenches in Spain. Among this group were writers like Milton Wolff, Alvah Bessie, William Herrick, and Edwin Rolfe, who, not content with merely writing prorepublican poems and editorials, attending benefit parties in Hollywood and Manhattan, or affixing their signatures to indignant circular letters, chose "to clothe their vision with flesh."[10]

The majority of prorepublican antifascist writers were innocent and well-meaning bystanders. Antifascism was another patently just cause. The Popular Front explanation for the "world importance" of the war made perfect sense. By contrast, writers who were more deeply involved in Communist-led antifascism were troubled by a dilemma. They employed the same rhetoric, but they knew and cared more about the complicated situation masked by the lofty slogans. They proudly held the banner of the Popular Front with Communists, but they did not forget to check the holy words emblazoned there against their bitter knowledge. At the heart of their predicament was a nagging apprehension about the true character of the Soviet regime and the wisdom of entering into an alliance with it. It was understandable that implacable anti-Communists harbored strong misgivings about the sincerity of Soviet Russia's volte-face, but seriously committed liberal writers themselves were also leery after having been jeered as self-deluded lackeys for capitalists throughout the Comintern's ultra-left Third Period. Needless to say, party loyalists were doing fine. They had already embraced Stalinism all the way. Those idealists had already bought into a farrago of exonerative arguments for the punishing consequences of Stalinism. Hence no need to prevaricate. But other liberals who wanted to play an active role in the Popular Front still had doubts about the Soviets, so they had to think more inventively. While the rhetoric of the Popular Front helped those apprehensive liberal writers toe the Popular Front line, the Soviets' actual conduct taxed their creative credulity, as damning evidence mounted throughout the war. After all, the Spanish Civil War (1936–1939) coincided with the Great Purge (1936–1938), the period when Stalinism at last bared its dreaded lineaments.

The anti-Communist propaganda further twisted the inner doubts of these nervous but deeply committed antifascists. During the civil war, in a direct challenge to the Popular Front line, anti-Communists put a diametrically opposed construction on its international import. The Popular Front government in Madrid (later in Valencia), they alleged, was a cat's paw of Soviet interventionism. Moscow's main aim was to control the Spanish government under the anodyne guise of a "People's Republic." The Iberian Peninsula was just the beginning; the dominos would fall in short order, giving rise to a new Europe pliable to Soviet designs. Anti-Communists with fertile imaginations even dreaded a prospect of the Red Empire conquering Latin America by using Spain as a springboard.[11] By this logic, American "innocents and stooges" enlisting in the International Brigade aided and abetted, however unconsciously, the Soviet plot for world revolution.[12] This storyline did not simply expire as the war drew to a close. The FBI raided the office of the Veterans of the Abraham Lincoln Brigade in February 1940. During World War II, despite Russia's new role as America's official ally, the military frequently relieved American veterans of the Spanish Civil War of important duties.[13] With the onset of the Cold War in 1945–1947, their record of "premature" antifascism became still more suspicious.[14] More and more Americans now viewed the Spanish Civil War retroactively as a dress rehearsal for the emerging bipolar confrontation between the free world and world Communism.[15]

The slighter the writer's contribution to the Popular Front was, the better shielded that writer was from these anti-Communist charges.

Restated otherwise, the more heartfelt the writer's sympathy was and the more committed he was to the cause of antifascism, the more that writer came to learn about facts difficult of incorporation into the Popular Front narrative. And consequently, the more worried he became if he made a right decision in allowing himself to work with Communists. Some quietly swallowed their doubts. Others reassured themselves that their collaboration with Communists was an alliance of convenience, subject to renegotiation or annulment once they won their common objective, the defeat of global fascism. Whatever the case, for these deeply committed fellow travelers, the war in Spain meant as much an inner struggle against gnawing concerns about their Communist allies as an actual combat against Franco's rebel armies. It is important to recapture this inner drama because it encapsulated the Popular Front's unintended contribution to the subsequent national consensus on the nature and purpose of World War II. The dream of antifascist international solidarity foundered on the rock of the realities of war and international politics, but the wreckage later supplied usable rhetorical materials. In this regard, Popular Front writers' inner turmoil reflected in a condensed fashion the way the Spanish Civil War fit into the evolution of the prewar culture.

Ernest Hemingway in Spain

Arguably no writer lived this psychological drama more intensely than Earnest Hemingway. Between 1937 and 1938, he visited Spain three times and spent a total of more than six months there. All told, his energetic coverage produced thirty-one dispatches, twenty-eight of which were published in major dailies (some of them to be reprinted in influential periodicals such as *Time* and *The New Republic*). As a founding member of the Popular Front venture Contemporary Historians, Hemingway advanced at least two thousand dollars (about thirty thousand in today's value) for the prorepublican propaganda documentary, *The Spanish Earth*, and collaborated with Dutch Communist filmmaker Joris Ivens during its shooting and postproduction.[16] He raised funds for ambulances, editorialized on the pages of left-leaning or Communist publications like Ken, *The New Masses*, and even *Pravda*, and wrote a play set in Madrid under siege, *The Fifth Column*, which premiered in early 1940. He labored for two years on *For Whom the Bell Tolls*, which came out in the fall of the same year to become a national best seller. Very few American writers and artists could match the depth and scope of his involvement, except those who actually enlisted in the International Brigade and fought the battles.

As already noted, writers' commitment to the Popular Front inevitably ensnared them in the paradox: the more they were involved, the less certain they became about the meaning of the war in Spain. Hemingway was no exception to this rule.[17] Unlike the bystanders like Kazin who contented themselves with interpreting the world historical significance of the war from a safe and comfortable distance, Hemingway and other Americans who visited Spain and beheld the face of battle had to reckon with glaring but inevitable contrasts between political explanations and their experience, between war talk and war itself. In private, Hemingway often gave voice to his reservations about the left's exclusive title to the "true" interpretation of the war. As he began working on *For Whom the Bell Tolls* in the spring of 1938, Hemingway told his Russian friend Ivan Kashkin how difficult it was to write "truly" about the war. The stark language he and other liberals brandished was just for public consumption: "We know war is bad. Yet sometimes it is necessary to fight. But still war is bad and any man who says it is not is a liar. But it is very complicated and difficult to write about truly."[18] Distancing himself from the openly prorepublican war correspondents like Louis Fischer and Herbert Matthews and from a surfeit of political commentaries issued by the Popular Front writers (the "ideology boys"), he would often defend his political neutrality and objectivity, as seen in this letter to Maxwell Perkins: "I am a writer. Not a Catholic writer, nor a Party writer nor anything but a writer."[19] The writer must be ready to buck the conventional wisdom retailed by both the Popular Front and anti-Communists. Following a prefabricated political narrative will compromise his professional integrity.

This discrepancy between Hemingway's public rhetoric and private doubts, a telltale sign of the impact of war on his political faith, produced the most important literary fruit of his experience in Spain, *For Whom the Bell Tolls*. War collided against politics in this novel, which took as its central concern the vertiginous impact of this collision on the morale of its main protagonist, an American volunteer fighter in Spain. Fictional as well as nonfictional accounts of war by the American veterans of the International Brigade, such as Alvah Bessie's *Men in Battle* (1938) and *The Un-Americans* (1957), Milton Wolff's *Another Hill* (1994), and William Herrick's *Hermanos!* (1964), give us a kaleidoscopic picture of how the belief systems of these volunteers coped with the clash of war with politics in Spain.[20] And yet none of these accounts study as honestly as did *For Whom the Bell Tolls* the ordeal of this psychological coping. Hemingway's was a story centering on war's corrective pressure on political beliefs and the limits of this pressure. The exigencies of combat present its protagonist, Robert Jordan, with an unanticipated opportunity to vet the two contradictory narratives, the Popular Front and anti-Communism. After he realizes they are both factitious, he improvises a new code (efficiency and pragmatism) to guide and redeem his conduct. But unbeknownst to Jordan in the fictional universe, and to Hemingway outside of it, this new rationale was also shared by Communists to justify their new policies, which could not be logically drawn from their original Popular Front line. The profile of a liberal internationalist that emerges from this novel is thus extraordinary. He is an idealist, a realist, and a gull all at once, but his gullibility is a curious kind, for which no sinister mastermind deserves full credit.

In July 1937, a few months after returning from his first assignment in Spain, Hemingway began his speech at the second congress of the League of American Writers by defining the writer as a discoverer and chronicler of "truth": "A writer's problem does not change. He himself changes, but his problem remains the same. It is always how to write truly and, having found what is true, to project it in such a way that it becomes a part of the experience of the person who reads it." By contrast, "Fascism is a lie told by bullies," a political movement that inverts truth and falsity systematically.[21] The proxy war between democracy and fascism in Spain equaled a literary battle between the custodians of truth and the cynical obfuscators.

For Whom the Bell Tolls recorded a slow demise of this pat equation. Himself a writer, one who has authored books on Spanish culture, the hero of the novel, Robert Jordan, is not only keenly conscious of the politicized character of the war but also wary about how it can distort his cognition of facts. He is a dynamite technician and a college professor from Montana, tasked to collaborate with a local guerrilla group behind the enemy lines to blow up a strategically important bridge as part of an elaborately orchestrated offensive. Behind this ostensible mission, however, the reader sees another mission, Jordan's self-assigned search for the truth of war beyond political arguments. Jordan, who "write[s] absolutely truly," in Soviet journalist Karlov's approving assessment, "liked to know how it really was; not how it was supposed to be."[22] Therefore, he has "no right to shut [his] eyes to any of it nor any right to forget any of it nor to soften it nor to change it" (304). All the way up to the end of the story, Jordan is preoccupied with aligning his concepts and percepts with the actuality of war exactly. We find him prostrate on the pine-needle floor of the forest, with one thighbone completely fractured. Delirious from pain, his consciousness is slipping fast. And still he is bothered that he has trouble counting exactly how many days have elapsed since he crossed into the enemy territory: "Keep it accurate, he said. Quite accurate" (466). This final self-admonition summarizes the hope that has been controlling Jordan's conduct since the very start of the novel.

Many hindrances lie athwart Jordan's path to absolute accuracy, however. He quickly learns that arguments by both sides often find evidence to strengthen themselves. Following the journalistic convention of ping-pong reporting, Hemingway gives equal space to allegations made by the two sides. If he gives out in passing elliptical information on the circumstances surrounding Maria's gang rape by the Falangists or the execution of Joaquín's family, the reader is also treated to Pilar's thirty-page narrative of the revolutionary terror at Ronda (99–129).[23] In one chapter, Jordan fatally shoots a Carlist officer; in the next, he discovers a letter from the officer's sister telling her brother that "she was happy he was doing away with the Reds to liberate Spain from the domination of the Marxist hordes" (302).[24] Jordan is at least self-critical enough to acknowledge that his evidence, both circumstantial and direct, allows scope for too many divergent readings to be explained away by a single paradigm: "Things he had come to know in this war were not so simple" (248).

A second lesson is that in a highly politicized war, "facts" are often lied about. The novel shows the characters living amid a cacophony of lies, where nothing is as it is said to be. When Maria tells Jordan that a piece of Nationalist propaganda alleges "there are hundreds of thousands" of Russian soldiers in Madrid, the latter dismisses it out of hand, calling it a lie: "Those are lies. There are very few" (249). When El Sordo's men tease Joaquín about his youthful devotion to Communism and tell him that la Passionaria has been hiding her "son thy age in Russia since the start of the movement," he cries indignantly, "It's a lie" (309). Occasionally, the narrator editorializes in order to expose a character as a liar. When André Marty, a paranoiac political commissar who sees lies and intrigues everywhere and shoots soldiers on the slightest suspicion, claims to have been a "gunner's mate" at the time that he famously led a mutiny during the Great War, the narrator obtrudes with the following commentary: "It was a lie. He had really been a chief yeoman at the time of the mutiny" (424). Militarily and politically, Jordan's and Hemingway's enemies are Nationalist rebels and their foreign allies. As an honest and independent writer-soldier, Jordan – and through him Hemingway – combat propagandists and mythmakers regardless of which side they are on.

Jordan's third lesson is that warding off the enemy's deception does not necessarily immunize him to the perils of voluntary fraud. Throughout, the novel notes Jordan's vigilance against the costly comfort of self-deception: "Don't lie to yourself, he thought. Nor make up literature about it" (287; for similar monologues, see 289, 304, 335, and 385). On the third day, right before the attack, Jordan is tempted to vindicate his senseless, almost suicidal mission by appealing to the Popular Front narrative: "Remember this that as long as we can hold them here we keep the fascists tied up. They can't attack any other country until they finish with us." But he quickly deconstructs this consoling storyline: "This is just a holding attack. You must not get illusions about it now" (432). This realism, however, all too often wilts in the face of Jordan's overwhelming emotional need to relax and "make up literature about" the war. As soon as he is fatally wounded and left behind by the guerrilla band to foil the enemies in hot pursuit, Jordan gives in to his impulse to idealize his imminent death and pretends to embrace a Popular Front slogan: "Stay with what you believe now. Don't get cynical … If we win here we will win everywhere" (466–67). Psychological need for the consolation of beliefs and symbols trumps the "cynical" appraisal of reality.

From the Importance of Winning to the Importance of Fighting Well

In the general context of war, fighters can attribute a discrepancy between facts and political explanations to misrecognition of facts, inaccuracies (deliberate or inadvertent) in the explanations, or both. Whatever the case, to the extent that they need some sort of narrative to boost their own morale and dignify their own action to themselves as well as to others, soldiers must beat a zigzag pathway, tallying narratives against empirical minutiae conscientiously while at the same time discounting radically untoward information that may upend their basic worldview. Jordan's predicament is a variation on what is commonly known as the paradox of "the truth of truth." To paraphrase Oliver Wendell Holmes, Jr., the veteran of another civil war who coined this nifty phrase: whereas any truth is provisional and might be debunked as the enemy's lie, the soldier must believe that his belief is true as long as he wants to believe in something.[25] Jordan *knows* that he knows the truth; he *believes* that he knows the truth of this truth. A faith exposes the political naïf to co-optation by bogus ideals and hence must be avoided by a truth-seeking writer-warrior such as Jordan, but he can ill afford the trade-off, namely the loss of his ability to spot and cling to any truth of war amid the chaos of lies. Belief begets truth, and truth in turn begets belief. To participate in this mutually guaranteeing relationship means exposing oneself to a host of untruths soliciting one's faith. "Bigotry is an odd thing. To be bigoted you have to be absolutely sure that you are right"(164), goes Jordan's gnomic injunction.

Jordan and Hemingway ultimately abandon this balancing act between empiricism and self-exhortation. And they do so by substituting the tactical mission (to work things out) for the cognitive one (to get things right). Dwight Macdonald noted in his review that Hemingway "instinct-ively ... tries to cut the subject down to something he *can* handle by restricting his view of the war to the activities of a small band of peasant guerillas behind Franco's lines."[26] Macdonald's emphasis on *can* is not entirely ill-placed, for the novel sidesteps the insoluble problem of object-ivity and accuracy by attending to the problem of action and its feasibility. Macdonald might also have wanted to italicize "handle" to accentuate its tactile quality. If the unvarnished truth of war is a prize that the soldier seeks using his eye, ear, and intellect, what is required to work things out is a pair of dexterous hands, nimble feet, and stout legs. The soldier sees the truth; he handles the problem.

Hemingway himself often stressed that his novel was concerned with the tactical decisions its hero makes on the ground, not his political opinions. In August 1940, a reporter from *The New York Times* visited Hemingway in a New York hotel room where he was correcting the galleys. Gustavo Duran (who commanded a regiment in the Segovia offensive) happened to be in the room. He was pontificating on how distinct military decisions were from civilian decisions: "The first duty of the commander is to make decisions ... It seems simple when you read it. You think, 'What is decision? Each day I decide what color shoes to wear, what to eat.' But decision, when the life or death of hundreds of men depend on your decision, that is much else." The difficulty of military decision was superlative, wholly unlike the decisions made in other profes-sions, such as business and politics, Duran explained, and that was why when a right tactical decision was made, it "pays off so well." Hemingway then chimed in: "That's what the new novel is about!"[27]

Jordan leaves the question of what is accurate for the question of what works. In the process, he comes to appreciate Hemingway's distinction between military and nonmilitary decisions. Like his creator, who was a military history buff, Jordan "had read on and studied the art of war ever since [he was] a boy" (335).[28] At one point, he dreams about his life after war and even flirts with Karlov's suggestion that he study at the Lenin Institute (339). Jordan is a university professor who reads the "Handbook of Marxism" (244), but he is also a flinty problem-solver (not a zealot who lets political doctrines get in the way of his pragmatism). He suppresses broad political considerations and abjures politics in favor of strategy, which is in turn discarded for still narrower tactical "problems" (35, 63, 161, 165, 226). Having already committed himself to the republican cause, Jordan declines to revisit the wisdom of his original political decision, nor does he question the authority to which he has decided to submit himself.

One reward that comes with a partitioning of tactical from political decisions is that Jordan can now make himself into an "instrument" and continue to fight with untroubled conscience. He acknowledges to himself how hopeless – and useless – his assignment is ("They were bad orders"). By his own admission, he is a disposable cog in a vast party-military machine, one of many mere "instruments to do your duty" (43). Jordan "was serving in a war and he gave absolute loyalty and as complete a performance as he could give while he was serving. But nobody owned his mind, nor his faculties for seeing and hearing, and if he were going to form judgments he would form them afterwards" (136). Two dualities stand out in this free-indirect internal monologue. The first sentence splits the continuum bridging the question of fighting well ("performance") and the question of the aim for which one supposedly wants to fight well. Jordan may be fighting for a just cause or an unjust cause (he cannot decide with absolute certitude), but that does not matter as long as he can comply with his orders as faithfully as possible. The second sentence strengthens a contradiction between cognition (his faculties for seeing) and judgment. By judgment Jordan clearly means political judgment, that is, the intellectual and moral decision on whether or not his tactics make good political sense, the judgment regarding whether or not his perform-ance and compliance further a rightful cause. These decisions over the goals and consequences of particular tactical maneuvers must not bother Jordan. Politicians and ethicists debate the ends. Generals and soldiers *are* the means.

Hemingway's signature style – concrete and literal in diction, short and conjunctive in syntax – is pressed into the service of giving formally matching expressions to Jordan's transformation from a moral and polit-ical agent into an instrument of force. Throughout the novel, figurative language rarely appears, which need cause no surprise, given the main protagonist's distrust of the elevated literary language: "Don't go roman-ticizing them [Spaniards]" (204); "Stop making dubious literature" (287); "Don't lie to yourself, he thought. Nor make up literature about it" (287). When figurative language is used, its straightforward artistic value serves a new intent, an antagonistic intent that torques literary conceits from inside and renders them parodic:

> The bombers were high now in fast, ugly arrow heads beating the sky apart with the noise of their motors. They *are* shaped like sharks, Robert Jordan thought, the wide-finned, sharp-nosed sharks of the Gulf Stream. But these, wide-finned in silver, roaring, the light mist of their propellers in the sun, these do not move like sharks. They move like no thing there has ever been. They move like mechanized doom. (87)

This hypnotic depiction of fascist airplanes flying over a high sierra reflecting the morning sun on their ominously glinting fuselages has been variously interpreted.[29] But these readings do not take into account the hidden polemical intention that the highly stylized diction is made to express. Robert Jordan quickly snaps out of his contemplation on "mechanized doom" and mocks his literary flair: "You ought to write, he told himself. Maybe you will again some time" (87). This line comes immediately after the ponderous simile "mechanized doom," which is out of key with the lean and athletic diction used throughout. The implied polemic against literature, stylization, and storytelling is impossible to miss. Mentally composing such an orotund prose can sabotage Jordan's mission.

As in the Nick Adams stories, so in *For Whom the Bell Tolls*, too, must the doing obviate the need to think, interpret, and explain. On the fields of battle, wordless activism must replace chatty hermeneutics. Otherwise, the soldier's mind would turn inward. He would worry about the correctness, not the effectiveness, of his action. If he has no choice but to give verbal meanings to deeds, his speech must aspire to the conditions of gestures and miming, strictly indexical or mimetic. The following scene shows Jordan demonstrating to Augustín how to install a machine gun properly: "'It must be farther,' he said, 'farther out. Good. Here. That will do until it can be done properly. There. Put the stones there. Here is one. Put another there at the side. Leave room for the muzzle to swing. The stone must be farther to this side. Anselmo. Get thee down to the cave and bring me an ax. Quickly'" (270). The pithy, staccato rhythm creates a sense of decisiveness without premeditation on the part of the commander. The silence of the addressee means that he is not supposed to debate but to follow the orders. "Farther out," "here," "there," "to this side" – these words are, essentially, the kind of locutions we associate with pedagogy and training. Because these context-dependent words cannot refer to anything predetermined, Jordan, presumably, accompanies them with nonverbal cues, such as gestures and eye movements. As a result,

Jordan's verbal instructions partake in natural referents. His pupils are better insured against misinterpretation.

In a scene depicting the direct confrontation between Jordan and the Carlist officer, Hemingway attempts to take war outside political stories:

> The horseman was almost opposite him now. He was riding a big gray gelding and he wore a khaki beret, a blanket cape like a poncho, and heavy black boots. From the scabbard on the right of his saddle projected the stock and the long oblong clip of a short automatic rifle. He had a young, hard face and at this moment he saw Robert Jordan.
>
> He reached his hand down toward the scabbard and as he swung low, turning and jerking at the scabbard, Robert Jordan saw the scarlet of the formalized device he wore on the left breast of his khaki blanket cape. (265)

Evidence supplants figurality. The fastidiously displayed signs, such as the uniform (a khaki beret), the openly carried weapon (a short automatic rifle), and the insignia (the formalized device), combine to lessen leeway for conjecture, codify the emotionally charged enmity into the rules of engagement, and protect Jordan against mistakes. Collectively these visual tokens amount to an overkill of tactical information, a stylistic inoculation against the blandishments of judgmentalism, moral or political. Jordan opens fire, "aiming at the center of his chest, a little lower than the device," as if to reassure himself of the legitimacy and legality of the killing. The language is parsimonious. Emotional and political meanings that require interpretation are studiedly eschewed. In an odd way, a sense of equality and camaraderie humanizes the enemy. The Carlist officer is no longer a political enemy fighting to impose his nefarious ideology. He is just another professional warrior like Jordan, doing his job.

Hemingway distinguished between fact and truth. In his terminology, "facts" of war could not substitute for "truth" of war. This does not mean that Hemingway was careless about factual fidelity; he took elaborate pains to get the facts straight for his novel. Hemingway did not witness the Segovia offensive, on which the story is based, but he and Martha Gellhorn toured the front in the high sierra of Guadarrama from late April to early May (the offensive was launched on May 10). The novel's descriptions of the terrain, troop movements, characters, and even the bridge must have been drawn from the actually existing things and people Hemingway witnessed. Gustavo Duran read the entire manuscript in order to weed out factual errors and false notes in dialogues.[30] During the galley reading, Hemingway attempted to find the most plausible designation for the cavalry regiment that beheads El Soldo and his band, but at the eleventh hour he instructed Perkins to use "Nth" for the cavalry for fear that "the business about the heads" would implicate the actual regiment.[31] Charles Scribner and Perkins worried that the political figures like Marty who appear in the novel by their real names might sue for libel and urged Hemingway to be flexible.[32] Their caution was a tribute to Hemingway's realism.

Realism in this sense (factual accuracy), however, had value only to the extent that it cleared the way for the different kind of reality, which he called "truth." He wrote in the introduction for a collection of war stories he edited: "A writer's job is to tell the truth. His standard of fidelity to the truth should be so high that his invention, out of his experience, should produce a truer account than anything factual can be." Mystifyingly, Hemingway did not take "true" and "factual" to mean the same thing. A writer must leave the fact for the truth, and that's what he or she is doing when inventing an account of war. Hemingway reached for an explanation: "For facts can be observed badly … but when a good writer is creating something, he has time and scope to make it of an absolute truth."[33] Facts can be observed badly; one can easily agree to this, especially insofar as facts on the battlefield are concerned. Whether this qualifies as a good reason for extricating the claim to truthfulness from the claim to factual accuracy is another matter. Moreover, for someone like Hemingway, who sacrificed so much to get to the front line and witness the facts of war, this was a bizarre line of argument to take. If a war writer's "job" was to tell the truth about war, and if facts could cause error and misrepresentation, why bother to go to Spain in the first place? To observe facts badly?

Fact prejudices "absolute" truthfulness. This postulate takes the form of a tension between truth and memory and resurfaces in Hemingway's private writing. Four letters Hemingway wrote to Perkins in 1939 are of particular value. In a letter sent on March 25, Hemingway giddily but also guiltily (because it was "bad luck" to talk about an ongoing work) reported the progress he was making with his new novel. He compared it with his short stories about the Spanish Civil War and assured Perkins that "[i]t is 20 times better than that Night Before Battle which was flat where this [*For Whom the Bell Tolls*] is rounded and recalled where this is invented."[34] In elevating the "invented" and "rounded" writing above the "recalled" and "flat" writing, Hemingway may have been recalling the advice Gertrude Stein gave at her Paris studio almost a decade earlier. "She [Stein] thinks the parts that fail are where I remember visually rather than make up," Hemingway wrote to Fitzgerald at the time.[35] However the case may be, Perkins must have been familiar with Hemingway's mistrust of writing from experience and memory. In another letter, Hemingway had insisted on including "Up in Michigan" in a collection of his short stories. Perkins was understandably wary of potential obscenity charges, but, Hemingway explained, that story was special because it marked his coming of age as a writer, the "beginning of all the naturalness I ever got." Until he wrote that story, he was unnatural because he "was writing from memory."[36] In another letter, Hemingway shared with Perkins his nightmare: "Last night I was caught in this retreat again in the goddamndest detail. I really must have a hell of an imagination. That's why I should *always* make up stories– *not* try to remember what happened."[37] In a letter posted in mid-April, Hemingway told Perkins how a friend in Havana, after reading the manuscript of *For Whom the Bell Tolls*, "tried to make me admit I'd seen all that stuff." Hemingway's answer: "Hell no, I made it up."[38]

The analogy that Hemingway presumed between writing well and fighting well indicates that his distinction between (invented) truth and (observed and recalled) fact was anything but a defensive disclaimer to avoid libel suits. The ethical question over the ends of war ought to have no relevance to an able fighter, a tactician. At issue is the efficacy of the soldier, not his moral deserts. Even the apparently honest urge to get facts straight, to divide a warring world into facts and falsehoods, can be detrimental to a good tactical decision. From a viewpoint of pure instrumentalism, there is still something sentimental and moralizing, something even callow and romantic, about a pretension to factual correctness, and this romanticism of epistemic correctness can be as damaging as the fanaticism of political correctness. In itself, accuracy is not the condition sine qua non of efficacy. Hemingway extended this line of reasoning to his theory of writing. If morals and facts make for a poor fighter, they will also make for a poor writer. His aesthetic stipulations about the truthful war novel were motivated by the analogy he saw between effective action and effective writing. Whether or not it worked tactically was the ultimate test.

Are You Now or Have You Ever Been a Member of ...

If the contemporary reception, both critical and favorable, that greeted *For Whom the Bell Tolls* serves as any guide, Hemingway succeeded in extracting the truth of battle out of a molten swirl of political lies. Jordan's literal-mindedness, evenhandedness, and zeal for the truth of war have helped the protagonist and the author of this novel contrast favorably with the dogmatism and pig-headedness of other prorepublican ideologues.

Since the book first appeared, a consensus has developed that Jordan's self-sacrifice and antifascist heroism spring from his idiosyncratic code of honor, his anarchic libertarianism, or strictly personal motives free of political obsessions. Jordan is, on this reading, politically neutral just as the United States, Britain, and France, which hewed to their nonintervention policy, were diplomatically neutral.

Feeling double-crossed by Hemingway's unflattering portraitures of Communist leaders like Dolores Ibárruri (309, 357–58) and André Marty (416–26), Communists and fellow travelers denounced Hemingway's bourgeois individualism and disowned, as much in sorrow as in anger, the literary celebrity they had utilized as a poster boy for the Popular Front.[39] Hemingway had written *To Have and Have Not* and other works dedicated to the cause of class struggle. He had endorsed the republican cause through *The Fifth Column* and his countless dispatches for the North American Newspaper Alliance (NANA) and opinion pieces for *The New Masses* and *Pravda*. The party thought that this prominent American novelist had promised to mature into a champion of social justice and international solidarity, but it was sadly mistaken. This kind of response was duplicated with a curious twist by anti-Stalinists like Edmund Wilson, who *liked* the novel for exactly the same reason. "Hemingway the artist is with us again," Wilson gushed in his book review, "and it is like having an old friend back."[40] These evaluations were accepted by another anti-Stalinist, Lionel Trilling, who judged the novel a "failure," again for exactly the same reason. Censuring Hemingway for the cult of experience, Trilling asserted that the "essential, inner dullness of the hero" rendered the novel a mere stream of picturesque scenes incapable of apprehending social and political contradictions.[41] The trivialization (or glorification) of Jordan as a sort of action-aesthete, a maverick uninstructed by any ideological dogmas, was to be set in stone by Carlos Baker's major study published at the height of the Cold War. Baker highly valued the same shortcoming that Trilling maintained was the source of Hemingway's failure: Hemingway and his mouthpiece Jordan believe in "the artistic 'neutrality' of one who puts humanity above politics and art above propaganda." "Robert Jordan is with, but not of, the communists."[42] Later scholars have seldom challenged this canonical reading.[43] When it comes to Jordan's association with Communists, they wax adulatory over Hemingway's "artistic integrity." Hemingway's impugnments of the Party ideologues were meant to sound the tocsin against totalitarianism.

However, contra the readings of these Stalinists, anti-Stalinists, and Cold War liberals, the hard truth that Jordan and Hemingway discern in the Spanish Civil War remains inside the framework of contemporary political conditions in several key respects. From the outset, the novel makes it clear that Robert Jordan is a guerrilla operative acting on direct orders from the Communists, who, as Hemingway knew, were increasingly placing the republican army under Soviet control by the Segovia offensive.[44] His civilian outfit must not be mistaken for a sartorial statement of political independence. Jordan does not wear a uniform or insignias because his specialty is in "*partizan* work" (7). He is directly answerable to "*Général Sovietique*" Golz, "who is the party as well as the army" (8, 162): "The orders do not come from you ... They come from Golz" (162). Rather than making a clenched-fist gesture of solidarity, he salutes Golz, Communist style.[45] The news source on which he relies most is *Mundo Obrero*, the Spanish Communist daily (245). His safe conduct carries two seals from the highest echelon of the republican army – one from *Servicio de Investigación Militar* (SIM), the Spanish counterpart of the NKVD (People's Commissariat for Internal Affairs), the power base for the Communists within the republican government; and the other from the general staff (10).[46] A few hundred pages later, the reader will discover that Jordan also possesses a seal of SIM itself so that, if need be, he can authenticate his messages (332).

On the point of the chain of command, nowhere can Hemingway be more explicit than in this passage: "He was under Communist discipline for the duration of the war. Here in Spain the Communists offered the best discipline and the soundest and sanest for the prosecution of the war" (163). Good generals "were Communists and they were disciplinarians" (234). Working with them "gave you [Jordan] a part in something that you could believe in wholly and completely and in which you felt an absolute brotherhood with the others who were engaged in it" (235). In this American dynamiter in Spain lingers little vestige of the deserter Frederic Henry, who makes his separate peace in the Great War. A more fitting archetype may be Philip Rawlings, the protagonist of *The Fifth Column*, a "grotesque romance of Republican terror."[47] Despite his protestation that nobody "owned his mind," Jordan has internalized the Communist discipline: "Turn off the thinking now, old timer, old comrade. You're a bridge-blower now. Not a thinker" (17; for similar passages of self-censorship, see 43, 135–36, 340, 394 and 433). Jordan's reluctance to intellectualize war bespeaks, not his political independence, but his devotion to the iron discipline of the Party.[48]

Jordan's partisanship also lurks behind his vindictive views on the lax discipline and political naiveté of anarchists – the Communists' nemesis in

Spain. Liberal writers who rushed to Spain were all bewildered by the factionalism that lacerated the Spanish left, especially the deadly in-fighting that broke out between the Communists and the anarchists.[49] George Orwell was sympathetic toward the anarchists and chronicled in *Homage to Catalonia* (1938), among many other Communist deviltries and depredations, the rigorous destruction of the *Partido Obrero de Unificación Marxista* (POUM) in Barcelona.[50] John Dos Passos, disillusioned by what he viewed as the importation of the Terror into Spain, wrote a novel of disillusionment, *Adventures of a Young Man* (1939), officially joining the ranks of the anti-Stalinists. Nonetheless, except for these dissidents, most writers including André Malraux and Gustave Regler took the side of the *Partido Comunista de España* (PCE). They had reservations about the ulterior intentions of the Soviets, but the Communists alone, they thought, had the expertise to overcome the notorious regionalism of Spanish politics, consolidate the central government, and "militarize" rabble militias. Hemingway was squarely in the camp of pro-Communists. Disagreements between Hemingway and Dos Passos, who together as members of Contemporary Historians visited Spain in the spring of 1937, escalated into a ferocious quarrel and ended their two-decade friend-ship, permanently.[51]

Hemingway ventriloquized his dim view of the anarchists through the protagonist and the narrator of the novel. Their inane utopianism comes in for particularly hearty condemnation (120, 126, 305, 377). When it comes to the deadly purge of the anarchists in Barcelona, Jordan, who "liked to know how it really was; not how it was supposed to be" (230), is unchar-acteristically credulous, swallowing Karlov's explanation uncritically: "It is all still comic opera. First it was the paradise of the crack-pots and the romantic revolutionists. Now it is the paradise of the fake soldier" (246–47). Confronted about whereabouts of the missing POUM general secretary Andreu Nin, Karlov blithely answers, "In Paris," which appar-ently meets Jordan's vaunted standards of accuracy and truthfulness (247).[52] Nin was in fact kidnapped and shot in a police cell in Valencia, presumably not before having undergone a customary NKVD interro-gation.[53] Like his protagonist, Hemingway was convinced that Nin was alive somewhere. So anti-Communist innuendos about his disappearance, such as General Krivitsky's charge that NKVD agents engineered the Barcelona uprising, threw him into a paroxysm of rage.[54] "Then there is Nin. Do you know where Nin is now? You ought to find that out before you write about his death," Hemingway snarled at the apostate Dos Passos in his breakup letter.[55]

Considered together, the chain of command Jordan follows and his rabid anti-anarchism show that he is a Stalinist guerrilla, motivated as much by his political preference as by soldierly professionalism. This reading does not require ignoring the novel's anomalies. For example,

> "He is a Communist," Maria said. "They are very serious *gente*."
> "Are you a Communist?"
> "No I am an anti-fascist."
> "For a long time?"
> "Since I have understood fascism." (66)

Prior scholars have adduced this dialogue to maintain that *For Whom the Bell Tolls* is "largely [a] nonpolitical novel" and its protagonist is an "intellectual free agent."[56] However, the inconsistency it introduces into Jordan's otherwise incisively drawn character calls for explanation. The little evidence we have suggests that in August 1940, Scribner and Perkins read the galleys and made extensive and substantial suggestions to Hemingway. In his August 26 letter to Perkins, Hemingway mentioned "a re-write of parts of galleys 21 (the Communist business)."[57] Galley 21 in question survives. It shows the original version of the "Communist business":

> "He is a Communist" Maria said. "They are very serious *gente*."
> "Are you a Communist?"
> "Yes."
> "For a long time?"
> "For two years now."[58]

Other galleys show that Hemingway made similar changes to mask or finesse Jordan's card-carrying status throughout the manuscript. The already quoted passage, "He was under communist discipline for the duration of war," for example, originally read: "He was a Communist for the duration of war."[59] The correspondence between Gellhorn and Scribner indicates that it was Scribner who suggested these changes. Hemingway was incapable of wanting to make these changes.[60]

Scribner's possible motive behind his last-minute urging is not hard to fathom. While Hemingway was at work on his novel, "Communist" ceased being synonymous with "anti-fascist." In August 1939, the Soviets abandoned the Popular Front strategy and signed the nonaggression pact with Germany. Given the nonintervention policy of England and France during the Spanish Civil War, a series of concessions they had recently made to Germany, and the way London and Paris strung Moscow along in the anti-Germany triple alliance negotiations, this move made strategic sense to the Soviet leadership.[61] Anti-Soviet socialists who had already spurned the Popular Front, like the intellectualized Marxists who gathered around *Partisan Review*, took this about-face in stride; the pact merely added to the fodder for their esoteric controversy over the character of Stalin's regime (the degenerated worker's state, the transitional society, the bureaucratic capitalist state, and some such).[62] Liberals and moderates were shocked; God failed them. Conservatives and reactionaries were having a field day; this unholy alliance between National Socialists and Bolsheviks finally confirmed their theory that political extremes always met. By August 1940, when Hemingway began correcting his galleys, there was a growing social trend to conflate the USSR with Germany, under such blanket terms as "Red Fascism," "Brown Bolshevism," and "totalitarianism." Once the pact was announced, the CPUSA jettisoned its Popular Front tactics without much ceremony and began to urge American liberals not to meddle in the "second imperialist war" (the Stalinist appellation for the Second World War, until June 1941), furthering the amalgamation of Communism and Nazism in the popular discourse of the day.[63] An open declaration of Jordan's party membership could have made it difficult to merchandize the novel to an American readership, which had just recently been rudely awakened from the bad dream of the liberal-Communist alliance.

Harder to understand but more relevant to our concern with the role that the Popular Front antifascism played in the gradual rise of the new American globalism is the question of why, as late as August 1940, when the nation's sense of the Spanish Civil War had decisively turned against the Popular Front line, Hemingway thought it fine to have a Communist hero for his most ambitious novel. Hemingway's obliviousness bears witness to how effectively the Popular Front storyline convinced fellow travelers of its nonideological and pragmatic character. The propaganda campaigns managed by the Comintern advertised the republican cause as the defense of bourgeois democracy, not as a revolutionary struggle between capital and labor.[64] To preempt any hysterical interpretation by British Tories, French conservatives, and American anti-Communists, prorepublican propaganda machines played up the republican government's coolness toward ideologues like anarchists and trade-unionists and touted its pragmatic prioritization of war over social revolution.[65] At the same time, the organizational genius and pragmatism of the PCE were made much of as a valuable asset for the republican government, which desperately needed to prove its viability to the world.[66] Robert Jordan adopts these propaganda boilerplates as a redemptory narrative for his actions (162–63, 285, 305). If Jordan occasionally convinces himself and the readers of the novel that he is a pragmatic republican, not a fanatic ideologue, as in the oft-cited passage in which Jordan literally quotes from the Declaration of Independence (305), it is not because Hemingway and Jordan have "no politics" but because the particular species of politics to which they insist they subscribe was designed by its architects to appear nonideological and liberal-pragmatic.

Jordan arrives in Spain, determined to find the truth of war, since he expects this truth to confirm him in the political suppositions that have originally inspired him. And yet, as he encounters inconvenient evidence that belies the Popular Front line (the massive Soviet intervention, atrocities on both sides, and sectarian battles between Communists and anarchists), Jordan's cognitive dissonance caused by this discrepancy grows more and more acute, to a point where he finds it necessary to rely on the second rationale – the importance of fighting well.

The first rationale – the civil war as a "holding attack" against global fascism – prompts Jordan to volunteer in the first place and exhorts him to stay in the fight. The second, fallback rationale – soldierly pragmatism – helps Jordan rationalize the action he continues to take after the persuasiveness of the first discourse wears off. Normatively, no new information leads Jordan to second-guess the primary rationale: it remains a just cause regardless of empirical evidence. But as the facts on the ground turn out to challenge the original war aims, he begins to shift his source of motivation and rewrite his canons of justification. The Spanish Civil War may be an internecine battle between two camps of totalitarians, Franco's supporters and the Communists, not a showdown between democracy and totalitarianism, but at least Jordan acquits himself well as an able soldier.

It is important to note that the second rationale of soldierly pragmatism is not different from the original rationale of antifascist internationalism in its political usefulness, namely in its redemptory and exhortatory function. This second discourse justifies Communists' agendas such as the prioritization of war, the deferment of land reform and other explosive revolutionary measures, or the "liquidation" of the "far left" "uncontrollables" and "Trotskyites" agitating for revolution "from below." When he tries to evade politics by immersing himself in tactical problems and capture the battle at its most literal dimensions, Jordan in fact switches out one political rationale for another. He may be fighting for different reasons, but both reasons serve their respective political goals. And it was Communists who authored both narratives, with the second one intended to cover the first wherever it broke down under the weight of war's reality.

There is a near-universal agreement among historians that the Spanish Civil War accelerated the reorientation of public attention from the economic calamity at home to the military conflicts abroad. This consensus is not entirely invalid. The hot debates over whether America should officially aid the Republican government in Spain primed Americans for a more capacious understanding of their country's global mission and for a sharper assessment of the Axis threat. Nevertheless, the inner struggle of the American antifascist fighters that this chapter has reconstructed suggests that this episode's real contribution to the prewar culture was in revealing the obstacle that Americans had yet to surmount on their way to internationalism. Despite the simplifying narrative of world democracy versus authoritarianism that the Popular Front movement retailed, in the final analysis, the Soviet-German rivalry, to which the Spanish Civil War drew the world's attention, complicated the emergence of an activist anti-Axis policy backed up by a militantly interventionist public opinion. The conflict in Spain as much exposed this complication as stimulated America's geopolitical-mindedness. Only by understanding this twofold significance of the civil war in Spain can we apprehend the unintended legacy of the Popular Front antifascism. Despite its many limitations, it implanted in the American mind an emotional framework, the idea that Americans could work with Communists against Fascists and Nazis, that would be reactivated when the United States had to form a grand alliance with Soviet Russia during World War II. Hemingway himself participated in this process of reactivation. During the world war, Hemingway rendered what little support he could to the government-led efforts to characterize the Red Army as tough freedom fighters and Stalin as its wise and benevolent leader. In 1942, Paramount decided to adapt *For Whom the Bell Tolls* for screen, and the task of adaptation fell on Dudley Nichols. Hemingway read an early draft of the script and made detailed and numerous suggestions, many of which were intended to play up the Soviet role in the Spanish Civil War that he had played down in the novel and to reinforce Franco's tie to the Axis Powers.[67] Even without the memory of the Popular Front antifascism, the Americans would still have accepted Soviet Russia as a democratic ally out of necessity during World War II, but the psychological resistance they would have had to surmount would have been much greater.

Some key prewar writers were completely spared Hemingway's gut-wrenching inner turmoil. They actually saw in the Spanish Civil War the ominous portent of an impending global struggle. Yet their anti-Communism meant that the Soviet influence, no matter how vociferously disavowed by the Party, over the anti-Franco Popular Front axiomatically ruled out the possibility of their publicly supporting the Spanish cause. One such writer was Robert Sherwood. In March 1938, when Hemingway was in Spain for his third and last assignment, Sherwood confided his frustration to his diary. "If the day comes when I have to choose between communism and fascism, then I choose death," so he dramatized his abomination of Communists, like a good dramatist.[68] The war in Spain forced such a melodramatic decision on many, and he chose silence. But silence would not be an option even for those who absented themselves from the debate sparked by the war in Spain when a next crisis threatened in Europe's geopolitical center – Czechoslovakia.

4

Munich on Broadway

A snapshot of the constantly changing map of Central Europe, taken at some point between the spring (the *Anschluss*) and the fall (the Munich Agreement) of 1938, should show Czechoslovakia, like a roughly hewed stone knife, plunged about halfway into the eastern flank of the Third Empire. Rising along the edge of this knife were the Sudeten mountains, which gave this narrow band of territory abutting Germany its name, "Sudetenland."

During the interwar years, wary of a possible German encroachment, that young republic situated in the heart of the geopolitically volatile *Mitteleuropa* built an excellent system of fortifications in the Sudetenland. Yet the population in that borderland was more than 90 percent ethnic German. Toward the end of the 1930s, conniving with Berlin, these ethnic Germans began agitating for self-rule, ultimately to reunite the Sudetenland with Germany. A chain of skirmishes, ultimatums, and counter-ultimatums was quickly set in motion. In September 1938, this culminated in the Munich Crisis. Britain and France blinked at the eleventh hour, selling their ally down the river. Czechoslovakia, the most westernized, the most militarily prepared democracy in a Central and Eastern Europe now dominated by autocratic regimes, fell into the German clutches.

This diplomatic catastrophe in slow motion sharpened the American sense of the escalating world anarchy in a way altogether different from the previous crises. During the Italo-Ethiopian War, most white Americans could easily convince themselves that the Italian aggression against a remote African kingdom had nothing to do with their country's security. During the Spanish Civil War, anti-Communists and Catholics could call into doubt the democratic credentials of the Popular Front government in Madrid by pointing to the widespread looting of churches and the Soviet military assistance. But it was impossible to interpret the destruction of Czechoslovakia in any other ways than as conclusive proof of Germany's insatiable territorial ambition and the terminal spinelessness of European democracies. With the Munich Crisis, the prewar culture entered a new phase.

The Munich Crisis and the Playwrights Company

While few writers believed that the United States should be held responsible for the appeasement policy authored by France and Britain, many did feel that the latest concession to Germany augured ill, even spelled disaster, for the future of their country. They followed with bated breath a stream of bulletins and communiqués from Berlin, London, Paris, Prague, and Moscow, through the radio.

The Munich Crisis was one of the first diplomatic events that were followed simultaneously around the world thanks to the advent of radio foreign news. During the crisis, the round-the-clock torrent of breaking news from Europe, translated and broadcast with commentaries by outspoken anti-Nazi radio commentators such as CBS's H. V. Kaltenborn and NBC's Walter Winchell, flooded the tens of millions of radio sets across the United States. Just in the last two weeks of September, when the tensions ran high, each major network broadcast about 150 shortwave pickups. At the same time, the Munich Crisis was boosting the production and sale of radio sets. During the negotiation, the industry sold more radio sets than during any other comparable period.[1] Diplomacy, once an arcane province of princes, ambassadors, and chancellors, was being conducted openly in the plain hearing of swelling multitudes of radio listeners around the world.

Among that ballooning population of radio news consumers was Robert Sherwood, who was just about to embark on the most phenomenal years of his career. His grotesque war satire, *Idiot's Delight* (1936), had just won him his first Pulitzer. During the rest of the prewar period, he would win two more for *Abe Lincoln in Illinois* (1938) and *There Shall Be No Night* (1940). After the war, a fourth would be awarded to his joint biography, *Roosevelt and Hopkins* (1948). In the fall of 1938, the alarums and excursions of the latest crisis in Europe were distracting him from his pressing duty, the rehearsal of *Abe Lincoln*. The Playwrights Company's second offering was scheduled to open in a month. Sherwood had tapped Elmer Rice, who also wrote such antifascist plays as *American Landscape* (1938) and *Flight to the West* (1940), to direct the play. In his memoir Rice recounts how the political crisis in Europe cast a dark shadow on the creative labors of these high-caliber Broadway playwrights: "We interrupted the rehearsal [of *Abe Lincoln*] one day long enough to listen to a short-wave broadcast from London. Neville Chamberlain, just back from Munich, said that the agreement reached there guaranteed 'peace in our time.'"² Sherwood's diary also records the tense atmosphere surrounding the rehearsal. The entry on September 19 reads: "I ought to be working on the Prairie Scene [the pivotal scene where Lincoln undergoes a dramatic transformation from an appeaser of the South to a crusader for liberty], but I can't think of anything but the shocking news that French & British 'statesmen,' meeting yesterday in London, decided to yield completely to Hitler's loud threat and betray Czechoslovakia." The entry two days later records his avowal to do battle against isolationists: "I must start to battle for one thing: the end of our isolation. There is no hope for humanity unless we participated vigorously in the concerns of the world and assume our proper place of leadership with all the grave responsibilities that go with it."³

As explored briefly in Chapter 1, Sherwood's espousal of America's world leadership was by no means foreordained. Having been first infatuated with and then later cruelly disappointed by the high-minded Wilsonian ideals like other liberal writers of his generation, Sherwood penned such antiwar classics as *The Road to Rome* (1927), *Waterloo Bridge* (1930), and *Idiot's Delight* during the interwar years. Even the Spanish Civil War could not draw him out of his protective shell of disillusion and enlightened cynicism. Unlike other liberal writers who rushed to join the Popular Front, Sherwood remained convinced throughout the civil war that his country had neither a mandate nor a capability to redress all the woes of the world.⁴ It was only toward the end of the 1930s, as the series of fateful events abroad appeared to conclude in the extirpation of democracies, that Sherwood finally came to accept America's special mission.⁵

Chief members of the Playwrights Company shared a belief that *Abe Lincoln* deeply resonated with the contemporary world. "Today we are in a period of crisis. The democracies of the world are menaced by the rising tide of totalitarianism which seeks to engulf our free institutions and to reduce us all to the level of servile, goose-stepping puppets, cowering under the shadow of terror and despotism," Rice stated in a document prepared for the play's publicity. Contemporary Americans, wrote Rice, may very well think about what Lincoln would have done had he been alive then: "More than ever eternal vigilance is the price of liberty. For this reason we turn with a special interest to another period of crisis when it seemed as though all that the founders of the Republic had fought for was to be dissolved in chaos and bloodshed."⁶ The director of the play reckoned that "another period of crisis" that shook the republic almost a century earlier offered his audience a lesson.

Maxwell Anderson was no less acutely aware of the contemporary significance of *Abe Lincoln*. One day during a rehearsal, Anderson commended to Sherwood's attention a passage in Lincoln's Peoria speech where Lincoln bemoaned the negative impact of the spread of slavery on America's "just influence in the world." He thought that the passage, adapted to suite the current situation, would improve the play because of its intriguing relevance.[7] On November 20, 1938, the Playwrights Company gave a benefit performance of Anderson-Weil operetta *Knickerbocker Holiday* and Sherwood's *Abe Lincoln* to raise funds for German refugees, at the Ethel Barrymore and the Plymouth Theatre, respectively.[8] During the intercession, Anderson rose from his seat and delivered a speech:

> It may be that, much as we dislike war, much as we may fear the effect of the war upon our own liberties, we may be unable to avoid a conflict with the dictatorship of Europe and Asia. Just as this nation once discovered that it could not endure half slave and half free, the earth as a whole may soon discover that it cannot exist half free and democratic, and half Nazie[*sic*] and enslaved.[9]

In contrast to Sherwood, Anderson had a libertarian streak. He tended to view Roosevelt, and the New Deal programs in general, askance. The bloated bureaucracy, the expansion of the executive branch, and the mammoth deficit spending all appeared to bear an ominous resemblance to European totalitarianism rather than to the bucolic republic envisioned by Thomas Jefferson or Henry Thoreau (he made a big public show of refusing to apply for a Social Security card in 1938; he voted for Wendell Willkie in 1940).[10] Nonetheless, on the matter of the threat the foreign dictators posed to his country, Anderson was falling in line with Sherwood's evaluation. In fact, Anderson's speech echoed almost verbatim a short speech Sherwood delivered at the Plymouth Theatre, only two blocks down Broadway. Scrambling Lincoln's 1854 Peoria speech with the 1858 "House Divided" speech, Sherwood argued that American appeasement reflected on the nation's credibility as the global upholder of democratic values: "[T]he policy of indifference to evil, that policy I cannot but hate. I hate it because it deprives our republic of its just influence in the world. We cannot forget those words of Lincoln's. We have come–reluctantly, as he did–to acknowledgement of the fact that our civilization cannot endure permanently–half Nazi–and half free."[11]

Also apparently Raymond Massey was conscious of the contemporary significance of the historical figure he played. One day while in rehearsal, Sherwood "showed Raymond Massey a passage from the Peoria speech, which seemed to have a direct bearing on the current situation," presumably the same passage that Anderson had initially brought to Sherwood's attention. They at once "decided to incorporate this into the speech which Mr. Massey delivered so brilliantly in the debate scene."[12] Offstage, Massey was busy with speeches warning of the coming crisis. And again one important motif running through all his speeches was the analogy between Nazi Germany and the Confederacy (and the parallel between Roosevelt and Lincoln).[13] At Christmas time in 1938, the Theater Arts Committee's campaign for aid to political refugees hosted an event in Union Square, New York City. Under the shadow of the statue of the Great Emancipator, whose emaciated face and lanky figure resembled himself very much, Massey paused to deliver a speech before he pressed the button to light up the Christmas tree:

> We know very well where Lincoln would stand if he were alive today. He would be with the persecuted and deprived people of Germany, of the Austria that was, of Spain and China, and against the arrogant men on horseback who are grinding them down into dust. Lincoln once said that this country could not endure permanently half slave and half free. But today, for better or for worse, the world has grown smaller–smaller in many ways than this country was in 1860 when Lincoln spoke those words. And looking about him at our divided modern world, Lincoln would surely have said: "mankind cannot endure permanently, half slave and half free."[14]

Lincoln was already fighting fascism and, by implication, Roosevelt was still fighting slavery.

Testimonies by those involved in the production of the play as well as the innumerous authorial glosses disseminated offstage suggest that Sherwood initially began working on *Abe Lincoln* in the spring of 1938 without any conscious political agenda, but by the time that the Munich Crisis came to a head in late September, he viewed his new historical drama as something more than a patriotic period play. Once he recognized the promise of his play's utility in his battle against the nation's timorousness, Sherwood, along with other principals of the company, retrofitted the pro-war message onto the play and made changes to the script to reinforce this message. Finally, after the play opened on October 5, the company launched the publicity campaign to instruct the audience how to decode its political message. Sherwood later maintained that *Abe Lincoln* was from its conception intended to propagandize for activist foreign policy against foreign dictators. Such recollections, however, should be taken as his post hoc attempts to exaggerate how premeditated the Playwrights Company's Lincoln campaign was.[15]

"President Quotes Lincoln"

In January 1940, about a year after the opening of *Abe Lincoln*, Robert Sherwood gained his first audience with Franklin D. Roosevelt. The motion picture adaptation of *Abe Lincoln* was scheduled to premiere on the following night in Washington, DC, and the successful New York theatrical producer Max Gordon and Sherwood's friend and Roosevelt's right-hand man Harry Hopkins arranged a dinner party in honor of Sherwood and a private screening at the White House.[16] Three days after the command night, Sherwood sent a note to Roosevelt, thanking him for his hospitality and wishing "with all my heart to offer my services, for whatever they're worth, to you in this crucial year and to the cause which is yours as surely as it was Lincoln's."[17] Enclosed was a copy of the Lincoln–Douglas debate that Sherwood used for his play. As Sherwood, who was soon to be inducted into Roosevelt's speech-writing team, explained in a letter to Massey, he wanted to "satisfy the president's craving for good material" for his speeches. Sherwood ended his letter to Massey on a conspiratorial note: "By the way, I think we should be very careful not to talk about this as any hint of this in the newspapers might well queer the whole project."[18]

By his first encounter with Roosevelt, Sherwood had already resolved to cast himself in the role of an interventionist firebrand and to enlist his glib pen and dramatic talents in his crusade against detractors of Roosevelt's foreign policy. A few weeks before the dinner party at the White House, when the Soviets began invading Finland, Sherwood poured out his frustration to the Kansas newspaperman and Roosevelt's confidant, William Allen White:

> In urging that the United States should send, at the earliest possible moment, the greatest possible force in ships, airplanes, munitions and men to the defense of Scandinavia, thereby committing an act of war against Soviet Russia, I realize that I'm exposing myself to dreadful charges. ... But the terrible truth is that when war comes home to you, you have to fight it; and this war has come home to me.[19]

Soon after this letter was posted, Sherwood pounded out the first draft of his pro-Finnish play, *There Shall Be No Night*. The play opened too late, a few days after Helsinki and Moscow signed a truce. Thanks to its topicality and the drawing power of Lynn Fontanne and Alfred Lunt, however, it proved to be a big commercial hit and considerably helped whip up the war fever among the public.[20] Two months later, in May 1940, as the *Wehrmacht* routed the Allies across Western Europe, Sherwood joined two interlocking advocacy groups, White's Committee to Defend America by Aiding the Allies and the Century Group.[21] He authored the White Committee's full-page "STOP HITLER NOW!" advertisement with some input from Rice and Anderson. In July 1940, on the morning after Paris fell before the German invaders, millions across the country opened their newspapers to find the bold-faced, all-capitalized imperative (the advertisement appeared on thirty-seven newspapers, whose total circulation reached eight million). They learned that Hitler's gamble was "nothing less than domination of the whole human race." They further learned that Britain and France were America's last line of defense. Should they fall, the United States would turn into a lone garrison state in a hostile world, and the perpetual vigilance and ballooning defense spending would ruin the democratic way of life. So, Sherwood's warning peaked with a command: send a postcard, a letter, or a telegram at once to the President of the United States and urge immediate aid to America's allies.[22]

When Sherwood met with Roosevelt back in January, he was already cognizant of how a divided public opinion forced the administration to take bolder foreign policies off the table. Soon after Sherwood's letter was delivered to the editorial office of the Emporia *Gazette*, White received a long personal letter from Roosevelt. White shared many of Roosevelt's concerns and in the fall of 1939 agreed to chair an interventionist pressure group, the Non-Partisan Committee for Peace through the Revision of the Neutrality Law. Sherwood was invited to join.[23] In his letter, Roosevelt confided to White that he was "getting to the point where I need a few helpful thoughts from the philosopher of Emporia." What disquieted him was the isolationist complacency of "public opinion over here ... patting itself on the back every morning and thanking God for the Atlantic Ocean (and the Pacific Ocean). ... [I]t really is essential to us to think in broader terms and, in effect, to warn the American people that they, too, should think of possible ultimate results in Europe and the Far East."[24] When he finally replied to Sherwood after Christmas, White, "in deepest confidence," apprised the playwright of the president's quandary: "I had a two page letter almost as long as yours from the president along the same lines exactly. Everyone who bothers to think at all straight about this world situation must come to the same conclusion that you and I come."[25]

White's reply to Roosevelt revealed the "same conclusion" at which Sherwood and White were arriving: "[I]f we can help the Allies surreptitiously, illicitly and down the alley by night, we ought to do it."[26]

His knowledge of Roosevelt's wish to educate the public about America's exposure to foreign wars most likely emboldened Sherwood to approach him a month later with his "project." Sherwood's letter to Roosevelt signaled his readiness to lead a propaganda campaign. He was well aware that Roosevelt's hands were tied because a government-sponsored propaganda campaign would recall to a suspicious public the abuses of the Creel Committee and other excesses during the Great War.[27] Eventually, Roosevelt rewarded Sherwood with direct access to the uppermost echelons in the administration, when in October 1940 he began to campaign in earnest for an unprecedented third term. Roosevelt took Sherwood up on his offer of "my services," and "Bob the Peroration Kid" joined Roosevelt's speech-writing team.[28] In the months that followed, Roosevelt more frequently referred to Lincoln.[29] References to Lincoln and the Civil War cropped up in all kinds of contexts – in carefully crafted major speeches as well as during his jocular banterings with the press corps:

THE PRESIDENT: I think there are a lot of people who haven't waked up to the danger. A great many people.
Q. Mr. President, if you were going to write a lead on that, how would you do it? (*Laughter*)
THE PRESIDENT: I'd say, "President Quotes Lincoln," – (*Laughter*) – "And Draws Parallel."[30]

Sherwood's influence on the presidential rhetoric seems undeniable. What remains to be measured is how wide a currency the Roosevelt–Lincoln parallel came to gain at the time. Since it is impossible to quantify i precisely, here we can do no more than cite some revealing quotes. Several of them come from the writers who will occupy center stage in Chapters 8 and 9.

First, in May 1940, Waldo Frank wrote the following in an essay, in which he explained why he was resigning from the editorial board of the shilly-shallying *New Republic*: "Whatever happens in Europe, I recommend a paraphrase of Lincoln's words on the eve of a less lethal, irrepressible conflict: *The world cannot permanently survive, half-fascist and half-free*. And we Americans, whether we like it or not, whether we believe it or not, will be forced to do something about it."[31]

Second and similarly, in July 1940, when the Democratic National Convention was about to meet in Chicago, Lewis Mumford, who had also just resigned from *The New Republic*, sent a telegram to Roosevelt:

"Upon your ability and willingness to exercise this leadership during the next few weeks will depend whether you will go down in history as the Buchanan or the Lincoln of the present world civil war."[32]

Third, in October 1940, Anne Morrow Lindbergh's best-selling isolationist apologia, *The Wave of the Future*, was published. An African-American reader in Chicago added her voice to the deluge of critical mail to the wife of the legendary aviator turned a leading spokesman for America First. Scoring this essayist for her defeatist view that in the ongoing crisis "the 'Forces of the Past' [democracies] are fighting a rearguard action against the 'Forces of the Future' [dictatorships],"[33] this reader drew a parallel between Nazi racism and American slavery: "Our country long ago dedicated itself to the belief that all men are born, free and equal, with certain inalienable rights, among them, life, liberty and the pursuit of happiness. Free press, freedom in religion, are imbedded in our way of national life. German, Italy, Russia can teach us nothing, and give us nothing, along this line. … Read Gettysburg address by Abraham Lincoln. The condition of peoples in these countries is that of serfdom."[34]

Fourth, in his diary entry of late July 1941, Henry Stimson, the most hard-line member of Roosevelt's cabinet, wrote: "The vacillations and the pulling back and forth, trying to make the Confederates fire the first shot. Well, that is what apparently the president is trying to do here."[35] Hitler had launched Barbarossa in June, the Japanese Imperial Army had descended on Southern Indochina just a few days before this diary entry, outflanking the Philippines. And the United States awaited the inevitable, watchfully waited for its enemies to "fire the first shot."

Fifth, in early January 1941, while laboring over the fourth draft of Roosevelt's third inaugural address, MacLeish, who was often called in to help Sherwood and Samuel Rosenman late at night, slipped in an indirect parallel between Lincoln and Roosevelt: "In Lincoln's day the task of the people was to preserve that nation from disintegration from within. In this day the task of the people is to save that nation and its institutions from assaults from without."[36] This reference, with only slight modification, stayed in the final address.

And last, throughout 1940, Reinhold Niebuhr, in a concerted move with his close friends Lewis Mumford and Waldo Frank, was immersed in his campaign against Christian pacifists. In mid-November 1940, a week after Roosevelt won reelection, he wrote to Mumford: "Funny, what you say about Roosevelt was the topic of a conversation between myself and my brother at Yale over the weekend. I used the pessimistic arguments which you advance and he used the optimistic ones and wondered whether

Roosevelt was any more the opportunist than Lincoln was. At least I think Lincoln possessed a degree of honesty which Roosevelt lacks."[37]

These six private remarks cited above, along with many other similar examples available, adumbrate the extent of the circulation of the Roosevelt–Lincoln couplet and map out a population of speakers so diverse as to encompass renowned cultural critics, the Librarian of Congress, the Secretary of War, and an African-American woman in Chicago. While this prevalence does not prove the efficacy of Sherwood's propaganda, it taxes credulity to deny the popular Pulitzer Prize–winning play, its motion picture adaptation, and frequent presidential mentions any degree of influence. In a book review of *Lincoln, Living Legend* (1940), a Lincoln biography by philosopher-politician T. V. Smith, one commentator, writing for *Partisan Review* (whose Trotskyism had led it to take an isolationist stance), remarked on "America's new pioneering crusade (now that Carl Sandburg, Robert Sherwood, and Raymond Massey have been mobilized) to make the world safe for Abraham Lincoln." The article went so far as to suggest that "this amazing Lincoln cult" was "so central to the developing war ideology in America today."[38] Writing for a much more staid and genteel venue, *Harper's Magazine*, Bernard DeVoto concurred. The "invocation" of "Father Lincoln" had become a new national religion.[39]

In the early 1930s, the exigencies of domestic politics made it signally beneficial for Roosevelt to be associated with Abraham Lincoln, as this comparison helped the Democratic Party peel off black voters in northern cities from the GOP, the party of the "Great Emancipator."[40] By contrast, the invocation of Lincoln on the eve of World War II strengthened Roosevelt's hand in a different way. The analogy implied that Lincoln reincarnated in Roosevelt, the Confederacy reemerged in the garb of the "gangster" states hell-bent on expanding their *Lebensraum*, and slavery transmogrified into "totalitarianism." By implication, obstreperous isolationists were modern-day Copperheads. At the same time, this analogy diverted the public from the odious comparison of the next war to the last war, a war in which isolationists regretted having participated.[41] Cultural historians, literary critics, and presidential historians all seem to agree that the Roosevelt–Lincoln parallelism as developed in Sherwood's play conveniently met all these disparate political needs.[42] The analogy, however, had one politically inconvenient implication: likening foreign dictatorships to the slave power presupposed the analogy between democratic nations and *black* slaves and the analogy between the Axis power and *white* supremacists. And so the interventionists downplayed these implications by presenting the Civil War in stark and abstract terms, as a battle between two irreconcilable principles, Liberty and Serfdom, all but stripping the Civil War of its racial aspects.

Lincoln the Appeaser

Still, these broad answers fall short of explaining how *exactly* the Civil War could be understood to be analogous to the new global war. Was there any other calculations that justified this comparison, save the irresistible temptation to deflect criticisms from the pacifists and isolationists with the patriotic appeal to freedom, slavery, and the Great Emancipator? A close examination of *Abe Lincoln in Illinois* reveals an even more audacious hope than is suggested by these timid considerations of small political advantage.

Reporting proudly to William Allen White that he had finally come to embrace America's world supremacy, Sherwood wrote that "it has taken me a long time to reach the boiling point, but I've reached it now."[43] This confession also encapsulates the storyline of *Abe Lincoln in Illinois*. Loosely based on Carl Sandburg's *Abraham Lincoln: The Prairie Years*, the play traces Lincoln's early career in Illinois, from Lincoln's early pacifism, through his gradual awakening to the evils of slavery and a mystical conversion experience, to his final departure to Washington as president-elect. Sherwood projected his own generation's youthful flirtation with pacifism onto Lincoln's early career. From his initial appearance onstage right up until Act II, Scene VII (where Lincoln reaches his boiling point), the play characterizes Lincoln consistently as "an artful dodger" (77), a feckless appeaser of slavery, "not a fighting man" (76).[44] Lincoln fears that he "might have to cast [his] vote on the terrible issue of war or peace" one day, but he already knows which way he will vote: "To go to war, for a tract of land, or a moral principle? Or to avoid war at all costs?"(77). Sherwood's Lincoln castigates radical abolitionists for the nation's polarization: "Freemen's League is a pack of hell-roaring fanatics" (68). If a civil war breaks out, "it'll be the abolitionists' own fault" (75). If Lincoln's complacency mirrors the pacifist temper that plagued liberals during the interwar years, his denunciation of abolitionists as "disturbing the peace" mimics the identical language employed by the pacifists and isolationists to accuse globalists like Sherwood and Roosevelt of "war-mongering."

The first half of the play also signalizes Lincoln's vacillation. Lincoln in the first half of the play is a pacifist with a bad conscience, or, as Carl Sandburg puts in his foreword to the published play, "an involved, baffling Hamlet of democracy" (xii). Lincoln "sit[s] up all night reading 'Hamlet' and brooding over his own fancied resemblance to that melancholy prince" (56).

Like Hamlet, he dithers while tormenting himself with a no less momentous question: to abolish slavery or not? He refuses to let the abolitionist propaganda disturb his peace of mind, with little success: "I'm minding my own business – that's what I'm doing! And there'd be no threat to the Union if others would do the same. And as to slavery – I'm sick and tired of this righteous talk about it" (106). His declaration of indifference ("minding my own business") is the tribute that hypocrisy pays to a better judgment (Lincoln *knows* that he is wrong). This portrayal of a conscience torn between abolitionism and appeasement, between the false comfort of the status quo and a necessarily violent but still righteous future, invites ready comparison with the nation during the Munich Crisis, polarized over the analogous question: to challenge foreign dictators or to stay neutral?

The great debate raging in Lincoln's mind reaches a crescendo in Act II, Scene VII, the "Prairie Scene," which finally satisfies the audience expectation that the narrative of reluctance and conversion has built up. What precipitates Lincoln's rebirth as a freedom fighter is the entry of his old friend Seth and his family. On their way to the western territories, they camp on the outskirts of New Salem and send for Lincoln so that he can offer a prayer for their dying child. When Seth tells Lincoln that his destination is Oregon, Lincoln is "*deeply impressed*" and plots Manifest Destiny on the westward journey of this pioneer farmer: "You'll be taking the frontier along with you" (117). At the same time, however, Lincoln also warns that the western territory where Seth and his household (including an ex-slave Seth has manumitted) hope to settle down may fall into the hands of Southern slaveholders. This revelation upsets Seth, who "*vehemently*" protests that the Oregon "territory has got to be free!" (119). He even threatens secession and declares: "If this country ain't strong enough to protect its citizens from slavery, then we'll cut loose from it and join with Canada. Or, better yet, we'll make a *new* country out there in the far west" (119). With Seth's proposal to render asunder the Union into a free nation and a slave nation, Sherwood's Lincoln reaches the boiling point. Lincoln "*suddenly rises*" and tells Seth that the white settlers like him who are advancing the nation's frontier westward "made me feel that I've got to do something, too, to keep you and your kind in the United States of America" (120).

Lincoln the Interventionist

A shrewd student of audience psychology, Sherwood omitted juridical technicalities of the slavery question for the sake of drama. But we know that, thanks to his thorough digestion of Sandburg's biography, Sherwood was quite knowledgeable about antebellum politics. The play's hesitant historical references sustain our inference that this conversion scene, out of which the entire play grew and which Sherwood revised again and again, dramatizes one decisive factor behind the escalation of the North–South conflict, that is, the extension of slavery into the western territories.[45] With this promotion of the slavery extension issue, *Abe Lincoln* affirms a more academic version of the Civil War's genesis. All influential explanations concur that the republic's westward expansion, the unstoppable population influx into the West, and the attendant need to organize territories as states conspired to inject the question of the legal status of slavery in the West into national politics.[46] The controversy over slavery's expansion, in turn, realigned national-political forces along the sectional divide and triggered a series of sectional clashes that climaxed in the Republican victory in 1860 and the outbreak of war in 1861. To consummate Manifest Destiny, the continental empire had to settle the debate over the fate of slavery in prospective members of the Union one way or the other. But being not so much about the prevailing status of slavery in member states of the Union as about the future of the nation, the debate came to be fought over hypothetical scenarios about possible consequences of admitting a new state as slave or free.[47] Southerners feared that prohibiting slavery in the West would lead to the extinction of the already existing slavery in the South. Northerners, on the other hand, internalized the symmetrical fear that in a Union dominated by the Slave Power majority, the area of freedom in the North may be encircled and ultimately conquered. Survival of liberty in the North was perceived to be contingent on its safety all across the continent.[48]

Sherwood's "Prairie Scene" simplifies these facts and calculations, condensing them bodily into a dramatic mise en scène.[49] The great prairie on "a clear, cool, moonlit evening" (109) reminds the audience of the westward growth of the nation. Sherwood acknowledged in the afterword that he "tried, all through this play, from the first scene on, to provide evidence of Lincoln's awareness of the West" (223). To this end, the dramatic narrative methodically distributes oblique allusions to the nation's westward expansion (37, 75, 77, 106). In this conversion scene, Sherwood finally gives concrete expression to "Lincoln's awareness of the West" and "his feeling of kinship for those who were to be its first settlers" (223).

A closely related historical event enters the conversion scene through Lincoln's forewarning about the legal status of slavery in Oregon, an allusion to the Dred Scott decision of 1857. The decision (which Lincoln called "an astonisher in legal history") voided Congressional prohibition of slavery in the territories. From this point on, at least in theory, where the bulk of the slavery controversies transpired, this decision could force a territory with an antislavery constitution, such as Oregon, to respect the property rights of slaveholders, including the human chattels they owned. What used to be a curious local institution, slavocracy, was now national, whereas liberty, once national, was provincialized.[50] This reversal kindled a paranoid fear in the North. The radical Republicans, toward whom Lincoln was drifting at the time, unleashed a firestorm of organized propaganda to warn the Northerners that the Supreme Court Justices, in cahoots with James Buchanan and Stephen Douglas, were laying the groundwork for the *nationalization of slavery*.[51]

In the play, Seth's return, with his ex-slave in tow, helps this scene perform its chief task: to spotlight the suppositional ("what if?") question of the spread of slavery into neutral space ("all the States of the future," as Herndon puts it [106]) as the prime determinant in Lincoln's decision making. The fearsome prospect of losing the West to the slave power effectuates Lincoln's conversion at long last–something a lifetime of exposure to the inhumanity of actually existing slavery, which pointedly includes "quite a shocking sight" (68) of chained slaves Lincoln witnesses on a boat, has failed to do. It is when the political disagreements over the extension and exclusion of slavery are elevated to the extravagant heights of speculation that Lincoln is forced to take a stance. In the play, Seth acts out one difficult alternative with his secessionist threat (we'll make a *new* country out there in the far west). But if disunion is out of the question, there is only one option left – the abolition of slavery in the entire Union and the unconditional subjugation of the South on the Northern terms.[52]

That Sherwood believed that these psychological and territorial considerations made the Civil War inevitable offers a clue to how he rationalized his case against appeasement. What alarmed him was not the existence of an antidemocratic political order in Eurasia but its (real or perceived) intention to expand into neutral countries. In *Abe Lincoln*, Sherwood represented North America as a closed space (after the frontier reached the Pacific, the nation's geographical contour seemed solidified). Similarly, to Sherwood and other internationalists of the time, the globe had become a finite space where the competition between democracies and despots was understood to be a zero-sum game. American freedom was conditional on world freedom.

Such a geostrategic calculation dovetails with Sherwood's characterization of the Slave Power as an enemy aiming to end the physical existence of the North. The choice of the empty and boundless prairie symbolizing the openness of the West as the backdrop for Lincoln's conversion disconnects this middle scene from the rest of the play. By evoking the palpable vacuity of the continent, this backdrop underscores the existential character of the threat posed by slavery. Lincoln prays for the dying child:

> Grant him the freedom of life. Do not condemn him to the imprisonment of death. Do not deny him his birthright. Let him know the sight of great plains and high mountains, of green valleys and wide rivers. For this little boy is an American, and these things belong to him, and he to them. … Oh God, to do the work that is before us. I ask you this favor, in the name of *your* son, Jesus Christ, who died upon the Cross to set men free. Amen (122).

Behind its deftly interwoven declamation and lyricism, this prayer achieves something political: Lincoln's prayer for the child's life shades into a prayer for the freedom of life. This seemingly innocent slippage, made possible by the phrase "freedom of life," entails something more than an indifferent alteration to the meanings of "life" and "freedom." The expression "free life," to take an obvious alternative, for example, summarily describes just one among diverse ways of life. It does not doubt that there are other ways of being alive, including the unfree way of life to which slaves are condemned. By subtle contrast, however, the expression "freedom of life" – note the possessive "of" – implies that being alive presupposes being free. Another pregnant phrase immediately follows: "the imprisonment of death." In our conventional understanding, death and bondage belong to different categories, because bondage means one way of being alive while death means ceasing to be alive. But, if being alive means being free, if freedom is a necessary condition of life, this equation of imprisonment and death does make sense. Thus, Lincoln's twofold plea for the "freedom of life" and against the "imprisonment of death" argues for the Lockean and Jeffersonian naturalization of freedom as a condition unalienable from life, an existential gift that Sherwood's Lincoln predictably refers to in the third sentence as "birthright."

Sherwood further exploited the term "birthright" as an opportunity to convert Lincoln's prayer for the freedom of life into a prayer for yet another unalienable right, the right to the vacant space in the West. Toward its conclusion, Lincoln's prayer presses a new demand: just as freedom belongs to life that the dying child is about to part with, so too the "great plains," "high mountains," "green valleys," and "wide rivers" "belong to him and he to them," because "this little boy is an American." The specific political value of the phrase "freedom of life" indicates that it is not "free space" in the legal sense, namely the space where slavery is criminalized, that is vindicated as the child's "birthright." This right is to something more abstract: the "freedom of space."[53] The concept of "birthright," which derives a moral title ("right") from the fact of "birth," thus conjoins the freedom of life with the freedom of *terra nullius*, the two inalienable rights equally menaced by slavery.

Here, it is worthwhile to pause and ponder the fact that Sherwood almost completely purged slavery of its racist implications. National Socialism, the gravest of all totalitarian threats, was an avowedly racist ideology, and hence highlighting racism of slavery should have helped the disseminators of the Roosevelt–Lincoln analogy. So thoroughly, however, did the play excise slavery's nature and function as an institution designed to produce victims through racial categories that slavery was virtually reduced to an abstract evil inimical to freedom (another abstraction). It is likely enough that this deracialization of the Civil War was a result of multiple factors, including Sherwood's almost congenital indifference to racial and civil rights issues. Nevertheless, readers alive to the political agendas behind the Roosevelt–Lincoln analogy should be able to see a more deliberate calculation. As already explored in Chapter 2, during the prewar years, black civil rights activists turned the national emergency into an opportunity. Tethering domestic racism to foreign fascism, they pressed for desegregation in the armed services and equal employment opportunity in the defense industry.[54] Black cooperation for the coming war against foreign fascism, the increasingly militant black leaders like A. Philip Randolph and Walter White made clear to the Roosevelt administration, was conditional on a vigorous war on domestic racism. And so, as Robert Sherwood himself would recall after the war, the interventionists anxious to rush the nation into war were caught in the middle. They could ill afford to aggravate traditionally militaristic Southern Democrats in Congress. These conservative (and usually racist) allies of Roosevelt's foreign policy feared that the civil rights leaders would use the coming war to draw untoward attention to domestic racism, especially the Jim Crow laws in the South.[55] Given Sherwood's awareness of these competing priorities and his insensitivity to race issues characteristic of someone whose social universe centered on the predominantly Anglo-Saxon establishment on the East Coast, his moral and political calculus was probably similar to Roosevelt's. The choice was between the coupling of domestic racism with foreign fascism and the deracialized reconstruction of the Civil War as an allegory of the timeless battle between abstract forces of "freedom" and "slavery." Sherwood saw the latter alternative as the more politically expedient.

Act III, Scene IX reenacts the Lincoln–Douglas debates of 1858. This scene also complicates Sherwood's geostrategic and deracialized reading of antebellum politics as a clash between the guardian of life and the army of death. Douglas assails his opponent along several lines, but the dominant thrust comes from his use of "popular sovereignty," the philosophical notion underpinning the Kansas-Nebraska Act he authored. Douglas's concluding remark summarizes it: "Let each State mind its own business and leave its neighbors alone. If we will stand by that principle, then Mr. Lincoln finds that this great republic can exist forever divided into free and slave states. We can go on as we have done, increasing in wealth, in population, in power, until we shall be the admiration and the terror of the world" (135).

Here, popular sovereignty appears as a direct antecedent of the policy of strict neutrality. Because the play opened immediately after the Munich Crisis, the risk of applying popular sovereignty globally must have been plain to the play's original audience. In the fashion that recalls the Lecompton constitution, the National Socialists had already engineered plebiscite victories in the Saar and Austria. To annex Sudetenland, Hitler and his satraps again appealed to the will of the ethnic Germans, and Daladier and Chamberlain cynically used this argument to cloak their appeasement policy with. The parallelism is as extensive as it is striking. In the 1850s, the Slave Power invoked the putative "will of the people" in the territories to extend their empire. In the 1930s, the new Slave Power, reconstituted in Europe, redeployed popular sovereignty to justify expansion through annexation. Just as in the 1850s in "Bleeding Kansas," a fraudulent minority of border ruffians sought to distort popular rule in order to incorporate this territory into the Southern camp, so too toward the end of the 1930s Henlein in Sudetenland, Quisling in Norway, Franco in Spain, and Nazi agents in Latin America plotted to hand over their countries to the totalitarian camp. Just as during the prewar years of the 1850s, indifferent doughfaces declared the compatibility of the two antithetical social orders, so too, during the prewar years of the 1930s appeasers argued that America should retreat into the Western Hemisphere and, in the words of a bitter critic of Roosevelt's foreign policy, "concentrate our attention on tilling our own garden."[56] Had Douglas reincarnated in the late 1930s, he would have applauded the appeasers and isolationists for respecting the small nations' right to self-determination, even if it meant the extension of the area under tyranny.

The rebuttal by Sherwood's Lincoln is a patchwork of quotations taken from Lincoln's own writings, most notably a letter to Joshua Speed in 1855, the Peoria speech, and several of the addresses Lincoln gave during his debates with Douglas. It contains passages with various bearings on the current political situation, not only international but also domestic. Nevertheless, the main brunt of Lincoln's counterattack falls on popular sovereignty, or "the complacent policy of indifference to evil" (139) as he calls it. Alerting the audience to the hazards of neutrality, Lincoln concludes: "There can be no distinction in the definitions of liberty as between one section and another, one race and another, one class and another. 'A house divided against itself cannot stand.' This government can not endure permanently, half slave and half free!" (149).

The scriptural quotation and the last sentence applying the metaphor of "house" to the Union are taken from the famous "House Divided" speech, the decisive speech that catapulted Lincoln from relative obscurity to national prominence. When it was delivered before the Republican Senate convention in June 1858, the scriptural quotation occurred at the beginning. But Sherwood moved it to the very end of his Lincoln's speech. This alteration eliminated the nuanced qualifications with which Lincoln softened his prophesy. Immediately after the quoted passage, the original speech continued: "Either the *opponents* of slavery, will arrest the further spread of it, and place it where the public mind shall rest in the belief that it is in the course of ultimate extinction; or its *advocates* will push it forward, till it shall become alike lawful in *all* the States, *old* as well as *new* – *North* as well as *South*."[57] The purpose of this long, meandering sentence was to reassure that by the metaphor of "house divided" Lincoln intended to convey nothing more than his expectation that quarantining slavery within the South would eventuate, "in God's good time," in the extinction of this peculiar institution throughout the Union.[58] By singling out the most incendiary and most reckless phrase out of the context and placing it at the very end of the climactic scene, Sherwood turned a prophesy into an ultimatum. Upon concluding that the sectional interests are irreconcilable, Lincoln emphatically *turns his back* to the audience, as if to underscore the final step he has just taken. The lights fade and the scene abruptly ends. The audience is left with a creeping sense of the impending crisis.

Lincoln said that the transcontinental republic *could* not tolerate dissimilar social orders. He did not say it *must* not. Like any good dramatists, Sherwood here made his case clearer than truth. All the same, perhaps, this unsurprising instance of artistic license elucidates the logical consequence which Lincoln's "house divided" metaphor entailed and which only Lincoln's worst enemies had the foresight to fear.[59] Regardless of Lincoln's political calculations, most paranoid southerners took his "house divided" rhetoric to prescribe (not simply describe) the territories expanding under federal sovereignty as a uniform space.[60] As Douglas alleged tirelessly throughout the debates, Lincoln's vatic statement that "this government cannot endure permanently, half slave and half free" rested on what Douglas disparagingly termed the "doctrine of Mr. Lincoln's of *uniformity*."[61] While Douglas envisioned the westward extension of the Union as a process through which various local governments were added to a loose federation, Lincoln scholar Harry Jaffa observes, Lincoln "thought in terms of greater homogeneity, because he thought in terms of sharply circumscribed boundaries."[62] The Union must "become *all* one thing, or *all* the other."[63] By uncovering the doctrine of uniformity shrouded in the heart of Lincoln's forecast, the debate scene now charges the Slave Power with the sin of diversity, in addition to the charge of mortal threat to the natural rights (to free space and free life) already made in the conversion scene.

The International Civil War

Sherwood's version of the Civil War's genesis was by no means canonical at that time. Nor was his estimation of its pertinence to the escalating international crisis. They competed against other rival theories. During the 1930s, historians sympathetic to the South like Avery Craven, Frank L. Owsley (one of the original contributors to the 1930 *I'll Take My Stand*), and James Randall discounted the inevitability of the North–South conflict and pinned a large share of war guilt on the self-righteous fanaticism of abolitionists and radical Republicans. Their revised view of the Civil War as an avoidable, needless war gained increasingly wider currency during the depression years.[64] A spike in the public's interest in regionalism no doubt facilitated the spread of this new theory.[65] Also the resurgence of the Lost Cause (Douglas Freeman's massive biography of Robert E. Lee came out in 1934) and a romanticized view of the antebellum Southern culture such as *Gone with the Wind* popularized helped along.[66] By the time that Sherwood converted to interventionism, the "avoidable war" thesis enjoyed impressive popularity.[67] In his presidential address at the 1940 meeting of the Mississippi Valley Historical Association, Randall compared World War II to the Civil War and urged the audience to consider how "the self-fulfilling prediction, the push-over, the twisted argument, the frustrated leader, the advocate of rule or ruin, and the reform-your-neighbor prophet" delivered an unwitting nation to disaster.[68] Zealotry of abolitionists, not slavery, caused the Civil War. By the same token, pro-war fanaticism of today's global abolitionists (reform-your-neighbor prophet), not foreign dictators, was rushing America into an avoidable war.

Taking strong exception to such pro-South revisionism, *Abe Lincoln* reinstated slavery, its philosophy of death and diversity, and its alleged expansionism at the origin of the causal chain leading to the outbreak of war. In an interview, Raymond Massey instructed the theatergoers to "substitute the word dictatorship for the word slavery throughout Sherwood's script."[69] According to this instruction, Lincoln's fear that freedom would perish in a divided Union must translate as a concern with America's precarious liberty in a divided world. Quoting from the "house divided" speech, War Secretary Stimson declared in June 1941 at West Point: "We are now facing exactly the same situation in the world at large which Abraham Lincoln faced within our nation eighty-three years ago when he pointed out that a nation divided upon such an issue could not remain divided. It must either become all one thing or all the other. The world today is divided between two camps and the issue between those camps is irreconcilable."[70] In the 1850s, the antislavery ideology imputed a monolithic design to the South.[71] Echoing the analogous fear, the supporters of Roosevelt's foreign policy projected the will to world domination onto dictatorships. In both cases, these crusaders for freedom nourished a chiliastic, zero-sum outlook on politics. A coming battle was bound to be the war of annihilation between free people and enslavers. Lincoln the Proto-Globalist contended that the Slave Power "conspired" to "nationalize slavery." Roosevelt the Neo-Abolitionist charged, sometimes citing cooked-up intelligence, that "totalitarian" regimes had a secret plan to internationalize terror and tyranny.[72] The playwright himself declared that "the world has grown too small to permit the survival in any one section of freedom of speech, or of religion, or other essential civil liberties, unless these rights are recognized and observed in all sections."[73] Only the general redemption of the whole world safeguarded American liberty.[74] Although many Americans were still uneasy about the radical claim that the Earth had become an indivisible, uniform space wherein an aggression on democracy anywhere impinged on American liberty, most of them had been already initiated into Lincoln's doctrine of uniformity, his sacralization of the nation as one and whole, free and united. These globalists used this easily recognizable self-concept as a heuristic device to ease the skeptics into a new worldview.

Just the same, however, this web of analogies cannot entirely justify Sherwood's desperation for the universal salvation of humankind. The rhetoric of the "house divided" asserted that free space was indivisible. Similarly, Roosevelt invoked Lincoln on numerous occasions and declared in the same breath, as he did in one of his most forthright addresses, that the "American people have made an unlimited commitment that there shall be a free world."[75] The implication was that the American people would remain enslaved until the entire world was liberated. The limit here imposed on American liberty appears counterintuitive, just as it did in Lincoln's and Roosevelt's times. In general, people *feel* free, to the degree that they do not doubt the reality of this sensation. Their knowledge of the existence elsewhere (for example, in the slave South or in Hitler's Germany) of the hordes of men and women subjected to state-sanctioned violence cannot entirely negate this feeling of freedom. As already suggested, in order to impugn the apparent infallibility of such an appeasement mentality, *Abe Lincoln* proposed the geostrategic analysis that called for a prudential consideration of American survival. The chief purpose of the "house divided" analogy was not to remind the nation that there existed large numbers of enslaved men and women awaiting liberation (the Northerners in the late 1850s and the Americans in the late 1930s were not innocent of such a reality and thus required no such reminder). The analogy was rather designed to insinuate that forces of slavery were driven by the expansionist impulse, which was in turn fueled by the existential hatred of free life and free space. But these strategic reasoning and existential angst are, as with any strategic arguments and any existential revelations, always debatable, not the least because they exaggerate the knowledge and foresight of the self-styled prophets. More fatally still, these motivational factors can only lead to the modest conclusion that the rising tides of international slavocracy must be stayed. They could not carry Americans all the way to the evangelical conclusion that the entire world must be liberated. A missing link needs to be found in order for this line of thinking to extend beyond this containment strategy and past the last vestiges of psychological inhibitions. A gap needs to be filled for this logic to consummate itself in the extravagant conclusion for which it yearns. What could have bridged, in Sherwood's mind, his strategic forecast to the soteriological dream of general salvation?

One way to locate this invisible link is by adopting the commonsensical but nonetheless valid distinction James Burnham once drew between the "formal meaning" and the "real meaning," the sly manipulation of which constitutes the essence of the language of politics.[76] The classic example

Burnham adduced was Dante's *De Monarchia*. This political pamphlet "formally" meant a plea for the world-state and eternal peace, but its "real" meaning was the selfish advocacy of Ghibelline interests in Florence made from a standpoint of a turncoat Bianchi exile. Similarly, we may speculate that the "house divided" slogan served as an exculpatory discourse, designed to suggest a specious concord between national interests and the welfare of the family of nations. War hawks of the time, including Sherwood himself, hoped to sell military intervention in distant lands to the American public by projecting the first line of defense away from the homeland, outward by degrees toward enemy territories, through intermediate geographical constructs such as "the New World," the "Western Hemisphere," or "Western civilization."[77] There is no qualitative difference between the gradual distension of the orbit of national security (by the summer of 1941, the American security zone would span vast tracts of the earth's surface from Guam to Greenland) and the globalization of the Civil War so long as the actual acreage of the sphere of national interests was at issue.[78] The latter merely and purely marked the logical and numerical extreme of the former. Despite their recent history of having been abused so grossly during the Great War, false universals were yet again being utilized as a stalking-horse to promote what were in reality particular local interests.

There is, however, another, less cynical explanation that can take into account how Lincoln, Sherwood, and Roosevelt transformed the meaning of freedom. Lincoln wrote in 1859: "This is a world of compensations; and he who would *be* no slave, must consent to *have* no slave. Those who deny freedom to others, deserve it not for themselves."[79] In the same vein, Sherwood's Lincoln warned the audience in the debate scene: "I advise you to watch out! When you have enslaved any of your fellow beings, dehumanized him, denied him all claim to the dignity of manhood, placed him among the beasts, among the damned, are you quite sure that the demon you have thus created, will not turn and rend *you?* When you begin qualifying freedom, watch out for the consequences to *you!*" (139).[80] These two assertions were concerned with neither the freedom of slaves nor the freedom of citizens living in free nations. Instead, they disputed the freedom of slaveholders, dictators, and other oppressors of human freedom. Manifestly, slaves were deprived of freedom. In addition, the strategic argument asserted that those living in the area of freedom also had their freedom "qualified" to the extent that they lived in fear of inherently expansionist slave regimes. But the new birth of freedom that Lincoln, Sherwood, and Roosevelt induced raised a more vexing question whether or not the enemies of human freedom were free. And by raising this question it nominated these freedom haters as a beneficiary of emancipation, in addition to those already enslaved and the bystanders like Americans living in the neutral countries, whose freedom was abridged by the mere existence of slavery in distance. It is not easy but very important to see that, in parallel with this expansion of the class of candidates deserving of forcible liberation, freedom ceased to be an inalienable right that all humans naturally possessed (until it was compromised by freedom-hating persons and institutions). Freedom redefined itself as an ideal way to be alive that can be achieved not by returning to the primeval state of nature but by obeying the higher law of freedom (the commandment: you shall not enslave fellow humans if you want to be free). The mandate for total victory ("either all free or all enslaved") could not have become licit without trading one meaning of freedom (natural right) for another (universal maxim).[81]

It may be helpful to describe this replacement in the familiar terms proposed by Isaiah Berlin: in mandating universal enforcement of the law of liberty, Lincoln, Sherwood, and Roosevelt shifted the meaning of liberty from the "negative" to the "positive" one.[82] In formulating "negative" liberty, Berlin drew on the liberal tradition in Britain. John Stuart Mill defined liberty as the sovereignty over one's own mind and body.[83] Before that, John Locke defined liberty as one's absolute prerogative to a slender terrain that encompassed one's life plus property.[84] These versions viewed negative liberty as a necessary condition for individual life. To the extent that property was the fruit of labor and to the extent that labor meant a purposeful application of corporal and cerebral energy – that is, life's power – these liberal thinkers also viewed negative liberty as a necessary condition for property.[85] They posited that life was a swirl of indeterminate energies that powered man's mental and physical activities. Any arbitrary power that imposed on this swirl harmed and potentially killed life. With life given such a high and independent value, its equation with negative liberty makes the latter appear inalienable. So much so that a strong version of this theory, Lock's for instance, attempted to argue that the individual cannot sell himself into slavery (yes, he can, although perhaps he shouldn't) or that the slave is in perpetual state of war against his master (he may not be, although perhaps he should be). The negative definition of liberty thus strengthens its case for the protection of liberty by minimizing the object of its application (life as the source of energies). And because of this, it also puts serious limits on liberty's projective power. It explains why the slave wants to rebel. It does not even claim to address the underlying problem: Why did his master want to enslave him in the first place?

By contrast, according to Berlin, positive liberty is a cognitive capability. It means self-mastery, namely the ability to master one's passions and to orient one's thoughts and actions rationally, that is, in such a way as to maximize one's well-being, however defined, within a community. Unlike negative liberty, this mental capability can detach itself from its host and its constituent parts, whether physical or psychological. And it can remotely organize the host's life. It is this remoteness, however internalized, of positive liberty from its gross material basis that tempts it to assume the role of universal legislator for its community. Given diversity of human propensities, the host's rationalized life encounters and often clashes with other people's lives. This friction inevitably diminishes the host's hard-earned well-being. To solve this problem, this individual's rational capability may try to externalize itself and command the community as the mind tries to command the body.

Those who believe in positive liberty, like Lincoln, Sherwood, and Roosevelt, are bound to find in self-mastery the only path to genuine freedom. Unlike negative liberty, which is premised on the uniqueness of individual existence (one's death is no one else's death), positive liberty can provide canons of conduct that the society (North America for Lincoln, the international community Roosevelt) must observe universally. For, all individuals being presupposed to possess reason, society discloses itself as a malleable object of betterment, whose shape the universal legislator can mold according to his rationally drawn design. Berlin broached this distinction in the context of the Cold War to illustrate the two contradictory philosophies behind the West and the East. Still, this distinction can also clarify the conceptual obstacle that the United States had to overcome when it chose to expand radically the federal sovereignty, first, in Lincoln's case, over the Southern states, and then, in Roosevelt case, over the rest of the world.

In the post-Munich world, which disclosed itself as a domestic space (a "house"), as a single, integrated field of operation in need of paternal guidance, there was born the new possibility that the nascent global sovereign could enforce the universal law of freedom firmly and, if necessary, coercively. It is a telling commentary on the historic import of the Munich Crisis that, three years before his country was dragged into the maelstrom, Sherwood's play summoned a new vision of national destiny and proposed an innovative reinterpretation of freedom that preemptively justified the subsequent appointment of the United States as the great emancipator of the world.[86] According to this new vision, war was always insurrection and the enemy was actually a rebel. This new type of asymmetrical conflict was fought not only for existential reasons (to defend, to attack) but more importantly to reform the rebel. Military expeditions to the distant battlefields would be mandated as a law enforcement action to keep the world (nothing less) free and united.[87] This is of course not to imply that Sherwood's play singlehandedly displaced the negative conception of liberty with the positive conception. Far from it. The play explored the ways to maximize negative liberty's projective power while, contradicting itself, it initiated a new thinking on using positive liberty to lure America onto the world stage. As controversies over "responsible" liberalism show in Chapters 8 and 9, the notion that the kind of liberty America was to defend in the next war was of a negative character had to die hard.

5

The War of Words

On September 1, 1939, Germany hurled 1.8 million troops against Poland along the 1,000-mile border. A "long dishonest decade," as W. H. Auden named the 1930s on this historic day, came to a shameful end. Realizing for once that the Munich agreement was a costly blunder, the French and British honored the sanctity of their alliance treaty with Poland and declared war on Germany on September 3. The "next war" finally came to Europe.

At 9:00 PM on that night, Roosevelt broadcast a fireside chat and spoke to "the whole of America." Roosevelt's first speech on the new European war bore two contradictory messages to the nation, so he had to perform a delicate balancing act. First and foremost, it was imperative to reassure a jittery nation that "the United States will keep out of this war."[1] The president gave millions of listeners "assurance and reassurance that every effort of your Government will be directed toward that end." Roosevelt reminded the warring European nations of the sacrosanct principle enshrined in the Monroe Doctrine: noninterference in the affairs of the Western Hemisphere by powers alien to the region. Europe, the president warned, must keep its war in the Old World. Otherwise, America would take every measure necessary to insulate itself from the general conflagration across the Atlantic.

Then, Roosevelt pivoted. Each passing day had shown the notion that the edenic New World was immune to the woes wasting the rest of the world a perilous delusion. Echoing Lincoln's "house divided" speech, Roosevelt enlightened the listeners on the basics of modern geopolitics: "When peace has been broken anywhere, the peace of all countries everywhere is in danger." We should not "shrug our shoulders," "ignore" those wars on other continents, and "go about [our] own business." "Passionately though we may desire detachment," Roosevelt spoke on behalf of America, "we are forced to realize that every word that comes through the air, every ship that sails the sea, every battle that is fought, does affect the American future."[2]

Roosevelt promised the course of neutrality and in the next breath instructed the public in the interconnectedness of world events. His promise contradicted his analysis, but Roosevelt, the shrewd student of public opinion, was here deliberately mimicking the divided voice of the American people, who refused to speak in unison throughout the prewar years. During the 1936 presidential election, Elmo Roper at *Fortune* and George Gallup at the American Institute of Public Opinion brought scientific precision to the art of polling. And their modernized polling methods once and for all changed how policies were formulated, how they were presented to the public, and how the government timed the release of politically sensitive news.[3] Elmo Roper and George Gallup not only made it feasible to measure such an elusive thing as the nation's zeitgeist and revived the old political force, "the People." Combined with the executive branch's new ability (thanks to the radio) to reach millions of firesides across the nation directly and instantly, the modern polling gave birth to a volatile form of mass politics predicated on a closer interaction between the central government and the People. Two weeks after the fireside chat, managing editor of *Fortune* Eric Hodgins sent to Roosevelt an advance copy of Roper's first poll since the eruption of war in Europe. The poll numbers vindicated Roosevelt's intuition. Roosevelt had said in the speech that "[t]his nation will remain a neutral nation, but I cannot ask that every American remain neutral in thought as well." The survey found that eight in ten Americans were actually unneutral in thought, saying that they would like to see England, France, and Poland win while only one percent favored German victory. This overwhelming sympathy for the Allies, however, did not translate into support for U.S. participation in the war on the side of the Allies. Roper found that a majority – 54 percent – disapproved of sending military forces to Europe under any circumstances. Two out of ten Americans favored supplying the Allies with materiel and refusing to ship anything to Germany. One out of thirteen favored sending troops to Europe (on the condition that it looked as though the Allies were losing). The approval rating for an immediate declaration of war on Germany stood at a piddling 3 percent.[4]

Although it would take World War II twenty-seven more long and climacteric months to reach the American shores, the next war at this point practically came to America, in the form of war of words – what later historians call the Great Debate. The final months of the prewar period would see American society riven by frenetic propaganda campaigns as pacifists, appeasers, and interventionists competed to capture the heart and the mind of their country. The public sphere would darken with manipulative messages, and that would hone the prewar writers' thinking about art, propaganda, and democracy.

"A Cinch to Be a Bestseller"

"dot-dot-dot, dash-dash-dash, dot-dot-dot" (SOS). Four days after Roosevelt's "unneutral in thought" address, Joe Bonham, a veteran of the Great War, began to beam his pacifist message to the national audience – by Morse code. On September 7, Dalton Trumbo's antiwar novel, *Johnny Got His Gun*, was published.

The novel came out when Trumbo was establishing his reputation in Hollywood as a fast-working, technically proficient screenwriter for B pictures. His dream of financial security was finally in sight. He knew he owed this to very little else but his own pluck, wits, and industry. A product of shabby, lower-middle-class gentility, Trumbo hailed from a small town in western Colorado. His mother was a Christian Scientist who yearned for Victorian respectability. Her husband, Orus Trumbo, was a man of regular school education with a teacher's certificate. His teaching career was brief. For much of his short and unlucky life, he worked at a string of precarious jobs like beekeeper, grocery clerk, shoe clerk, and some such, whose pay and prestige never matched his gentlemanly integrity and cultivated tastes (on the day of wedding he bought a set of Shakespeare). Understandably, fear of financial ruination and vague cultural aspiration would shape his oldest son's life course. Already exhibiting his talent for verbal eloquence, Trumbo was an active and popular student. In high school he led his debate team to regional championship twice and worked as a cub reporter with byline for a local newspaper. After his father was laid off from a shoe store in the mid-1920s, his family decided to move to Los Angeles seeking better jobs. Quitting the University of Colorado, Boulder only after a year, Trumbo joined his family there. Soon his anemic father died an excruciatingly painful death. Barely twenty years of age, Trumbo found himself head of the family. To provide for his mother and two younger sisters he worked at a bakery for next eight years, but he could not succeed in extinguishing his dream of becoming a writer. As the nation plunged into the depression, he quit his job and began freelancing. His writings showed promise, as attested by the fact that *The Saturday Evening Post* took two stories. It was only a matter of time before Trumbo worked for movie studios. Motion pictures just started talking a few years ago, and the industry had a voracious appetite for new talents. Trumbo's first job at Warner Bros. as a reader led to screenwriting contracts at Columbia, MGM, and RKO, and with each move came a substantial raise and new expensive habits like a chauffeured Chrysler Imperial. His swift rise in Hollywood was unsurprising, for essentially Trumbo was a fabulist. A flamboyant and gallant believer in happy endings, he saw life as a story, and this made for a supremely useful talent in an industry that sold the same belief. As the new crisis brew in Europe, Trumbo was about to embark on his most critically acclaimed years, which would be abruptly terminated by the blacklisting in 1947, a fallout from his involvement in the labor struggle that polarized Hollywood between Communists and anti-Communists.[5]

Trumbo had many traits in common with other high-profile prewar authors. Among them were speed and compulsiveness, or the ability concentrate, to the total exclusion of others, on tasks at hand. His statute in his hometown Grand Junction, Colorado does homage to this trait, depicting him at his typewriter in a bathtub, his favorite place to write and smoke. Trumbo often said that he struggled to teach himself how to write. It is certainly understandable that he wanted to emphasize hard work. But most indications are that like other prewar writers he was gifted with a phenomenal facility in language, which in his case also manifested itself in his equally phenomenal volubility in conversations. Even in Hollywood, the town of fabulists fast with words, his sure way with language was legendary. Another notable trait was his professionalism, his faith in craft. He honored conventions and respected techniques. They were not dead rules constricting the living imagination. Accordingly he applied himself to their mastery. This attitude was particularly advantageous because he mostly worked in B-units throughout the 1930s. Trumbo thrived thanks to ingenuity rather than originality.

Johnny Got His Gun, his third novel, featured arguably the most disfigured and deformed hero in the annals of the American novel: a quadruple amputee who has also lost much of his face, "a dead man with a mind that could still think."[6] A tongueless, eyeless, noseless, and earless basket case, Joe Bonham slowly awakens in a hospital and, after realizing the extent of his injuries, begins his lone struggle to reconnect with the outside world. He hits on an ingenious strategy: tapping signals with his head in Morse code. The entire novel unfolds in Bonham's consciousness, with daydreams, hallucinations, and flashbacks to his idyllic childhood in a small Colorado town interspersed throughout. The story builds up suspense as it draws to the climax where Bonham at long last establishes contact with his doctors and requests to be exhibited to the public as a graphic indictment of the horrors of war. The military authorities, however, reject his plea. The novel ends with Johnny breaking out of the fictional world.

Joe Bonham (by this point he completely merges with the didactic author) instigates the readers to "get their guns" and stage a mass mutiny in the event that war-profiting oligarchs again force an unnecessary war on a peace-loving republic.

As the author and his publisher J. B. Lippincott knew, the turn of events across the Atlantic was bound to goose up the book's sales. Striking a cord with a nation frightened by the prospect of involvement in another world war, *Johnny* proved much more successful than his previous works. At the end of the second week, the initial printing of 3,000 copies had sold out, the second printing of 1,500 was nearly gone, and a third printing of 1,500 was already ordered.[7] Six days after the publication, on September 13, Congress was called into extraordinary session to discuss revision of the Neutrality Act. On that day, a reader in Massachusetts wrote to Trumbo that it was impossible to miss the book's "application to these times." This reader's letter closed with a supplication: "Would that Congress, Senate, President and all would read it before they meet."[8] Some key players in the ensuing Congressional battle were in a position to answer. Back in mid-April, the publisher mailed bound galley copies of the novel to Senator Key Pittman, who, as head of the Foreign Relations Committee, would prepare a tentative proposal for a revised Neutrality Act in September. The publisher also sent copies to other public figures, most notably Senator William E. Borah, the legendary progressive-isolationist warhorse, who was to mobilize his impeccable nationalist bona fides and phenomenal oratorical gift for his last stand against Roosevelt's internationalism.[9]

Johnny Got His Gun could not have been timelier. And its timeliness was a result of careful calculation. Over the course of the writing, the negotiation with potential publishers, and the galley reading, Trumbo evinced a keen interest in the timeliness rather than the timelessness of his work. Trumbo had the entire manuscript in fairly good shape by the Munich Crisis.[10] Going behind Elsie McKeogh, his agent, he let a representative of Lippincott consider the manuscript, although the right of first refusal belonged to Alfred Knopf, who had published his previous novel *Washington Jitters*, a frivolous satire of the New Deal bureaucracy. A protracted negotiation between McKeogh and Trumbo ensued. The former was piqued by her client's ethically questionable behavior. The latter was unapologetic. Outraged by what he considered unfairly low royalties and Knopf's tepid effort to promote his last book, Trumbo deemed himself in the right. He was "in a firm, decisive, grasping mood" and wanted to bargain hard with the publishers, convinced that his new novel was a "cinch to be a best-seller": "You see from the outset I'm operating upon my firm conviction I've got a winner. I think it's a book we can bargain with. ... I want to be damned tough–isn't that every writer's dream?"[11] In the end, McKeogh prevailed, and in mid-February Trumbo submitted the manuscript to Knopf.

Two weeks after the treaty of Munich was signed, Trumbo guiltily confided to McKeogh: "From the selfish viewpoint I am relieved about the turn of events in Europe because for a time it seemed to me that pro-war sentiment would completely swamp the book."[12] A Hollywood writer with sympathies for Communism (he officially joined the Party in 1943), Trumbo was no supporter of Chamberlain and Daladier, who were more interested in deflecting Hitler's military might eastward against the Bolsheviks than in resisting Germany's escalating demands. Nonetheless, with an impassioned antiwar manuscript on his hands, he calculated that any delay tactics by the European appeasers should be welcomed. Had the war erupted in the fall of 1938, public sentiment would have been consumed by war fever by the time his book was ready for the press.

In February of the following year, Knopf still sat on Trumbo's manuscript. Though the European situation had stabilized somewhat, the war could still come any day. Knopf's characteristically leisurely way with his writers' manuscripts was squandering the precious time Trumbo earned at the sacrifice of Czechoslovakia. This frazzled his nerves no end. After occupying the Sudetenland, Hitler tore up the treaty and went on to dismember Moravia and Bohemia in March. The new European war could come at any moment. In a flight of paranoia, Trumbo confided to his agent his fear that Alfred Knopf, party to the East Coast cabal of warmongers, was trying to keep his pacifist novel in cold storage indefinitely:

> One of the things that disturbs me is the fact that there is growing up in this country among liberals and intellectuals a strong pro-war sentiment. They appear to view war as the only salvation for democracy, whereas I see it as a sure destruction for the kind of democracy we know at present. These perfectly sincere war-mongers are becoming louder, more influential and even more dangerous. If Knopf were in sympathy with them – and I suspect that he might be – he would certainly be out of sympathy with "Johnny Got His Gun." In such an event he might deliberately delay a decision, and if he decided to publish it he might further delay its ultimate appearance. If the book is any good at all it is good as an argument against war; and it will be utterly valueless if the country is either in war or in favor of war by the time it is published.[13]

In spring, Knopf finally decided against the book.[14] Immensely relieved, the author and his agent in eager haste offered the manuscript to

Lippincott in early March.[15] In Europe, at least on the surface, the high political tension was showing signs of cooling off. For both Trumbo and his new publisher, it was now a time to wait. Aiming for a perfect timing, Lippincott reversed its previous decision and suggested to Trumbo that they delay the publication: "The bound books will be ready approximately the first of June. If there is evidence that the U.S. will be drawn into war before fall, we can publish the book on very short notice. … I think that the fall will be more timely for a war book than the present. If there's war in Europe and America is endeavoring to stay out of it, the appeal of JONNY GOT HIS GUN would be infinitely stronger than the present. It looks as though things are now as quiet as they will be for some time."[16] Trumbo's antiwar novel would gain the widest audience and therewith throw the weight of its didactic power into the scale of national debate most decisively when public opinion on the war hung in the balance. Trumbo took his publisher's advice, and thenceforth until September channeled his idle energy into a series of fruitless attempts to serialize the novel. Besides generating additional revenues, a serialization, he thought, would help the book's reception in the fall.[17]

Democracy and Art in the Age of Propaganda

Writing to Trumbo, one reader lauded *Johnny Got His Gun* as "the strongest piece of anti-war propaganda available at present."[18] A proper appreciation of the strength of Trumbo's "anti-war propaganda" requires that we situate Trumbo's achievement in the context of two contemporary debates. One had to do with the role of propaganda in a democracy. The other revolved around art's relation to propaganda.

The outbreak of the new European war ignited the Great Debate, which clove the nation into pro-Allies interventionists and those insisting on neutrality and isolation. Predictably, these two sides deployed a full battery of propaganda techniques that had been invented during the Great War and perfected later during the interwar decades by a new generation of symbol manipulators working in the increasingly respectable and lucrative industries of advertising and public relations.[19] Soon, however, the brazen use of semantic chicaneries hit the point of diminishing returns. In no time the public, which found itself lost in the blizzard of manipulative messages, responded by discounting the accuracy of any information and the sincerity of any policy proposals. Sensing that the mass paranoia was causing a breakdown in mass communications, the heterodox Freudian political scientist Harold Lasswell wrote in 1940:

"At the moment the American public has symptoms of a light anxiety neurosis on the subject of propaganda. Citizens on the eve of the next world war exercised due diligence against all sources of information. Citizens may convince themselves that it is hopeless to get the truth about public affairs."[20] Many prewar writers wondered if they lived in a post-truth society. "There is no longer any truth. Truth is a prostitute of power," Reinhold Niebuhr despaired just a few weeks after the outbreak of the new European war. Listening to the German propaganda night after night "makes one finally question one's own sanity" and wonder: "What kind of a world is this anyway in which sweet has become bitter and bitter sweet, white has become black and black white?"[21] The president of the Institute for Propaganda Analysis had an answer: "We live in a propaganda age. Public opinion no longer is formulated by the slow process of what Professor John Dewey calls shared experience. In our time public opinion is primarily a response to propaganda stimuli."[22] John Dewey himself, the indefatigable champion of the fundamental reasonableness of public opinion, appeared blindsided by a de-enlightening of his beloved community. "In every important matter," he wrote, "the words used have to be read in reverse." The progressive dream of non-dogmatic, good-faith, and evidence-based public deliberation withered away in the face of "complete inversions of truth," which "produce[ed] a state of daze that endures long enough to enable its creators to accomplish their will while darkness still prevails."[23]

While writing her rebuttal to Anne Morrow Lindbergh's bestseller *The Wave of the Future* (1940), Edna St. Vincent Millay reached the same conclusion. "During the last few years," Millay complained, "words have changed their function completely, and serve, with no strain or effort of the mind, to present to every imagination a picture quite the opposite to that which they formerly presented."[24] Archibald MacLeish also voiced his worry over the debasement of public language. Speaking through Roosevelt in one of the speeches he ghostwrote during the 1940 presidential campaign, the Librarian of Congress warned the nation not to confuse rhetoric with reality. "Certain techniques of propaganda, created and developed in dictator countries, have been imported into this campaign," MacLeish's script read. "It is the very simple technique of repeating and repeating and repeating falsehoods, with the idea that by constant repetition and reiteration, with no contradiction, the misstatements will finally come to be believed."[25] Like a real combat zone, the war of words engendered a fog, a miasma that dazed and confused the otherwise rational participants in the democratic process and drove them paranoid. A young

David Riesman observed. "[T]he fear of propaganda [has] created a large number of citizens who don't believe what they read in the papers, and who feel surrounded by conspiracies and lies."[26] "This is very bad for the English language," quipped T. S. Eliot.[27] The anxiety over the debasement of public language and the fear of psycho-linguistic manipulation spread well beyond narrow circles of professional writers. Bestsellers like Thurman Arnold's *The Symbols of Government* (1935; four printings through 1941), Stuart Chase's *The Tyranny of Words* (1938), and S. I. Hayakawa's *Language in Action* (1939; revised three times by 1941) debunked the rational and autonomous citizen as an obsolete fiction and shocked a wide reading public with the theory that modern man was a "child," a "savage," a patient in the "insane asylum" "affected by the social disease of slavery to symbols."[28] Anyone adept at manipulating emotionally potent symbols could gain access to the mind and heart of the democratic citizen and control his views and attitudes at will. The popularity of such books itself indicated that the public was already primed for their message by the late 1930s.[29]

In such a climate, the prewar writers took to handling words like "truth" or "facts" with scare quotes, as if they were pollutants, to be gripped with a pair of tweezers. Warring factions touted their "truth" about the coming war, but it was just another "lie," cloaked in the patriotic language of national interest or the altruistic gospel of world peace. The angry speaker of Langston Hughes's antiwar poem "Comment on War," published in the *Crisis* in June 1940, was typical:

> Let us kill off youth
> For the sake of *truth*
>
> We who are old know what truth is –
> *Truth* is a bundle of vicious lies
> Tied together and sterilized –
> A war-makers' bait for unwise youth
> To kill off each other
> For the sake of
> *Truth*.[30]

The Word itself was among the first casualties in the war of words. The strength of Trumbo's "anti-war propaganda" must be measured against its contemporary social climate where the efficacy of words, Trumbo's tool of the trade, was declining precipitously. Trumbo should have been aware that it took him exceptional artistic savvy to outsmart his competitors and woo a leery and nervous public to his version of the future.

The other contemporary debate, the one over whether art should serve propagandistic ends, supplies another context within which the ingenuity of Trumbo's approach to verbal manipulation must be evaluated. Trumbo did not directly participate in this theoretical controversy. It was very much an intramural affair among left-wing intellectuals initiated into the arcana of philosophical Marxism, quite removed from Trumbo's more quotidian but nonetheless equally felt concerns for the proletariat. All the same, since *Johnny Got His Gun* was a propaganda novel rather than a nonfiction propaganda tract, a great many questions this debate raised help us see the intentions behind Trumbo's artistic choices, obscured to the eye of later generations, that made his novel such a triumph as art and propaganda.

Under the depression conditions, the debate among politically radical-ized writers and artists over the implications of their agreed-on slogans such as "all art is propaganda" and "art is a class weapon" (the John Reed Club's motto) intensified all the way to the actual coming of World War II.[31] It was commonly accepted that art was not completely divorced from politics and further that there was some sort of transmission mechanism connecting "superstructure" (art and politics) to "base" (the real economy). The strictly "mechanic" conception of art and politics (that they passively reflected what mattered commercially and technologically) had few adher-ents. Even so, how art's impact, mediated by politics, on social relations and modes of production occurred remained to most disputants an enigma shrouded in layers of mysteries.

One unpopular view, the *agitational* understanding of the relation between art and propaganda, held that arts and letters transmuted them-selves into an event by causing the spectator, the listener, the singer, and the reader to take an immediate action desired by the author. Should they fail to cause a direct action, went its weaker version, works of art at least could change the recipient's mind by disposing it for or against particular policies, institutions, and customs. One important effect of agitational arts was obviously of a psychological nature namely that of rousing fighting spirits and scaring the enemy. This became explicit in performed arts. Skits played at the factory gates or labor songs chanted on the waterfronts exhorted the workers to choose a particular course of action or adhere to the course of action that they had already decided to adopt for reasons that may not have been directly connected to these songs or skits. Despite its clearly observable efficacy, however, commentators on art and propaganda during the prewar years were largely critical of agitational arts. This unpopularity was confusing. After all, these writers never repudiated the basic premise that art was a "weapon" in the social struggle. In intent as well as in effect, agitational arts exhorted and incited, and to this extent they understood the metaphor of "weapon" literally. It was inconsistent to liken art to a weapon and then mock and berate the "utilitarianism" of agitational arts designed to facilitate a direct change in reality by agitating the audience mentally. Whence this inconsistency?

Polemical terms like "utilitarianism" masked the fact that most active participants in this controversy, such as Mike Gold, V. F. Calverton, Joseph Freeman, James T. Farrell, Granville Hicks, Malcolm Cowley, and Philip Rahv, covertly set apart good types of utility from bad. While direct action (or at least mental agitation) immediately established the effectiveness of agitational arts, the truly valuable kind of social utility to which the new art for the revolutionary class must aspire became known only little by little, gradually, imperceptibly, and marginally, over a long period of time. These theoreticians' terminologies were variegated and belabored, but bluntly put, their favorite version–what might be called the *epistemic* justification of propaganda art–argued that art works as a weapon in the social struggle should reveal the secret springs that set in motion the vast and intricate mechanism behind the ever intensifying capitalist crisis. And it should further light up the many ways in which this crisis affected a particular individual at a particular time in a particular place in a particular manner. These philosophical Marxists' indebtedness to German idealism, particularly the Hegelian characterization of art as marriage of the singular and the universal, is plain to see, although the intellectual pedigree of their opinion remained unconscious to most. According to the consensus among politically engaged writers, a consensus from which Dalton Trumbo dissented, dialectical materialism debunked classic liberalism as the bourgeoisie's self-serving alibi and finally tore the veil off the hidden motor driving history–the strains, pressures, and contradictions arising ceaselessly and inexorably from property relations and productive forces. However, the consensus ran on, objective knowledge about history and society proffered by this exact science was, while universally applicable and accessible to reason, liable to leave the human heart cold. Therefore, it behooved the nascent revolutionary art to flesh out this objective truth – the working class would inevitably triumph precisely because its exploitation was inevitable – with living characters and colorful circumstances.

The proletariat had no ideals to realize, said Marx.[32] The sentimental pandering to subjective longings had to be replaced by the blood-and-flesh realization of inescapable vicissitudes. The truly effective propaganda art thus illustrated the general law of history with "living" particulars. It did not agitate. Nor did it passively mirror. What it did was arm the workers with a clear and humanized understanding of their own destiny so that they could modify their values and behaviors in such a way as to hasten its resolution – the self-ruination of capitalism.[33] It was the creative contradiction embedded in dialectical materialism, the exact science of the ineluctable, that called for these stipulations about the truly effective propaganda art. The cognitively empowering kind of propaganda art changed history, despite the immutability of its basic laws, by flashing a living image of the scientifically discovered idea about economic history. Theorized thus, propaganda art was at once explanatory and transformative. It was no less preparation for action than inducement to action. By contrast, agitational arts not only failed to edify but also hampered efficient organization of energies and strategies to bring about the structural social change. For they mistook private wishes for objective trends of history.

The majority of leftist writers were content with these platitudinous dicta on art's theoretic and transformative office in the ongoing class struggle. Art was propaganda, insofar as art bent the trajectory of social change in the long run. The problem almost posed itself: What kind of transmission belt linked art to social change, or, by implication, knowledge to action? Most American participants in the debate over the social efficacy of art looked away from this blindingly obvious question. Their reflections bluntly and abruptly juxtaposed art and society, insight and structure, without any interpolating gradients. Someone had to fill in that truncated space.

"The Strongest Piece of Anti-War Propaganda"

Trumbo ingeniously responded to the challenge that provoked the first of these two controversies: how to overcome the skepticism of the democratic citizenry that was aware that it lived in the age of propaganda. According to the contemporary scholarship on propaganda, the key to mass persuasion lay in the recognizability and predictability, not the inventiveness of messages. Skilled propagandists had to know how to craft such suggestions and messages as would reaffirm the audience's preexisting prejudices.[34] Early communication scholars reached this conclusion after conducting extensive content analysis, but that was just an old saw to any successful entertainers. As Irving Berlin famously noted, "A song to become popular should not establish any new ideas – it must be a means of expression for sentiments already in vogue."[35] Himself a highly successful entertainer,

Trumbo followed this sure rule. *Johnny Got His Gun* rehearsed the old norms, sayings, and sentiments against war instead of inventing new ways to condemn war. The novel, for instance, infantilizes soldiers and sentimentalizes their filial attachment to their coddling mothers: "They died crying in their minds like little babies … They died whimpering for the voice of a mother a father a wife and a child" (121); "It was like a full-grown man suddenly being stuffed back into his mother's body. … That was exactly like the womb except a baby in his mother's body could look forward to the time when it would live" (83). These two quotes are just two examples taken from an impressively large stock of comparisons that highlight the youthfulness and helplessness of dying soldiers. Trapped in his ravaged body, Joe Bonham compares himself to a baby in the womb struggling to get out. As he regains consciousness and the severity of his injuries dawns on him, Bonham begs his mother to take him out of a nightmare: "Mother where are you? Hurry mother hurry hurry hurry and wake me up. I'm having a nightmare mother where are you? Hurry mother. I'm down here. Here mother. Here in the darkness. Pick me up Rockabye baby" (65; for similar comparisons, see 92, 129, 197, 209). What the soldier in a vegetative state (though he is conscious unbeknownst to the doctors and nurses) longs for desperately is his mother's nurturing affection. It is an open question whether facts really support the age-old belief that women oppose war more than men do due to their socialization to childbearing responsibilities. But this should matter little so long as Trumbo's wish to reinforce the prevalent idea of the mother as a pacific noncombatant is clearly recognized in this babe-soldier figure. Additionally, the infantalization of the soldier implies the feminization of the reader. This meshes well with the traditional division of gender roles in the war narrative, wherein men bring back from the front a story of savagery, heroism, and sacrifice to women at home.[36]

Another popular sentiment against war that the novel abets to its advantage is a populist distrust of military adventures overseas. Trumbo's selection of a fictional town, Shale City, Colorado, as Bonham's hometown almost gives the game away. More than a biographical coincidence, the Midwest's reputation as the bastion of progressivism and isolationism, fueled by the populist resentment against internationalist financial interests in the East, appears to have been decisive in Trumbo's design. As in Frederick Jackson Turner's frontier thesis, the Midwest in the novel doubles as the incubator of the classic ethos of democracy and as the bulwark against the corrupting influences of commerce and banking. Bonham's household is a laboratory of economic self-rule. In the backyard, chickens lay eggs, stands of bees supply honey, and a cow gives fresh milk daily, from which Bonham's mother makes butter and ice cream. His father's garden produces "lettuce and beans and peas and carrots and onions and beets and radishes" (107). However, the novel evokes the cornucopia of organic produces and praises the average citizen's resource-fulness, only to remind us of his pathetic powerlessness in the face of the undemocratic forces of money economy: "All these things they had and yet his father was a failure. His father couldn't make any money" (109). To participate in the money-making game, the independent, self-sufficient yeoman has to join a frighteningly vast network of exchange, credit, and distribution, but because the market is rigged to favor a sinister cabal of financiers on Wall Street and their stooges in Washington, DC, this everyman ends up losing even little things of modest use-value he has produced. It is a reasoning like this that prompts Bonham to redraw drastically the geography of national and personal interests:

> This was no war for you. This thing wasn't any of your business. What do you care about making the world safe for democracy? All you wanted to do Joe was to live. You were born and raised in the good healthy country of Colorado and you had no more to do with Germany or England or France or even with Washington D.C. than you had to do with the man in the moon. (25)

The phrase "the good healthy country of Colorado" and the comparison of Washington, DC, to European countries draw in the sprawling compass of American interests. Washington, DC, where "the little old guy with the book who figures all day long and all night long and never makes a mistake" (185) conspires with financiers and industrialists to conscript the wholesome youths of Shale City, Colorado, in an irrelevant foreign war, is no less outside the orbit of America's core interests than are Europe and the moon.

While the isolationist temper of the Midwest traced its origins to the populist movement, another antiwar discourse that Trumbo picked up was of much more recent vintage: the Great War revisionism. As discussed in Chapter 1, in the aftermath of the last war, the syndrome of disillusion-ment struck its young and progressive supporters. During the interwar years, this collective mood found academic confirmation in the revisionist scholarship by men like Harry Elmer Barnes, Charles Beard, C. Hartley Grattan, and Walter Millis.[37] Since the late 1920s, sensationalistic exposés and solid historical scholarship conspired to disseminate the view that a gullible America was swindled into the last war by munitions makers, international bankers, and propagandists on the British payroll. A 1939 poll by Gallup, conducted a few weeks before the publication of *Johnny Got His Gun*, asked why the United States entered the last war. A plurality (34 percent) of those polled agreed with the statement: "America was the victim of propaganda and selfish interests."[38] In highbrow literary circles, this revisionist regret spawned a bevy of gloomy war novels that revolted against Victorian gentrification and glorification of war: John Dos Passos's *Three Soldiers* (1920), E. E. cummings's *The Enormous Room* (1922), William Faulkner's *Soldier's Pay* (1926), Hemingway's *A Farewell to Arms* (1929) and his short stories about disillusioned veterans like "Soldier's Home," "A Natural History of the Dead," and "Big Two-Hearted River," William March's *Company K* (1933), and countless others.[39] Collectively, these literary byproducts of what Dos Passos called the "Great Sham" painted a resolutely cheerless picture of the last war and convinced great numbers of intellectuals that noble slogans and uplifting perorations on liberty and democracy must be subjected to the most cynical appraisal.

Echoing a (fictional) spokesman of this generation, Frederic Henry of *A Farewell to Arms*, Bonham savages the "highfaluting words" that he blames for bamboozling America into a war of choice: "If they weren't fighting for liberty they were fighting for independence or democracy or freedom or decency or honor or their native land or something else that didn't mean anything. The war was to make the world safe for democracy for the little countries for everybody. If the war was over now then the world must be all safe for democracy. Was it?" (116). The problem with these abstract words is that unlike "houses and tables" (117), they cannot refer to anything objective. The pure notionality of democratic slogans inflates the war aims for which the soldier sacrifices his life while masking the paucity of their concrete content: "[W]hen you change your women to all the women in the world why you begin to defend women in the bulk. To do that you have to fight in the bulk. And by that time you're fighting for a word again" (118). The debunking of idealistic words was a double-edged sword for the novelist, who still had to depend on language to press a case for pacifism. At least *some* words had to be true. Trumbo's solution was to discard words with abstract connotations (e.g., "the war to end all wars") in favor of granular, detailed descriptions of everyday pleasures and creature comforts, which only peace could guarantee.

During the prewar years, the disgust with the stupendous waste of blood and goodwill in the last war and the distrust of the patriotic language united to spread another argument against the coming war: that the next war was bound to reprise the last war. Even well before the new European war broke out, the analogy between the next and last war had spread to be adopted by countless pacifists and appeasers. Still contrite for his war enthusiasm, Hemingway wrote in 1935: "[N]o country but one's own is worth fighting for. Never again should this country be put into a European war through mistaken idealism, through propaganda, through the desire to back our creditors, or through the wish of anyone through war, notoriously the health of the state, to make a going concern out of a mismanaged one."[40] Likewise, Charles A. Beard, proponent of continental isolationism, hoped that its evident similarity to the last war would help Americans to make a hardheaded appraisal of their interests in the next war: "If our efforts to right historic wrongs and bring peace and reason to Europe in 1917–1919 have not taught American citizens anything, no words of mine can add to their education."[41] Editors of *The New Republic*, the unofficial organ of Wilsonian one-worldism two decades ago, were now repentant. They admonished war hawks and hotheads to "take more pains to remember the deep shock to the sense of human dignity which was suffered by the incurring of such losses twenty-five years ago for causes which turned out to be deception and illusion."[42] As the randomness of these quotes should suggest, no one monopolized this equation between the last and the next war. It was one of many antiwar commonplaces circulating freely just as Trumbo was casting about for useful themes for his new novel in 1938–1939.

Trumbo elaborates this analogy near the climax of the novel. The hospital's rejection of Bonham's request to be taken out on a nationwide tour as an antiwar exhibit triggers the following epiphany:

> Why? Why? Why?
>   And then suddenly he saw. He had a vision of himself as a new kind of Christ as a man who carries within himself all the seeds of a new order of things. He was the new messiah of the battlefields saying to people as I am so shall you be. For he had seen the future he had tasted it and now he was living it. He had seen the airplanes flying in the sky he had seen the skies of the future filled with them black with them and now he saw the horror beneath. He saw a world of lovers forever parted of dreams never consummated of plans that never turned into reality. He saw a world of dead fathers and crippled brothers and crazy screaming sons. He saw a world of armless mothers clasping headless babies to their breasts trying to scream out their grief from throats that were cancerous with gas. He saw starved cities black and cold and motionless and the only things in this whole dead terrible world that made a move or a sound were the airplanes that blackened the sky and far off against the horizon the thunder of the big guns and the puffs that rose from barren tortured earth when their shells exploded.

> That was it he had it he understood it now he had told them his secret and in denying him they had told him theirs.
>
> He was the future he was a perfect picture of the future and they were afraid to let anyone see what the future was like. Already they were looking ahead they were figuring the future and somewhere in the future they saw war. (248–49)

Bonham's epiphany fuses the last war and the next war. By equivocating between remembrance and prediction, the passage makes it impossible for the reader to decide whether Bonham is witnessing the last war or hallucinating the next war. Bonham's prophesy-memory instructs Americans teetering on the brink of another world war to remember the future.

The miscellany of antiwar sentiments and arguments that Trumbo borrowed for his novel were available in various media and formats, ranging from newspapers, magazines, and pamphlets to political speeches and radio broadcasts. The wide availability of the novel's political contents most likely added to the acceptability of Trumbo's political message. Yet this also came with an disadvantage because the banality of Trumbo's antiwar arguments could hazard the novel's potential to change the reader's mind with striking arguments. *Johnny Got His Gun* slipped through these two horns of dilemma by packaging a reaffirmation of clichés as the revelation of a private truth.

At the end of the novel, it is revealed that the doctors and nurses have known all along the "secrets" that Bonham struggles to disclose to the world. Prior to his breakthrough, Bonham boasts that "I know the truth and you don't you fools. You fools you fools you fools" (240). His main source of frustration then is not his ignorance but the conspiracy of the military authorities ("they") to muzzle him. Perhaps we will recall that, in one of the letters to his agent, Trumbo vented his suspicion that Alfred Knopf, in cahoots with the pro-war East Coast establishment, was intentionally delaying decision on his manuscript. Reasoning similarly, Bonham attributes his nurse's incomprehension first and then the doctor's rejection of his request to a sinister plot: "They were trying to shut him up" (192); "They were plotting against him out there in the darkness" (193). The hospital's final answer to Bonham ("What You Ask Is Against Regulation") catalyzes the final moment of enlightenment: "That was it he had it he understood it now he had told them his secret and in denying him they had told them theirs" (249). But if Bonham's message to the world was a "secret," it was an open secret, a collection of well-worn antiwar commonplaces. In other words, Trumbo privatized publicly accepted ideas with one hand and gave them back to the novel's first readers with the other hand, as if they were esoteric truths only accessible to those who had experienced the most extreme horrors of war.

These horrors are indeed so extreme that they approximate the state of death. This near-death condition of the hero permits the novel to style itself a narrative of resurrection, by figuring Bonham as a "dead man with a mind that could still think" (122), Lazarus, and the Messiah. He is a "new kind of Christ" (248). Behold the man, and the telltale marks of the ravages of the last war will reveal to you the truth about the next war. The first half of the novel is entitled, "Book I: The Dead," the second half, "Book II: The Living." Given the circumstances responsible for Bonham's virtual death, the association of silence with death redounds to the authority of Bonham's antiwar opinions and the authenticity of his suffering. A discourse on war often feeds on the reader's deference to the veteran-hero. The veteran's status as a survivor of rare, extreme experiences, as a witness to extraordinary violence, gives him a special right and duty to publicize the ugly truth of war, a truth deserving of universal and respectful hearing that transcends the partisan line. Often, the degree of physical injuries he sustains is a function of the authority of the disclosed knowledge. The more severely injured the veteran is, the more moral legitimacy is accorded to his pronouncements. Trumbo turns up one variable in this equation (the degree and extent of injuries) to its theoretical extreme, to the point where the veteran, stuck in a limbo between the dead and the living, can form opinions but cannot communicate them. While Trumbo maximizes the interest of the narrated experience and the validity of Bonham's political opinions, the hero's ability to tell his story gets minimized. Having created this contradiction, Trumbo offers to dissolve it with the patently literary convention – psychological realism, or the illusion of unmediated access to the mind of the fictional character.

Psychological realism served Trumbo well in his efforts to solve the problem of selling a public suffering from propaganda fatigue on his political argument. Furthermore, the novel's ability to let the reader live Johnny's mental states vicariously helped Trumbo overcome the challenge debated in the second of the two overlapping controversies: how to bring a clear understanding of the mysterious mechanism whereby insight turned into structural change to bear on the creation of a propaganda artwork. To see how this was the case, we must turn to another historical context – the emergence of the "people's culture" during the prewar years.

6

The People's Culture

Changing Minds: From Persuasion to Simulation

The marks of violence seared on Bonham's body understandably transfix us. But by so doing they distract us from some clear implications of the novel's genre: psychological realism.[1] Without recognizing the novel's reliance on this tradition, it is all but impossible for us to know what gave Trumbo's pacifist tale considerable edge over other nonfictional vehicles of propaganda, whether pro-war or antiwar.

The wildly implausible premise of the novel gives Trumbo a license to employ a whole host of techniques for rendering what is often defined in contradistinction to the all too visible body: the hidden operations of the mind.[2] Throughout the novel, the default stance of narration is the one of an omniscient storyteller speaking through a central "point of view" character, in this case Joe Bonham. Certainly Trumbo bends elementary rules of the genre in a few notable ways, but never against the grain. For instance, while a point-of-view character typically refracts a variety of sense data, Bonham's injuries block out all perceptions but touch. This exiguity of perceptual inputs firmly deposits the dramatic center of the novel within the hero's consciousness. The novel also exaggerates the hero's near-total immobility, isolation, and passivity. Historically, up to the heyday of high modernism, all these three characteristics (isolation, passivity, immobility) had become more and more pronounced in tandem with the increasing sophistication of techniques for probing into consciousness and the unconscious. Innovators and pioneers in this genre calculated that the more isolated, passive, and immobile the protagonists were, the more effectively they could showcase the terrific potential of their lexical and syntactic implements.[3] In the figure of a totally incapacitated war veteran, this innermost dynamic of psychological realism was carried to its logical conclusion.

The immobility of the point-of-view character enables Trumbo to carry another assumption of psychological realism to its limits. Throughout, the storyteller sidles closely along Bonham. And thanks to their closeness, the fictional world keeps time with the experience of reading. In most psychological novels, the reader's glimpses into the inner life of the center-of-consciousness character remain glimpses. They are sooner or later followed by summations and commentaries by the narrator or descriptions of objective facts, such as outward gestures and expressions of the character. And these transitions serve to signal to the reader that the narrator has exited the inner life of the hero. Trumbo, however, radicalizes psychological realism's tendency to concentrate the story on the mind of the protagonist and completely does away with these external descriptions. By making this choice, Trumbo releases his readers from the onerous labor of imaginatively constructing Bonham's continuous mental life from a discrete series of momentary glimpses. And thanks to the reader's total immersion in the mental milieu of the main protagonist, the tempo of the experience of reading answers the tempo of Bonham's thinking.

Throughout the novel, Trumbo depends on the three most basic techniques to present the fictional mind: psycho-narration (thought-report), quoted (internal) monologue (commonly known as "stream of consciousness"), and free indirect thought (free indirect speech that is not spoken). And yet even these undergo substantial modification.[4] The first convention is the most extensively used, as in the following passage, which depicts Bonham straining to find out the extent of injuries to his face:

> He began to reach out with the nerves of his face. He began to strain to feel the nothingness that was there. Where his mouth and nose had been there must be nothing but a hole covered with bandages. He was trying to find out how far up that hole went. He was trying to feel the edges of the hole. He was grasping with the nerves and pores of his face to follow the borders of that hole and see how far up they extended. (63)

Syntactically, all sentences but the second are constructed similarly. The reader first encounters the subject ("he") of a mental experience at the beginning of the sentence, who next engages in a purposive mental action (his mind "begins" something), and the reader finishes the sentence with the discovery of the object at which the character's attention is directed ("the nothingness that was there," "a hole covered with bandages," and so on). The word order directly mimics the pace and direction of Bonham's mental action depicted here, that is, the mind's purposeful focusing of attention on its own contents. Despite the fact that these sentences are rendered in the third person and in the past tense (a combination that usually stresses the narrator' detachment from the character's mind), the narrator's knowledge scarcely deviates from Bonham's self-knowledge. Because the reader's knowledge does not deviate from the narrator's either, passages like this end up suturing together Johnny, the narrator, and the reader.

The second sentence in the quoted passage exemplifies another familiar convention – free indirect thought. Assuming the transition here bespeaks a deliberate choice, one can make reasonable guesses as to why. Trumbo could have written: "*He thought that* where his mouth and nose had been there must be nothing but a hole covered with bandages." This construction would have reduced the mental experience to an independent proposition ("that…"), which must be attributed to Bonham, from whose inner life the narrator and the reader are now alienated. By contrast, free indirect thought allows the narrator to dispense with introductory verb phrases ("he felt," "he supposed," "he sensed," and so forth). A proposition is now dyed with the sense that it is being felt subjectively from inside. The illusion of immediacy thus created strengthens the cohesion that obtains between Bonham and the reader. And this technique manages to do all this without isolating this sentence from the rest of the passage. For the third person in the past tense infuses this sentence with the narrator's voice and weaves it into its textual surroundings.

The third and last technique to render psychological activities of a character is quoted internal monologue. It is used throughout *Johnny Got His Gun* less frequently than the two other techniques. And when he uses it, Trumbo modifies it so as to keep up the surface continuity and evenness in the texture of his prose. Two examples:

> He didn't have the courage to ask himself even so simple a question as how long will it be before the nurse understands what I am doing? (188)

> He thought to himself with a kind of hysterical happiness four years maybe five maybe six years I don't know how many years but I've been alone through all of them. He thought all my good work is gone all my way of keeping time has been forgotten but I don't care I am no longer alone. (207)

The first example depicts Bonham wondering when his nurse will understand that he is sending a message in Morse code. The second example occurs soon after his nurse finally responds to Bonham's message. The nurse draws letters (M.E.R.R.Y.C.H.R.I.S.T.M.A.S) on his chest with her finger. In both, the sentence starts in the voice of the narrator and segues both in tense and person to internal monologue. In both, too, this shift coincides with mental agitation. In the first passage, Bonham's frustration (*how long?*) with the nurse's inability to recognize his signals occasions the shift to the first-person and the present tense. In the second example, it is a "kind of hysterical happiness" that triggers the transition. In this case, the breathless syntax imitating Bonham's thought-language (four years maybe five maybe six years) prepares the reader for the eventual shift in tense and person and, when the "I" finally appears, mitigates its abruptness.

Taken together, these three quite hackneyed tricks for creating the illusion of direct access to the mental state of fictional characters enriches our sense of Bonham's consciousness. Our act of reading and Bonham's act of feeling and thinking almost completely converge when the story catches the mind in the act of reciting:

> Lie and lay. Now I lay me down to sleep. I lay these flowers on the table. I lie them on the table. I lie down to sleep. He laid there for three hours. I lie this book down. What the hell why not put it down and be done with it? Who is there? Whom is there? Of whom to who of who to whom. Between you and I and the gatepost. Between you and me. Between us that's much better. There is nobody like she. There's nobody like she is. There's nobody like her is. Nobody like her (127).

By the very nature of recitation by rote memory, in this and other similar passages thoughts become words. A moment like this shows Trumbo most effectively sparing us the labor of interpreting words. As Bonham's mind gains in aliveness, our need for new input about his thought process drops to the bare minimum, just enough to maintain a requisite level of immersion and obliviousness. The mental energy tied up to the priorities of interpretation is now reallocated to role-playing, until reading shades into mirroring. Both Bonham's mental states and the reader's consciousness that simulates them meet in the unbroken series of the reader's responses to the novel. Bonham and the reader come to share a co-consciousness.

Here seems to lie the key difference between miscellaneous antiwar opinions circulating in the prewar culture and Bonham's hatred of war. Unlike nonfictional writings on the next war, Trumbo's novel could train the readers to unlearn their skepticism toward propaganda. Encountering the same antiwar arguments presented in a public debate, the novel's initial readers suffering propaganda fatigue had to raise a slew of critical questions regarding their meaning, truth-value, logic, effects, and intention: Is it true? Does it make sense? What are probable effects of this message? Is someone behind this message intending to manipulate me? But all the important formal choices Trumbo made spared these readers this kind of due diligence when faced with Bonham's deeply felt versions. In the final three pages, Bohnam begins to speak in the name of "we," and this pacifist collective calls for a mutiny against the warmongering government: "Put the guns into our hands and we will use them" (251). Gesturing toward a mental and vocal solidarity between the audience and fictional characters, agitprop literature of the 1930s typically culminated in a chorus. But critics alive to the novel's political end and its aesthetic means should also notice Trumbo's dream being grammatically realized in this final swelling of the person, from "he" to "we." Bonham's was a fictional mind through and through. Nonetheless, what happened when the audience's minds reflected it was not so much persuasion of one mind by another as the proliferation of tens of thousands of kindred minds. Populating the reading public with countless Joe Bonhams – that is, becoming popular in the literal sense of the term – was the novel's ultimate mission.

The Prewar Culture as the People's Culture

The prewar writers shared one characteristic: with a few exceptions, all were "popular" writers addressing their works to the "middlebrow" audience. The term "middling," not in its pejorative sense but in its literal sense of being in the middle, between the avant-garde and kitsch, between high art and lowly trash, befits most of the writers who appear in this book. In his 1934 book *ABC of Reading*, Ezra Pound proposed to "distinguish two totally different kinds of writing."

> A   Books a man reads to develop his capacities: in order to know more and perceive more, and more quickly, than he did before he read them.

And

> B   Books that are intended and that serve as REPOSE, dope opiates, mental beds.[5]

This was an ill-timed proposal, because the middle of the 1930s exactly coincided with the blurring of such an unequivocal distinction by middlebrow writers. Rarely were their works so shockingly complex as to detract from their recreational value. At the same time, they were audacious and sophisticated enough to enable their readers "to know more and perceive more, and more quickly." Fusing these distinct functions, middlebrow writers during the prewar years carved out a profitable middle ground. On the lower end, these prewar middlebrow writers fastidiously dissociated themselves from the hacks and dope-peddlers of commercialized culture, although, as professional writers gaining a livelihood solely by writing, they did write, partially but necessarily, for money. They tended to avoid venues of the lowest cultural and social prestige. Claiming that their products were works of art, as distinguished from light entertainment, they wrote for respectable magazines and publishers. Their intended audience consisted of those not only literate but cultured, who were enthusiastic as much about the literary quality of the products they consumed as about their amusement value. On the upper side, these writers distanced themselves from practitioners of high modernism who loved art for the sake of art. This self-distancing did not bother them too much, because they knew that focusing on psychological idiosyncrasies of the eccentric artist-hero or experimenting with aesthetic properties of a literary medium meant losing access to the national market, a dilemma personified in the hero of Clifford Odets's 1937 play *Golden Boy*, who vacillates between classic music and prizefighting, the former symbolizing art and the latter the culture industry. Whether they were commenting on the impending war or not, it mattered to the prewar popular writers that they be read widely.

The middling reading public rewarded them with accolades and awards. *Johnny Got His Gun* won the American Booksellers Award, the precursor to the National Book Award. Edna St. Vincent Millay, Stephen Vincent Bénet, and Archibald MacLeish all won a Pulitzer Prize for poetry. Pearl S. Buck won hers for *The Good Earth*, which was also a Book of the Month selection. The most astonishing was Sherwood, who won three Pulitzer Prizes during the prewar years. The Pulitzer committee unanimously recommended Hemingway's *For Whom the Bell Tolls* in 1941, but Columbia's president Nicholas Butler overrode the decision.

While popular authors and bestsellers had been fixtures of American literary culture since the nineteenth century, the social and cultural function those middlebrow authors of the 1930s fulfilled was historically unprecedented. Their lives and careers straddled two traditionally antithetical categories: popularity and prestige. They were respectable, an intermediate status that defined itself against the popular but illegitimate (plebian amusement) and the unpopular but prestigious (high art). And their transcendence over the highbrow-lowbrow dualism – which, according to Lawrence Levine's influential thesis, solidified itself around the turn of the century, precisely the time period when all these prewar writers were born–became possible in the first two decades of the new century thanks to a confluence of interlocking long-term transformations. First of all, the expansion of public education led to the rise of literacy, which led to the growth of the reading public and a greater market demand for cultural commodities. Second, mechanization and automation (the "second industrial revolution") resulted in the steady reduction of working hours and the increase of "leisure" hours. Third, the new industry of advertising promoted greater discretionary consumer spending. As a result of all these, throughout the 1930s, a decade better known for socioeconomic suffering and labor unrest, proletarian lives were increasingly commercialized and the profit motive penetrated deeper into the realm of "culture."[6] The age of mass destitution coincided with the golden age of mass culture, the new middle-class culture for the people and about the people.[7] The two most important new technologies of mass entertainment illustrate this coincidence. It was at this juncture in the evolution of the people's culture that radio and motion picture reached their zenith in terms of social influence and aesthetic sophistication. Throughout the 1930s, under crisis conditions, the trends that became salient in the previous decade – the embourgeoisement of the proletariat, the absorption of Art into Culture, and the popularization of Culture through standardization, industrialization, and commercialization – accelerated.

Trumbo and his coworkers in Hollywood were among the chief beneficiaries of this agglutination of culture with business, brokered by what some recent émigrés called with abomination "the culture industry" (Max Horkheimer arrived in the United States in 1934; Theodor Adorno in 1938). And yet most of Trumbo's peers maintained a conflicted attitude toward their success and often bewailed melodramatically the soul-destroying prostitution of their talents.[8] Exiled modernists in Hollywood who disdained moguls and caliphs and tycoons of moviedom could not reconcile themselves to the paradox that the culture industry overpaid them for underutilizing what they prized as their rare artistic endowments.[9] As Raymond Chandler put it his screed against the studio system, "the essence of this system [is] that it seeks to exploit a talent without permitting it the right to be a talent."[10] The studio system kept their muse in chains, and these writers thought they could not afford the ransom – their fabulous salaries. Objectively, theirs was not such a terrible bargain, but most chafed and complained. During the first two decades of the new century, in lonely garrets and noisy cafés, these modernists worked hard to avoid shoehorning life into desiccated and hypocritical formulas. And all of a sudden, their new employer commanded them to let all that romantic toiling go. In 1935, F. Scott Fitzgerald was still complaining to his agent about whoring his gift of words for the studio system: "it simply fails to use what qualities I have."[11] By 1939, he had learned to live with the terrible truth: "This is not art. ... This is an industry."[12] Those who let the system devour themselves alive had to reckon with the fact that it was on the condition that they waived their cherished aesthetics and ethics ("originality," "individuality," "independence," and so on) that they were promised an obscene sum of money. And because their acceptance was not unconscious but willed, self-denial felt like self-mutilation to Trumbo's co-orkers in the culture industry. The more successful they were as Hollywood hacks, the more spiteful they became. Clifford Odets, who made $2,500 (more than $30,000 in today's value) a week during his first stint in Hollywood in 1935, lamented the studio system's conformism: "What goes – and this is very bad – is a loss of the sense of the unique self; forgetting to keep one's point of view, forgetting an essential difference between one's self and most other people."[13] From Ben Hecht, Chicago-bohemian turned the highest-paid writer in Hollywood, we learn that all those modernists lived with "the guilt of violating their culture."[14] Compensation should be commensurable to the quality of work. But when one's assigned task was to "sell out," that is, the premeditated debasing of the very quality of work, the people's culture was basically asking them to commit a crime against nature.

Dalton Trumbo was more serene. He seldom misrecognized his work in the culture industry as art. He accepted the same hierarchy of aesthetic values as his modernist colleagues, but his acceptance did not result in so much self-tormenting or crabbing. Unlike quondam bohemians ("queer owls with causes at stake," Trumbo joshed them) leading ambivalent existence in Hollywood, Trumbo excelled at writing for screen without feeling guilty about it. Just about a half-year after the publication of *Johnny Got His Gun*, he was still tied up by a contract with RKO, which prevented him from accepting more lucrative deals. In frustration, he wrote to McKeogh that "I daily receive offers of work in other studios at twice my present salary, and you can imagine how frantic I get at the thought of so much gold slipping by me without being able to clutch so much as a farthing of it."[15] A year later, he finally negotiated an annual contract with Paramount (most writers contracted on weekly or project basis). The studio was to pay him a weekly salary of $1,250 (an amount enough to buy a new car in the depression decade), and he was entitled to a twelve-week vacation. In case the studio was interested in any original material that Trumbo might produce during his vacation, Paramount had an option to buy it at ten thousand dollars per story (an unusual concession because any new materials that writers produced during their contracts usually belonged to their employers, on the theory that they wrote new stories on the studio's time).[16]

Trumbo enjoyed all these rewards without blaming himself for "violating culture" or losing the sense of the "unique self." Actually, he could not stand the spiteful modernist literati simultaneously selling out and bitching, the East Coast writers descending on a post-silent cinema Hollywood that had to manufacture romantic dialogues, clever one-liners, and adaptations of literary works at an industrial clip. "It is, no doubt," Trumbo wrote in 1933, "the magnificent treatment they have received from Hollywood which prompts the literati to abuse the town. Knowing in their hearts that they have been palming off inferior merchandise for enormous prices, they are so shrewish as to despise the gullibility of the purchaser."[17] Trumbo was nonchalant whether his instinct for the popular and the saleable embarrassed his aspiration to gain recognition as a serious novelist. All his novels read like novelized movies (many of them were quickly adapted for screen), but he did not see this as a flaw. Nor did he interpret the kitschness of his novels as a stigma, as proof of capitulation in the face of some vast conspiracy against high art and all the values that it symbolized: freedom, individuality, spontaneity, perceptiveness.

As far as moviemaking was concerned, Trumbo acknowledged, art and business were indeed inseparable. "Hollywood is a business which is an art, and an art which is a business," he wrote in 1933. Hollywood *was* a hybrid of art and industry, and so to hold its mongrel nature accountable for anything it did was "tantamount to solving a crime by declaring that murder has been done." Hence, neither as a novelist nor as a screenwriter did Trumbo bear popular culture, the industry that peddled it, and the people who consumed it any ill will. Because he wished to be successful in the new people's culture, he wished it to be successful. Hollywood needed good businessmen and good artists, both of them, and it appeared to him that there was no shortage of talented artists. The artistic quality of movies thus worried him much less than the industry's business practices. Rather than complaining that Hollywood's pandering to the people's coarse tastes befouled national culture, he would want to talk about how investment bankers in New York who had no expertise in moviemaking, nepotism, and the contract system united to create financial difficulties at many studios, thereby preventing men and women with right ideas, like Trumbo, from being "rewarded more richly."[18]

As personified in Trumbo's career, the ascent of "popular" writers and artists who purveyed vital content for the people's culture was rapid and unmistakable. This meant that the expansion of the new mass-based culture, a cultural united front that leagued art with kitsch, had to contend with a backlash sooner or later. As literary historian Janice Radway has shown, the resistance against culture's absorption of art came as early as the mid-1920s when the pejorative term "middlebrow" became part of the American vernacular. The backlash continued to wax more and more strident through the 1930s.[19] Critics of the people's culture, construed as a national and popular way of life shared by the people (not "classes") who enjoyed economically affordable and aesthetically accessible entertainment products, came from various backgrounds and pursued conflicting political goals. But the poet-critic like John Crowe Ransom and Allen Tate in the South rebelling against what they perceived as the inhumanity of Northern industrial capitalism while incubating basic ideas that would eventually found New Criticism, the Eliotic Trotskyites, those anti-Stalinist leftists based in New York for whom the avant-garde at once heralded and completed the coming world revolution, and a number of early communications scholars associated with the Institute for Social Research, which relocated from Vienna to New York City in 1934 – these writers skeptical of the people's culture were united in their belief that the industrialization and popularization of culture were part of a global trend toward what Dwight MacDonald called in 1941 "totalitarian cultural values," a trend that increasingly diminished artistic, and by extension human, freedom.[20] Aesthetic ideals resistant to external standards set by the markets and the government, they thought, made art and modern individuals more alive, more free, more democratic, less susceptible to the seduction of authoritarian regimentation.[21] Attacks on the people's culture initially arose out of concern with aesthetic autonomy but as the menace of totalitarianism began casting a long shadow on the public imagination during the prewar years, these aesthetic and economic analyses of the culture industry started bleeding into the national debate over the nature of the impending world war and America's role therein.

Binding together these prewar critics was a sense that the people's culture derived from a new capitalist order now reaching what they vaguely called a "late," "monopolistic," "collectivist," or "advanced" stage. Iconoclastic critics of late capitalism in the prewar years, such as Joseph Schumpeter, Adolf Berle, Gardiner Means, Peter Drucker, Friedrich Pollock, Max Horkheimer, and James Burnham, welcomed, rued, or otherwise proposed strategies to manage the passing of the heroic age of buccaneering nineteenth-century capitalism. They explained, and the critics of popular culture listened avidly, how the spread of monopolistic practices and the vanishing investment opportunities facilitated each other; how the growing "bigness" in industry called forth a corresponding tendency in the organized labor and the administrative state; how the separation of corporate management from ownership, coupled with new mores hostile to the nineteenth-century ethic of competition that buttressed the mythos of entrepreneurship, doomed the bourgeoisie.[22]

The prewar critics of the people's culture reasoned that the downfall of the bourgeoisie had to entail the decline of its nemesis – bohemia. If a historian of the original bohemia in mid-nineteenth century Paris is correct, "the Bohemian style only works in a capitalism with a myth of itself, a belief in its future."[23] Their antagonistic relationship had been also a form of symbiosis. In the bygone era, "contradictions" between the bourgeoisie and the proletariat allowed the third social group of bohemians to indulge in antisocial gestures of disaffection and revolt. To the eyes of the aesthetes, the contradiction between property ownership and dispossession was laughably insignificant because capital and labor both emphasized the same ethic of practicality, industriousness, and efficiency. By contrast, the supernal virtues in the autonomous realm of Bohemia were impracticality, idleness, and inefficiency.[24] Capitalists and the working class battled over surplus value. Bohemian artists impugned the value of value as such. Bohemians may strive like workers and factory owners, but their striving always led them away from productive goals, toward an internal enrichment paid for by the rigorous pauperization of their social value. "An important aspect of the artist's 'efficiency,'" Kenneth Burke, the archetypal bohemian of a Jazz-Age Greenwich Village, wrote in 1931, "resides not in an accumulation of products, but in a ceaseless indwelling, a patient process of becoming expert in himself."[25] This indwelling expertise enabled bohemians to advance arts and letters along their internally necessitated lines of growth through formal experimentations.

Even so, no sooner did these three groups settle in a strange ménage à trois than cultural trends in America became driven more and more by the new type of cultural workers, whose careers spanned traditionally distinct classes, media, and genres. In a "late" or "state" capitalism that was consolidating itself as the new world war impended, the proletariat toiling on shop floors and work sites were indistinguishable from stock brokers, secretaries, shop clerks (like Trumbo's father), and managers who staffed mammoth corporations whose ownership was diffused through numberless and faceless stockholders. The economic inequality was glaring, surely. But to the extent these prewar Americans all consumed inexpensive cultural commodities – Book of the Month selections, Pulitzer Prize – winning bestsellers, radio plays, operas and classic music on the radio, motion pictures, cartoons in newspapers – they were members of the same national culture that transcended class, regional, and even racial differences.²⁶ The "overmastering reality of our age [was] the decompos-ition of the bourgeois synthesis in all fields," observed Dwight MacDonald on the eve of Pearl Harbor.²⁷ Walls separating various classes of art were crumbling on all sides. On one side, the industrialization of artistic expression and the integrated national market combined to democratize and vulgarized high art. In the age of "technological reproducibility," cheap imitations sans aura were universally available.²⁸ On another side, light entertainment, which had met the recreational needs of the plebeians in the nineteenth century, was intellectualized and dignified, that is, made palatable for the patricians, who had lost their class integrity as they were absorbed into the American *Volksgemeinschaft*. Like Norman Rockwell's illustrations for *The Saturday Evening Post*, the people's culture was respectable, fit for consumption by all people from all walks of life.

In his postwar essay, "The Legacy of the 30's," Robert Warshow, a young member of the New York Intellectuals, singled out the decom-position of the bourgeois synthesis and the attendant fusion of highbrow with lowbrow as the central problem that frightened his generation: in the 1930s "the mass culture of the educated classes – the culture of the 'middle-brow,' as it has sometimes been called – had come into existence. For the first time, popular culture was able to draw its ideological support from the most advanced sectors of society. If this represented a lowering of the level of serious culture, it also raised the level – or at least the tone – of popular culture. This is precisely what made it a 'problem.'"²⁹ The mass market, catering to anonymous, "average" citizens, neither plebian nor patrician, neither proletarian nor bourgeois, had an insatiable demand for cultural contents. Writers and artists faced a choice: Should they work for or against the people's culture?

The period leading up to the new world war saw the deepening entangle-ment of the mutually reciprocating changes: the great convergence of high and low or art and culture, the mechanization of artistic creation, the permeation of the national market by the new media of mass entertainment, the rise of popular culture as a way of life of a modernizing people, and the growth of dictatorships abroad that magnified these national-popular trends in the perception of their critics. This development offers a fresh vantage point from which to reconsider the debate, already touched upon in the previous chapter, over art's relation to propaganda. Such a reconsideration would expose how the theoretical Marxists' hostility to agitational arts was bound up with their alienation from the people's culture. Art works circulating in popular culture were actually soporifics to stupefy the masses, and so they could never negate the status quo, these critics thought.³⁰

During the Popular Front years (1935–1939), Stalinists abandoned class sectarianism and embraced the people's culture in the name of antifascism, but anti-Stalinists persisted in their attack on culture's absorption of art in the name of "the people." Actually, their criticisms grew more venomous as their alienation from the national-popular synthesis deepened. Commercial culture was formulaic and schematic, they said. The culture industry audience-tested private experience and social reality and edited out any upsetting truths.[31] Workers like Dalton Trumbo in this industry cut spontaneous experiences along formulaic lines and set titillating fragments together to fit a predictable storyline. Popular artists performed the labor of experiencing the world in order to spare the consumers that labor, so that the consumers could just roam the market for the fruits of the labor of experiencing that matched their tastes most closely (by contrast, the avant-garde artist did not experience the world vicariously for his audience but instead imitated the process of experiencing). The people's culture never failed to reproduce the actual. Nor did it ever frustrate expectations. For the people had been trained to expect that particular species of the actual.[32] The people's culture was popular by virtue of being popular.

In the estimate of these critics, then, the way the people consumed standardized entertainment products demonstrated beyond any doubt that artwork fulfilled social and political functions, mostly of degrading, narcotizing, and exploitative kinds. Art was a "class weapon," and in late capitalism it was the new ruling class – the malevolent confederacy of bureaucrats, managers, financial interests, and popular artists in the employ of the culture industry – that was exploiting most fully the political potential of art and entertainment. Struggle always presupposes the distinction between the oppressors and the oppressed, and one of the disturbing consequences of late capitalism during the prewar years was that it blurred this distinction. So the detractors of the people's culture had difficulty answering basic questions about the instrumentality of art. Who were the oppressors? Who were the victims? Middlebrow bestsellers, movies, radio shows, popular music, pulp magazines, short stories and cartoons in popular "slicks" were all roundly denounced as "propaganda." "The encouragement of kitsch is merely another of the inexpensive ways in which totalitarian regimes seek to ingratiate themselves with their subjects," Clement Greenberg said in 1939, and it is worth remembering that these writers seriously thought that an America readying itself for the impending global war was as "totalitarian" as Germany and Russia.[33] Yet the visage of the "regimes" and "their masses" remained rather elusive, especially so in the case of their American incarnations.

The same vagueness undermined their championing of the archenemy of the people – the avant-garde. Those who felt threatened by the narcotized masses invested the avant-garde with several distinct characteristics. First and foremost, it had to be unpopular, or even militantly antipopular. The people were actually the enemy of the vanguards, both in politics and aesthetics. Second, while the popularization of culture was an international trend, America–a traditionally barren ground for an oppositional elite culture–was in the most advanced stage.[34] Third, the avant-garde was against stasis. Rather than petrified culture, its inclination toward formal purification gave the avant-garde an odd dynamism, for the genuine sorts of art evolved by working out their own formal potentials and intrinsic propensities. Purism and dynamism needed each other, and so wherever one was missing, the other was not to be found. Thus, one feature of the people's culture, syncretism (between art and nonart, or among different artistic media such as movie, radio, and literature), caused stasis. Conversely, once arts stopped advancing, priorities and considerations foreign to their innermost logic started creeping into them.[35] And last, the most extravagant versions of this backlash against the people's culture on the eve of World War II predicted that the avant-garde could flourish only when the world revolution was at hand. Under Stalinism, National Socialism, Fascism, and the New Deal, the people's culture tended toward the same goals: the persecution of the avant-garde as the enemy of the *volk* and the triumph of middlebrow realism. The imminent world war would be fought among late or state capitalist powers that were morally, culturally, and economically indistinguishable. The critics of the people's culture connected the dots. The decline of the avant-garde and the growth of totalitarian mass society in the advanced industrial nations throughout the 1930s appeared to account for each other. A fight for the avant-garde meant a fight against the culture industry, against the transformation of free, spontaneous, and critical individuals into the regimented national community. Highbrows and vanguards were fighting for freedom, individuality, spontaneity – qualities and values that were human, liberal, and truly democratic. Disturbingly, however, the increasingly popular view of the next war as a battle between America the land of free and diabolical totalitarian regimes obscured the critical importance of this real fight for human and artistic freedom that cut across superficial regime variations.

It was not a coincidence that these attackers on the people's culture were also against the use of art for agitational purposes. Agitation controlled the audience instead of emancipating it. To that extent, it retarded the advent of an ideal society where its members would be spontaneous and perceptive. It was its efficacy as a device of social control that these critics found most alarming. Similarly, their exaggerated estimate of the revolutionary potential of the avant-garde dovetails with their tendency to espouse the use of art as a political weapon on the epistemic grounds. For in both arguments, art's political utility was claimed to reside in its ability to correct cognitive mistakes that late capitalism and the people's culture forced on the workers regarding what was truly in their economic and spiritual interest.

Becoming Popular

An epitome and beneficiary of every baneful tendency in the new people's culture, Dalton Trumbo embodied what made the people's culture appear so threatening to these leftists and modernists who claimed to have the best interest of the people at heart. Like many other successful popular writers of the time, Trumbo was a rhetorical writer, in the sense that he used his art kinetically, in order to move the people. To him, art was a weapon. Or an even more apt metaphor may be some sort of psychotropic drug. The ultimate test for him was efficacy, that is, whether he could bring change to the audience's mood, opinion, comportment, and ultimately their conduct. He would not see anything derogatory in the metaphor of narcotics that the critics used to warn of the addictive influence of mass entertainment. Mind control was exactly what art was supposed to do, as far as Trumbo was concerned, and as we have already seen, to this end, he took advantage of a suite of conventional and innovative techniques. An array of tricks perfected by the tradition of psychological realism instructed him in how best to induce the reader to simulate the psychological state of a fictional character. And through simulation, illusion, and identification, *Johnny Got His Gun* succeeded, where a didactic appeal to reason or an experimental highbrow art would have surely failed, in eliciting desired political reactions from its readers.

Moreover, to cement the identification between the fictional character and the reader, Trumbo went beyond a mere tweaking of compositional formulas. He collaborated with social values and the popular symbols associated with those values. His novel forged connection between Joe Bonham and the reader not through singular experience but through collectively shared values. Joe Bonham met the reader through a sentimental fraternity to which they both belonged. Trumbo perhaps chose to reach *I* of the reader through *we* because he gathered that what seemed like a unique private soul was in fact a sum of multiple affiliations with overlapping social groups. In the era of general suspiciousness against propaganda, public relations, advertising, and the narcotizing influences of the culture industry, the road to the heavily guarded citadel of *I* ran through unguarded drawbridges by which a suspicious citizenry remained in touch with the communities of agreeable values and recognizable arguments. If the writer wanted to infiltrate the reader's mind with new ideas and orientations, his best chance was in camouflaging them in appropriate (namely, disarming) symbols. Ideas and orientations, no mater how objectively correct, no matter how advantageous to the people, would refuse to catch on as long as they were cloaked in inappropriate (namely, uninteresting) symbols. As Kenneth Burke, the slyest commentator on the burgeoning people's culture, tenaciously explained in a succession of books, *Counter-Point* (1931), *Permanence and Change* (1934), *Attitudes Toward History* (1937), and *The Philosophy of Literary Form* (1941), the key was in exploitation of a subtle difference between what was in the people's best interests and what they were actually interested in.[36]

According to its determined foes, the people's culture was a theater of "mass deception." When evaluated against Trumbo's practices, such a criticism reveals its own errors as well as the correctness – no, the appropriateness – of the way Trumbo dealt with a particular combination of developments that confronted the insiders and outsiders of the culture industry. Whatever its cognitive merits, the "false consciousness" thesis, elaborated and propagated by Georg Lukács following the failure of the Bolshevik revolution to spread to more industrially advanced parts of Europe, was a tactical error. As a didactic message brought to the deceived masses, the charge of delusion was not merely ineffectual but counter-productive. No citizen was interested in learning that he was deceived and by implication stupid, sloppy, and gullible. When the outsiders frontally attacked a host of delusions the deceived masses had bought into, the masses would inevitably cling to them more desperately. And what seemed like a case of "infantile disorder" (as Lenin dubbed ultra-left sectarianism) reveals itself as an act of bad faith, for those critics of the people's culture were initiated into the arcana of Freudianism more thoroughly than Trumbo or any other middlebrow writers.[37] They most likely knew that their criticism would not effect an iota of change in the masses' false consciousness. The primary function of any polarizing language, like that of "mass deception," was to shore up the in-group morale of the already undeceived friends, not to propitiate angry mobs or to enlighten self-satisfied gulls.

In 1936, in response to a draft of Walter Benjamin's artwork essay, Theodor Adorno wrote that the debate between Benjamin and himself over the revolutionary potential of the people's culture in the age of mechanical reproducibility needed "a true accounting of the relationship of the intellectuals to the working class," and Adorno had this to say about the political consciousness of "the working class": "actual workers ... have absolutely no advantage over the bourgeois except their interest in the revolution, but otherwise bear all the marks of mutilation of the typical bourgeois character."[38] Adorno here conceded that the proletariat at least had an "interest in the revolution" but elsewhere, in most of his denunciatory writings on the popular, he wrote as though he believed that the proletariat, completely narcotized by the culture industry, had an interest in *thwarting* the revolution. His mistrust of the proletariat was widely shared among a majority of the critics troubled by the coming war among super late capitalist powers, Stalin's Russia, Hitler's Germany, and Roosevelt's America. In a complete reversal of Lenin's plea to transform the international war into the civil war during the last war, these belligerents in the next war would use their respective people's cultures to co-opt the revolutionary energy and whip it up into volkisch frenzy. While it is easy to cavil with their assessment of the political consciousness of the working class, the critical point that Trumbo's fascination with rhetoric illuminates is that these critics prescribed a treatment that was not even consistent with their original diagnosis. For if, as they supposed, the proletariat, as mutilated in its political and cultural character as the bourgeoisie, was indifferent, or even hostile, to the revolution, then that would only redound to the importance of the foxy manipulation of popular symbols and popular media.

Some of the most emotional critics of mass culture, for instance, also took the most extreme position against America's mandate in the coming war. Like Trumbo, they opposed Roosevelt's pro-Allies policy. Like Trumbo, their sympathies lay with workers, who were despite themselves being dragooned into a capitalist war. But their proposal and the language in which it was couched could not have been more dramatically different from Trumbo's. As late as the summer of 1941, the two most eloquent detractors of the people's culture and late capitalism, Dwight Macdonald and Clement Greenberg, counseled defeatism of sorts as the best way forward for their country. As always, their argument was syllogistically unassailable. "Only socialism can win this war. Only uncompromising, unambiguous and unflagging opposition to Churchill and Roosevelt can win socialism." Ergo the American workers must organize and overthrow the proto-fascist capitalism in the United States before cooperating with the nation's military buildup.[39] One problem, which was typical of their writings, was that their major premise – "only socialism can win this war"– was not grounded in reality. But so were other "propositions on the war" that writers of all ideological leanings publicized at that time. A more fatal problem was that, regardless of its factual accuracy or predictive value, an absolute majority of the American people were not interested in hearing that only socialism could defeat the Axis powers.

For sure, the sort of sentimental pacifism and patriotic isolationism that Trumbo espoused may have been equally inadequate as analysis of object-ive trends and national interests. And yet Trumbo was at least intelligent enough to do his point of view a favor by making it entertaining and instructive. The question was how to wheedle, not how to polarize and antagonize. And he found the answer in opportunistic majoritarianism, not in haughty rejectionism of the mass culture critics. And he was supremely qualified for this task, for his experience in Hollywood had instilled in him "the childish conception that the principal function of an expressive medium is to tell a tall tale in an interesting fashion."[40] He did not sharpen the antithesis between the truth of war revealed in his novel and the gullibility of a public who easily forgot their class interest in a bout of nationalism. Instead, he synthesized – and in many passages already examined, synchronized – the attitude of the patriotic antiwar working-class hero and the attitude of the reader through grammatical devices as well as through a miscellany of clichés and common sayings that sounded good to ordinary Americans.

Politically radicalized intellectuals who felt excluded from the culture of the workers they wanted to help deplored that commercialized cultural productions were "schematic" and "formulaic." Schematized and formu-laic art endlessly reproduced same blatant lies. Hollywood, "This Isle of Do-What's-Done-Before," as Dorothy Parker mocked it, told the same stories over and over, with hardly distinguishable characters, settings, and plots.[41] "Every film is a preview of the next, which promises yet again to unite the same heroic couple under the same exotic sun," fumed Adorno and Horkheimer. "Anyone arriving late cannot tell whether he is watching the trailer or the real thing."[42] In a culture that reproduced the same perpetually, it was impossible to obtain a genuinely new revolutionary vantage point. By contrast, middlebrow writers with leftist agendas, like Dalton Trumbo, operated on the assumption that there was no such thing as a genuinely unprecedented perspective on late capitalism that antedated schemas and formulas. The masses' experience was severely conventional-ized. Therefore, it could not be restored to a pre-conventional state without losing its political interest. Conventions, or schemas, patterns, formulas, oriented the people's attitudes toward a historical situation. In dealing with art or reality, the audience recognized a situation when that situation was labeled by easily recognizable categories like "mother," "son," "villain," "hero," "American," "un-American," and so on. These labels may be evaluated according to their appropriateness but never according to their accuracy because labels motivated action rather than depicted reality. Action was based on cognition. Cognition was always recognition. Recognition presupposed prejudice, which was entwined with preexisting schemas. Schemas then formed a vital link in the transmission loop that connected a social situation to a citizen's action. A critic could stipulate unilaterally that schemas were bad for art. But if that critic agreed to art's political instrumentality, which all critics of the people's culture did, it was logical to work with clichés, slogans, stock characters, and formulaic plots.

Unable to love the people they wanted to love, the critics of the popular and the national, in their unrelieved guilt and bitterness, neglected a number of subtle distinctions among the various ways in which popular experience in the era of late capitalism, mass culture, and total global war was schematized, the distinctions that were visible only to the artists competing in the free market without relinquishing their political agendas, such as Dalton Trumbo. The distinction between what was to a reader's interests and what was in his interest was one of them. Another distinction of practical moment to popular writers and artists was the one between being popular and becoming popular.[43] The fact that popular culture was popular by virtue of being popular did not warrant the conclusion the alienated intellectuals drew, that in the people's culture art necessarily stagnated. Over time, tried-and-proven methods of schematizing a situation wore out and became less stimulative and less popular. Being popular did entail being formulaic, and yet formulas were neither eternal nor immutable. The task of political artists was to identify incipient popularity in unpopular formulas and signs of senescence in popular formulas. And having grasped the drift of the people's culture, they could call the political enemy the most unpopular names while promoting desired programs through association with popular symbols. Little wonder then that Dalton Trumbo excelled at such a job. His was a middlebrow art – popular, formulaic, and syncretic (he wrote fiction with the expectation that his novels would be adapted to such other mediums as screen, theater, and radio). He constantly had to attune his sensibilities to the mean of the national-popular. In the process he enjoyed the rewards of being popular and paid the price of being ephemeral. There is no doubt that many cultural workers with Trumbo's endowment cynically sold out and engaged in reproduction of the sameness, producing popular works for no other reasons than that they were popular. Throughout his prolific career, Trumbo, too, often did just that. But in writing *Johnny Go His Gun*, he also exploited his knowledge of the popular, so as to make pacifism and isolationism more popular.

7

Across the Pacific

For much of the prewar period, the most disturbing rumors of war always came from Europe. The Atlantic still provided the front window on world affairs for depression-era Americans. Of a series of Japanese aggressions across the Pacific, including the establishment of a puppet regime in Manchuria in 1931, the invasion of China in 1937, and the advance into Indochina in 1941, only distant echoes reached an America uneasily peering at the darkening war clouds over Madrid, Munich, Prague, Warsaw, Helsinki, Paris, and London.

There were, however, certain trends and conditions that collectively managed to insert China's decade-long fight into a variety of prewar debates. The fact that it was not a transatlantic attack by a European power but the U.S.–Japan competition for hegemony in China that finally plunged America into World War II is clear evidence of Asia's importance to the United States.[1] America refused to go to war over Ethiopia, Spain, Czechoslovakia, Poland, Finland, France, and finally even Britain. But when Japan's ambition to extend its sphere of control from China into South East Asia became clear, the United States took measures that at least policy makers knew could provoke Japan to an act of war.[2] Although they knew and cared less about Far Eastern affairs than they did European politics, ever since the invention of the Open Door policy in the last decade of the previous century, a great mass of Americans had tended to be more sensitive to Japanese expansionism than to the ongoing battle among European powers for control of the continent. This tendency only strengthened during the depression decade when public animus against the main adversary of the Great War receded in parallel with Americans' deepening regret over their country's last foreign intervention. Throughout the 1930s, by contrast, the impression of Japan as traditional foe-to-be remained vivid and provocative in public as well as official imagination.[3]

The pro-Chinese coverage by newsreels, magazine articles, and journalists' dispatches also helped the Japanese invasion of China become one of the pivotal prewar developments, especially after the conflict's escalation into a full-blown war in 1937. To later generations familiar with the obviously biased pro-Chinese and anti-Japanese propaganda of the war years, the media coverage during the prewar period may seem surprisingly objective and detached. Just the same, Japanese atrocities juxtaposed with Chinese heroism in extreme adversity inevitably recruited public sympathy toward the latter.[4] Another impetus behind the Asian war's gradual intrusion into public consciousness was a host of highly visible pro-Chinese campaigns by such anti-Japanese pressure groups as United China Relief and the American Committee for Non-Participation in Japanese Aggression, all funded and staffed by people with strong ties with China – missionaries and businessmen and their sympathizers in the publishing industry, Hollywood, and the radio networks.[5] Exploiting means of mass persuasion no different from those used by partisans of other foreign causes, such as rallies, galas, editorials, circular letters, and pamphlets, these organizations alerted Americans to the unfolding humanitarian crisis in East Asia and America's complicity in Japanese aggression (through sales of strategically valuable materials such as oil and scrap iron) and called for the boycott of Japan's export items like silk.[6]

All these conditions favorable to America's more active involvement in Far Eastern affairs, however, were countervailed by unfavorable trends that blunted the Sino-Japanese War's impact. According to a survey taken in 1937, 95 percent of those Americans who had any opinion sympathized with China (more than half of those polled had no opinion at all). And yet, according to another survey conducted shortly after Japan's attack on Pearl Harbor, 59 percent of Americans could not find China on the map (more people were able to find Iceland).[7] These two statistics combine to indicate that, unlike Europe, to a substantial majority of Americans, Asia was still a sentimental blur, a terra incognita existing somewhere beyond the Pacific. Asia's relative obscurity in the American mind was further exacerbated by the racial and religious difference between white Americans and the Chinese. If Germany's aerial bombardment of British cities could not convince great numbers of Americans that the British were fighting their country's war, China's resistance against another Asian nation faced even greater difficulty in attracting sympathy and support. In this regard, the war in Asia was akin to the Italo-Ethiopian War, except for the fact that a pro-Chinese force comparable to the African-American partisans of the Ethiopian cause simply did not exist in the United States.

The weak kinship between America and China was moreover complicated by the frail national unity of the latter. The Sino-Japanese War was also a three-cornered fight. The Chinese Communists and the Nationalists battled each other off and on throughout the decade for control over China, with each telling the other that their common enemy was the empire of Japan. As in the case of the Spanish Civil War, neither side in the Chinese civil war could be easily portrayed as innocent freedom fighters, the Communists for obvious reasons and the Nationalists because of their alleged corruption, military ineptness, and authoritarianism. This posed a problem when writers tried to fit this conflict into the simple narrative of the free world versus world tyranny. After his trip to China, Hemingway summed up this dilemma in his detailed report to Treasury Secretary Henry Morgenthau, who oversaw complicated schemes of circumventing Congress to send financial aid to China:

> [T]here will be no permanent settlement of the Communist problem in China until an agreement between the Generalissimo's Government and the Soviet Union settles definite limits to the territories the Communist forces are to occupy. Until then the Communists, as good Chinese, will fight against the Japanese but as good Communists they will attempt to extend their sphere of influence in China no matter what territorial limits they may accept on paper.

Naturally, Hemingway continued, this kind of analysis could reveal to the Americans "an atmosphere of civil war, [so] I didn't publish it [in his essays for *Collier's Collier*'].''[8]

And a last complicating factor was the fact that American sympathy for the Chinese cause was dulled by a sober calculation of economic and strategic interests in the Far East. Despite the U.S. commitment to China's sovereignty and integrity since the turn of the century, officials in the Roosevelt administration recognized Japan's vital interests in China, particularly in Manchuria. After all, the Japanese invasion did not dramatically impinge on what little interests the United States held in the region.[9] Although the symbolic and emotional factors surely guided the general public's attitude toward Asia, the difficulty of appealing to America's self-interests hampered the efforts to persuade the hesitant and confused nation that the Japanese aggression in Asia was but one local battle in a globe-wide showdown between the free world and dictators.

As with the Ethiopian crisis and the Spanish Civil War, then, the significance of the war across the Pacific to the evolution of the prewar culture was twofold. On the one hand, the debates over Japan's potential threat to U.S. security and China's qualification for U.S. aid, simmering over the course of the depression decade until it came to the boiling point in late 1941, schooled the United States in novel ways to synthesize events across the Atlantic and events across the Pacific and imagine its global mission on a truly planetary scale. In this sense, this episode must be given importance equal to climacteric events in Europe. On the other hand, the fact that America ended up waiting until the Japanese fired the first shot bears testimony to the potency of lingering inhibitions that contorted America's road to the new world war. In search of the best site to study this ambivalence and ambiguity, I again turn to a literary engagement – Pearl Buck's championing of democratic China.

Pearl S. Buck's Asia

Predictably, writers, artists, and intellectuals paid much more attention to the crisis across the Pacific than did ordinary Americans. In new periodicals like *Amerasia*, founded by Frederick Vanderbilt Field, *Pacific Affairs*, edited by Owen Lattimore, and *Asia*, edited by Richard Walsh, Pearl Buck's second husband, a new generation of China specialists presented serious commentaries that applied powerful theories such as class, modes of production, imperialism, patterns of land ownership, nutrition, literacy, and so forth to the terrible aches of modernity ravaging Asia. Meanwhile, journalists like Agnes Smedley, Edgar Snow, his wife Helen, writing often under "Nym Wales," and Theodore White, Henry Luce's alter ego in China, supplied Americans with a steady stream of reports on the intermittent outbursts of hostilities between the Nationalists and the Communists, the resilience of Mao's guerrilla armies, and the Japanese campaigns against both Communist- and Nationalist-held areas.[10] Writers and artists with no special tie to Asia also rushed to cover Japan's reign of terror and atrocities. Margaret Bourke-White visited China with her husband Erskine Caldwell and dispatched pictures to United China Relief. Some veterans of the Spanish Civil War headed to the Orient, too. Robert Capa took photos for *Life*. Joris Ivens teamed up with Contemporary Historians again and traveled to China in 1938 to shoot a pro-Communist propaganda film, *400 Million*. For a brief moment, Hankow, and then Chungking, the wartime capitals of the Nationalist government, assumed a romantic glow, a new Madrid of sorts, riveting the attention of antifascist liberals around the world.[11] In the spring of 1941, Hemingway and Martha Gellhorn flew to Chungking, hop-scotching from Hawaii to Wake to Guam to Hong Kong. They traveled around China for three months to cover the Nationalist fronts for *Collier's*.

Towering over all these China commentators was Pearl S. Buck. In 1931, Buck, who grew up in China as a "mishkid" like Luce, White, and John Hersey and was about to return to the United States permanently, published her first novel, *The Good Earth*, to a tremendous commercial success. The book topped various bestseller lists for two years.[12] It won the Pulitzer Prize, was made into a Broadway play, and adapted for the Oscar-winning motion picture in 1937. The same year, Buck was also awarded the Nobel Prize in Literature. In a national poll in 1937 that asked the respondents to name "the most interesting book you have ever read," *The Good Earth* ranked the fourth, after the Bible, *Gone with the Wind*, and *Anthony Adverse*.[13] By the end of the depression decade, Buck had published six more full-length novels, all of them bestsellers. Five of these were set in China and incorporated references to the ongoing political turmoil in the Far East. Her books were at the same time serialized and her short stories regularly featured in glossy middlebrow magazines such as *Collier's, Ladies' Home Journal, Cosmopolitan, Women's Home Companion*, and *Good Housekeeping*. A keen observer of China's struggle for national independence and a sympathetic chronicler of the plights of Chinese peasants with unrivaled access to the people's culture, Pearl S. Buck left a deeper imprint on the American perception of China than anyone else in the 1930s.

Her idea of America's stake in the war in Asia also happened to be more complex than those of her contemporaries. Her views mirrored widely available conventional opinions, but coinciding in one individual, they made Buck's stance unpredictable. First, her position was colored by her deeply ingrained pacifism, a kind that was naïve but fairly common among her contemporaries. With a visceral aversion to violence, she would not accept that force could be a policy tool to undo tangles of aggression and counter-aggression among the nation-states. The nation must not fight sword with sword, so she would argue like Christian pacifists, although she always protested that she was no pacifist.[14] This inclination was compounded by her idée fixe that war was a clash between two antagonistic tribes possessed by such primitive emotions as the drive for destruction, revenge, and conquest or antipathy toward unfamiliar cultures and races.[15] Consequently, Buck seldom described the Asian war as a black-and-white battle between the Chinese innocents and the Japanese evildoers. Knowledgeable about the common people of China, she took an oddly neutral stance regarding their struggle against Japanese imperialism.

A second piece in the makeup of Buck's worldview was her burning rage against Western hypocrisy. Partly a reaction to the sordid realities that she witnessed while growing up in China, such as the missionaries' paternalistic attitude toward Chinese heathens and the rapacious and arrogant behaviors of foreign merchants and militaries, Buck mistrusted the motives of the Western powers meddling in Chinese affairs ostensibly to help the Chinese educate themselves, build, be healthy, be Christians. However noble their intentions may have been, their long record of imperial wrongdoings inspired absolutely no confidence. Aid through private charities was one thing. Western nations dispatching gunboats to help the Chinese repel the Japanese invaders was quite another.

A third complicating factor was Buck's antiracism, which often disregarded the traditional boundaries of empires and nation-states. The single most important reason why Buck was not only skeptical but even critical of U.S. aid to Britain during the prewar years was that she simply did not see any moral distinction that the likes of Churchill and Eden presumed between the British Empire and the Third Reich.[16] To the American partisans of the British cause who pointed to the *Kristallnacht*, Buck could point to Britain's colonial misdoings in Africa and Asia no less icily than did Padmore, Du Bois, and Bunche. Buck's globe-girthing color line cut through the United States. From the black perspective, lynch mobs in the South or Roosevelt's unwillingness to back antilynching bills at the risk of alienating the gung-ho Southern Democrats made a mockery of the assertion that the United States was a democracy, whereas Germany was a racist autocracy. America must achieve a more perfect democracy at home before intervening in foreign wars, across the Pacific or the Atlantic. For sure, Japan's colonialism had racist elements, but the Japanese and the Chinese were both Asians after all. Their shared skin color meant much in Buck's thinking, which often attached overpowering importance to the East-West contrast.[17]

Buck's strange evenhandedness was much on display in her 1937 novel, *Patriot*. Set in China and Japan, the novel is a Pan-Asian revolutionary romance that tests the political commitment of a young Chinese Communist. When his father gets wind of an imminent Nationalist crackdown on Communists in Shanghai, the protagonist, I-wan, flees to Japan where he marries a Japanese woman, the daughter of his father's business partner. But once the Japanese invasion begins, I-wan decides to return to his homeland as an aide-de-camp to Chiang Kai-shek, after an anguished vacillation between his adopted country and his country of birth. The politics of the novel is hard to pin down. Buck sought to include both Japanese and Chinese points of view in order to condemn war as a work of the universal and primordial evil. The novel was later adapted into a radio-play by the Mercury Theater on the Air. Orson Welles, who played I-wan, interviewed Buck and asked if it is "possible to feel sympathy for the Chinese and the Japanese and at the same time understand them both." Buck replied: "[N]o matter who is the aggressor and who is the attacked, both are the victims and both lose in the end."[18]

"I am not a pacifist but…"

Combined, her sympathies for the suffering of the Chinese, naïve pacifism, mistrust of the West's motives, odd neutrality between the Japanese and the Chinese, and her habit of thinking along the color line made for a volatile political-literary activist. Nothing illustrates this volatility better than her strained relationship with the pro-Chinese lobby organization, the American Committee for Non-Participation in Japanese Aggression in China (ACNPJAC). The new war in Asia was officially called the Sino-Japanese Incident because neither side ever formally declared war. This gave Roosevelt an excuse for not invoking the Neutrality Act, so that the United States could continue to export arms to the Chinese.[19] A motley group of pro-Chinese Americans comprising missionaries, educators, businessmen, and diplomats with experience in China, however, believed that the non-invocation of the Neutrality Act did not sufficiently redress the great harm that the United States did to China by supplying, according to one estimate, "56% of all the materials essential for war purposes that Japan bought abroad" in 1938.[20] In late 1938, they proceeded to form the ACNPJAC, for the purpose of redeeming America's unwitting but reprehensible complicity in Japan's rampage.

   Under the leadership of Harry Price (another mishkid), the Committee devoted its slender resources to pressuring the government to enact a discriminatory embargo bill specifically targeting Japan. To this end, the Committee lobbied through useful contacts within the administration and Congress, but it also solicited endorsement from prominent authors, Hollywood actors, and famed foreign correspondents and mounted vigorous campaigns to educate public opinion. It was against this backdrop that the Committee approached Buck in the spring of 1939, with high hopes for the visibility she could bring to their endeavors.

   On April 10, 1939, the Committee contacted Buck's editor at the John Day Company, inquiring if she could give a speech at the Stop Arming Japan Rally in Manhattan on April 25. Although her appearance was requested on a short notice, Buck readily obliged because she "heartily believe[d], of course, in stopping shipment or armaments to countries engaged in war."²¹ Her acceptance takes on great significance, considering the fact that at the time she was inundated with dozens of requests for public speaking engagements and she almost always begged off these invitations, citing some inoffensive reasons. But the casual line just quoted, which was added almost as an afterthought at the end of her brief note, contained a germ of misunderstanding between Buck and the Committee. A full-blown disagreement would sprout out of it in November.

In her speech, which was broadcast on WQXR (one of the earliest FM station covering the New York metropolitan area), Buck repeated all the obligatory statistics about America's unwitting contribution to the Japanese aggression in China and took inventory of strategic materiel that kept flowing across the Pacific to massacre the Chinese. As a matter of principle, the American people all wanted to be "on the actual side of liberty anywhere."²² But, as a matter of fact, bombs made from scrap iron the United States sold to Japan were raining from the Chinese sky. Whence this disparity between the ideal and the fact? Buck had an unsurprising word to solve this conundrum – "profits." According to Buck, "when they ["individual Americans"] determine that business is in their control, as it is, when they choose liberty for the Chinese rather than profits for themselves, this war in the Orient will stop." What stands out is a glaring contrast between her near-complete silence about Japan's culpability and her optimistic forecast that the war in China would cease once U.S. businessmen gave up "profits."

Concurrently to this rally and unbeknownst to Buck, Harry Price, executive secretary of the Committee, was helping Senator Key Pittman, chairman of the Foreign Relations Committee, draft the Senate Joint Resolution 123. If adopted, the resolution, which was introduced two days after Buck's speech, would authorize the president to lay an embargo on foreign trade with any country that violated the Nine Power Treaty. In practical terms, this could only mean that Roosevelt would have executive authority to restrict shipment of strategic materiel to Japan, for the Japanese invasion of China had to be construed as violation of a provision in the Nine Power Treaty that guaranteed the territorial integrity and sovereignty of China.²³ The timing of the Stop Arming Japan Rally in New York was decided to reinforce public backing to this parallel maneuver taking place behind closed doors in Washington.

If the ultimate goal of the China allies inside and outside the government was a discretionary embargo on trade with Japan, the principal goal of interventionists concerned with the European crisis was to revise or repeal altogether the Neutrality Act. America's allies around the world needed American arms. The ACNPJAC, however, felt that this drive for nullification did nothing to address the mayhem breaking out across the Pacific. The nub of the issue was that Japan and China were not officially at war. Hence the debate over how to revise the Neutrality Act, which only applied to belligerents at war, was of little relevance to the Far Eastern situation. The Pittman resolution mentioned earlier was devised as a means to inject the Pacific viewpoint into various war-related congressional debates that seemed woefully Eurocentric. The method that worked well in the Atlantic did not work in the Pacific.

Her letters and her speech at the rally indicate that Buck was under the impression that the Committee was lobbying to expand the existing Neutrality Act to cover non-contraband goods including scrap iron and oil. As already noted, at the very end of her first letter accepting the request, Buck added that she "heartily believe[s], of course, in stopping shipment of armaments to countries engaged in war." Buck here appears to have willfully misinterpreted the Committee's objective. The Committee was interested in punishing Japan through a narrowly tailored policy (embargo on strategic materiel), not in keeping America neutral regarding all the regional conflicts breaking out across the globe. Her mock assent as expressed in the phrase "of course" hints that Buck was in fact aware of and uneasy with her own wishful interpretation. Her unease would soon harden into regret.

Following Hitler's invasion of Poland, the Committee threw itself into another flurry of aggressive campaigns. Congress, which had met for the special session at Roosevelt's request, was debating the proposal to repeal the arms embargo. If passed, the revised Neutrality Act would enable the French and British to purchase arms and munitions in the United States on cash-and-carry basis (no U.S. loans, no use of U.S. vessels). From the viewpoint of pro-Chinese Americans, this would do little to right the wrongs America had been perpetrating in the Orient. China's problem had not been that it was disallowed to purchase American arms but that it lacked ships, convoys, and cash to import them. The whole situation made it imperative for the Committee to force the Pacific point of view into the debate in Congress, which was understandably preoccupied with the new war across the Atlantic. It was in this new context that the Committee solicited from Buck a letter of endorsement of embargo on Japan to enclose with 10,000 fliers it was about to mail to its members across the nation.

On October 11, when Buck met with Harry Price in New York City, the latter suggested that Buck write a letter of appeal, arguing for the immediate halt on U.S. export to Japan.[24] Buck procrastinated until she received a second reminder from Price about two weeks later.[25] Her reply, when it finally came, was hesitant and circumspect: "I have been honestly so confused by the issues which it presents that I am not sure that I ought write it."[26] The eruption of the European war in the previous month had compelled her to think out the full implications of an embargo "The situation in regard to Europe is such that I feel that if we put what amounts to an embargo on Japan, we are really discriminating against Japan and that in itself is an act of war." Surely, Harry Price should have been the last person to gainsay Buck's legalistic construal of an embargo on Japan as a possible *casus belli*. But these China hands habitually underestimated that resource-scarce Empire's fear of a gradual strangulation by trade sanctions. Instead of recklessly lashing out, they expected, Japan would scale back its aggression in East Asia to get back in America's good graces.

To Buck's self-deprecating request to send her "anything that might clarify me on this particular phase of this subject," Price responded with a four-page letter brimful of bold arguments. The embargo could not be a *casus belli*, according to Price's understanding, because the Nine Power Treaty gave the United States a mandate to "provide the fullest and most unembarrassed opportunity to China to develop and maintain for herself an effective and stable government." As regards Buck's concern for the risk of war, Price reminded her that it was too late to entertain because the United States was *already* in a war "to the hilt" – against China. If the only alternatives open to the United States were a proxy war against China (through shipment of oil and iron to Japan) and a war with China against Japan, which war should America fight?[27]

By that time, however, Buck had already decided against endorsing economic sanctions on Japan, concluding that embargo indeed amounted to an act of war. Apparently, it was only after a long and agonized deliberation that she made up her mind. Early November, in a latter to Emma Edmunds White, her oldest and most trusted friend, Buck confided: "I have been thinking so much about this whole subject of war and what I as one individual can say or do that would be of any use. I feel so strongly that women can prevent war by refusing by all means to allow men to resort to it, but there is so much to think out and reason through when one takes a stand."[28] As was her wont, she hedged her antiwar stance with a consequentialist argument, to the effect that she did not oppose the use of force "on the grounds of pacificism [*sic*] or even religion but on the solid grounds of practical accomplishment of any desired end, that war is so completely useless." Yet, her categorical renouncement of "the force of war machines and methods" only gave the lie to her hollow claim that

"I am not a pacifist." Soon after, the pro-Chinese lobbyists finally heard back from Buck. In her final reply, she came out as a staunch opponent of embargo on Japan: "[B]y every possible means I believe my own country should stay out of any war. I am not a pacifist but I simply do not believe that wars do any good in finally solving problems. To me, an embargo is an act of war in that it is no use unless it is enforced and it cannot be enforced unless by warlike measures."[29] Here again Buck foreswore any pacifist motives. Her defensiveness is mystifying, and what she thought would qualify her position as non-pacifist is unclear, because she never stipulated under what conditions she condoned the use of force.

In another letter to the Committee, Buck shed light on her reasoning from a slightly different angle:

> I cannot overcome my conviction that an embargo is an act of war and unless it is made universal against all countries engaged in war, I cannot see that it is a proper weapon to be used. If we should establish, as a matter of principle, that we would not ship arms to any belligerent country, I would come out for that heart and soul, but to declare such an embargo only against Japan is another matter that involves more than China.[30]

An embargo against Japan must be part and parcel of the universal policy of unilateral abstention from any foreign war. In fact, the conclusion she finally reached should not have been surprising to Buck herself. The isolationist fantasy of a unilateral withdrawal from the world, arising out of the belief that the overstretched network of business interests, military bases, and missionary activities could potentially ensnare America in a foreign war in which the ordinary citizens had no real stake, was one of the recurring themes in her political writings.[31] In her most unguardedly isolationist mood, Buck recorded the following thoughts:

> Granted, however, the moral of the hour in the west that no western nation will participate in the war between Chinese and Japan, what is the true basis for the policy of dignified non-participation? Or is it simply this; a government must recognize in this modern day its prestige no longer rests upon old chivalric attitude towards its flag on nationals. Prestige rests solely upon the power of internal prosperity, of peace, of self-regulation. Only a barbarous nation needs to shout and protest for its prestige's sake. ... A strong and sensible [sic] should make it clear to those of its nationals who choose to live and do business abroad that they must take the risks of their countries to which they go. The tax payers cannot justly be called upon to pay for a guard to protect those who voluntarily wander outside their country for their own personal satisfactions, either moral or material. Once this policy is made clear, there will be no more "incidents." It is the

absurd self-importance of those individuals who, going abroad to make money, preach their gospels, consider themselves as representatives of their nations, which involves their governments and fellow citizens in this entangle which they dread.[32]

Prominent throughout what appears to have been a rough, somewhat incoherent speech draft are the hallmark ideas of isolationism, such as the priority of domestic prosperity over economic and political expansion overseas, the fiscal burden the protection of the expanding sphere of interests could levy on "tax payers," and finally the fear lest the protection of U.S. nationals in the trade and missionary outposts should lead to a *casus* (incident) that could be used as a pretext to call the nation to arms.

The question, then, that needs answering is why did Buck initially endorse an embargo against Japan. The answer seems to lie in the fact that the Committee's program of "non-participation" in a foreign war had the advantage of implying, erroneously, that an embargo was not an entry but an exit strategy that would reduce America's exposure to international affairs. The popularity of the Committee's program among many Americans, who were neither doctrinaire pacifists nor internationalists, banked on this isolationist connotation, and the Committee exploited this ambiguity to their advantage.[33] With a strong pacifist streak in it, Buck's heart was initially captivated by the prospect of bringing about a peaceful conclusion to the Sino-Japanese Incident through withdrawal of American support to one side of the conflict. Soon, however, Buck came to see embargo under a different light, which was perhaps thrown by the new European war and the imminent possibility of American involvement. A discriminatory embargo on Japan, she came to recognize, would facilitate U.S. aid to the European imperial powers she utterly despised (France and Britain), a policy that was a far cry from what was implied by the passive-sounding decoy term "non-participation." If an embargo was calculated to be selectively invoked against those nations that Roosevelt deemed America's enemy, it would precipitate rather than forefend foreign entanglements.

Flight into China

One of the intellectual leanings that controlled Buck's unexpectedly timid stance on America's capability to thwart Japan and aid China was her progressive politics on racism and imperialism. Her refugee play *Flight into China* (1939) dramatized how her antiracism and anticolonialism paradoxically resulted in her distaste for activist foreign policy. Staged by Lee

Strasberg, himself a German Jew who had recently emigrated to the United States, *Flight into China* explored the topical theme of Jewish identity and the refugee crisis. The drama is set in a café in the Shanghai International Settlement. Reinhart, a German Jew, arrives in Shanghai after narrowly fleeing Hitler's Germany. As he explains to Mollie, a Chinese flapper he meets at the café, he broke up with his Jewish girlfriend, who opted for America, and came to China because he is frightened by race prejudices in the United States: "Who knows what will happen in America if there are too many Jews? I said [to his Jewish girlfriend] I wasn't going to any country that hadn't already proved it would not persecute a race. ... They kill Negroes there. ... If they kill the black, they can also kill the Jew."[34] Then, into the café wanders a Chinese curio vendor with vestiges of stereotypically Jewish characteristics. Through Mollie acting as his interpreter, Reinhart learns from the vendor that in the eighteenth century a small group of Jews settled in Hunan, from whom he descends. As the Chinese-Jewish curio vendor, who has lost his ethnic and religious heritage and has been assimilated into the Han race, answers Reinhart's questions and recapitulates his genealogy, the lights go out downstage and a romance centering on a Jewish man and a Chinese girl in the mid-nineteenth century begins to unfold upstage.

At the center of the curio vendor's narrative is a young Jewish man, David, the narrator's distant ancestor. He is trapped in a dilemma between his love for a comely Chinese girl and his filial obligation to his superficial and fluttery mother, who contrives an elaborate scheme to marry her son to the daughter of a poor rabbi in order to preserve her family's tribal integrity. With her aquiline nose, large liquid eyes, and cloudy dark hair, Leah, David's fiancée, is intended as an easily recognizable symbol of Jewish purity. Sanctimonious and tempestuous, Leah is a female Moses, who dreams of a day when she and her husband will raise Jewish armies, break loose from the bondage in a gentile land, and go on a military expedition to succor the persecuted Jews the world over. By comparison, Kwei-lan, the Chinese girl with whom David is really in love, is a carefree, spoiled, somewhat slow-witted daughter of a rich Chinese merchant. Ultimately, David spurns his mother and chooses Kwei-lan, preferring assimilation to the tribal priorities of faith and blood. Then the scene returns to the café in the Settlement.

Reinhart is horrified by the rather absurd yarn just narrated by the curio vendor. What disquiets him no less is the very physiognomy of the curio vendor, an end result of the long history of assimilation, miscegenation, and racial amnesia. Mollie implores Reinhart to stay with her and dance.

But in an access of assimilation-phobia, Reinhart leaps out of the café. He is now determined to emigrate to America, presumably to reunite with his Jewish girlfriend, a decision that is the exact inverse of David's choice.[35] With the example of the curio vendor, Reinhart can now better appreciate the usefulness of racist hatred and the cult of tribal purity from which he originally fled. Only the animosity of gentiles safeguards racial and religious distinctions. Before turning away from Mollie, who stands for the elemental force of the Chinese melting pot, Reinhart fashions a cross out of a piece of paper and brandishes it before the vendor's face. When he realizes that even this murderous symbol cannot stir up any flicker of distant memory in the curio vendor, Reinhart perversely renews his appreciation of anti-Semitism: "We've been kept alive by this cross. This cross, the death, the sorrow it has brought upon my people – the hatred – that's what's kept us alive until this day. Why, the hatred of the nations – it's saved us!"[36] As the curtain falls, the audience sees a slobbering Japanese soldier laying his lecherous hand on the defenseless Chinese maiden abandoned by Reinhart, who has just been revealed to have internalized the same myth of consanguinity that has originally forced him into exile.

The setting of the play in China and its unusual plot marks off Buck's play from much of refugee literature produced during these years. Unlike Elmer Rice's refugee play *Flight to the West*, Varian Fry's reportage *Surrender on Demand*, or Martha Gellhorn's novel *A Stricken Field*, which all purveyed suspenseful stories featuring intrepid underground partisans, Gestapo deviltries, and narrow escapes, Buck called attention to the trans-Siberian flow of Jewish refugees. *Flight into China* is also unusual for its hero's initial refusal to flee to America. Reinhart has doubts about the United States because of its racist treatment of African Americans. This unavoidably implies an analogy of victimhood between African Americans and Jews. And this analogy in turn implies that America and Nazi Germany are both implicated in a sort of worldwide racism. The play gives this innuendo another ironical twist. Near the end Reinhart changes his mind and departs for the United States, not because China is exposed as a racist country inhospitable to Jewish refugees, but for the contrary reason. China, he discovers to his consternation, is the one true melting pot, an inclusive society that has transcended the divisive identity politics battening on pathological attachments to race, religion, and nationality. But complete assimilation, of which the Jewish-Chinese curio vendor serves as a nauseatingly clear emblem, dissolves identity and diversity into a uniform mass of the people. Faced with this fearsome prospect, Reinhart realizes that racial antipathy, which keeps diversity alive, is the necessary condition of race-based identity. It is this tragic knowledge that impels Reinhart to his Flight into America.

The play's setting and plot leave room for conflicting interpretations. The Shanghai International Settlement was unlike other well-known overseas territories held by imperial powers, such as Hong Kong or Gibraltar. It was a land of ambiguity. Independent of and belonging to all participating nations, this territory was administered by a quasi-democratic board of representatives from Britain, the United States, Japan, and other colonial powers.[37] A western café in the Settlement was thus a pointed reminder that Western powers and Japan could unilaterally carve out a zone of extraterritoriality in the midst of Asia's mainland. Furthermore, it was this colonial status of the international zone that enabled tens of thousands of Jews who were rejected entry by Western nations to seek sanctuary there.[38] If anything, then, the International Zone in Shanghai demonstrated the imperial encroachment on Chinese sovereignty and its unintended consequence for the Jews. Colonial extraterritoriality was saving the victims of Nazi racism.

These discordant meanings of the setting were most likely inadvertent. But the plot of the play also sends confusing signals. The play's portrayal of race relations in the United States is flatly negative ("They kill Negroes there"). The didactic author clearly disapproves of Reinhart's panicked flight into America. One inference to be drawn from this is that Buck may also have approved of David's choice of Kwei-lan over his fiancée, the daughter of the beggared rabbi. Following David's example, Reinhart should also choose Mollie over his Jewish girlfriend and stay in China. It seems a short step from here to more unsettling implications: that as a German citizen, Reinhart should have mated with an Aryan woman in the first place; that by extension the Jews in Germany should have assimilated into the Aryan race through interracial marriage, just as the Jews in China did; and that perhaps the German Jews were partially to blame for Hitler's persecution.[39]

Buck's main point was that, unlike Germany or America, China had an exceptional history of harmonious racial assimilation, a highly arguable point factually. But that would still leave unresolved the prior question of whether or not racial minorities *ought to* assimilate if given a chance to do so by a dominant social, ethnic, and religious group. This hint of assimilationism did not escape some initial readers of the play. Later, producer Gertrude Macy would recall Katherine Cornell as telling her that Guthrie McClintic (Cornell's husband) "couldn't get [financial] backing for it [*Flight into China*] because N.Y. Jews didn't want to encourage Jewish assimilation."[40]

Chinese Melting Pot

The play's espousal of racial and cultural assimilation was at once old-fashioned and radical. Buck did not see any intrinsic value in racial homogeneity or racial diversity. The touchstone of interracial comity had to decide which of the two was desirable. In other words, difference or sameness assumed importance only to the extent that either helped forestall interracial strife. Buck thought that equality through diversity was fine and desirable. For her, difference was not intrinsically harmful. But in reality, diversity engendered tribal animosity and often turned into hierarchy. Therefore, her thinking unfolded, equality through uniformity emerged as the best and most practical policy. This was in essence a variant of traditional assimilationism, not dissimilar in its logical structure to the Americanization movement of the 1910s and 1920s – only more radical. It was founded on the premise that humankind shared a certain basic identity despite sharp differences on the surface. These visible differences were not only illusory, that is, cognitive errors. They were also detrimental to peace and justice. They tended to make people lose sight of the essential equality and unity underlying different groups and treat other peoples differently than they themselves would rather be treated. And thus, the basic claim of this worldview was at once factual and moral, insofar as it asserted that it reflected the reality more accurately than racism *and* bolstered one's capacity for empathy. Buck took this conventional view in an unconventional direction, however, when she relocated the center for this cognitively and ethically correct understanding of humanity from its traditional homeland, the Occident, to the Orient. In Europe, the birthplace of the Enlightenment, Germans killed Jews and burned synagogues. Jews, on their part, internalized racial antipathy and, like Reinhart, adamantly refused to assimilate, perpetuating the cycle of bondage and vagabondage. In America, supposedly a land free from racial hierarchy, whites lynched Negroes. It was the Chinese, Buck's literary works stressed, who were more egalitarian and color-blind than Euro-Americans. More deeply than any other cultures, Chinese culture appreciated the fundamental sameness of all seemingly different social groups.

As enacted in *Flight into China*, Buck's dream of racial harmony in China tempered her sense of America's (and the West's) natural and moral superiority. Her play held China, not the United States, as a paragon of universal humanism among a host of regimes unable to harmonize their internal racial and cultural divisions. China was the last bulwark against the waves of racism engulfing the world. This Chinese exceptionalism, when pieced together with the previous discussion of Buck's vacillation regarding the embargo question and pacifism, suggests that inclinations characteristic of pacifism such as the distrust of munitions industry and the categorical renunciation of force cannot exhaustively explain her decision, reached about two months after the opening of the play, to oppose the embargo on Japan. The play championed China's oceanic capacity to abolish diversity, thereby warding off racially and culturally motivated violence arising from within. The play at the same time exposed America's and Europe's failure to meld internal differences into a homogeneous and nonhierarchical society, the failure primarily responsible for the world anarchy of the 1930s.[41] Buck's celebration of Chinese melting pot indicates that she thought it was not only unnecessary for but presumptuous of the United States, itself an inadequately democratic nation that still had a lot to gain from the example of racial harmony in China, to aid the Chinese. Given this view of China as the last beacon of hope in a world ravaged by race-motivated aggressions, it was inevitable, regardless of her pacifism, that Buck eventually came out strongly against U.S. involvement in Far Eastern affairs. To her mind, American intervention would not promote democracy against totalitarian aggressors but distract itself from domestic reform.

Buck's fantasy of Chinese melting pot bridged her pro-Chinese literature with her pacifist politics. Chinese guerrillas harassing Japanese invaders that Buck immortalized in her war stories were not America's junior associates in its global war on dictators.[42] They actually offered a model that America must emulate. After listening to the "Four Freedoms" speech in December 1940, she wrote to Roosevelt: "Far too many who long to believe in our leaders are prevented by these two questions as yet unanswered: why is India not a free dominion, if England is a true democracy, and why in the United States do those in authority ignore the oppression by stupid prejudice of a whole race in our nation? Shall those who are to lead us to devote our whole selves to the cause of liberty not even speak out against these grave denials of democracy to a portion of our own peoples?"[43] In an op-ed column written a year later, she condemned America's "lack of principle and action" to a much wider audience, with more causticity and less indulgence: "If the United States is to include subject and ruler peoples, then let us be honest about it and change the Constitution and make it plain that Negroes cannot share the privilege of the white people. True, we would then be totalitarian rather than democratic; but if that is what we want, let us say so and let us tell the Negro so. ... With all the evils that Hitlerism has, at least it has one virtue, that it makes no pretense of loving its fellowman and of wanting all people to be free and equal."[44] The United States was unexceptional in that, like other imperial powers, it had yet to atone for its own original sin of racism. It lacked the vital qualification to ally itself with China.[45]

Buck's unquestioning trust in the superiority of Chinese civilization sometimes led her to a less-than-realistic assessment of the military odds against which the Chinese were fighting. About two weeks after the opening of *Flight into China*, Buck wrote to Roosevelt, commending to his notice a peace proposal issued by Wang Ching-Wei, a recent tergiversator from the Nationalist government proposing a negotiated peace with Japan.[46] Called a traitor, a madman, and worse by the Nationalists and the Communists alike, Wang was installed in Nanjing as "acting president" of the "recognized government" propped up by Japanese generals in early 1940.[47] What China needed from the United States was, Buck miscalculated, not military aid or economic sanction against Japan, but "mediation." Out of step with the analyses of most China hands, Buck's approval of the Wang plan betrayed more than her naiveté. Her decision was guided by her recognition of China's lone qualification as a resilient, dynamic, and egalitarian society and the general depravity of Western powers. In practice, of course, Americans were in a position to proffer moral and material support to China. The instrumental role Buck played in various China relief organizations offers proof that her faith in China's moral and natural superiority seldom led her to overlook the slightest opportunity to send humanitarian aid to China. Nevertheless, this faith, when commingled with her unforgivingly dim view of America's spurious democracy (she was particularly critical of the segregation in the military), compelled her to occupy the same political position as other pacifists and isolationists who reached the same conclusion starting from the different premise – the chauvinistic pretension to America's exceptional probity.

The profoundly private vision buried in the nucleus of Buck's artistic creations was incongruous with their impact outward. This incongruity counsels us to pause. If we want to analyze social energies charged in prewar literary productions, we should be mindful of the hazards and opportunities inherent in such an indirect operation. Buck's influence on the public's attitude toward the plight of the Chinese, if such a slippery quantity can be measured, must have been net positive. Given her unmatched access to the middlebrow consumers of the people's culture, it is safe to say that no single figure contributed more to the gradual gelling of the public sentiment that China's foe might become someday America's. And yet, the course of action that she envisioned for her country swerved away from the direction in which her favorable and sympathetic portraits of the heroic Chinese prodded her readers. This irony is even better appreciated if it is compared to a more unequivocal case like Henry Luce, another mishkid with the power to mold public opinion rivaling Buck's. The man who thought that "I probably gained a too romantic, too idealistic view of America [because of his upbringing among 'good' missionaries in China]" made public statements about the inevitability and desirability of America's global leadership in strict accordance with his innermost conviction. Without hesitation his readers took his statements at their face value. And many of them were impressed, if not enthralled, by his arguments.[48] Straightforward propaganda pieces like Luce's are of historical value because they enable historians to ferret out sources of public sentiments and map out channels of influence. But Buck's politically inspired cultural productions, in a way analogous to Schuyler's and Hemingway's, remind us that a fuller history of the prewar culture must incorporate works of art that preserve suppressed doubts, aborted thoughts, and half-glimpsed wishes that usually could not survive the oversimplifying process required of effective propaganda. As a rule, what we discover in them is a highly personal and often solitary experience that failed to get fully socialized, but such a private complication was as much part of the reality of the prewar culture as were the broad and conventionalized reactions of the masses.

8

The Axis Conquest of Europe I

So here I am, in the middle way, having had twenty years—
Twenty years largely wasted, the years of *l'entre deux guerres*—
Trying to learn to use words, and every attempt
Is a wholly new start, and a different kind of failure
Because one has only learnt to get the better of words
For the thing one no longer has to say, or the way in which
One is no longer disposed to say it....
T. S. Eliot, "East Coker" (1940)

Since the German-Russian division of Poland in September 1939, a noticeable calm had fell over the Continent. Some in the press soon took to calling the new conflict the "Phony War." There were abroad even rumors of early negotiated peace. This false hope was dashed in the spring next year, when Germany carried the conflict across its northern and western borders. The Phony War finally flared into a general conflagration. The Danish government fell within the day, Norway in June. To the west, overrunning the Low Countries, the German troops broke into France. The trapped British Expeditionary Force evacuated at Dunkirk as May turned into June. Ten days later, Italian troops massing behind the Alps pounced on their distressed northern neighbor, and just three days after that the German troops were goose-stepping down the boulevards in Paris. The Battle of Britain began in no time. *Luftwaffe* carried destruction to cities in the hope of bringing the British morale to its knees, but with the improved anti-air weaponry and a regrouped RAF, Britain was to repel the German onslaught. In the Far Eastern theater, Japan hotfoot exploited the weakening grip of the British, French, and Dutch metropoles on their oriental empires. In July, its new cabinet hammered out a strategic guideline that confirmed as its official policy the tightening of the alliance with a triumphant Berlin-Rome axis and a further expansion into Southeast Asia.

The Axis conquest of the Continent threw the American home front into paroxysms of war hysteria. On May 19, Robert Sherwood wrote to

William Allen White that the question confronting the American people was not how to stay out of war but "how to keep war out of *us*."[1] "There is no doubt in my mind that this country is in the most critical situation since we won our independence," Harold Ickes confided to his diary in a burst of hyperbole on May 26. He wondered: "[W]hat we would do if a threat were made, that we knew might be carried out, to bomb Washington and Baltimore and Philadelphia and New York and other cities…?"[2] A wave of febrile nationalism surged over the country. Filling the vacuum left by the government's abstention from public-opinion control, propagandists outside government stepped up their efforts to alert the public to the gravity of the situation. Commenting on one such project aiming to distribute syndicated columns by prominent authors expressing "The 'American Case' as opposed to the Totalitarian or Nazi Case," Hemingway complained to Maxwell Perkins: "There is so much panic and hysteria and shit going around now I don't feel like any flagwaving stuff."[3] If the sudden flare-up of patriotism annoyed Hemingway, it distressed pacifists like Pearl Buck. Plays like Sherwood's *There Shall Be No Night*, which Buck found "so pro-war," fanned the nation's desire to repent its isolationist mistakes and supererogate. Buck told a friend: "It is getting increasingly unpopular already to be against intervention. Dick [her husband, Richard Walsh] and I are both resolved that nothing will change us, however, even though all around us, friends and family are changing."[4] Another Anglophobe, Ezra Pound, had written Buck in January that "I take it from your 'The Patriot' that you object to needless mass murder. I doubt if anyone in American [*sic*] realizes how much trouble was taken to get this war started, and what difficulty the sons of hell are having to keep it going."[5] With Italy, his adopted country, on the verge of entering war on the German side, Pound now unleashed blistering invectives on "Churchill and his gigolos" in an essay that cropped up in a Japanese daily just a week after Mussolini's armies marched into southern France. Pound warned the English-speaking readers of this obscure Japanese newspaper: "There are still Anglomaniacs and usuro-maniacs in America who like us to stick our hands into the fire. For England?"[6]

France fell like a house of cards. Bracing for a likely German invasion across the Channel, London asked Washington for superannuated destroyers in exchange for the lease on British bases in Canada and the Caribbean. The British Empire could fall any day, taking with it free security in the Atlantic that Americans had long come to take for granted. Should the French Navy and the British Navy fall in the German hands, that would thrust the impossible – the German invasion of the Western

Hemisphere – well into the realm of possibility. From spring to summer, the administration made a series of military appropriations requests to Congress. The latter, sorry that they had been too stingy with national defense throughout the 1930s, did not disappoint Roosevelt. A few days after the fall of Paris, Congress quickly passed the Two-Ocean Navy Act, and in early fall, the Selective Training and Service Act became the law of the land. The first peacetime conscription in American history officially put the nation on war footing, more than a year before the actual commencement of hostilities with the Axis powers. The Almanac Singers (Pete Seeger, Woody Guthrie, Lee Hays, and Millard Lampell) released a new antiwar song forthwith:

> It was on a Saturday night and the moon was shining bright
> They passed the conscription bill
> And the people they did say for many miles away
> 'Twas the President and his boys on Capitol Hill.
> CHORUS:
> Oh, Franklin Roosevelt told the people how he felt
> We damned near believed what he said
> He said, "I hate war, and so does Eleanor
> But we won't be safe 'till everybody's dead."[7]

Herewith climaxes our anticipatory history of World War II. Following the Allies' rout on the Continent, the major premises of the national debate underwent an irrevocable change. At contention were no longer questions of *if*: *if* America entered the war; *if* the crisis beyond national borders had any bearing on the survival of the America Way of Life; *if* America's enemies oceans away made attempts on the Western Hemisphere. Narrowly tailored questions over timing and strategies displaced these big conditionals. In the mid-1930s, the "next war" was an enigma into which the intrepid and the timid read their hopes and dreads. A half-decade later, that future took definite shape. Rumors, predictions, and imaginings met facts. The limelight dimmed on prophets while soldiers, generals, and architects of postwar peace made to take center stage.

In this atmosphere of national emergency, the stern and often strident language of "responsible" liberalism gained wide acceptance in the intellectual community. This and the next chapters examine motivating forces behind this new language by looking at activities of its three most visible spokesmen: Archibald MacLeish, Lewis Mumford, and Waldo Frank. Their charge that liberals' irresponsibility was at the root of world anarchy and America's military and spiritual underpreparedness shines a bright light on some lingering impediments that Americans, especially those of liberal persuasion, had to manage before embracing a new global responsibility that circumstances had devolved upon their republic.

The Backlash: Democracy without Liberalism?

By the late 1930s, "liberalism" came to connote two partially contradictory meanings.[8] In *Liberalism and Social Action* (1935), John Dewey traced the evolution of the term's meanings:

> Gradually a change came over the spirit and meaning of liberalism. It came surely, if gradually, to be disassociated from the *laissez faire* creed and to be associated with the use of governmental action for aid to those at economic disadvantage and for alleviation of their conditions. In this country, save for a small band of adherents to earlier liberalism, ideas and policies of this general type have virtually come to define the meaning of liberal faith.[9]

This distinction was hardly lost on prewar critics of liberalism. But when they began singling out liberalism as the main culprit for the unchecked growth of totalitarianism abroad, they extracted a common definitive thread that ran through these two forms of liberal impulse and gave this extraction a catchy and tendentious name–irresponsibility. In this term of universal opprobrium prewar critics of liberalism sought to imprison a spontaneous philosophy that had always controlled the liberal mindset: the optimistic faith, prevalent among cultural and intellectual elites in the previous three decades or longer, in the betterment of human and social well-being through rational introspection, public enlightenment, and social planning. On September 1, 1939, Reinhold Niebuhr wrote in his diary: "The liberals with their simple ideas of progress, through education – how wrong they have been!"[10] This exclamation summed up the dominant sentiment that governed much of the critique of liberalism appearing at that time. The self-styled "responsibles" held that their touching cheerfulness led liberals to neglect certain tragic constants like aggression, violence, and destruction in the politics of nation-states. But rooted in the deepest stratum of human constitution, they contended, *animus dominandi* could not be wished away by the pious incantation of liberal prayers. The liberal neglect of this species-specific (animals, the responsible liberals pointed out, exhibited more ethical and cooperative dispositions than did humans) penchant for irrational cruelty was fatally irresponsible, went their typical allegation.

This sanctimonious parole of "responsibility" did not suddenly spring out of the tense political atmosphere of 1940. It gained strength in tandem with the gradual emergence of illiberalism, which was in turn part of the prewar revival of religious sensibilities. Attacks on liberalism, in other words, reflected the broader attacks on secularism. Throughout the lead-up to World War II, the American perspective on the world crisis took on an increasingly religious complexion. The following comment by Anne O'Hare McCormick crystallized the nation's heightened religious temper: "The present war is fought for many ends. It is fought on various fronts with new methods. In a way, it is a war too big to fight, at least with military weapons, for the reason that its fundamental issue cannot be resolved on a battlefield, and everybody knows it. In the broadest sense it is a religious issue."[11] Those in the government did not scruple to inject religious overtones into the cacophonous debates. The Four Freedoms that Roosevelt said he would like to see prevail "everywhere in the world" pointedly included freedom of worship. The administration designated September 8, 1940 as "Day of Prayer for Peace," and the commander-in-chief personally urged "the people of the United States, of all creeds and denominations, to pray on that day, in their churches or at their homes, on the high seas or wherever they may be, beseeching the Ruler of the universe to bless our republic, to make us reverently grateful for our heritage and firm in its defense, and to grant to this land and to the troubled world a righteous, enduring peace."[12] In his message to the Christian Endeavor Convention meeting in Atlantic City in July 1941, Roosevelt declared that Americans must "work and pray for the establishment of an international order in which the spirit of Christ shall rule." "Let us," he said, "unite in labor and in prayer to hasten its coming."[13] Three months later, Roosevelt told the nation that the government had recently obtained the German Reich's secret plan to outlaw all religions in the event it successfully conquered the Western Hemisphere. Given Germany's avowed hostility to Christian civilization, Hitler's war was no less religious than territorial. At a meeting with foreign mission organizations in January 1940, Roosevelt reportedly said: "I was one of those foolish persons who used not to believe in foreign missions. I now see that it is an all-important task of the Church, if the world is to be made peaceful."[14]

In reading these statements, the question of sincerity must be taken seriously, particularly so when Roosevelt was their issuer. But Adolf Berle at the State Department, for one, did not feel that Roosevelt's consistent characterization of war aims in religious terms and his diagnosis of the spiritual roots of the global crisis were not entirely contrived for public consumption. During the Christmas season of 1939, Berle confided to his diary that the "real reason [for Roosevelt's proposal to send Myron C. Taylor, the special envoy to Vatican] is something more than diplomatic. The President is convinced that there is something more than merely mechanics wrong with Europe. Somehow or other we have to tap the underlying philosophical necessities of the situation."[15] In a letter to Pope Pius XII drafted by Berle and corrected by Roosevelt, the president's conviction was much in evidence: "[O]nly by friendly association between the seekers of light and the seekers of peace everywhere can the forces of evil be overcome."[16]

Unsurprisingly, this solemn atmosphere emboldened religious thinkers to attack secularism and the liberal worldview back of it. Never entirely reconciled to liberals' secular pragmatism, Catholicism flexed its intellectual muscles. Although culture, business, and politics in America were still dominated by Protestants, by the prewar years, Catholic political theory had entered one of the most energetic periods in its entire history. Catholics' increasing political clout as a crucial member of the New Deal coalition no doubt energized Catholic intellectuals. But the more proximate cause of this Catholic insurgency was the wartime influx of European thinkers, such as German Catholics Waldemar Gurian and Götz Briefs and exiles from France such as Yves R. Simon and Jacques Maritain.[17] Two important secularized Jews with Thomist sympathies, Mortimer Adler and Walter Lippmann, helped along.[18] These writers, all in close association with the new journal Gurian founded at the University of Notre Dame, *Review of Politics*, collectively designed during the prewar years an impressive system of ideas. First, Catholic theory of democracy faulted liberalism for its anarchic, nonconformist individualism. In order to manage the twin problems of depression and war, the theory went, the modern individual must be embedded in overlapping communities of varying sizes (family, tribe, church, town, and so on). Second, Catholics charged that in the liberal society the state and the individual confronted each other without mediation, which made governance and representation irrational and volatile. By bolstering mediating communal units, Americans must turn this two-dimensional structure into an organic hierarchy. Third, these Catholic critics denied the liberal belief that social organization did not require authority because the individual could self-rule. On the contrary, they held, the individual would be helpless without guidance from authority figures in a variety of small and large communities to which it belonged. And fourth, they insisted on the limits of the rule of law and the necessity of the rule of man. The decision over what was best for the community and the decision over practical strategies to achieve that common good were prudential, that is, they had to be both ethically and epistemically correct. And since these decisions must face a complex of unpredictable conditions, the decision-making process could never be codified legalistically. Ultimately, in all sorts of communities, someone possessing integrity and wisdom must be invested with the authority to make final decisions. Although these profoundly antiliberal arguments were usually presented in a dense and technical language of neo-Thomism, during the closing years of the prewar period they exerted strong influence on secular critics of liberalism.[19]

Meanwhile, the backlash against liberalism was also gathering momentum among recovering modernists in Protestantism. In the pessimistic and desperate climate of post–Great War Europe, there arose neo-orthodoxy, a new theological school of thought that rediscovered Augustinian doctrines that optimistic moderns would rather forget, such as the sinfulness of human nature and the absolute transcendence of God from culture and society. During the interwar decades, this new theology quickly crossed the ocean and provoked the liberal clergy in America to take a sober measure of the efficacy of human reason. By the mid-1930s, dour murmurs were issuing from ex-modernists, including Henry P. Van Dusen, Francis Miller, Reinhold Niebuhr, Henry Sloan Coffin, Justin Wroe Nixon, and John C. Bennett. With the approach of Word War II, the critique of liberalism by these Protestant realists grew shrill, culminating with the 1941 launch of Niebuhr's interventionist journal *Christianity and Crisis*. In words dripping with condescension, these hardboiled theologians skewered the Panglossian and effete pacifism of their fellow liberal Christians. They wanted to bust the myth of national innocence, they said, for Americans' coyness with their country's preponderant power stemmed from a holier-than-thou exceptionalism. America was a normal and sinful nation like any others, Protestant realists asserted, and so it should not be ashamed of involvement in great power politics. Power, which was the coefficient of freedom, was indeed dangerous. Motives behind the exercise of power were always mixed. Consequences of that exercise were always unpredictable. But it was irresponsible of America to wash hands of power politics unilaterally. If power could be misused, it could be also bent to good works. The responsible thing for America to do then was to deploy its supernal puissance, hoping for the best. If it later arrived that power *was* misused, then America would do its utmost to right its wrongs. That was also part of being responsible. And anyway, divine providence would measure the sins of the warmhearted on different scales.[20]

The critics of liberalism I am here lumping together under the moniker "responsible liberals" were a motley and fractious crew. At the core of this heterogeneous group were Protestant realists and neo-Thomists and their

secular allies such as Harvard political scientist William Y. Elliott, Mortimer Adler, Robert Hutchins, Walter Lippmann, Archibald MacLeish,
Lewis Mumford, and Waldo Frank. This core was then surrounded by a
fairly wide penumbra of allied journalists, commentators, and pundits who
picked up the language and posturing of responsible liberalism as much for
its sensationalism and newsworthiness as out of personal convictions.
Obviously, these thinkers and writers disagreed over a variety of social
and doctrinal issues. Internal harmony was lacking. And yet, these responsible liberals still constituted a distinct cohort, to the extent that they were
united in their profound animosity toward the common enemy. Their
attacks largely concentrated around two allegedly most fatal weaknesses of
liberalism: pluralism and instrumentalism. Liberals had traditionally
claimed that the clash of competing interests was not only inevitable but
also could be eased and soothed through bargaining to the mutual profit of
all concerned. Monism would be bad for democracy and capitalism.
Pluralism would be beneficial for everyone. In the 1930s, however, the
increasingly restive proletariat challenging the liberal economy (free
market) at home and the rise of undemocratic powers defying liberal
internationalism (free trade) abroad took a sharp exception to fundamental
assumptions beneath the liberal consensus, including pluralism itself. Not
all opinions, not all interests, after all, were welcome to the political
process, particularly those that incited people to intolerance of social
diversity. Some extreme demagogues and intransigent interest groups
threatening the process of negotiation and compromise had to be suppressed peremptorily. In short, the principle of liberal pluralism could be
extended to all political positions but those aiming to abolish that
principle. In the late 1930s, the realization that the liberal tolerance of
plurality had limits led many traditional liberals to acknowledge willy-nilly
that pluralism had reposed on the supremacy of liberalism in the domestic
and international arenas during the belle epoch. For so many years one
could celebrate diversity and champion conflict precisely because there was
no real diversity or conflict in the ideological order.

   The depression and the approach of war also highlighted the possibility
that liberals could not uphold liberalism for instrumentalist reasons.
Instrumentalism was a science of means wherein ends were always given.
It made no pretense to guiding people through the process of selecting
ends. The praiseworthiness of ends fell outside its purview. Instrumentalists therefore could not ground their defense of liberalism on its intrinsic
attributes. They could support liberalism, only to the extent that it
conduced to the end they all desired, that is, the democratic goal of

improving the material and spiritual welfare of the greatest number of citizens. Yet throughout the depression years, it was becoming unclear whether liberalism promised, let alone delivered, democratic fruits. As far as their rhetoric was to be believed, Fascists, Bolsheviks, and Nazis did not espouse any deviant goals for their political communities. America's enemies all professed that they aspired to be the government of the people, by the people, for the people. Actually, in the international war of words that preceded the shooting war, they turned the tables on liberal democracies. Dictators said that their national communities were more "democratic." Mussolini claimed that Italian Fascism realized a "true democracy." Goebbels asserted that the Third Reich was "the most ennobled form of a modern democratic state." Stalin declared the Soviet constitution of 1936 "the only constitution that is democratic to the limit."[21] "Curiously enough," Thurman Arnold, soon to be appointed to head the antitrust division of the Justice Department, observed in 1937, "in all this holy war against Communism and Fascism to make the world safe for our prevailing divinity, we find very little spiritual conflict about the principles of democracy. Democracy was accepted as a political fact, not as something to be chosen or rejected."[22] Totalitarians argued that they invented ideas and principles ("the dictatorship of the proletariat," *Volksgemeinschaft*) that enabled them to realize a polity more democratic than the traditional democracies based on liberal principles. Liberal instrumentalists did not feel obligated to refute such claims until the prewar years, thanks to a historic coincidence between liberalism and democracy and the misleading impression this coincidence created, namely that liberty axiomatically produced democratic consequences. Since the late nineteenth century, the instrumentalist justification had sufficed for liberals because liberal principles and institutions (individualism, civil liberties, pluralism, compromise, competition, and so on) did seem to benefit the nation democratically. Manifestly, even during the halcyon days of the American belle epoch, that was not the case at all for vast numbers of citizens such as the 12 million descendents of slaves or the economically exploited. Yet voices of the dispossessed were sufficiently disciplined by Jim Crow or the legal system protecting the sanctity of private property and free enterprise to sustain the illusion of harmony between liberalism and democracy. During the depression decade, however, the crescendos of illiberal claims to democratic achievements shook up liberal complacency. Traditional liberals, who used to think that they could justify their espousal of liberalism instrumentally, were now faced with the question whether they should practice their preaching and follow their line of argument to its logical conclusion: the abandonment of liberalism, which had proved not as good at increasing the general welfare of society as previously supposed.

In genesis, then, responsible liberalism was a negative movement. It was defined more by what it wanted to pull away from than by what it wanted to push toward. Born in the last two decades of the previous century like their irresponsible friends and colleagues, a clear majority of liberal hawks were reared on the toothsome milk of cheery progressivism. This common upbringing meant that when the responsible liberals such as Mumford, MacLeish, Adler, and Niebuhr assailed the irresponsible variant of liberalism, they were actually attacking their own younger selves. Contempt commingled with remorse and self-disgust therefore crept into much of the abuse that these responsible, tough-minded liberals heaped on the heresy of naïve liberalism. Having been mugged by the harsh reality of liberal powerlessness in the face of the depression and the war, these grownups renounced their shameful past and redirected the full measure of their self-hatred against the annoyingly innocent peers who remained unmoved in their faith in liberalism. Their extraordinary animus gave away their unacknowledged complicity in the problem.

Responsible liberalism was also a negative movement for another, more mundane reason. Liberal hawks spent more ammunition attacking soft-headed liberals at home than their external enemy, dictatorships abroad. Clearly, it was not liberalism, whether of an irresponsible kind or not, but totalitarianism that menaced the American Way of Life. Totalitarianism deserved at least as much criticism as liberalism. But the self-evidence of the case made it less urgent and less interesting to attack Nazis, Fascists, and Communists. So, the responsible liberals' pent-up frustration with America's hesitation found a vent in their hot denunciation of well-meaning liberals, comprising a still-solid majority in intellectual circles at that time. These critics could have made more constructive use of their polemical energy. For example, they could have analyzed how the end of optimistic liberalism corresponded with the emergence of a new totalitarian society where political ideas dictated economic rules. Actually, many European émigré jurists, sociologists, economists, and psychologists who were also critical of nineteenth-century liberalism (Karl Loewenstein, Franz Neumann, Friedrich Pollock, Emil Lederer, Karl Polanyi, Joseph Schumpeter, Erich Fromm, Eric Voegelin, Arnold Brecht, Albert Salomon, and Peter Drucker) began doing just that around the same time.[23] But for such a global analysis, these liberal warhawks were ill-prepared in training and lacked motivation.

They also could have reserved their venomous philippics for another enemy of liberalism, those reactionaries opposing the New Deal, "liberals" in Dewey's first sense who clung to the doctrine of *laissez faire* and *moins gouverner*. These villains, however, did not present a target worthy of serious criticism. After all is said and done, the responsible liberals, including neo-Thomists and Protestant realists, were liberals in Dewey's second sense. That is, they were progressives, no matter how reactionary they occasionally sounded when discoursing on noneconomic issues. Hence they never doubted that the old variant of economic liberalism had already been discredited by the free market's inability to self-adjust during the depression years. Any critical ammunition used to impugn this bankrupt theory would be a great waste. By contrast, liberalism construed as an innocent faith in social reform and world peace through rational planning, legal norms, and enlightened debate was still widely popular among writers and intellectuals. The responsibles understood better than anyone else the irresistible allure of this faith because they themselves had been captive to it until recently. Absence of ideological enemies deserving refutation, their lingering shame and outrage (they had been shown the fool), their need to overcompensate, their conviction that liberals should know better, and their hope that optimistic liberals were still open to persuasion – these mixed feelings and considerations impelled MacLeish, Mumford, and Frank to a frenzied assault on liberalism.

MacLeish: Responsible and Dangerous

Soon after the outbreak of the new European war, Roosevelt appointed this prolific poet with a Harvard law degree the new Librarian of Congress. His nomination originally came from his Harvard mentor and new Supreme Court Justice, Felix Frankfurter, who had already managed to place in the sprawling empire of federal bureaucracy his prized protégés such as Tom Corcoran, Benjamin Cohen, Nathan Margold, Felix Cohen, and David Lilienthal. Given his instinct for self-promotion and his diligently cultivated network of well-placed liberal elites in the East Coast establishment, it was perhaps a matter of time that MacLeish joined this hejira of young lawyers to the only town in a depression-era America that could give full scope to their brainpowers, idealism, and fascination with power. Until the United States officially entered war, MacLeish would put to good use his marginal position in Washington and badger his way into the center of the national debate over the responsibility of liberals in times of national emergency.

Some unkind critics may charge that MacLeish's poetry suffered from excessive derivativeness, from signs of trying too hard to appear au courant. Edmund Wilson concluded his thorough and sadistic parody, "The Omelet of A. MacLeish" (1939), with these lines:

> *A clean and clever lad*
> > *who is doing*
> > > *his best*
> > > > *to get on...*[24]

Many of his poems surely betrayed his insecurity, his appropriation so blatant. Withal, MacLeish's sin of unoriginality should also be measured by his wish to be the tribune of his generation. As he sang in "Sentiments for a Dedication" (1929),

> I speak to my own time
> To none other
> I say Remember me Remember me this one rhyme
> I say Remember me among you in that land my brothers[25]

He became, by choice as much as by temperament, an echo of "my own time." During the last war, like so many Ivy Leaguers of the time (he was at Yale), MacLeish interpreted American involvement in idealistic Wilsonian terms and served in France enthusiastically first as a volunteer ambulance driver and then as a field artillery commander. The realities of war, however, soon embittered him (his brother, a pilot, was killed in action). During the postwar decade, joining other lieutenants of the Lost Generation in Paris and the Riviera, MacLeish swung to art-for-art's-sake aestheticism. As the Jazz Age drew to a close, he repatriated along with most of his fellow expatriate writers, only to witness his country plunge into the abyss of economic depression. Love of politics returned to MacLeish, as he began working as an editor for *Fortune*. Alongside such diverse talents reaching their primes as James Agee, Margaret Bourke-White, Robert Cantwell, Whittaker Chambers, John Chamberlain, Walker Evans, and Dwight Macdonald, MacLeish wrote a wealth of copy for columns addressing New Deal policies.[26] Unlike some of his more sensitive brethren who thought their creative energies were sucked up by Henry Luce's media empire, MacLeish remained a prolific poet all along. With seemingly preternatural ease he kept publishing collections of poems, librettos, dramas, and radio plays that probed into first the economic catastrophe at home and then soon the menace of foreign dictators.[27] When the Soviets launched the Popular Front in 1935, MacLeish joined the bandwagon with characteristic celerity. With other fellow travelers like Herman Schulmin, Ernest Hemingway, and John Dos Passos he founded the antifascist film production venture, Contemporary Historians, through which he helped finance *The Spanish Earth* and *The 400 Million*.[28] In 1937, as the world's attention was trained on the civil war in Spain, MacLeish stood shoulder to shoulder with Earl Browder as a principal organizer of the Second Congress of the League of American Writers at Carnegie Hall. After a screening of *The Spanish Earth*, MacLeish and Hemingway got on their soapbox. "Fascism is a lie told by bullies," Hemingway lambasted. "The War is ours," MacLeish declaimed. Soon, however, the precarious antifascist alliance between MacLeish and the Communists unraveled, reflecting the general disillusionment with Stalinism among his generation between 1937 and 1939. The Nazi-Soviet Pact in the fall of 1939 officially annulled MacLeish's common-law alliance with Soviet-led antifascism, which anyway came about at an opportune moment. Shortly after, Frankfurter sounded him out about the opening at the Library of Congress. At forty-eight, Archibald MacLeish went to Washington.

His swelling interest in international affairs during the prewar years also inspired him to a new theory of poetry. MacLeish was one of those poets who could not poetize without intellectualizing. Even in the 1920s, when he was under the spell of high modernism, his poems were seldom without theory or message. One famous piece from this period, "Ars Poetica" (1926), putatively about craft and poetics, began with one prescription ("A poem should be palpable and mute") and ended with another ("A poem should not mean,/ But be").[29] Didacticism argued against itself, even while aestheticism argued against itself. The events of the 1930s tempered his aestheticism. Modern poetry should be like "public speech," went a new preaching, which he expounded in a series of writings on poetics and politics. Pioneers of modernism, Pound and Eliot, revolted against highfalutin mannerism of Victorian poetry, in order to revitalize poetry by restoring demotic voice to it. But their achievements did not effect a clean break with that which they revolted against. The task for public-minded poets of the 1930s was to extend this movement until it finally realizes its ideals such as public engagement, openness, maturity, and realism.[30] The 1930s, a season of political passion, saw the meeting of private and public experiences:

> The single individual, whether he so wishes or not, has become part of a world which contains also Austria and Czechoslovakia and China and Spain. The victories of tyrants and the resistance of peoples halfway round

the world are as near to him as the ticking of the clock on the mantel. What happens in his morning paper happens in his blood all day, and Madrid, Nanking, Prague, are names as close to him as the names by which he counts his dearest losses.

The traditional poet, a mooning soul-searcher preoccupied with lyric trivia and precious reveries, could not rise to the challenges posed by the new age of iron. The new bard, the new herald bringing news to the culture and the mainstream, had to join the crowds in the streets. A fully realized modern poetry must be equal to the urgent task of giving form to the new type of experience where public events met the individual with the nearness of private feelings. And that would call for, MacLeish ominously predicted, "the responsible and dangerous language of acceptance and belief."[31]

MacLeish was talking about poetics, not homiletics. But more often than not, he would put to test his new theory of the "responsible and dangerous language" not in his poems (his poetic production dwindled to almost nil during this period) but in patriotic homilies he delivered in his self-assigned capacity as Roosevelt's propaganda czar. Nine days after the onset of the German spring offensive, MacLeish delivered a hard-hitting speech, titled "The Irresponsibles," at the meeting of the American Philosophical Society in New York. Calling college professors in the audience "irresponsibles" to their face, his speech was at once an incendiary *j'accuse* directed at academics' anemic reaction to the plight of democracies overseas and a self-righteous command to repent their guilt. In this speech, MacLeish rehashed and reinforced an argument that had been more or less latent in his previous criticism of fascism. The conflict between dictatorships and America's allies in Europe, he said, was "spiritual" or "cultural," as distinguished from exclusively economic or purely political. The coming war with totalitarian systems would involve "the defense of culture – the defense truly, and in the most literal terms, of civilization as men have known it for the last two thousand years."[32] In this new *Weltanschauungskrieg*, therefore, not statesmen and policy makers, but the guardians of spiritual values, namely the very audience whom he was addressing, had to shoulder the main burden.

The root cause of the spiritual torpidity of the American professoriate, MacLeish went on to venture, was in the partition of the kingdom of learning between "two castes" of specialists – scholars and writers. Scholars, with their institutional base in the modern research university, modeled their inquiry in accordance with various scientific canons such as objectivity and value-neutrality. The cult of these ideals engendered an intellectual atmosphere in which final judgment was indefinitely deferred and the relativistic view of truth fomented disagreements. And ultimately this permissive and pluralistic culture periled national security, for what. What the nation needed was a snap judgment, a quick identification of the enemy by the use of cultural knowledge and spiritual intuition. If scholars followed the example of scientists, MacLeish continued, writers affected the attitude of painters. The painter's method required cool detachment from the object of representation. Painters saw "the world as a god sees it – without morality, without care, without judgment."[33] This painterly affectation conveniently concealed American writers' cowardice and callousness toward moral and human crises abroad.

This speech marked an opening salvo in a war of attrition between MacLeish and the "Irresponsibles." In late May, the British Expeditionary Force were evacuating at Dunkirk while Hitler's armies converged on Paris. Against this menacing backdrop MacLeish dropped another bombshell at the annual meeting of the American Association for Adult Education. His address, entitled "Post-War Writers and Pre-War Readers," alleged that pacifism fatally infected the American youth across college campuses. The morale of the nation wilted because young people took a cynical view of the civilizational clash between totalitarianism and democracy. College students' lack of the "moral conviction that fascism is evil and that a free society of free men is worth fighting for" had a much deeper source than could be eradicated by some lectures on geopolitics and world trade. The real source of their indifference lay in their loss of faith in "all slogans, all tags – even all words."[34] Lofty abstractions such as "freedom" and "democracy" now embarrassed young Americans.

This diagnosis was followed by the most controversial part of the speech – his allegation that "the post-war writers" lured these gullible children down the unpatriotic path of moral lethargy. Gratuitous as this theory may seem, MacLeish was able to dress it up with fairly damning citations gleaned from a host of antiwar novels and the historical scholarship on propaganda campaigns during the Great War. While drafting the speech, he compiled two long lists. One listed famous antiwar novels, both American and European, that painted a disillusioning picture of the Great War: Henri Barbusse's *Under Fire* (1916; English translation in 1926), John Dos Passos's *Three Soldiers* (1921), E. E. Cummings's *The Enormous Room* (1922), Laurence Stallings's *Plumes* (1924), William Faulkner's *Soldier's Pay* (1926), Ford Madox Ford's *Last Post* (1928), Richard Aldington's *Death of a Hero* (1929), and Hemingway's *A Farewell to Arms* (1929), to name but a few prominent entries.[35] The other list covered such classics of the revisionist historiography as Harry Elmer Barnes's *The Genesis of the*

World War (1929), Walter Millis's *Road to War* (1935), and Charles Callan Tansill's *America Goes to War* (1938).

In his actual speech MacLeish singled out Barbusse, Andreas Latzko (a Hungarian pacifist writer), Dos Passos, Ford, Hemingway, Erich Maria Remarque, and Aldington as the prime culprits for the emasculation of young Americans. Dos Passos and Hemingway, MacLeish's collaborators at Contemporary Historians, had the special honor of having long excerpts quoted from their novels. What those postwar writers wrote "was disastrous as education for a generation which would be obliged to face the threat of fascism in its adult years." "Perhaps," he suggested, "writers, having so great a responsibility to the future, must not weaken the validity of the Word even when the deceptions of the Word have injured them." "Perhaps," he ventured a stage further, "the luxury of the complete confession, the uttermost despair, the farthest doubt should be denied themselves by writers living in any but the most orderly and settled times."[36]

These two hard-hitting speeches ("Mr. MacLeish's brave mea culpa," as headlined by *The New York Times*), delivered in swift succession at a time Americans were terrorized by the apparent invincibility of Hitler's armies, raised a furor.[37] Wise men weighed in. Robert Sherwood, who had read the draft of "The Irresponsibles" and showed it to Elmer Rice and Maxwell Anderson, wrote to MacLeish, expressing solidarity and bewailing the incurable stupidity of pacifists and isolationists:

> This is so terribly true. ... When I wrote the play "Abe Lincoln in Illinois," I did so primarily for the purpose of expressing (in your words) "the conviction that there are final things for which democracy will fight." Lincoln, it seemed to me, was the supreme non-isolationist in his essential faith. However, time and again, people writing approvingly of my play, said "It teaches a great lesson in Americanism—that we can sustain our democracy by minding our own business and keeping out of Europe's wars." Discouraging is a faint word for it.[38]

While himself a radical relativist suspicious of any forms of dogmatic thinking, philosopher-politician T. V. Smith at the University of Chicago, now serving his first and only Congressional term, read "The Irresponsibles" into the Congressional Record on June 21.[39] Ralph Barton Perry, a disciple of William James now organizing a series of morale-raising events on Harvard campus, lauded MacLeish, writing that "I much admire your Nation article on 'The Irresponsibles.' Certainly the negations of the youth of to-day are largely the product of the irresponsible a-moralism of their elders."[40] From Cambridge, Massachusetts, also responded Bernard DeVoto, who was taking part in the local branch of the Committee to

Defend America through Aids to the Allies. DeVoto reported that the "uproar that followed your double-barreled attack washed round the greater part of my ten thousand miles." Joining MacLeish's campaign for moral rearmament of spineless college students, DeVoto wrote, he was going to borrow some of MacLeish's ideas for a keynote address he was asked to deliver at the annual meeting of the Modern Language Association in December.[41] Editors of *Life* solicited responses from various novelists and historians including those named in MacLeish's address. Dismissing MacLeish's finger-pointing as a symptom of a "very bad conscience," Hemingway trotted out his record of antifascist exploits: "If MacLeish had been at Guadalajara, Jarama, Madrid, Teruel, first and second battles of the Ebro [as Hemingway had], he might feel better." Richard Aldington declared MacLeish's theory that the postwar writers demoralized the prewar readers a "typical highbrow delusion." The delusion of MacLeish's kind should have been more aptly called middlebrow, but no matter. Flattering as MacLeish's attribution of enormous influence to his novel was, Aldington pointed out that "[m]ost people in America have never heard of the writers MacLeish mentions." MacLeish also managed to elicit some hearty nods and enthusiastic plaudits. Maxwell Anderson not only agreed with MacLeish but also took this opportunity to call for the immediate dispatch of military aid to the Allies: "If we do not instantly help the Allies to the fullest possible extent it is likely that we shall have to face a hostile world alone."[42]

Inexplicably, MacLeish passed over *Johnny Got His Gun*. But Dalton Trumbo responded anyway. His comment appeared in the *Life* round-table. The real reason why words like "democracy" and "liberty" ceased to inspire the youth was that facts had exposed them to be a travesty unworthy of sincere worship. In order to make democracy worth fighting for, therefore, it "becomes an immediate imperative for us to broaden our democratic base" through socialist programs.[43] This terse rebuttal was apparently not enough for Trumbo. His 1941 novel *Remarkable Andrew: Being a Chronicle of a Literal Man* features a MacLeish spoof, district attorney Beamish, who spearheads a town-wide witch hunt for pacifists and dissidents. In the court scene where defendant Andrew Long, accused of all kinds of un-American activities, and prosecutor Beamish face off, Trumbo mercilessly burlesques Beamish's penchant for slogans and idealistic abstractions. Long cites solid facts, verifiable dates, and unmistakable numbers. By contrast, Beamish's address to the jury is a gelatinous concoction of emotional symbols (the land of the free, the home of the brave) whose function is not descriptive but purely stimulative. Finding

A Farewell to Arms and *All Quiet on the Western Front* in Long's bookshelf, Beamish, like the Librarian of Congress, requests severe sentence for the "writers who have corrupted him": "In this time of national emergency, we must not be too particular about freedom of the press and speech lest through it we lose all freedom entirely."[44] Beamish's exalted peroration debases itself due to its outrageous verbosity and volubility. Beamish (MacLeish) inadvertently vindicates the younger generation's mistrust of the Word. The youth of the prewar years lost faith in noble slogans for good reason.[45]

The indefatigable MacLeish continued to stump the country down to the eve of Pearl Harbor, mostly harping on the same motifs found in these speeches: the spiritual character of the coming war between totalitarian dictatorships and the United States and how qualities prized as virtues by liberals such as detachment, neutrality, moral relativism, disinterested objectivity, and distrust of fanatic faith sapped the public's morale. "In a struggle which is truly fought, whatever the economic interpreters and the dialectical materialists may say to the contrary, across the countries of the spirit, can those who hold those countries remain neutral?" he demanded everywhere he went.[46]

When not on the speech circuit, MacLeish performed sundry administrative duties at the Library during the day and hobnobbed at night with movers and shakers of the nation's capital, commingling recreation with politicking. Thanks to his exceptional fluency in schmoozing and unerring nose for effective back channels, MacLeish swiftly raised his profile despite the marginal office he held. Frankfurter remained his closest ally, and most of the time MacLeish found himself in the company of hard-charging New Dealers. One night in the spring of 1940, MacLeish hosted a dinner party for Ralph Ingersoll, his former boss at *Fortune* now preparing to launch *PM*, a progressive-interventionist newspaper. In attendance were Frankfurter; another Supreme Court appointee by Roosevelt, William O. Douglas; Attorney General Robert Jackson; Solicitor General Francis Biddle; Secretary of the Interior Harold Ickes; Dean Acheson; Benjamin Cohen, the master draftsman responsible for many of epoch-making New Deal bills; and Tom Corcoran, Ben Cohen's gregarious Irish alter ego.[47] Another dinner MacLeish hosted for Henry Luce was attended by Acheson, Biddle, Frankfurter, Special Assistant to Secretary of War Robert Lovett, Robert Patterson, who was to be promoted to Under Secretary of War in December, and William O. Douglas.[48] Ingersoll, Luce, Acheson, Patterson, Lovett and, Ben Cohen – one gets an intimate glimpse into the East Coast government-press complex.

In the early summer of 1940, these president's men were pessimistic about the chance of British survival, tense about America's preparedness against a possible German attempt on the Western Hemisphere, and all frustrated by Roosevelt's excruciatingly circumspect approach to the isolationist-interventionist debate. Frankfurter, all for a stiffer policy against Germany, was "not really rational these days on the European situation," according to Harold Ickes.[49] Ickes himself had long been the lone foreign policy hard-liner in the cabinet. Robert Jackson cajoled legal experts at the Justice Department to find loopholes, obscure precedents, and creative techniques to legalize various executive actions aimed at aiding the allies that were condemned by Roosevelt's congressional enemies as dictatorial.[50] Under the leadership of new Secretary of War Stimson, Patterson and Lovett were tackling a cluster of extremely complicated problems requiring the surest administrative hands: the British procurement of U.S. armaments, the problem of bottlenecks, the expansion of production capacity, and the creation of a full-fledged Air Corps.[51] The two remaining fixtures in the MacLeish circle, Dean Acheson and Ben Cohen were connected to the Century Group, a Manhattan-based interventionist group comprising Anglophile New Dealers, ministers, businessmen, and journalists. In June and July, this exclusive advocacy group, whose membership included Henry Luce, Robert Sherwood, Lewis Mumford, William Allen White, Francis P. Miller, and Henry Sloan Coffin, was ratcheting up a campaign to convince Roosevelt that Britain was foredoomed unless the United States released its overage destroyers built during the Great War to be deployed by the British in their defense of the Channel. Acheson was soon to be appointed Assistant Secretary of War.[52] Respected as "the lawyer's lawyer" among the wonkish New Dealers, Cohen kept coaxing Roosevelt into leasing overage destroyers to Britain.[53]

MacLeish's self-assigned role was basically that of what one sneering commentator dubbed "the armchair fist-waver," a strategically apoplectic purveyor of patriotic clichés and hortatory banalities.[54] But he sometimes stepped out of his armchair and muscled his way into the decision-making process. His escapades usually ended up adding to Roosevelt's political headaches. Here the Century Group's campaign for the destroyer-for-base deal serves as a good illustration. MacLeish had already surprised his friends, right after Paris fell, by coming out as a strong proponent of the immediate declaration of war on Germany.[55] By late July, using the secret information harvested from a classified British intelligence report that was leaked by the British Embassy and circulated among the members of the

Century Group, MacLeish's former employer Henry Luce was urging Roosevelt to release the superannuated destroyers to the British in exchange for the use of British bases in North America.[56] Concurrently, brandishing the same information, MacLeish was nagging Ickes to persuade Roosevelt to release the destroyers. MacLeish also apprised Ickes of the existence of a "group of writers, radio people and publicists who are eager to go out on a nationwide campaign of education."[57] Among numerous factors that went into the destroyer deal was a political liability to which Roosevelt, running for a third term, could be exposed if his opponent, Wendell Willkie, although himself supportive of aid to the Allies, exploited the issue for political gains.[58] MacLeish sounded out Russell Davenport, his former colleague at *Fortune* who was then working as a campaign manager for Willkie, to see if the latter could give assurance that he would make no public criticism if the administration requested Congress to release the destroyers. In early August, Arthur Krock got wind of this attempted collusion and exposed it in his *New York Times* column.[59]

MacLeish's activities as a rhetorician and an operative help clarify the nature of the connection between cultural symbols and politics in the prewar culture. MacLeish spun a fine and pleasant web of patriotic homilies for pubic consumption, but when he wanted to influence decision makers he took recourse to familiar techniques of the politician: reorienting others' behavior by appeal to the sense of friendship, obligation, hope for future favors, and strategic considerations. MacLeish's switching between two registers of persuasion can be understood to exemplify how power and language interacted. While emotional arguments purveyed by master rhetoricians like MacLeish and Sherwood cumulatively shaped the climate of opinion, many consequential decisions made during the prewar years that dramatically expanded the ambit of America's global commitments were products of strategic thinking shared among a closely knit network of insiders. "Rational" decision makers were not of course entirely immune to the blandishment of cultural symbols, which could anesthetize their inhibitions or radicalize their impulses. These idealistic Machiavellians in government, from Roosevelt downward, were highly literate people who read (many even wrote) books, understood difficult concepts, and appreciated the force of words. But at the same time, homilies supplied by professional rhetoricians often served an expedient explanation for the decision already taken for other – usually political but often military – reasons. Roosevelt's third-term nomination acceptance speech is a perfect example. Roosevelt had made up his mind to run again; he used MacLeish's memorandum to justify the decision he had already made.[60]

Lewis Mumford's Lucid Fanaticism

In retracing the notable episodes in MacLeish's offensive against irresponsible liberals, I placed special emphasis on one facet of his thinking – his vaguely religious view that the new type of war America was about to enter was fought over the "countries of the spirit" as much as over physical territories. It is important to understand why he did not specify what he meant by the "sprit" of democracy. His spread-eagle perorations were always short on specifics and long on ringing slogans, feel-good bromides, and memorable one-liners. As other adept manipulators of popular symbols like Trumbo and Irving Berlin well understood, banality was exactly MacLeish's point. MacLeish's writings on democracy and liberalism from this period, although many were later printed in popular magazines and some read into the Congressional record, were usually designed as public addresses to various audiences. And those original contexts dictated his method: he was determined to be rhetorical, not analytical, not even communicative. He used language kinetically, not informatively. His chief task was to move people, in the sense of influencing the mental states of his listeners, producing a desired disposition in them, and stimulating them to action. How his words sounded was more important to him than what those words meant. Instead of enlightening, he aimed to scare, browbeat, flatter, or incite. By reacting angrily to an outrageous spectacle MacLeish made of himself, his mockers paid tribute to his finely honed sense for publicity.

MacLeish also had as many sympathizers. Among the most active of them were Lewis Mumford and Waldo Frank. These two militant anti-fascists had been closely associated with *The New Republic* in their capacity as contributing editors throughout the 1930s. But when the war came in September 1939 they realized that the pro-war *New Republic* of 1917 was no more. By late December, despairing of the timorous foreign policy stance of this weekly, they decided to submit a joint resignation. That would, they calculated, force the editors to publish their letters of protest.[61] They had their wish. Urging reconsideration, editor-in-chief Bruce Bliven proposed to Mumford and Frank that the magazine provide ample space so that they could air their grievances. Frank and Mumford accepted this challenge, with an understanding that they would anyway resign in the event that the magazine showed no sign of remorse for its anti-British bias.[62] As the German armies swept through Western Europe, Mumford's "The Corruption of Liberalism" appeared in the April 29 issue, followed by Frank's "Our Guilt in Fascism" in the next issue. The editorial responses that accompanied each article critically pointed out that those two self-styled antifascists were more like crypto-fascists encouraging the emulation of the enemy's method.[63] Mumford and Frank promptly resigned and their letters of resignation were published in the following issues. Two more disaffected liberals abandoned their irresponsible confrères and joined the swelling rank of responsibles.

Mumford's "The Corruption of Liberalism" was a document of extraordinary intensity that bordered on fanaticism. At once a manifesto, a religious confession, and a treatise on political economy, the essay marked the culmination of the author's long career as one of the most extreme firebrands of democratic militancy. A polymath whose fields of interest spanned literacy criticism, architecture, and urban sociology, Mumford had always been an ardent nationalist, in the sense that his love for America as a land of special promise always motivated his investigations. The fierce controversies over domestic and international crises throughout the 1930s only deepened this preexisting tendency. Mumford's first call for the declaration of war on Germany came early, even before the Munich Crisis. His "Call to Arms" appeared in *The New Republic* in May 1938, in which Mumford exhorted his readers: "To arms! Gather together your strength and prepare for action. Strike first against fascism; and strike hard. But strike."[64] Ever since, Mumford took it upon himself to convert the public from pacifism to a new religion of hard-boiled liberalism.

There was something obsessive about Mumford's reaction to the approach of war. His acute distress over the international situation and what he saw as America's irresponsible cowardice almost shattered his nerves. By the spring of 1940, he was suffering from nightmares of "an German invasion of England, and of face-to-face confrontation with Hitler." A year later, Mumford would purchase a rifle so that he could lead an American resistance movement should the United States come under German occupation.[65] Numerous letters of remonstrance and denunciation he fired off to his liberal friends during this period, all displaying a characteristic mixture of pompous rectitude and calculated offensiveness, show how the slightest sign of demurral on the part of his correspondents drove him to the brink of insane fury. Because his liberal friends mostly refused to take a pro-war stance, his feeling of isolation mounted. His language grew livid and vituperative. If his friends and associates disagreed with his spiritual analyses, he did not hesitate to impugn their patriotism. When the American Artists' Congress announced a resolution for complete neutrality, Mumford dispatched his letter of resignation: "I not merely disagree with this policy: but I repudiate it with complete contempt for the reasons and the motives and the political groups behind it. Your statement might have been written by Father Coughlin or Earl Browder or Goebbels. It shows that the members now in control of the Congress are, intentionally or passively, the allies of fascism and the enemies of democracy."[66] When he chanced on a short passage of endorsement by Frank Lloyd Wright in an isolationist pamphlet, Mumford terminated their two-decade friendship with this letter:

> It is hard to lose a friend by his physical death; but it is even more painful to lose him by his spiritual death: above all at such a time as this, when one looked to Frank Lloyd Wright to be a leader of the fight for freedom, wherever it might be threatened, and a defender of democracy, in every country where men still were faithful to the ideals of humanity. Instead, you advocate a slave's safety, and a coward's withdrawal.
>
> You shrink into your selfish ego; you are willing to abandon to their terrible fate the conquered, the helpless, the humiliated, the suffering: you carefully refrain from offending, if only by a passing reference, those Nazi overlords to whom in your heart you, like Lindbergh, have already freely given the fruits of victory. You dishonor all the generous impulses you once ennobled. Be silent! Lest you bring upon yourself some greater shame.[67]

It is impossible today to recapture the seriousness with which these responsible liberals wrote these censures and instigations, how exhausting their thankless labor was, and how personally they took what were after all foreign wars raging in distant lands. But their correspondences indicate that their not so infrequent loss of self-control was quite unfeigned. They were, they felt with vain self-pity, victims of their own perspicacity. They belonged to a band of persecuted soothsayers battering away the thick foreheads of the American Pharisees with their prophesies of doom.

"Call to Arms" was soon expanded into a full-length book, *Men Must Act* (1939). Throughout the book, as its hectoring title left no doubt, Mumford commanded complacent Americans to take action against fascism without delay. Imputing a conspiratorial design for world conquest to Germany, Japan, and Italy, he argued that "these fascist countries are no longer simply political states: they are states of mind. ... As a propulsive system of beliefs, fascism aims at world dominion."[68] New technologies, most notably airplane, brought this ancient dream of world conquest within reach for modern dictators. "Isolationism assumes that the United States is today what England was in the nineteenth century: a tight little island." But in fact, the "mere potentiality of German or Italian bombing squadrons, making their way to the cities of the Atlantic seaboard will, within a few years, have a *momentous political* effect."[69] In a psychological sense, "the airplane has done away with geographic isolation: above all, it has done away with psychological isolation." In the new age when the military conflict turned as much on psychological brinksmanship as on the marshalling of soldiers on the battlefield, the strategic advantages lay with the country that could credibly threaten a devastating first strike against the enemy.[70] The "notion that we should not lift a hand in our own defense until a troopship laden with invaders lies off Sandy Hook is" simply "fatuous."[71] Therefore, the United States must strike first – with unilateral imposition of economic sanctions on the fascist countries as well as with unstinting aid to the democracies around the world. As for the liberal fear that war would bring about an American *Gleichschaltung* and inevitably curtail civil liberties, Mumford invoked the analogy of "suicide" favored by these tough-minded liberals. Liberty was not an idea but a way of life. Freedom had no value in absence of men, women, and institutions that lived it: "It is not freedom we seek but a society of free men."[72] To sacrifice the flesh-and-blood people of freedom to save the abstract principle amounted to an irresponsible act of suicide.

In the first few weeks of 1940, Mumford found himself behind a podium. He was delivering a series of public lectures at the School of Arts and Sciences of Columbia University. His address contained various strains of arguments that recapitulated his hawkish views previously expressed since his "call to arms" in May 1938. They also foreshadowed his masterwork, "The Corruption of Liberalism," to be published in a matter of months. Ponderously and misleadingly titled "A Brief Outline of Hell," his not-so-brief lectures drew a parallel between the decline and fall of the Roman Empire and the ongoing international cataclysm. Mumford highlighted five common symptoms afflicting the past and the present alike: recrudescence of irrationality, leader worship, surrender of personal freedom, collapse of law and order, and indifference to violence and cruelty. The last symptom – indifference to violence and cruelty – was particularly serious in America. Mumford was referring to the nation's tendency to let the cocoon of geographic insularity desensitize itself to the sufferings overseas. Not only did this callousness make Americans even more reluctant to confront the aggressor nations. It also diverted them from the fact that the four other types of corruption and disintegration were gnawing at the spiritual foundation of their own country. He wrote: "We in America, clinging to the illusion of isolation, fancying that we are outside these processes of disintegration and by the exercise of a circumspect and pharisaical virtue will escape the evils of our time – we in America are only, by our ignorance, our apathy, our capacity for self-delusion, showing how completely we suffer from the disease that is wasting the rest of the world."[73] Although rendered in lower case, the epithet "pharisaical" still manages to impart a religious overtone to Mumford's quarrel with the "irresponsibility" of liberal pacifists. Like the Pharisees, isolationists believed that the strict observance of the law of the land would buy their salvation, but this pretentious innocence actually damned America. Mumford's religious analogy in effect compared America's benevolent world leadership to the New Testament promise of universal salvation. The inevitable implication was that on a spiritual plane the holier-than-thou attitude of isolationists descended from something grotesquely unchristian, namely the tribal provinciality of the Judaic law.

It was soon after this public address that Mumford, along with Frank, tendered his resignation to *The New Republic*. Writing to Henry Luce in response to a widely discussed *Fortune* article that called on the church to guide its confused flock to see the light of the new globalism, Mumford explained his reasoning behind his decision to break with the irresponsibles at *The New Republic*. His long letter was plangent with laments about how the pacifist mentality pervaded liberal circles, his intellectual homeland in the past two decades:

> I think that your first appeal to the church should be extended by a second appeal and criticism of the writers and philosophers and artists of our time, whose defection from their own spiritual allegiances and insights has been just as serious as that of the clergy. When a Charles Beard or a Van Wyck Brooks is an isolationist, he undermines that universal society which the great spirits in every culture have been building up in every age. … I am so deeply concerned over this condition in American letters, exhibited by those whom I have been proud to call friends and colleagues, that as a gesture of clarification on my own part I resigned, on the day Kaizer sent me the Fortune editorial, from the New Republic, as contributing editor. There are a handful of people who feel the way I do on this subject: Waldo Frank is one and Reinhold Niebuhr – to whom I hope a copy of the Fortune editorial has been sent – is another. But for the most part, the American intellectual stands condemned, for his actions and even more for his inaction, for his faithlessness to the spirit and for his failure to hear, to see, and to speak those truths which all men of good will must share.[74]

What stands out in this letter is Mumford's pretension to prophetic foresight, which probably derived from the neo-Thomist emphasis on authority. This boastful note, often disguised in a complaining voice, recurred throughout his correspondence. Writing to Waldo Frank of the readers who had written him to thank for helping them see the folly of isolationism, Mumford wrote:

> [W]hat makes me very humble, is the depths that the book [*Faith for Living*] has touched in many other people, not merely you and Van Wyck

and Oko and Rosenstock-Huessy, but even among unknown people, who write me out of nowhere to confess – as if to a father confessor – their sins and declare their repentance. It makes one feel that if your political leaders were not too corrupt to tell the truth, they might awaken a response that would really save the soul of America.[75]

Mumford rejected the naturalistic explanation of American isolationism. Isolationism was not merely an ill-informed political opinion, a faulty economic calculation, or a strategic blunder. Everyone was entitled to fallibility, including irresponsible liberals. Deeper than the inherent limitations of human foresight, the popularity of isolationism and pacifism among liberals was rooted in a certain kind of sinfulness, a spiritual fallenness.

Like MacLeish's broadsides against irresponsible academics, these letters let conservatives off the hook while putting the responsibility squarely on the shoulders of the liberal custodians of America's soul – progressive intellectuals and the modernist clergy. Here, Richard Aldington's dismissal ("typical highbrow delusion") of MacLeish's charge could be extended to Mumford's ravings against the *trahison des clercs*. These responsible liberals had a self-servingly inflated estimation of the utility of the cultural and religious clergy in the coming battle against diabolic dictators. His resignation from *The New Republic*, a coterie weekly for liberal intellectuals, took on a sacrificial meaning. Mumford, for it could be only he (and like-minded shepherds like MacLeish, Reinhold Niebuhr, and Frank), submitted himself to the cross and atoned for the sins of all other corrupt liberals. Those liberals were more sinful than conservatives who balked at responsible assertion of America's benevolent power for their own benighted reasons, for liberals should know better. By contrast, conservatives were, paradoxically, innocent to the extent they were beyond redemption. The corruption of the best became the worst.

That was the purport of his next essay, "The Corruption of Liberalism." Between 1940 and 1941, critics of liberalism told and retold a story of "corruption." Suffering from a plethora of internal infirmities ("confusion," "inner doubts," "contradictions," "self-deception," "self-betrayal," "protective illusions"), liberalism, inaugurated with the best of intentions, had perverted itself. Mumford led this trend. In this essay Mumford named the best turned into the worst through corruption "pragmatic liberalism," the dominant ethos of the interwar years. This debased strain of liberalism, Mumford declared, weakened America, because liberals and pragmatists had failed to lay a philosophical foundation fertile in fighting faiths and actionable ideals. This failure made U.S. foreign policy timid and passive in the face of the "worldwide resurgence of barbarism." Mumford was well aware that liberals already had enough detractors. In Europe throughout the 1920s and the 1930s, the legitimacy of liberalism had been called into question by Marxists on the far left and by conservative revolutionaries on the far right. And the Soviet-German Non-Aggression Pact officially signaled that, at last, "these extremes have met in their attack on liberalism."[76] Mumford intended to hold no brief for these totalitarian critics of pragmatic liberalism. Nevertheless, he had no interest in salvaging it either. Rather, Mumford's object was to change the subject. He argued that perhaps liberalism deserved such abuse from its ideological rivals. The fact of abuse was turned into the guilt of pragmatic liberalism and the exoneration of its enemies.

Mumford festooned this then-popular tale of liberalism's fall from grace with minor arguments against its other weaknesses. The most annoying among them were its optimistic attitude toward history and its cheerful belief in human goodness. The present was not only different from the past. The present was better than the past. So pragmatists and liberals thought. Certainly the world was still occasionally subjected to destructive convulsions. But this did not deter liberal pragmatists. They prayerfully told themselves that these sporadic episodes were simply due to imperfect social arrangements. They would surely improve as science uncovered hidden natural laws, technology vanquished scarcity, education enlightened the ignorant, and administrative expertise rationalized institutions. Yet the assumption that one could fix ills and woes of society as though society had been a malfunctioning machine also allowed liberals to discount the possibility that spiritual questions may divide peoples, derail history, and plunge humanity back into the Stone Age. This liberal faith in progress battened on the view, canonical among the Social Gospellers, that human nature was perfectible. The United States, originally a country of righteous puritans, had shed off its Calvinist tradition, and Americans of that time believed that humans were by nature good. Such an attitude fed the wishful thinking (the "color-blindness to moral values") that democracies could negotiate with their nemesis, that despots were open to persuasion and rational inquiry and so coercion was unnecessary. This illusion turned out to be fatal. When one encountered a venomous snake in one's path, one must not ponder this mortal enemy abstractedly, without experiencing fear or rage. The appropriate reaction was not to analyze the situation philosophically but to strike the reptile's head reflexively. An indecisive American public must snap out of its obsession with observation, analysis, and debate. They should realize that they could not analyze away the satanic.[77]

The doctrine of human perfectibility also impaired the nation's will to confront its implacable enemies because it obscured the fact that Americans themselves were no different – they were humans, fallen, out of grace, evil by nature, like National Socialists, Fascists, Bolsheviks, and the Japanese militarists. Americans were not "angels." Those who saw in the current global conflict a battle between angels and Satan were

> secretly complimenting themselves upon virtues and purities that neither they nor their countrymen possess; they are guilty of that most typical liberal sin, the sin of Pharisaism. It is because we, too, are not without guilt that we may, in the interest of preserving humanity from more abject humiliations, oppose Hitler and Stalin with a clean heart. To be too virtuous to live is one of the characteristic moral perversions of liberalism in our generation.[78]

This was Reinhold Niebuhr's signature idea. For him isolationism was at bottom just another case of "self-righteousness ... the basic human sin."[79] In early February, Mumford reported to Frank of a long conversation he just had with Niebuhr: "Niebuhr and I had a good talk that same night: on all matters political and social we see eye to eye, and there must be something deeply akin in our religious and moral premises, too, to bring us so close to the same conclusions."[80] These critics indeed saw "eye to eye." Niebuhr, Mumford, Frank, and other critics of liberalism (with an important exception of MacLeish, who usually avoided this grim message that could undermine his otherwise sunny chant for America's democratic genius) saw "Pharisaism" as the root cause of America's political paralysis. Americans' overconfidence in their innocence fulfilled a versatile function in far-ranging debates during the prewar years. That is to say, it provided an unpredictable rationale for both globalism and isolationism. On the one hand, by turning on America's innocence and incorruptibility, the simple-minded advocates of America's global leadership like Henry Luce rationalized their wish to impose their moral vision on the rest of the world and shape the postwar peace. Isolationists, on the other hand, invoked American innocence to bolster their argument that the fallen world was simply undeserving of American ministration. The responsible liberals' attack on Pharisaism was calculated to pre-empt this second argument for their country's unilateral withdrawal from the world. The idea, popular among liberal pacifists, that the United States was immune from problems, no matter how cancerous, devouring the world beyond the edenic New World had a deeper religious source in their belief that their country was too holy to meddle in the sordid affairs outside its borders. Against these innocents and exceptionalists, Mumford, Niebuhr, and Frank argued that what gave the United States a license to decide the ongoing battle between democrats and totalitarians was not its immaculate moral credentials. America had to lead because its moral preening was a sham, because it was equally entrapped in gross circumstances of politics. Nation-states were all sinners in the hands of angry God, and America was no exception.

By early May, it was becoming clear that the British campaign in Scandinavia was ending in an utter debacle. Americans grew even more skeptical about the British will to commit itself to the war to the hilt. One such skeptic, Mumford subsisted on a steady diet of the successive editions of newspapers and the endless stream of radio foreign news pick-ups.[81] Mumford suggested to Frank in a letter released on May 30 that the United States perhaps could not afford the luxury of holding onto its interests in the Far East. Dabbling in war game, Frank and Mumford anxiously debated whether a bulk of the fleet stationed in Hawaii to check a possible Japanese attempt on the European possessions in Southeast Asia must be transferred to the Atlantic. Germans could storm the Panama Canal any minute, they feared.[82]

As May turned into June, Mumford began revising "The Corruption of Liberalism" into a pamphlet. The new manuscript ballooned apace to a book length by the time Paris fell. In late July, he began correcting the galleys "under utmost pressure." The European situation was harrying these responsibles. In early July, Niebuhr complained to Mumford about a strange fatigue: "The international situation is so desperately bad that I can hardly think or live. I have never recovered my health sufficiently to face it properly. … I desperately need the invigoration of your mind and heart. I'm constantly skirting the edges of despair."[83] Mumford similarly complained to Frank of severe mental strains. Only his hope that his new book would do a tremendous service to his country kept him going: "[O]ut of the sky a new call came upon my time which I could not refuse, because it was one of those voluntary efforts to awaken the public mind from its torpor, one might almost say its infantile paralysis, upon which the very survival of our civilization may depend."[84] By July 26, his "private Blitzkrieg [was] over," and his new book was on the presses.[85] But the imminent possibility of the fall of the British Empire caused him black despair: "[N]o matter whether Hitler conquers or loses, it seems to me that we are in for another Dark Ages; for as you have said the same dark forces that have come to the surface in Germany, Italy, and Russia are present everywhere."[86] His writing marathon lasted for six weeks without a remission, until *Faith for Living* was finally published in late August.

Faith for Living amplified the charges against liberal intellectuals set forth in "The Corruption of Liberalism." Among many themes elaborated further, the most noteworthy was the idea of democracy as a distinct culture, the way of life of a particular people. As already highlighted again and again, Frank, MacLeish, Mumford, and their allies equated national security with the defense of "culture." Since by "culture" they meant to designate a certain pattern of life shaped by common purposes and repudiated the liberal definition of culture as an aggregate of artificial treasures, their call to arms amounted to a call for the development and conservation of a system of values. Mumford offered the following defin- ition of "values" in the middle of the book:

> Values are not added to a world that exists independently without values: on the contrary, that seemingly independent world was finally abstracted, after centuries of patient study, from the world of values, a world of impulse and purpose and life, in which man primarily lives. Values are not cemented on to the ugly structure of physical existence as in a bad piece of architec- ture, without affecting either the function or the design. Values are, on the contrary, present from the very beginning. This is true in the development of all culture; and it is true in the development of the human personality within a particular culture.[87]

This passage contains several important ideas that by the late 1930s had become commonplaces among cultural critics, anthropologists, and neo- Freudians. The first theme concerned the reversal of order in which facts and values emerged in human experience. The optimistic faith in science, Mumford and other major cultural critics of the late 1930s argued, encour- aged science-worshipping liberals to treat the world as a collection of value- neutral facts, events, and things. They were mistaken, however, because the so-called physical universe was really an abstract notion hoisted upon the actually lived environment. Humans always understood facts, events, and things through their usage. Objects came into existence as objects at the same time that their contributions to human designs were revealed. Value (the varying usefulness of objects) was primary; the object devoid of values contemplated from a disinterested standpoint was secondary, or in truth, a fiction. The individual, Mumford wrote, "knows life from the beginning, not as a fact in the raw, but only as he makes use of the society about him and uses the tools and instruments and modes of expression that society has developed and conserved. Words, gestures, abstract symbols of number, grammar, logic come to him first, though of course without these labels."[88]

His second point was that there was no such thing as the "individual" any more than there was an objective fact. Just as fact was always value-laden, so too the individual was always a person with particular interests, a member of a community affiliated with other members through a web of traditional ties: "All our values are both personal and communal; who shall say where one begins and the other leaves off?"[89] Mumford's contemporaries, neo-Freudians like Abram Kardiner, Karen Horney, and Erich Fromm and anthropologists allied with the Culture and Personality School like Margaret Mead, Ruth Benedict, Melville Herskovits, and Ashley Montagu, would not have gone that far. Those leading culturalists of the late 1930s, all to a varying extent accepting the Freudian orthodoxy, believed in the universality of certain primary cravings that cut across different cultural systems. But like the Catholic critics of liberalism, Mumford wanted to make a bolder claim, that a personal impulse, even in its earliest stages, was always already molded by communal conventions. The notion of pre-cultural, pre-communal instinct, some naked, untamed, and universal drive, was "a phantasm, an aberration of the mind" smuggled back into reality like the notion of value-neutral fact.[90] Under this logic, the antagonistic relation between social norms and individual desires revealed itself to be a result of a fictitious bifurcation of something originally one and whole, that is, values. Communal criteria deciding what was useful and what was useless, what was valuable and what was valueless, answered, not battled, personal needs. The problem arose when liberal rationalists alembicated social norms and personal needs out of "values," a fusion of personality and culture. In fine, Mumford's extreme cultural relativism rejected the notion that values could be traced back to universal and eternal sources, such as God, Nature, Reason, and the Pleasure Principle. Driven out of these realms, values wandered the temporal terrain of concrete order, which Mumford called "tradition," "heritage," or "inheritance." Far from forcing them into homelessness, the banishment from their universalistic strongholds made values more at home with humans. Values now dwelt in the concrete habitat where those who were living, those who were dead, and those who were to be born established an eternal partnership.

Pitting their spiritual and cultural interpretation of the global crisis against the liberals' rationalistic and materialistic view, the responsibles told their nation that the coming war was about values, and certain values such as individualism and freedom were superior to the enemy's values. Mumford's theory of values reveals that their charge that liberalism's value neutrality could not vindicate America's moral and cultural superiority and thus disallowed America to "distinguish between barbarism and civiliza-tion" was another way of saying that liberalism could not conceive liberal democracy as a tradition in which a free people lived a free life.[91] Liberals first tried the supposedly unsentimental argument that democracies and dictatorships both fought war for tangible spoils, not for noble ideals. When this argument collapsed under the weight of the overwhelming moral difference between democracy and totalitarianism, liberals usually ran to the other extreme, arguing that America had to fight for two extremely diaphanous values, freedom of the individual and freedom of the world. And this fallback argument prevented liberals from supporting the defense of freedom as a cultural inheritance, as distinguished from freedom as an abstract and universally applicable right. But if the American people understood a liberal value like freedom as a local value embodied in a race of congenitally free persons, if liberal democracy was embraced as an autochthonous life form, America would be more fiercely motivated to defend it because, like any organism, liberal democracy could perish without appropriate care.

Such a nationalization of liberal values, while understandable as a debater's tactic, came with some disadvantages, which undercut these liberal hawks' cry for a preventive strike against America's enemies. As discussed in Chapter 4 regarding the two notions of liberty, negative and positive, the Achilles' heel of democratic nationalism was that it could not motivate foreign wars in absence of strong evidence suggesting a clear and present danger to the national community, something that was very hard to prove to everyone's satisfaction in the age of propaganda. That was why, contradicting themselves, these advocates of democratic nationalism would often assert that America's core values were also global values, an argument fundamentally at odds with the other justification for militant democracy, that democracy and liberty were autochthonous values. Here, rather than mock these responsible liberals for their opportunistic inconsistency, we should appreciate that responsible liberalism was trapped between the two horns of a dilemma. On the one hand, American democracy needed to become an aboriginal mythos in order for it to overcome liberalism's ingrained nonjudgmentalism and sharpen the contradiction between the self and the foe. On the other hand, a totally particularized society would run the risk of degenerating into an insular tribe, incapable of projecting its first line of defense globally. It was to slip out of this dilemma that these cultural warriors and liberal warhawks argued that democracy was not an export article and, in the next breath, that the law of their country had to be globally enforced.

9

The Axis Conquest of Europe – II

A rather more romantic figure was Waldo Frank. Three years and six years senior of MacLeish and Mumford, respectively, Frank broke into the New York literary scene during the Great War as an associate editor of the short-lived but incredibly ambitious magazine *The Seven Arts*. Essays on American culture Frank solicited for this magazine and Frank's own widely discussed 1919 manifesto *Our America* captured the nascent zeitgeist of cultural self-determination, announcing "our" culture's confident independence from European civilization. His screed against the defilement of the national spirit by a peculiarly American admixture of puritanism and capitalism, and his cry for the unshackling of the subconscious life force from love of money and hate of sex resonated with the young and insurgent literati.[1] Although his turgid prose and bizarre Lawrencean cosmology befuddled many a reader, Frank was without a doubt the most intrepid tribune of the Jazz Age, the solar plexus of the rising generation of romantic primitivists.[2]

The hopefulness of the Roaring Twenties soon dimmed into the murky atmosphere of the depression decade, but Frank, always critical of capitalism and machine, adapted to the leftward drift of culture without awkward self-consciousness. In the presidential election of 1932, he campaigned for Foster and Ford. Four years later, he again supported the Communist ticket, Browder and Foster, and covered their nationwide campaign. During 1935–1936, at the outset of the Popular Front period, Frank served as chairman of the League of American Writers. Soon, however, his alliance with Communists began to fray, more or less following the broad pattern of the American writers' collective exodus from the Party-led antifascism. After the Roosevelt recession of 1937–1938, the economy got back on a steady upward path by 1939–1940, thanks largely to the massive government spending on defense, and with it the urgency of social revolution abated considerably. As the ills and woes within showed signs of subsiding, the threats from without to "our America" began to consume Frank.

The Guilt of Irresponsible Liberals

In early February, Frank was putting final touches to the manuscript of *Chart for Rough Waters* when Bruce Bliven responded to the Frank-Mumford joint resignation letter with the suggestion that *The New Republic* offer them an ample space to lambaste the liberal isolationists. These mutinous contributors could not have wished for a better chance. However, Frank's initial reaction was a heavy groan of an overworked man. Frank grieved to Mumford: "This long article to the NR is a nightmare: You know at what strain I wrote my book, finishing it just on the deadline: Feb. 1. Since then, I've had no respite from all kinds of work and problems. . . . I am simply at this moment in no shape to do even a bad article."[3] He asked Mumford to stay the release of his article so that he could buy "a day or two of just breathing before I can get into passable shape."

Written back-to-back within a month, Frank's *Chart for Rough Waters* and his protest piece "Our Guilt in Fascism" for *The New Republic* laid out grandiose arguments for America's limited intervention. Frank opened his book with this question: "How deep is our separateness from Europe?" Europe for Europeans, America for Americans, so antiwar liberals and selfish unilateralists argued, but how sound was that instruction? To make a case for the unity of North Atlantic civilization, Frank enumerated geopolitical consequences of a British downfall to American security. Frank was not a geostrategist but a critic, however. So his argument hit its stride only later, when he proceeded from his rather ably done conspectus of geographic and economic facts to an inquest into spiritual pathologies afflicting liberalism. "We are not separate from Europe," in his view, because "many of the psycho-cultural as well as many of the economic causes of war are already within us." "[W]e cannot be neutral, whatever we want and say, because what is happening tonight in London, Berlin, Moscow, in the fields and seas of battle, in the diplomatic and economic warfare the world over, exists in us as a virulent potential." The European war was actually but a local front in a worldwide "revolution": "Now, whether or not you agree that this is a World War and we are in it, I think, reader, you will find it hard to doubt that the world crisis is a revolution and that we are in it. In fact, we've been in it a long time."[4] His historical perspective ("for a long time"), like Mumford's, was very truly long. The rise of totalitarianism and the decay of Western liberalism, Frank thought, began with the advent of modernity, roughly defined as the historical period characterized by secularization and industrialization. Modernization had delivered tangible material benefits, but at what cost? At the sacrifice of human spirituality. Modern individuals replaced religion with science and the organic community of neighbors with the inorganic aggregate of faceless consumers. All this ended in the "humiliation of man." The psychically damaged masses revolted finally, giving birth to modern dictatorship:

> Man has been "humiliated" by the age of the machine and reason and individualism, not because the machine is evil, not because the individual is absolutely false, not because reason and a life of reason are wrong: *but because, as they have expressed themselves, the individual and reason and the machine represent a halfway house in the growth of man, a transition world from which man is challenged by his own growth to emerge in order to live more consciously in the depths of his whole nature; and from which at the same time he is pulled back and down, being still left with too many cultural tools and concepts of his unconscious past.*[5]

With the pride of a man who boasted that "there is no writing in it [his short stories] that anybody with a high-school education cannot read," Hemingway once said that Frank "writes a language so badly he cannot make a clear statement."[6] The passage quoted above showcases well his notorious predilection for mystical jargons that bemused his contemporaries. His allegedly congenital inability to "make a clear statement" aside, there was certainly a sort of erudite turgidity going berserk to Frank's prose. It was poetic in the sense that his train of thought was shot through with gaps and leaps. The reasoning was seldom spelled out, with a string of non sequiturs substituting for demonstration. But his prose at the same time managed to appear learned and prophetic. The whole impression was that his sentences were written in curiously compressed shorthand, each symbol keyed to a large body of arguments that would require several paragraphs to be thoroughly unpacked.

"Person" and "individual" were two such code words, largely taken from Emmanuel Mounier's personalism and neo-Thomism. The "person" was a human being who was religious, understood his station in the world in relation to the fellow members of the community. The "person" was not a monster of ingratitude besotted with the grandeur of autonomous and rational selfhood. Hence he did not vainly imagine that he stood above the hallowed values of the community but recognized his debts to the nurturing environment. The person was in a sense a medieval man, extinct in the age of reason and machine. All this was meant by Frank's gnomic definition: "The individual integrated in his Cosmos, I call *the person*."[7] The "individual," conversely, stood denounced as a disintegrated "person." This new type of vainglorious human being had replaced the person over the course of the West's modernization and liberalization. The individual understood himself as a self-regulating and self-referential sovereign secure in his imperial belief that he was not only independent of but in possession of mastery over external impediments to his freedom: "The individual has a 'soul'; it is stringently separate from the group; and its rightness – *its own* – is the one true value."[8] But the recent series of man-made disasters had shown the individual's sublime "rightness" a self-serving fancy, a protective delusion masking the individual's enslavement to the mechanized, deterministic civilization. The West defined the individual in idealistic or materialistic terms. And yet both versions of the human were actually complicit in the murder of the integrated "person," for both doctrines broke the totality of a human being into parts and exalted one piece, whether mindless flesh or disembodied reason, over the other.

Frank seems to stray too far afield in search of the origins of the new world war and in the process has forgotten about his point of departure. Yet he justified rehearsing his pet theory of the person's fall from his unity with cosmos, by pointing out that shortsighted preoccupations with superficial technical failures in political economy had produced only "desperate remedies," which had all proven ineffective. These "desperate remedies" were sold to the public under two labels: reformist liberalism and revolutionary communism. Looking back on the 1930s, which saw Frank's faith in these two "isms" diminish year after year, Frank finally concluded that these two political philosophies were simply not equal to the task of checking the spread of extremism on the far right. As Frank saw it, their inadequacy was due to the fact that:

> These two schools of change and revolution [liberalism and communism] had the same basic value and the same basic methods to attain it as the conservatives of the modern age which they hoped to better. They either believed in a God who, like Voltaire's, was a mere figurehead of empiric rationalism or they denied God point-blank. They believed in the efficacy and autonomy of reason, in the goodness of the individual will. They were optimists: haters of the tragic sense of life which they equated with incompetence, and despisers of the mystic intuitions which they confounded with ignorance and muddle. And their supreme value, like their enemy's, the exploiters, was well-being.[9]

The affinity of Frank's assessment of the frailties of liberalism and communism to Mumford's and MacLeish's is plain to see. All three censured these two "isms" for their faith in reason and human goodness. Communists and liberals could not discern the evil nature of fascism because they sacrificed pre-rational intuition for empiric rationalism. Rationalism and empiricism may be good in the sense that they helped promote the "supreme value" of "well-being," namely the satisfaction of materialistic needs. But the price these "optimists" paid was the atrophy of the faculty to intuit moral values, a critically important weapon in a global war fought across the countries of the spirit.

Dictatorship's competitive edge over American democracy came from the former's rhetoric of overcoming reason, optimism, and materialistic culture. This assessment informed Frank's prescription: to defeat Fascists and National Socialists, the United States must follow its enemy's example and scuttle once and for all the sinking ship of liberalism and capitalism. This suggestion, however, fanned a fear very much essential to the liberals' hesitation, and Frank and his colleagues knew it. It was one thing to study the enemy's methods; quite another to become the enemy. It was precisely this fear of mutual mimicry that motivated various versions of pacifism. Even John Dewey now tacked to pacifism and wrote that "if the United States is drawn into the next war we shall have in effect if not in name a fascist government in this country."[10] The popularity of such a fear was quite understandable, given the disastrous consequences of the last war for civil liberties. Therefore, so as to make their counsel that America curtail civil rights and liberal values look less scary, the responsible liberals had to invent a bunch of heuristic analogies, many of them rather comically desperate. Mumford explained:

> The notion that if one fights fascism one will become fascist has been one of the most popular aids to the spread of fascism. One might just as well say that an honest house-holder who confronts a burglar with a revolver will in turn become a burglar if he shoots.[11]

In *Chart for Rough Waters*, Frank cited three counter examples to allay the fear of "becoming the enemy":

> It [pacifism] claims that there is no sense in warring against Fascism, because if we won, we would come out of it fascisized. ... [But] it is nonsense to say that it will lose its values even if it wins the war. When the Christians under Charles Martel beat back the Arabs at Tours, did France turn Moslem? When we threw King George's redcoats out of these States, did we proceed to choose a monarch? When the North went into victorious battle against the slave South, did it readopt chattel slavery?[12]

Ultimately, from his "cultural-philosophical-psychological" standpoint, Frank could not see any distinction among the three ideological end results of modernity: communism on the left, fascism on the right, and liberalism in the middle.[13] He viewed them as three superficially differing evidences of modernity's tendency toward self-destruction. Over the course of modernization, the "individual" superseded the "person," reason mastered nature, and *Gesellschaft* supplanted *Gemeinschaft*. This created all kinds of woeful distortions in the psyche of moderns and in the way they organized society. Liberalism, Communism, and National Socialism, however, asserted in chorus that these distortions and imbalances could be adjusted through more modernization, not less. Hitler's Germany may have been different from a liberal America, but only to the extent that the former had already attained a more advanced stage in suicidal modernity. This kinship between liberalism and totalitarianism posed a problem for hawkish responsibles. How could the United States wage war against the international conspiracy of dictators if the difference between the self and the foe was that of degree, not of kind? As Frank wrote, "The dire *justice* in fascism must therefore be avowed. ... Fascism's anti-democracy, anti-justice, anti-reason, etc, are the virulent rage of men's energies against the modern concepts of democracy, justice, reason, that have been turned into *caricature*."[14] Totalitarianism was not the enemy of liberal democracy but the avenger of blood. Modern had turned their articles of faith into "caricature." And out of spite and rage against the phony freedom of modern liberal society, men and women in Europe launched a powerful movement to avenge themselves on the betrayal of modernity and liberalism. Insofar as totalitarians vowed to destroy the corrupt liberalism, they were inadvertently aiding America.

How to fight a war against one's simulacra without killing oneself – this question understandably complicated Frank's argument. In Frank's case for America's responsible exercise of world leadership, two cagey movements stalked each other. On one side, Frank said that America's moral character was immaculate and inviolable. Therefore, studying the enemy would not lead to adopting the enemy's methods. Frank was here appeasing those "pharisaical" Americans who believed that their country must stay aloof of the fratricidal Europeans. On the other side, he had a sterner argument couched in the language of shared guilt. The real enemy – the corruption of liberalism – was within and the dictators abroad helpfully pointed Americans to their internal enemy. The task of liberals in America was thus twofold. Repent and reform. In the meantime, however, do not forget to prepare to cross the Atlantic to slay the god of revenge, as He was now hell-bent on destroying all variants of liberalism, root and branch, perverted or not. The problem at the root of the ongoing world revolution could be resolved only through liberalism's total self-transformation. That would transform the kinship between liberalism and totalitarianism into inimicality.

This double-talk betokened the complexity of the question that strained responsible liberalism. Here again we see that America's self-righteousness provided a political-theological justification for and against internationalism. The myth of America's singularity mandated the imposition of its moral vision upon the world and at the same time offered a pretext for barricading itself in the Western Hemisphere and forsaking the rest of the hapless world. Either way, from the faith in American innocence flowed the same corollary: the outside world was no sooner acknowledged than was dismissed. Whether America veered toward a puritanical withdrawal from the world or lunged toward an evangelic crusade across the world, the world anyway vanished through neglect or conquest. With his repeated reassurance that the impending war would not "fascisize" America, Frank turned to American exceptionalism for a strong rationale for foreign military adventures. Of course, however, pandering to America's vainglorious self-opinion could backfire because unilateral isolationists may appropriate it to their advantage. Therefore, Frank, illogically, had to hedge this risk by telling his reader that the United States was "guilty" like any other European countries.

Freedom Is Culture

Despite differences in phraseology, all these interrelated versions of the critique of liberal irresponsibility seem to have sprung from a single fount. What was it?

One of the noteworthy things about responsible liberalism was the fact that these pro-Allies liberals searched for the origins of isolationism far – very far from the present crisis. Vertiginous indeed is the breadth and depth of the historical vistas within which they set their pressing questions. A variety of ills plaguing the United States and the world were traced to their most distant sources. At times, it looked as though some sort of competition was on, all contestants trying to discover the remotest possible and the least conceivable cause for the pathology of liberal isolationism. In this regard, these responsible liberals formed part of an extensive group of contemporary thinkers similarly writing on the origins of the escalating world anarchy and America's place therein. Many books on the approach of the second world war that were either published or began to be researched during the prewar years, such as T. S. Eliot's *The Idea of a Christian Society* (1939), Peter Drucker's *The End of Economic Man* (1939), Reinhold Niebuhr's *Europe's Catastrophe* (1940) and *The Nature and Destiny of Man* (1941–1943), James Burnham's *The Managerial Revolution* (1941),

Karl Polanyi's *The Great Transformation* (1944; written in 1939–1943), Joseph Schumpeter's *Capitalism, Socialism, Democracy* (1942; written in 1940–1941), and Pitirim Sorokin's *The Crisis of Our Age* (1941), all set forth breathtakingly grandiose explanations for the two entwined cataclysms: the global depression and the global war. To their eyes, now empowered by hindsight, it became crushingly clear that all pivotal events in the last millennium foreran the impasse in which liberal democracy found itself in the 1930s. Terrifying phrases like "catastrophe," "world revolution," "apocalypse," "anarchy," and "the end of Western civilization" adorned these thinkers' analyses. While no doubt some of the alarm expressed in these topical tomes was faked to jolt somnambulant Americans, most writers sincerely suspected that the ongoing world crisis portended something unprecedented, a departure from cycles of wars, revolutions, and depressions that had ravaged the West in the past.

By 1940, American intellectuals had been sufficiently acquainted with the nonlinear view of history. Popularized by Oswald Spengler and Arnold Toynbee during the interwar decades, this view took "civilization" as the basic unit of study and analyzed their birth-growth-senescence cycles. There was no such thing as universal history through which customs, inventions, and institutions of the "natural people" gradually revealed the true nature of humankind, a unitary world history whose various developmental phases were represented by civilizations around the world (with the one in Europe ahead of all others). Civilizations were rather like organic life forms. Each distinct from all others, they were born, grew, matured, declined, and perished. The prewar thinkers witnessing the escalation of the global depression into the global war feared that, like extinct civilizations and ruined empires that archeologists studied, Western civilization may perish, to be replaced by a wholly new civilization.[15] The laconic opening sentence in Polanyi's *The Great Transformation* set the tone for this group of doomful books: "Nineteenth century civilization has collapsed."[16] "In times past," Carl Becker struck a worried note in 1941, "certain civilizations, long established, brilliant and prosperous and seemingly secure against mischance, slowly decayed and either disappeared altogether or were transformed past recognition and forgotten. What has happened many times in the history of mankind may happen again."[17] Sociologist Sorokin similarly saw in the approach of war the end of modern "sensate" civilization. Eight centuries ago, a new civilization founded on the principle that only the objects revealed to senses were real and valuable displaced medieval civilization founded on the belief in the reality of the ideational, the invisible, the ineffable, and the supernatural. Now the modern sensualist ethos, which had driven economic growth and political liberalization, consummated its innermost propensity and began falling apart at the hands of the most fervid adherents to the cult of the sensual: Nazis and Bolsheviks.[18]

T. S. Eliot, in his own tract of the times, *The Idea of a Christian Society*, also understood the ongoing "world revolution" to mark the end of modernity. The book, which was based on a series of lectures he gave in May 1939 and published after the outbreak of the European war, opened with a disclaimer that it wasn't "intended to be either an anti-communist or an anti-fascist manifesto."[19] That was an accurate statement of purpose because the book was meant as an antiliberal manifesto, the latest installment in his decade-long campaign against "a society like ours, worm-eaten with Liberalism."[20] The battle in progress between totalitalianism and liberal democracy was of a religious and ideological character through and through, according to Eliot. It was a war of godless Pagans against god-fearing Christians. Secular liberals in the West were "neutral," torn between fascination with the efficiency of totalitarian systems and mistrust of Christianity, but the day had finally come when they must choose between these two sharply divergent alternatives: "Our choice is now not between one abstract form and another, but between a pagan, and necessarily stunted culture, and a religious, and necessarily imperfect culture."[21] As long as secular liberals ("neutrals") refused to accept the spiritual explanation of the world crisis and reverse the course of secularization, their fate was sealed. Echoing his confrères on the other side of the Atlantic, Eliot traced the ultimate cause of the current international crisis to the modernization and liberalization of the Western world, the arduous process of human emancipation from scarcity and superstitions, which began in the eighteenth century and gradually turned into blind enslavement to the new myth of scientism and industrialism in the nineteenth century. Liberalism was the idea at the back of everything, from industrialization to mechanization, secularization, and possessive individualism, which combined to poison society with commercialism and silly mass culture, to ruin the pristine environment in the countryside, and to make everyone's spiritual life vacuous. Neo-paganism – totalitarianism – must be understood as a reaction against this spiritual and social impoverishment poverty. "We cannot effectively denounce the enemy without understanding him; we cannot understand him unless we understand ourselves, and our own weaknesses and sins," and only Christianity could teach godless liberals this tragic sense of one's own sinfulness, an absolute moral prerequisite in the new global crusade.[22]

Niebuhr also offered a breathtakingly stringent (or simplistic) historical analysis of forces behind the decline and fall of Western civilization. "The easy conscience of modern man" was responsible for the peaceableness and feebleness of liberalism, he told his Scottish audience in his 1939 Gifford Lecture. Since the advent of the Renaissance, various theories of man, such as idealism, materialism, and irrational romanticism, for all their bickerings to the contrary, had conspired to make Westerners forget the most important contribution of Christianity to the study of man: man was by nature evil. Built on the fatuous wishful thinking that man was incapable of committing aggression against his neighbor with full knowledge of his own sinfulness, Western civilization perforce degraded into National Socialism, a spiritual expression of collective egoism, or liberal-capitalist democracy where individual egoism devastated the common purpose.[23] Niebuhr concluded that appeasement and isolationism were part and parcel of the main tenets of modern liberalism such as the optimistic faith in progress, the belief in perfectibility of human nature, and secularism that conveniently absolved humankind of original sin. He even pushed back the date of the birth of American isolationism to the end of the Middle Ages. At the obscure end of the long chain of guilt and culpability, Niebuhr descried Leonardo and Pico della Mirandola. Irresponsible liberals in America were direct descendents of these Renaissance men.[24]

Mumford was merely practicing the same long-range historicism when he recounted the genealogy of Western philosophy that improbably identified liberal isolationism as a "child of Voltaire and Rousseau."[25] A host of liberal attitudes associated with the Enlightenment, ranging from optimism and political naïveté to the presumption of scientific objectivity, abetted liberal irresponsibility, he concluded. Waldo Frank concurred. Frank thought he traced the etiological origin of liberals' terminal spinelessness to the age of reason, machine, and individualism. The end of the Middle Ages coincided with the beginning of the "humiliation of man," which set in motion a chain of events culminating in liberalism's internal corruption, which by turn called forth its own avenger, totalitarianism. Of all these responsible liberals, MacLeish was the most present-minded.[26] He found the origin of liberal irresponsibility in the vicinity of the Roaring Twenties, especially in idealistic writers' overreaction to the disappointing consequences of the last war. All the same, even this polemicist sometimes acknowledged that the crisis of confidence in democratic slogans originated in the Victorian era or in long-term secular trends such as the overspecialization of intellectual roles.[27]

Frank, MacLeish, Mumford (or the Triumvirate of Treachery, as *The New Masses* dubbed them), and their allies were united in the recognition that liberals in the Western democracies brought on the current predicament themselves and therefore should be deservedly punished. They declared the downfall of the Western liberal tradition a case of "suicide" and "corruption." Such recurring terms as "suicide," "corruption," and "self-betrayal" show that they sought the cause of the crisis in the internal workings of liberal democracy and did not blame some abrupt intrusion of exogenous forces. Liberalism's mortal enemy was itself. And this self-diagnosis at once daunted and invigorated these responsible liberals. They had to discipline the slackers and saboteurs within, those irresponsible, whether pacifists, appeasers, isolationists, or disillusioned postwar writers, in addition to fighting, as the shock troops of democratic values, the ideological battle against totalitarian propaganda. It stood to reason, these writers calculated, that, beyond rebutting slanders against American democracy disseminated by dictatorships abroad and defeatist counsels coming from within, they had to strike the logical fountainhead from which fascism, Bolshevism, and liberalism arose.

All the same, these writers' epic scope of analysis did not always keep them above scapegoating handier suspects. The debate between the responsibles and the irresponsibles frequently became ad hominem. Harsh words were aimed at liberalism as a hodgepodge of self-congratulations and gutless apologies, certainly, but these words anyway hit the actual persons, accidentally or not. The liberal hawks all eagerly made an example of sitting targets – usually innocent bystanders – such as Christian pacifists, well-meaning fellow travelers, college professors, or the Lost Generation novelists. Along the way, these writers resigned from magazines, had falling-outs with their long-time friends, and irrevocably alienated themselves from the liberal-modernist consensus.

So there was a grain of truth in the charge that these responsibles were a sort of intellectual bullies – or "intellectual cops" as James T. Farrell called them – roughing up liberal namby-pambies.[28] But they were occasionally brave enough to take on formidable adversaries with impeccable records of Americanism. Their concerted attack on John Dewey was a case in point. These critics of liberalism agreed one with another that John Dewey's philosophy epitomized the most pernicious aspects of liberal irresponsibility. Frank's *Chart for Rough Waters* mentioned Dewey five times, always to disparage.[29] Frank claimed that Dewey "accept[s] the thesis that human reason is a product solely of empiric environmental factors." His mind was accused of being "as sterile today as was decadent scholasticism when the seventeenth-century masters of these worshipers of science arose against it." He was an "antiphilosopher" who "despised metaphysics and religion," a "great creator" of "techniques of knowledge, not creator of value."[30] The name of Dewey rarely turned up in Mumford's tirades against corrupt liberals. Mumford acknowledged that America's spiritual torpor resulted from a long tradition of widespread beliefs that "do not belong to any philosophical group or political party."[31] But his choice of the phrase "pragmatic liberalism" to designate this faceless culprit signaled that he had Dewey's pragmatism squarely in his mind. Niebuhr also attacked Dewey's "naïve answer" to the complex problem of human capacity to do evil. To him pragmatism was a prima facie example of the "easy conscience of modern man." "Dewey is in fact less conscious of the social perils of self-love than either Locke or Hume," and Niebuhr attributed this regression in the understanding of the "perils of self-love" to Dewey's optimistic belief in science: "Professor Dewey has a touching faith in the possibility of achieving the same results in the field of social relations which intelligence achieved in the mastery of nature."[32]

In most intergenerational disputes, it is the anxiety of influence, not some substantive difference in values and goals, that fuels young rebels' rage against their mentors. The responsible liberals' insurgency against the idol their generation once deliriously worshiped was no exception. Pragmatism exerted enormous influence on liberal intellectuals in the post-progressive era, roughly from the mid-1910s to the early 1930s. And its reign, significantly, coincided with the formative years when these much younger critics (Frank, b. 1889; MacLeish, b. 1892; Niebuhr, b. 1892; Mumford, b. 1895) developed their intellectual outlooks on basic social and philosophical questions. In 1925, Mumford wrote to Van Wyck Brooks that "I was brought up, so to speak, on pragmatism."[33] Frank's first wife, Margaret Naumburg was a progressive educator who studied with Dewey at Columbia. Starting his career under the influence of Social Gospel, Niebuhr was similarly smitten by the Deweyan faith in the democratization through public enlightenment in his early years.[34] Dewey's influence is evident in their writings on culture and personality, which rarely deviated from the most attractive part of Dewey's brand of pragmatism, his faith in the essential connection between democracy and the cultivation of personal potentials. Little wonder, then, that although these patriots and warhawks tracked the origins of liberal irresponsibility to distant ancestors such as Galileo, Bacon, Locke, Rousseau, Bentham, Comte, and other venerable European thinkers, they chose to lash out against the only surviving founder of pragmatism, John Dewey, almost twice their age. Their accusation that pragmatism was the philosophical and emotional basis of America's appeasement policy had an aspect of cutting the umbilical cord still connecting these younger writers to their intellectual progenitor.

The timing of their simultaneous assaults on science and pragmatism is significant. A pugnacious coterie of prophetic liberals soured on the hopefulness of the interwar years, roughly around the same time, when America was on the brink of entering a new world war.[35] They came to espouse a view that modern science, and its cardinal virtues such as objectivity, experimentalism, and free communication, prejudiced national security. This backlash against modern science and its philosophical hand-maiden, pragmatism, cautions us against construing the responsible liberals' denunciations of the fanatic irrationality of totalitarianism as an endorsement of Western civilization erected on the foundation of experimental science. These writers did not apprehend in the morality play then unfolding on the global stage a battle between rationality and irrationality or science and atavistic neo-medievalism. The two contending forces were both irrational, driven by the "final judgment and absolute belief" that no scientific inquiry, because it was an open-ended and never-ending undertaking, could ever hope to empirically certify. The real fault lines ran between two spiritual orders, not between myth and method.

Because these critics of liberalism were at least as much interested in burning their intellectual progenitor in effigy as in sizing up his the real strength, their gibes at this doyen of American philosophy usually ended up obscuring ways in which Dewey's ideas could be adapted to meet the demands of the new age. In October 1939, Dewey, at the age of eighty, published *Freedom and Culture*, a pragmatist's reply to the charge that pragmatism, science, and liberalism had become a liability for the nation's survival. In the chapter entitled "Science and Free Culture," Dewey reaffirmed his faith in the culture of science and wrote that among its "obvious elements" were

> willingness to hold belief in suspense, ability to doubt until evidence is obtained; willingness to go where evidence points instead of putting first a personally preferred conclusion; ability to hold ideas in solution and use them as hypotheses to be tested instead of as dogmas to be asserted; and (possibly the most distinctive of all) enjoyment of new fields for inquiry and of new problems.[36]

At first glance, this passage turns responsible liberalism upside down and praises as virtues all the alleged weakness of liberalism. For the responsibles, these "obvious elements of the spirit of scientific inquiry" were the worst characteristics of liberal irresponsibility. MacLeish, for one, compared the "irresponsibility" of pacifist professors to the neutrality of scientists: "[T]he irresponsibility of the scholar is the irresponsibility of the scientist upon whose laboratory insulation he has patterned all his work. . . . His words of praise are the laboratory words – objectivity, detachment, dispassion. His pride is to be scientific, neuter, skeptical, detached – superior to final judgment or absolute belief."[37]

However, Dewey's claim that "enjoyment of new fields for inquiry and of new problems" was the "most distinctive" scientific attitude suggests that for him science was not just a means but a value in itself. Dewey wanted to show that the choice the responsible liberals forced upon the nation was a false one. Science was an enjoyable activity in itself, and Americans could educe a tribal myth out of it. This chief wager of the book appears to have eluded not just the responsibles but even those sympathetic to Dewey's lifelong undertaking to anchor democratic values in pragmatism. In the fall of 1940, Charles Merriam was teaching a graduate seminar on democracy at Harvard as a visiting professor. Among his assigned readings was *Freedom and Culture*. After one class session, Merriam wrote to Dewey, asking for clarification:

> I am giving a seminar on 'Democracy' this fall, and at our last session we reviewed your Freedom and Culture. Students kept insistently raising the question how Dr. Dewey proposes to derive values from science. I did the best I could to explain, but I am not sure I was wholly successful. I suggested to one of the principal reviewers that he write you, but his student timidity could not be overcome. . . . Consequently, I am writing on behalf of these student reviewers to ask if you could indicate more sharply the ways and means of going about the task of evolving values from science. Perhaps you have written on this subject, passages which have escaped me.[38]

The students' puzzlement is mystifying, because from the outset of the book Dewey explained why, far from being a value-free instrument subservient to human whims, science had "intrinsic moral potentiality."[39] Although science began as a quest for general laws, formulated with mathematical stringency free of moral and cultural values,

> in some persons and to some degree science has already created a new morale – which is equivalent to the creation of new desires and new ends. The existence of the scientific attitude and spirit, even upon a limited scale, is proof that science is capable of developing a distinctive type of disposition and purpose: a type that goes far beyond provision of more effective means for realizing desires which exist independently of any effect of science.[40]

Science was not just an ensemble of given facts and cold methods, uprooted, transportable, indiscriminate. It was in fact a complex of embodied practices followed with ritualistic precision in the lives of teachers, pupils, and researchers. As a way of life, it was spreading to wider segments of the American population primarily through schools but also through other institutions of mass enlightenment. Modern science was, then, not a jumble of techniques that humanity universally employed, but pointed people to particular ends, valuable in themselves, which a particular community consciously or unconsciously preferred, to the exclusion of other, incompatible ends. To be scientific or to be antiscience – that was an ethical question. The propagation of "scientific attitude" as value was crucial for the "fate of democracy" at this historical juncture because the "very agencies that a century and a half ago were looked upon as those that were sure to advance the cause of democratic freedom," such as high literacy, public education, and freedom of the press, ended up creating more openings for cynical propagandists and inadvertently undermined democracy from within. To counter the culture of "pseudo-public opinion" and to restore an enlightened republic where transparency, objectivity, and impartiality were respected, nay, desired, it was imperative that public intellectuals recruit more and more people to the new religion of science. Should this culturalization, or nationalization, of scientific rationality fail, the "practical alternative is competition and conflict between unintelligent forces for control of desire."[41]

Dewey's was an undertaking to rework science into a democratic esprit de corps, a common culture, something substantive that the youths of the nation could and would find worth fighting, even dying, for. Emotional interest, which had been expunged from reason, would return to modern scientists the moment they realized that they belonged to a cultural tribe whose task went beyond nonjudgmental perception, classification, and reproduction of the actual. An interest group consisting of scientists, technicians, and professors could be as militant as the believers in *Blut und Boden*. Two months into the new war in Europe, Dewey wrote: "[A]s teachers and scholars we too are soldiers in a cause which is as definitely ours as that of any nation at war in Europe is that of the soldiers who are fighting in its special behalf."[42] Science and mental aptitudes associated with it could be made excitingly desirable, objects of conscientious choice and loyal attachment. It was a moral choice whether one believed, as communal values, in "free inquiry, free assembly and free communication."[43] Freedom meant commitment to *a* culture.[44]

Mumford argued, in concert with his associates, that "[u]ntil we rebuild values our activities, no matter how rationalized and refined, or however impregnated with science, will remain insensate: that is, dull, blind, unresponsive to the needs of personality."[45] But if a "world of values" was something a person and a community inherited, nurtured, and passed down to the next generation, there should have been no reason that various attitudes and character traits of a free liberal, such as instrumentalism and experimentalism, could not be adopted, slowly and gradually through social usage, into the existing family of traditional values such as honor, magnanimity, and courage. That was the main point of Sidney Hook, Dewey's most ardent and unblinking follower.[46] These neo-medievalists said they wanted a "renewal," "rediscovery," and "revitalization" of uniquely American values. But they refused to admit scientific impulses, pragmatic habits, and liberal desires into the existing assemblage of positive values. By ignoring the need for a "creation" of new national values, these responsible liberals were at best contradicting their own definition of culture as a living tradition and at worst indulging in an empty gesture of religious revivalism. The cultural "potentiality" of science in fact could be a welcome addition to the moral arsenal of democracy. Nothing prevented Americans from provincializing science into the content of a local myth. America could be liberal and responsible at the same time.

Liberty *and* Union

> MENTOR
> Emphasize the "*and*."
>   ABE
> "Liberty *and* Union, now and forever, one and inseparable!"
>   Robert Sherwood, *Abe Lincoln in Illinois* (1938)

As this controversy reveals, responsible liberalism was mainly driven by the unease about the liberal proposition that a democratic society could operate without unanimous agreement on "fundamentals" in the ideological order. Even in a decade that supposedly exposed capitalism's inability to self-adjust, liberalism's favorite metaphor for society remained that of unregulated but unintentionally harmonious marketplace. Reminded by the rise of totalitarian systems of the danger of oppressive monism, liberals even more earnestly praised the genius of pluralism and competition throughout the prewar period. In a liberal democracy, they said, self-interested groups, who were politically on an equal footing with one another, haggled with each other to forward their agendas. These factions were fundamentally at odds with each other. Human motives were contingent and diverse and so it was all too natural that free people were wayward, quarrelsome, and recalcitrant. Certainly, these selfish social groups employed the rhetoric of "rights" and "common good," but when they did so they did not mean it. They were merely socializing their radically particularistic desires, wants, and opinions in order to prevail in the democratic process.[47]

The responsible liberals did not hesitate to question this Madisonian celebration of pluralism at practical levels. The lessons learned from the depression and from the failure to mobilize the fractured nation for the coming war taught them that some sort of centripetal force was desirable and that liberalism was congenitally incapable of envisioning a mechanism to generate such a force. Moreover, the absence of the monolithic national will was bound up with the nation's inability to make decisions promptly and act on them. The problem of expeditious decision making vexed America as it edged toward the brink of war. The speed in arriving at and executing a decision may not have been the most important factor in administrating domestic programs. But timely decision was of critical importance to a nation seeking to survive in the normless international system. The nineteenth-century liberal world order, underwritten by the gold standard and the British Royal Navy, was no more. Autarky, currency war, and protectionism were on the rise. Under such circumstances, the reflexes of the nation were the sine qua non of survival. But the intransigence of an isolationist Congress and the anti–New Deal behaviors of the Supreme Court exposed the difficulty of speedy decision making. The far-sighted precautions invented in the eighteenth century to forestall the recrudescence of monarchy now hamstrung the executive branch, which resulted in America's ineptitude at checking the growth of the autarkic empires with an apparently insatiable zest for territorial expansion. If, the liberal hawks wished, the commander in chief only could liquidate treasonous partisans in Congress and censor the pernicious propaganda of the isolationist press!

So even measured by the pragmatic standards of liberals, their social theory did not work. But the most urgent charges of the responsible liberals were of a psychological nature. Describing the psychic disintegration of modern liberals, Frank wrote:

> Man is not a mere congeries of physical and social atoms to be comfortably arranged by the pragmatic mind. Man is indissolubly involved in the depths and heights of the universe; is attached to its ineluctable dynamic movement; and yet is rooted in its immobile wholeness.[48]

Eliot used the same term "congeries" to describe the disintegration of modern liberal society:

> Was our society, which had always been so assured of its superiority and rectitude, so confident of its unexamined premisses, assembled round anything more permanent than a congeries of banks, insurance companies and industries, and had it any belief more essential than a belief in compound interest and the maintenance of dividends?[49]

These two observations on the anomie of liberal society echoed each other. Liberals and liberal societies were a "congeries," an omnium gatherum of discrete components merely "arranged" and "assembled." On the one hand, the liberal community was not bound into a whole by inherited ties such as customs, common values, guilds, common houses of worship, and consanguinity as opposed to such accidental connections as occupations (mostly unskilled), mass-produced consumer goods, and leisure activities. On the other hand, people who lived in such a community were internally fragmented. That is to say, dissociated from each other, desires and purposes controlling the members of the liberal society did not hang together in their reciprocal subordination to an ultimate goal. Placing these two quotations side by side, we can see clearly that the responsible liberals were concerned that the liberal society and the liberal individual facilitated each other's disintegration. Frank deplored that modern man was reduced to a "mere congeries of physical and social atoms" while in Eliot's lecture on the future of theocratic society it was liberal society that was held to have degenerated into a "congeries of banks, insurance companies and industries." These two writers were merely addressing the two different manifestations of the same sickness. America had to cure culture and personality both, at the same time. In a newly rediscovered "our America," Frank hoped, "social justice becomes a coefficient of individual health."[50]

The fragmentation of society and individual could not be healed by economic policy, political reform, or even psychological counseling. In the proposal for an abortive magazine, Frank, Niebuhr, and Mumford tried to sell their project to potential sponsors primarily as a "cultural project." The opening line of their prospectus read: "This magazine will be dedicated to the essential task of modern society – that of staying the forces of barbarism and laying the foundations for an organic and personal human culture."[51] For these writers culture denoted a way to look at social organization and the mental health of the individual. They needed to avail themselves of a new method – the intermediate level of analysis where one could explain how psychological ills of individuals transmuted into societal problems and vice versa. Not only did liberalism motivate people to create the lawless markets, the partisan press, and the culture industry, which connived with one another to fragment human psyche and community. By denying that there was such a thing as a common culture based on shared substantive values, liberalism also made it impossible to analyze these societal and psychological issues in the comprehensive reality of mutual penetration. This carried an enormous risk because, as these liberal hawks saw it, the present world crisis "is in essence a cultural crisis – a revolt of certain classes, certain conditions of men against the inherited culture of the West and all common culture."[52] Even if the Americans could defeat their foreign enemies by dint of their sheer productive power, their country was still doomed as long as the illness that infected both America and foreign dictatorships remained untreated.

The fact that the theme of cultural nationalism came to interest so many intellectuals in the prewar period serves as a useful gloss on the essential difference between the crisis in the domestic economy and the international crisis. In dealing with domestic problems like the depression, a political decision reached through the intricate mechanism of federalism, bicameralism, the two-party system, universal suffrage, and checks-and-balances did not need to be unanimous. What mattered was whether a proposition got enough votes – a majority (or just a plurality in many decisions). If the decision, when implemented, worked, that marked another triumph for democracy. If it did not, that was no cause for worry because citizens and their representatives could start haggling and debating all over again until reaching another decision. But when the United States dealt with the rapacious competitors in world politics, and when the government must decide on foreign policy, enough votes were not enough. Thus, while, in the democratic formulation of a domestic policy, dissenting opinions did not invalidate the final decision, still less the democratic process whereby the community reached its final decision, dissension did cast a reflection on the authenticity of the collective decision when the liberal community voted on foreign policy. The vote, insofar as it bore on key matters of state, had to be unanimous, so the responsible liberals maintained. The liberal community might have a majority opinion, but never a common interest. This was all well in times of peace, but during wartime, the nation had to break through the threshold separating *many* from *all*. It needed to close the qualitative gap between the majority interest and the common purpose.

W. H. Auden, a friend of Eliot's and Niebuhr's, who had recently immigrated to the United States with MacLeish's help, explained this conundrum as an unavoidable conflict between two kinds of freedom.[53] On June 17, just four days after the fall of Paris, Auden delivered a commencement speech at Smith College. His speech, entitled "Free or Romantic?", treated the Class of 1940 to his metaphysical reflections on what was happening in Europe. He began by defining freedom in two ways. From the standpoint of each constituent of a community, freedom meant the right of that constituent member to satisfy its needs and develop its potential, unhindered by the laws of the community to which it belonged. This kind of freedom was a freedom *from* communal restraints. If one turned the perspective inside out and observed the community from the vantage point of the whole, freedom was "synonymous with unity, through harmonious agreement of the parts." Freedom, in this second definition, denoted a type of freedom that the community could attain only when all its constituents voluntarily accepted the objective logic of collective priorities. Evidently, these two types of freedom could clash with each other. Each of the parts of the nation could experience freedom, in the communal sense of the term, as necessity, as burdensome, even enslaving norms. On the other hand, the nation grudged freedom in the individual sense of the term because individual freedom also included the freedom to transgress communal rules, a transgression that hampered the free production of unanimity in the national community.[54]

Auden's disquisition may have struck the youthful graduates as too abstract to be relevant to the horror of the Western world going up in flames again. But his metaphysical inquiry actually "has more connection with Hitler's Stukas than you may realize," reassured Auden. The present war had its deepest root in a metaphysical cause, for the ongoing conflict was between an "open society" and a "closed society." By the former, Auden had in mind a society that preserved the habitual tension between the two contradictory kinds of freedom. It was a society that could maintain balance between tyranny of the regimented masses and anarchy of atomic individuals. No existing society was perfectly open. But, having immigrated to the United States, Auden found a society that he thought came closest to the ideal of an open society that "believes that . . . the truth is best arrived at by free controversy." In contrast, a closed society was a totalitarian society. It was "romantic" in the sense that a closed society was characterized by "laziness," "impatience," or some sorts of wild spiritual abandon. Perhaps, Auden echoed Eliot, "heretic" better expressed what he meant by "romantic." Under a romantic or heretic system, freedom had to designate either the absolute free will of the individual or the stifling collectivism. There was no tension between the two types of freedom.

The scale had been tipped in one direction or the other throughout history. In the nineteenth century, for example, the scale was tilted dangerously on the side of individual freedom, and the result of this imbalance was the nightmare of laissez-faire fundamentalism. But the regnant romanticism of the interwar decades had been the other type, the absolute triumph of the collective will over individual freedom.[55]

Could an open society, where individual freedom and the collectivity's will were deliberately left in tension, defend itself against a closed society? Although formulated differently and variously, this question was also uppermost in the minds of MacLeish, Frank, Mumford, and their responsible friends. Around this central question crystallized a complex of related questions that exercised them: How could the government of laws defend itself against the government of men, rules against exception, and the dynamic but inefficient society against the regimented and efficient society? To Mumford, liberal organizations such as the ACLU did not seem to appreciate the tension between individual liberty and the freedom of the collectivity and a host of problems this tension raised in times of national emergency. In November 1940, someone at the ACLU made a blunder of inviting this antiliberal firebrand to join. Mumford naturally declined and characteristically went out of his way to add insult to injury:

> Today we have a twofold job on our hands: one is to guard our constitutional rights against those who would, for base reasons, curtail them; and the other is to guard them against those who by an absolutist interpretation of freedom would use the principle of free speech as a cloak for treason: thus employing freedom to destroy freedom. By upholding the latter American Civil Liberties Union shows an almost pathological inability to understand the nature of the dangers that now confront democracy.[56]

MacLeish was no less keenly aware of this dilemma. In one of the many speeches he delivered in the spring of 1940, he observed that the question the United States faced was "whether it can survive in competition with a more efficient way of government and a more efficient way of life which achieves its efficiency precisely by suppressing and destroying and eliminating all those human values which democracy was created to achieve."[57] The question was not rhetorical. MacLeish seems to have been genuinely perturbed by this problem, as indicated by his tortured conclusion: "Only liberty which is strong enough to defend itself is strong enough to be truly liberty and truly tolerant."[58] At first glance, liberty "strong enough to defend itself" looks like just another question-begging tautology that sounded good, the kind of patriotic rhetoric MacLeish honed to a point.

Yet, whether intended or not, MacLeish's formulation did capture the essence of the contradiction between Auden's two varieties of freedom: negative liberty of the individual constantly had to defend itself against the free and harmonious action of the collectivity while the latter, collective freedom, constantly had to defend itself against individual freedom. Two freedoms, each defending itself against the other, realized a synthesis that was "truly liberty and truly tolerant."

Faced by the identical problem, Mumford, in the chapter entitled "Prospect for Survival" in *Faith for Living*, flirted with the idea of a "totalitarian democracy." The international crisis demanded economic and political sacrifices of the American people. So "for the duration of the war," "[t]he totalitarian element will be inescapable." But no sooner did he float this idea than Mumford retreated in the next paragraph: "But the democracy is also real; for the purpose that must be safeguarded at every step is the right of free citizens to exercise rational choice and decision, to live under a system of law instead of a personal despotism, to freely choose or reject their governors." In the paragraphs immediately following, Mumford claimed that he had discovered a magic formula for marrying totalitarian sacrifice to democratic freedom. The "large scale sacrifice" of individual rights would cease to be perceived as such if and when the nation "erect[s] a *common* goal of living." The general will and the particular needs of the individual, then, would harmonize, each resolving itself into the other. And this unlikely marriage of two freedoms required something drastic on the order of a Great Awakening. America had to pursue, Mumford wrote, the "psychological possibility of a large-scale conversion," that is, to press toward "a conversion, deep-seated, organic, and religious in essence, so that no part of political or personal existence will be untouched by it."[59]

In a nutshell, these various proposals amounted to a nationalization of freedom, a redefinition of freedom as a culturally habituated mode of living and desiring. These remedies, prescribed variously by Mumford, Dewey, Eliot, Auden, Frank, and MacLeish, proposed to use national culture as a solvent that fused the law of the country and individual liberty. Culture denoted a local and concrete order wherein common values and desires were conserved – passed down – through extensive public use, that is, through parenting, education, and other forms of acculturation. And once all Americans internalized a common purpose, thanks to the "large-scale conversion," they could be as free as they wanted without hindering the harmony, unity, and freedom of their country. In the nation "united and free," disparate social units (citizens, families, churches, schools, trade unions, corporations, political parties, and so on down to the largest unit, the state) were placed in an exact correspondence and symmetry with one another, because they all wanted the same things. This national whole was inclusive to the extent that anyone was admitted to it as long as he or she swore an oath of allegiance, or was habituated, to its hierarchy of cultural values. At the same time, this community was exclusive since no one had a title to membership by positive rights. Only the converts were allowed to join. By dissipating into each other, the two freedoms gave birth to the American Way of Life.

The responsibles criticized liberalism not only because it delayed the decision-making process of the community but also because, regardless of its swiftness, any decision the liberal community made looked weak when confronted with the hostile decision of other nonliberal communities. Hidden in the nucleus of the liberal conceptualization of freedom was the assumption that there was something intrinsically good and sound about political disagreements and conflicts of interests, and liberals failed to bring this assumption to the fullest clarity by acknowledging that such an intrinsic good could be posited only as a value upheld by all members of the national community. American citizens could always agree to disagree, but they must not transcend the horizon of the fundamental agreement that grounded plurality and individualism. But the emergence of the avowed enemies of liberal democracy, the liberal warhawks argued, had revealed this hidden proviso.

The main protagonists of these two chapters were haunted by this revelation. A domestic policy choice that gained the assent of the majority was considered legitimate as long as it got enough votes. Yet a foreign policy lost its legitimacy even if it was legal and backed by the majority vote unless it expressed the sameness permeating the community. The liberal-pluralist mechanics of decision making (party politics, local rule, horse-trading, log-rolling) were designed on the assumption that the two types of freedom would never harmonize. Liberalism, in other words, could not allow the participants in the ritual of decision making to achieve their goals through self-sacrifice, for the religious and deeply illiberal concepts like "conversion" and "sacrifice" threatened the principle of liberal-pluralist society. The systematic elimination of the various stages of self-negation in the collective decision-making process of a liberal democracy ensured that the national community remained a "congeries" of autonomous bystanders with bizarre preferences and volatile commitments dissociated from one another, a rabble of lost individuals uninterested in sublimating their multitudinous desires collectively into the legitimate political will through self-negation (or sacrifice, conversion, awakening).[60] The collective decision, democratically arrived at by bargaining and compromise, may be able to get itself legislated, but it could never rise to the monolithic agreement ("metaphysical purpose") that gave the decisive edge to Nazis, Fascists, and Bolsheviks.[61] It may be legal, but its legitimacy would remain a sham in the eyes of America's mortal enemies.

The American Lebensraum

Freedom requires and will require far greater living space than Tyranny.

Henry Luce (1941)

We will never know just how many American owners of shortwave radios actually listened in.

The last of the prewar years opened with Roosevelt's "Four Freedoms" speech (January 6, 1941), in which he called for not just the promotion of these novel freedoms but their enforcement "everywhere in the world."[1] The nation's rearmament, both material and moral, quickly overshadowed the lingering concerns over economic recovery. With as yet almost a full year until Pearl Harbor, the U.S. government officially declared its determination to turn the nation into the arsenal of democracy.

And just about the same time, propaganda shortwave programs that Rome had been flashing to America to drive a wedge between the British and Americans began featuring an unfamiliar voice: "Ezra Pound, the famous American economist, poet, and commentator."

Of all the writers who explored America's stake in World War II before that war actually came, Ezra Pound stands out as by far the most extraordinary case. Critics have copiously wrote about his support for fascist Italy, his identification of Mussolini's corporatist project with the American Revolution, his obsession with crackpot monetary and fiscal theories like Social Credit, and most disturbingly the burgeoning of his old phobia of usury into full-blown anti-Semitism.[2] All the same, the truly unhinged quality of his radio broadcasts has yet to be assessed in light of their prewar circumstances.

Once the war broke out in Europe, Pound, who had been living in Italy for the entire depression decade, began a one-man letter-writing campaign. He pestered fellow writers, Cabinet members, and senators with letters blasting the sneaky pro-British policy of "Roosenstein," "Jewsfeldt," or

"Roosevelt and kikery."[3] It chills us to read Pound telling in a letter to Lothrop Stoddard, "If Hitler can free the French and English people from their usurers he will lay the basis for a lasting peace in Europe."[4] Hitler proceeded to gratify Pound's wish in less than two years. What is surprising to the later generations who know of the treason indictment brought against him in 1943 in absentia and Pound's insanity plea after he was captured in 1945 is that many even took the trouble to respond to such blatherings. Harold Ickes wondered "whether it [Pound's letter] is a lyric or merely modernistic prose" in his reply to a letter in which Pound anathematized, no doubt for his Jewishness, Henry Morgenthau – "that uusp unspeakable 'colleague' to use a mild expression of yr/ Mr Morgenthau (may god eliminate him)."[5] Some, like Germanophile H. L. Mencken, who was waging his own anti-Allies campaign from his editorial perch at the *Baltimore Sun*, commiserated with Pound: "Imbecility is enjoying a colossal triumph in this great nation. Not only is Roosevelt falling for every fraud of the British propaganda bureau; he is also taking Congress with him. Yet worse, the newspapers have abdicated all their rights as the opposition and go along with loud hosannas."[6] Pound also found a sympathetic correspondent in Anglophobe Pearl Buck, who responded with a fulsome assent to Pound's economic theory that bankers and monopolists pushed nations into war for profit: "It is extremely valuable to me to have at my hand what you say about the war. I am sure that it is true, and there are more than a few of us in this country who are writing and saying all we can to make it known."[7]

Pound abandoned his hope to build a pro-fascist Committee of Correspondence when on the high seas the British Navy stepped up interception of the mail originating from the areas under Axis control.[8] He then turned to the shortwave radio to reach the audience in North America, to break to Americans "news of the real Europe instead of ... fairy tales from the Anglo-Jewish legends."[9] In January 1941, Pound broadcast his first message from Rome in the program *American Hour* in which he attacked the arbitrary extension of the U.S. sphere of vital interests: "Today OUR American frontiers are neither on the Danube nor on the Yangtze–I wonder [if] there are any adults left in America." Pound went on to rant and fulminate in a series of demented broadcasts for the remainder of 1941.[10] By the end of the year, he had broadcast a few dozen vitriolic speeches savaging Roosevelt and Churchill. In a sign of his deepening addiction to German propaganda, an anti-Semitic undertone would presently dominate his broadcasts after summer.

Pound's was arguably the most nauseating literary propaganda performance during the prewar years, for these broadcasts were performance indeed. Foreign broadcast monitors working for the Federal Communications Commission kept track of Pound's raging madness. Listening to these old recordings we catch a certain cadence in his recitals (Pound always scripted his broadcasts) – serpentine, repetitious, without clear punctuation, an incantation of putrid mantras.[11] Whoever happened to tune in heard Pound's attacks on the Jews, Roosevelt, Churchill, or Anthony Eden muffled by a thick layer of cackling noise, which sometimes rendered a whole broadcast unintelligible. It was all "rambling," "confused," "turgid," and "disorganized," as the federal monitors posted at listening centers across the country observed.[12] It is impossible to estimate how many Americans Pound's messages reached and of those how many he successfully got to consider "why mothers in Montana and Minnesota should send their sons out to die for the Rothschilds."[13] In light of the fact that a typical broadcast by Father Coughlin, which was more coherent in delivery but no less nefarious in content, could draw millions of listeners in the 1930s, one should not underestimate how much Pound's broadcasts resonated with his American audience.

For all their bad reception and barely intelligible delivery, Pound's broadcasts played on some of the most deep-seated prejudices that buttressed American isolationism: anti-Semitism, Anglophobia, the "devil theory of war," and the tradition of unilateralism. Americans arguing for isolation took pains to distance themselves from anti-Semitic isolationists who practically bought into Hitler's argument that Germany was waging a war of annihilation against the nemesis of European civilization, the "Jewish Bolshevism." But Charles Lindbergh's infamous Des Moines speech, in which he suggested that "the British, the Jewish, or the Administration" were "agitating for war," indicates the popularity of the view that the Jews both at home and abroad were trying to plunge the United States into war against Nazi Germany to the prejudice of its national interests.[14] The foul abuse that Pound hurled at British imperialists also flattered America's self-image as an anti-imperial lone eagle while also confirming the widespread regret that the United States was dragooned into the last war to defend Britain's imperial interests. The notion that a sinister cabal of international financiers and monopoly capitalists engineered the new world war was anything but a far-out opinion at that time. Many Americans stopped short of identifying that cabal with the "international Jewry," as Nazi propagandists and Ezra Pound openly did. Nonetheless the American public opinion was amply primed for Pound's racial and economic interpretations.[15]

Furthermore, Pound's counsel of American neutrality harmonized with the traditional unilateralism whose roots extended back to the founding of the republic. Ever since Washington's farewell address enjoining the republic against foreign entanglements, the fear of losing freedom of action in foreign policy had gripped wide and vocal segments of the public at critical times when the nation's international commitment was tested. In the first third of the twentieth century, its influence was on the wane, as this sort of nationalistic unilateralism was retreating to its traditional redoubts, the Midwest and the west where populism and nativism still held strong sway (although he grew up in Philadelphia, Pound was born in Idaho, and he self-consciously referred to his western origin throughout his career). All the same, at moments of national hesitation when America vacillated between international responsibility and haughty isolation, as during the debate over Article X of the League of Nations charter, these unilateralists held a casting vote. Their claim that collective security was un-American, even treasonous, still held residual attraction for the nation's ethos during the prewar period. In selecting his correspondents, Pound was predictably drawn to those politicians who were steeped in this tradition. Robert Taft, William Borah, George Tinkham, Burton Wheeler, Gerald Nye, Arthur Vandenberg (before his widely publicized recantation of the isolationist dogma during the war), Jerry Voorhis, and Henry Wallace made strange bedfellows, except for their distrust of the East Coast internationalist establishment.[16]

Pound's transition from his euphoric embrace of cosmopolitanism in the late 1910s to his anti-Semitic isolationism was facilitated by several factors, some proximate, some distant. His espousal of unilateralism most likely was reinforced by his new mania for early American history, his adoration for the founding fathers (Jefferson and Adams in particular), and his fetishization of the Constitution.[17] Pound's study of early American history and his analysis of contemporary geopolitics influenced each other, as evidenced by both his broadcasts and the "Adams Cantos" (1939). For him, Adams was a paragon of wise go-it-alone-ism. In Pound's version, Adams firmly believed that the very simple principle, "Keep out of Europe," should govern American foreign policy all the time. Hamilton may be interested in playing his "game" that would have "got us entangled with Britain," but Adams was unswervingly for "eternal neutrality in all wars in Europe."[18] These "fathers of our American republic left us a heritage. It was to keep out of foreign affairs."[19] Adams's foresight served as a foil to Roosevelt's perfidy. Pro-British Roosevelt was a traitor, a traducer of the Constitution. His pro-Allies policy was not a mistake but a wicked scheme to hand American sovereignty over to the Jewish-dominated world-state. Roosevelt and his globalist cronies "have learned nothing even from their parents, let alone grandparents." "As John Adams said, not one of 'em is capable of understanding any constitution whatever. But they seem also to have lost what was known by our forebears. An alliance with France *or* England wd/ put an end to our system of liberty."[20]

Pound's idealization of the early republic also helped radicalize his anti-Semitism. For Pound and many other conservative unilateralists, the America to which Washington bid his farewell represented an agrarian utopia where its citizens were all landed and thus independent, which further meant rational, moral, and public-minded. The Constitution crystalized the eternal values that permeated that utopia. In the myth of republican decline to which they subscribed, however, that fresh and healthy society soon began rotting away, as it moved from agrarian economy to monetized economy, from democracy to oligarchy, and from republic to empire, under corrosive influences of commerce and modernity. These modernizing forces were all encapsulated in *Neschek* (Hebrew for "usury"), Pound's not-so-innocent catch-all term. Having corrupted America's republican character, usurers now schemed to embroil America in a web of foreign entanglements. A fragment that he wrote in 1941 began thus:

> The Evil is Usury, *neschek*
> the serpent
> *neschek* whose name is known, the defiler,
> beyond race and against race
> the defiler
> Tóχos hic mali medium est
> Here is the core of evil, the burning hell without let-up,
> The canker corrupting all things, Fafnir the worm
> Syphilis of the State, of all kingdoms[21]

This stanza points us to another source of Pound's anti-Semitism, namely the traditional characterization of the Jew as, to quote Hitler, "the anti-man, the creature of another god … a creature outside nature and alien to nature."[22] If Pound's choice of the Hebrew word and his allusion to well poisoning leave any room for ambiguity, "beyond race and against race" unmasks the identity of this great Evil variously called serpent, toxin, canker, defiler, syphilis of the State. He was the Jew. Anti-Semitism in general, and its German variant adopted by the National Socialists and their followers (including Pound) in particular, was unlike other forms of racism in that antipathy to the Jew was rooted in the fear of what anti-Semites imagined as the Jew's deracinated, cosmopolitan character.[23] The Jew had no nation but he was in every nation. The Jews did not form a distinct race because they lived as a parasite in all races. This alleged rootlessness certainly facilitated the conflation between the wandering Jew and the wandering Capital: money and Jews both transcended national borders and racial differences. During the prewar years, this potent stereotype encouraged unilateral isolationists to scapegoat the Jew. Many of them embraced the devil theory of war that blamed bankers, speculators, and merchants of death for war. They were also gripped by the deep-seated fear of losing freedom of action on account of alliance with foreign powers. The fantasy of the global cabal of Jewish bankers trying to pit the nations of the world against one another for profit graphically lent color to these abstract worries.

Lastly and most importantly, anti-Semitism resonated with Pound because of its affinity to his long-held poetics, which can be seen as a cluster of six correlated feelings. First was a distrust of rhetoric. By rhetoric Pound meant a certain abuse of language. Being rhetorical meant using language to persuade people, to change their mental state. Because its origin and effect were both purely mental, it could not capture a poetic fact, which existed objectively.[24] Second was a distaste for symbolism or expressing something in terms of something else. Pound attacked symbolism because when the poet treated language as a symbolic system, he or she was merely following lines of conventional association. The symbolist played a linguistic game, which took him or her away from life.[25] Third was apathy toward abstraction. Pound insisted on avoiding abstract words because they had no referents. They were empty words devoid of concrete particulars.[26] Fourth was an impulse to efficiency. This impulse presupposed the distinction drawn above between empty and meaningful words. Pound thought that certain words were just pure sounds without corresponding meanings, and that using them rhetorically reduced the intensity of his poetry. The poet had to be selective, so that he or she could intend as much meaning as possible in the fewest possible words.[27] Fifth was a faith in objectivity. Pound said many times that the subject matter of a poem objectively existed. His main task was not to create imaginatively something that did not exist but to discover exact expressions for things that already existed in the modern world.[28] Sixth and last was a passion for fullness. Pound believed that people tended to use words without intending anything directly. From this tendency resulted the fustian verbalism of pre-1914 poetry. To avoid this, Pound tried to use fewer words and fill them up with intended meanings more intensely.[29] All these orientations were related to one another because they arose out of Pound's essentialism, his lifelong belief that words ought to have the essential, nonarbitrary tie to the poetic facts to which they referred. There were of course many words without referents.

These words were malignant words, to be extirpated from one's language. Pound understood money and interest in an analogous way. Usury made money out of money. Its operation was analogous to a bad poem wherein empty words multiplied, with even more empty words proliferating along lines of conventional association, taking this bad poem farther away from concrete particulars. By this analogy, Pound's brash, didactic, and exterminationist attitude toward inferior poesy was transferred to usurers, and by extension to the Jew. And when the National Socialists and their sympathizers used the figure of the Jew to put a face on the alleged international conspiracy to drag the United States into the new world war, and when his study of the founding fathers convinced him that Thomas Jefferson and John Adams were proto-isolationists, Pound was easily led to a virulent variant of anti-Semitic isolationism. Up to that point, Pound had tirelessly battled the lazy logic of symbolic substitution. But his anti-Roosevelt stance of 1941 was a sheer flummery, the end-point in the long chain of one careless substitution after another.

By some curious coincidence, Pound's last prewar broadcast fell on December 7. Pound counseled American isolation and warned against the perils of imperial overreach: "My idea of a state of empire is more like a hedgehog or porcupine – chunky and well defended. I don't cotton to the idea of my country bein' an octupus [*sic*], weak in the tentacles and suffering from stomach ulcers and colic gastritis."[30] Pound signed off at 12:24 PM Eastern Standard Time. Twenty-four minutes later, the first wave of Japanese bombers descended on Pearl Harbor.

These prewar years marked a watershed of singular significance in modern U.S. history. Within the Western Hemisphere, the United States had already commanded geopolitical supremacy since the late nineteenth century, when the Monroe Doctrine transmogrified from the legitimacy principle for the political independence of new republics in Latin America into the pseudo-legal instrument of U.S. penetration into their domestic politics. In the prewar years, the challenge posed by the two autarkic empires on the western and eastern edges of Eurasia began to lure this regional hegemon out of the comfort and security of its hemispheric stronghold protected by the two oceans. Seduced by the prospect of the American Century, America fought against itself. Prudes and innocents in the New World had to overcome a great number of residual inhibitions before anointing themselves as the Great Emancipator of the World.

Tellingly, the phrase "the American Century" was a product of the prewar culture. Henry Luce's manifesto by the same title was published in the February 17, 1941, issue of *Life*. If the Lend-Lease bill then debated on the floor of Congress meant, for all intents and purposes, America's unofficial declaration of war, Luce's essay, read by millions of Americans, marked the moment when the nation's posture toward the impending crisis finally tipped from avoidance and vacillation to clear-eyed resolve.

Luce played various rhetorical roles in this essay (with significant help from MacLeish, who prepared for Luce a number of memos).[31] He was a cheerleader reminding the nation of its promise and fundamental goodness. Alternately, he was also a fugleman demonstrating to a hesitant nation how to move and think as if it owned the twentieth century. And to those recusants balking at America's ascension to world supremacy, Luce played the Devil's advocate, telling them, on the summit of a high mountain, that all the kingdoms of the world were theirs for the taking.

Whatever else Luce did, the essay's main aim was not to lay out facts and analyses. Rather, Luce's goal was hortatory and therapeutic. He deliberately presented his case for the American Century as something self-evident that the Americans willfully ignored. "The American Century" was not a forecast. It was the ratification of a fait accompli. "We are *in* the war," so he notified his readers. "The trouble is not with the facts." The "trouble is that clear and honest inferences have not been drawn from the facts." What little sentiment of isolationism still lingered, then, reflected misrecognition of the drift of world history. And this misrecognition resulted from a psychological blockage that prevented Americans from giving a proper name to the opportunity within their grasp, to the desire they secretly nursed and nurtured. Because America was not in error but in denial, more statistics about world trade or more revelations about the evils of totalitarianism would not sway the nation's mind to internationalism. America had been true to the facts. But its citizens had been "false to" themselves. This was Luce's pet argument. In his preface for Boothe's *Margin for Error*, he had already written:

> It [the audience's self-congratulatory reaction to his wife's play] proved not that the American people were honestly confused (for as the self-admittedly best-informed people in history they knew what it was all about) but that they *desired* to be confused, were at great pains to confuse themselves, applaud the confusion, hoped that they might painlessly confuse themselves straight through World War II.[32]

What was needed, then, was honesty with oneself. Only the unflinching reckoning with what America had already become "in spite of ourselves" could lead Luce's country out of "the whole mass of deceits and self-deceits in which we have been living." World War II was "not *primarily* [war] of necessity and survival." It was a war of choice. Therefore, the question before America was: "Do we *want* to be in this war?" Or even better, because America already wanted to be in this war but denied itself this shameful desire, the real question was: Did America *want to want* world leadership?

Luce also pressed his case along other lines. He did acknowledge some fears that were often voiced by those frightened by the prospect of the American Century. America's post–Great War foreign policy did leave room to be desired and must not be repeated after the next war. The expansion of the federal government in the last decade was indeed worrisome, and the next war may increase people's dependency on big government. Luce tried to raise the nation's consciousness with facts. Wasn't there "already an immense American internationalism"? "American jazz, Hollywood movies, American slang, American machines and patented products are in fact the only things that every community in the world, from Zanzibar to Hamburg, recognizes in common." And he appealed to the nation's enlightened self-interest, too. Since the American people were fighting this war through the proxy, the British Empire, they were allowed little say in formulating war aims. But now dependent on the arsenal of democracy across the Atlantic, the British had already accepted their status as "junior partner" in any future Anglo-American alliance. "[W]hat we want will be okay with them," Luce told the readers. "We fight no wars except our wars," and the last thing that the Americans were fighting for was another century of Pax Britannica. America had better set its own terms so that its ideals, values, and interests would shape the coming peace. In the final analysis, however, all these facts, concessions, and calculations were meant as therapeutic devices, to cajole and bait the Americans out of shyness, confusion, and guilt to a more positive and confident evaluation of who they had become, what they were already capable of.

The quality that most stood out in Luce's brazen-faced manifesto was vagueness. The essay did not urge any position on the pressing policy issues such as the Lend-Lease or a preventive war on the Axis powers. In making the audacious case for American capability and responsibility for solving all the problems of the world, Luce mainly addressed Americans' commonsense morality, cultural pride, and evangelical optimism. No concrete policy was recommended. The essay made it sound as though as soon as Americans mentally converted to Luce's vision of the American Century, that vision would become the agent of global salvation and do the rest of the hard work: "It now becomes our time to be the powerhouse from which the ideals spread throughout the world and do their mysterious work of lifting the life of mankind from the level of the beasts to what the Psalmist called a little lower than the angels."[33] Luce's idealism – giving ideas efficacy – reflected the inordinate importance the prewar culture accorded to ideas. At the same time, this vagueness helped the essay absorb and repackage in the extremely elastic slogan all the controversial changes that had taken place as America anticipated the next world war for half a decade.

The full gamut of emotions associated with the Great War had to be abreacted. "You'll never catch me hoping again!" chanted angrily the disappointed writers, artists, and intellectuals during the interwar decades. Most of them now in their forties, they still wanted the same things that they wanted in their idealistic youth, but once burned, they were afraid to hope, afraid to want. It took their dried-up willingness of heart half a decade of escalating global calamity to quicken again. Many remained too frightened to hope to their bitter ends.

The illusion of geographical immunity from attacks by powers alien to the Western Hemisphere had to be dispelled. This required a mass reeducation of the Americans' sense of their place in the world by training their ability to grasp the world as a spherical object, to conceptualize the interconnections among distant locations, and to understand tactical and strategic marvels that new technologies had made feasible. Roosevelt played the role of the nation's geography teacher with enthusiasm, enlightening the public through his fireside chats. And his supporters, within the government and without, often in concert, assisted his efforts with their own initiatives. Europe was unshakably lodged at the center of the emergent global consciousness, but throughout the prewar years, traditionally peripheral regions – Asia and Africa – began slowly snapping into focus in America's mental picture of the world.

The Italian aggression in Africa forced on other rival colonial powers the choice between two alternatives: condone Italian colonialism or condemn it and reconsider their own colonial policy. The Western colonial powers tried to wiggle out of this dilemma without embarrassment. In the event they ended up in a compromised position closer to the latter than the former. Anticolonialism spread and accelerated throughout the prewar years. In the United States, the anti-Axis rhetoric based on universalistic ideals created an opening for African Americans. They could harass their own government to choose between two alternatives: brook totalitarianism or attack it and reform its own racist treatment of black citizens. The racist nation attempted to argue its way out of this quandary but ended up in a position much closer to the latter than it wished. Anticolonialism and antiracism, finally conjoined during the prewar years, became integral part of America's vision for the postwar global order, first in rhetoric but eventually in policy.

Communists and anti-Communists locked horns over who really must lead the global coalition against Germany, Italy, and Japan. Initially, the Popular Front rhetoric appeared successful. It persuaded many prewar writers that the Soviets had the requisite foresight, expertise, and courage to rally the liberal democracies against the dictatorships. However, the consolidation of Stalinism during the Great Purge and the Soviet alliance with Hitler's Germany in 1939 combined to change the dominant narrative of Soviet-led antifascist coalition. The USSR was gradually absorbed into the nebulous notion of "totalitarianism" in the American imagination. Although Soviet Russia would again join the Allies as a "democracy" during World War II and indeed defeat Nazi Germany at stupendous costs, the fatal wounds it incurred during the prewar years to its self-assigned role as the most legitimate champion of world freedom and world justice would continue to fester during the Cold War.

Responsible liberals attempted to break the myth of liberal innocence, calculating that Americans' coyness with their own nation's preponderant power was rooted in the naïve, holier-than-thou exceptionalism. America was a normal nation, they argued, and so it should not be ashamed of involvement in great power politics.

Various concepts of liberty crystalized around two definitions: freedom as the American Way of Life and freedom as a universal law. Logically, they contradicted each other. Singly, each also had weaknesses as an argument for America's world leadership. Combined opportunistically, they spared the American people a troublesome look at the incoherency at the heart of their most sacrosanct value.

Collectively, these emergent opinions, attitudes, and feelings laid the intellectual groundwork for the American *Lebensraum*. Conceptual and emotional frameworks that would shape the official and popular definition of national interest and guide America's dealings with the world through-out the rest of the twentieth century were built before the American entry into World War II. When opportunities presented themselves during and after the war (the power vacuum on the Continent and in the Pacific; the dismantling of the British imperial system), America was ready to seize them not only because the military and industrial hardware (production capacity, military bases, the atomic bomb, and other physical furnishings necessary for empire building) was at hand but also because the intellectual know-how was in place, having already been invented and audience-tested in the crucible of the prewar culture. This is not to assert the primacy of ideology in twentieth-century U.S. foreign policy. Nor should ideology be narrowly understood as "blueprint," "program," or still less "grand strategy." As a rule, goals, capabilities, and conditions stand in a dialectical relation. Goals pressure the nations to create new capabilities and change conditions; existing capabilities and conditions at the same time make certain goals more thinkable and desirable than others. The prewar years were an extraordinary period when America had to relearn how to dream, a period when visions and desires lagged behind conditions and capabilities. The prewar writers thought up visions commensurate to America's capabilities and world conditions. They made new policies, practices, and commitments seem in the interest of the American public.

The legacy of the prewar culture is most easily discernible in postwar U.S. interventions in three key areas: Western Europe, East Asia, and the Middle East. At critical moments, the language of the American Century helped policy makers suppress inhibitions and remove psychological obstacles. It served as a putative reason, a soporific lullaby, substituting for an original (and often economic) motive that was usually offensive to the belief system of the decision makers. Second, thanks to their creative and selective credulity, this new, expansive sense of America's world leadership was able to prod the United States toward more radical options than could have been adopted in its absence. Architects of the American Century were not simply cynical. Cynicism is just a set of motivational terms that rests on the vitality of aspirations as much as idealism does.[34] And finally, even when the cheerleaders of America's world hegemony did not believe in their own cheers, the slew of precepts, symbols, and storylines that the prewar culture had tested and refined furnished rationalizations that justified official policies to the public. They proved useful PR tools.

Meanwhile, isolationism fatally lost influence in America's political culture. Since the end of World War II, the national temper several times swung to isolationism after unpopular wars. But even the lessons of Vietnam and the second Gulf War have proved unable to revert the nation back to the era when the United States was satiated with hemispheric leadership. Old-fashioned nationalists who take exception to this consensus are marginalized as irrelevant troglodytes and allowed little real influence on policy making and public opinion.

In sum, the prewar culture irremovably changed Americans' deepest assumptions about their nation's role in the world. Separated by this tectonic shift, today's Americans can no longer calculate their relation with the nations outside the hemisphere the way their grandparents did. Surely, it is not out of the realm of possibility that the United States will withdraw its forces and commitments across the Atlantic and the Pacific and drastically contract its *Lebensraum*. With the emergence of a counter-hegemonic alliance in Eurasia or a catastrophic collapse of the domestic economy, America may retire to the Western Hemisphere and primarily focus on nipping the emergence of a Eurasian power by playing the game of great power politics. *Pace* the doomsayers busily writing premature obituaries for the American Century, however, these eventualities remain unlikely if not inconceivable. This means that there is little chance that a fiery and protracted debate over national purpose, something on the order of those that raged during the run-up to World War II, will be reprised anytime soon. For the foreseeable future, Americans will continue to live in the nation whose character and mission were established through the war of words that the main protagonists of this book fought.

Notes

NOTES TO PROLOGUE

1 Franklin D. Roosevelt, *The Public Papers and Addresses of Franklin D. Roosevelt*, vol. 10 (New York: Harper, 1941), pp. 385, 386, 387, 391, 385, 386, 389.

2 This vignette relies on: "To the Photo Editor," The Committee to Defend America by Aiding the Allies Records, Folder 7, Box 35, Mudd Library, Princeton University; "Freedom Rally Thrills 17,000," *The New York Times*, October 6, 1941, 1; "America 'Must Sweat' to Top Nazi Output, Knudsen Warns," *The Washington Post*, October 6, 1941, 1; Ben Hecht and Charles MacArthur, *Fun to Be Free* (New York: Dramatists Play Service, 1941).

3 See Sheryl Kaskowitz, *God Bless America: The Surprising History of an Iconic Song* (New York: Oxford University Press, 2013), pp. 33–43; Laurence Bergreen, *As Thousands Cheer: The Life of Irving Berlin* (New York: Da Capo Press, 1996), pp. 156–63, 369–70.

4 Wallace Stevens, "The Irrational Element in Poetry," in Frank Kermode and Joan Richardson (eds.), *Wallace Stevens: Collected Poetry and Prose* (New York: The Library of America, 1997), pp. 788, 789.

5 Wallace Stevens, "The Noble Rider and the Sound of Words," in *Wallace Stevens: Collected Poetry and Prose*, pp. 656, 659, 660, 665. These expressed Stevens's theory, or wish. Whether he practiced his preaching in his poetry is altogether a different problem. For analyses of this problem, see Alan Filreis, *Modernism from Right to Left: Wallace Stevens, the Thirties, and Literary Radicalism* (Cambridge: Cambridge University Press, 1994). Chapter 1 is particularly germane to topics considered in the present book.

6 Archibald MacLeish, "Libraries in the Contemporary Crisis," in *A Time To Speak: The Selected Prose of Archibald MacLeish* (Boston: Houghton Mifflin, 1941), p. 122.

7 Gordon Hutner, *What America Read: Taste, Class, and the Novel, 1920–1960* (Chapel Hill: University of North Carolina Press, 2009), p. 189.

8 Malcolm Cowley, "A Farewell to the 1930s," *The New Republic*, November 8, 1939, 42, 43.

9 Matthew Josephson, *Infidel in the Temple: A Memoir of the Nineteen-Thirties* (New York: Alfred Knopf, 1967), p. 405.

10 Because he believed that another war would undercut the black civil rights movement, Wright opposed U.S. entry into war after the outbreak of the European war ("not my people's war"), which conformed to the CPUSA's official line. Yet when Germany invaded the Soviet Union in June 1940, the Party line switched overnight from nonintervention to intervention. Wishing to remain within the Party, Wright reluctantly toned down his public stance against American participation. See Richard Wright, "U.S. Negroes Greet You," *Daily Worker*, September 1, 1941, 7. For the Party's censorship of Wright's acceptance speech at the Spingarn Medal ceremony, see Hazel Rowley, *Richard Wright: The Life and Times* (New York: Henry Holt, 2001), pp. 252–254.

11 Steinbeck's resistance novel, *The Moon Is Down*, was eventually published in early 1942, after America's official entry into war. For more details regarding Steinbeck's deepening immersion in pro-democracy propaganda activities, see Jackson J. Benson, *John Steinbeck, Writer* (New York: Viking, 1984), pp. 458, 465, 486–92.

12 On isolationism in the 1930s, see Wayne S. Cole, *Roosevelt and Isolationists, 1932–45* (Lincoln: University of Nebraska Press, 1983); Justus D. Doenecke, *Storm on the Horizon: The Challenge to American Intervention, 1939–1941* (Lanham: Rowman and Littlefield, 2000); Manfred Jonas, *Isolationism in America, 1935–1941* (Ithaca: Cornell University Press, 1966).

13 The question of where to locate the "point of no return" has exercised generations of historians. Some classic works by new left historians, such as William Appleman Williams's *The Tragedy of American Diplomacy* (Cleveland: World Publishing, 1955) and Victor Kiernan's *America, the New Imperialism* (London: Zed Press, 1978), have traced origins of America's expansionist impulse all the way back to the colonial period. Other scholars have proposed other watershed moments. Frank Ninkovich's *Global Dawn* (Cambridge, MA: Harvard University Press, 2009) identifies the Gilded Age as a catalytic moment, while Christopher Nichols's *Promise and Peril* (Cambridge, MA: Harvard University Press, 2011) nominates the first three decades of the twentieth century as a period when internationalist ideas wrestled with and eventually gained the upper hand of the isolationist tradition. One of the implications of the present book is a rebalancing of these existing emphases. Colin Dueck's *Reluctant Crusaders* (Princeton: Princeton University Press, 2008) and Christopher Layne's *The Peace of Illusions* (Ithaca: Cornell University Press, 2007) have recognized the critical importance of the prewar years.

14 My decision to study the evolution of a new globalism during the prewar years in the sphere of commercialized mass culture is considerably indebted to Michael Denning's similar decision in his study of the "age of CIO," which significantly but not entirely coincides with the prewar years. See Denning's concise but detailed discussion of the consolidation of a new "cultural apparatus" in the first three decades of the twentieth century and its simultaneously or alternatingly complementary and oppositional relationship with the Popular Front movement in *The Cultural Front: The Laboring of American Culture in the Twentieth Century* (London: Verso, 1997), pp. 38–50.

15 With a few exceptions, the most influential cultural medium of the 1930s, movies, are not considered here, not because the cinema cannot be included in literary culture however flexibly defined (it can, actually, particularly in the context of 1930s American culture). The main reason is that, unlike the print culture, theater, and, to a lesser extent, radio, Hollywood failed to make its influences felt in a host of prewar controversies. This failure can be ultimately attributed to a single cause, the Production Code, which enjoined studios from addressing sensitive issues that could have diplomatic implications. On major studios' response to foreign threats, especially those coming from Germany, see Michael E. Birdwell, *Celluloid Soldiers: The Warner Bros. Campaign Against Nazism* (New York: NYU Press, 2000); Thomas Doherty, *Hollywood and Hitler, 1933–1939* (New York: Columbia University Press, 2013).

16 Archibald MacLeish, "The American Writers and the New World," *The Yale Review* 31 (1941), 76.

17 Hans Bak (ed.), *The Long Voyage: Selected Letters of Malcolm Cowley, 1915–1987* (Cambridge, MA: Harvard University Press, 2014), p. 295.

NOTES TO CHAPTER 1

1 On the coinage of the neologism "totalitarianism" during the prewar years, see Les K. Adler and Thomas G. Paterson, "Red Fascism: The Merger of Nazi Germany and Soviet Russia in the American Image of Totalitarianism," *American Historical Review* 75 (1970), 1051; Abbott Gleason, *Totalitarianism: The Inner History of the Cold War* (Oxford: Oxford University Press, 1995), pp. 49–58; Thomas R. Maddux, "Red Fascism, Brown Bolshevism: The American Image of Totalitarianism in the 1930s," *Historian* 40 (1977), 86–87; Benjamin L. Alpers, *Dictators, Democracy, and American Public Culture: Envisioning the Totalitarian Enemy, 1920s–1950s* (Chapel Hill: University of North Carolina Press, 2003), pp. 130–31; Thomas E. Lifka, *The Concept of "Totalitarianism" and American Foreign Policy, 1938–1939* (New York: Garland, 1988).

2 Arthur Schlesinger Jr., "Back to the Womb?: Isolationism's Renewed Threat," *Foreign Affairs* 74 (1995), 4.

3 Akira Iriye, *The Globalizing of America, 1913–1945, vol. 3, The Cambridge History of American Foreign Relations* (New York: Cambridge University Press, 1993), pp. 164–69. The German-originated term "geopolitics" entered the popular lexicon exactly at this juncture. See Gearóid Ó Tuathail, *Critical Geopolitics: The Politics of Writing Global Space* (Minneapolis: University of Minnesota Press, 1996), chapter 4.

4 For data on isolationism among various demographics, especially on its popularity in the Midwest, see George L. Grassmuck, *Sectional Biases in Congress on Foreign Policy* (Baltimore: The Johns Hopkins University Press, 1951), pp. 141–74; Leroy N. Rieselbach, *The Roots of Isolationism: Congressional Voting and Presidential Leadership in Foreign Policy* (Indianapolis: Bobbs-Merrill, 1966);

Richard Franklin Bensel, *Sectionalism and American Political Development, 1880–1980* (Madison: The University of Wisconsin Press, 1984), pp. 104–28.

5 Alan K. Henrikson, "The Map as an 'Idea': The Role of Cartographic Imagery During the Second World War," *The American Geographer* 2 (1975), 22.

6 The best overviews of U.S. foreign policy during this period are Waldo Heinrich, *Threshold of War: Franklin D. Roosevelt and American Entry into WWII* (New York: Oxford University Press, 1988); Patrick J. Hearden, *Roosevelt Confronts Hitler: America's Entry into World War II* (Dekalb: Northern Illinois University Press, 1987); David Reynolds, *From Munich to Pearl Harbor* (Chicago: Ivan R. Dee, 2001).

7 Marc Trachtenberg, *The Craft of International History: A Guide to Method* (Princeton: Princeton University Press, 2006), pp. 136–39.

8 Virginia Carr, *Dos Passos: A Life* (Garden City: Doubleday, 1984), pp. 136, 145.

9 For the syndrome of disillusionment and cynicism that pervaded the liberal community following the Versailles settlement, see Stuart I. Rochester, *American Liberal Disillusionment* (University Park: Pennsylvania State University Press, 1977); Manfred Jonas, *Isolationism in America, 1935–1941* (Ithaca: Cornell University Press, 1966), pp. 26–30; Robert Osgood, *Ideals and Self-Interest in America's Foreign Relations* (Chicago: University of Chicago Press, 1953), pp. 307–425.

10 "The Week," *The New Republic*, September 13, 1939, 141.

11 Ernest Hemingway, *A Farewell to Arms* (New York: Scribner's, 2003), p. 184; *The Complete Short Stories of Ernest Hemingway* (New York: Scribner's, 2003), p. 112.

12 "old men's lies" from "Hugh Selwyn Mauberley" in *The Selected Poems of Ezra Pound* (New York: New Direction, 1957), p. 64. For Pound's initial reaction to the war, see A. David Moody, *Ezra Pound: Poet* (Oxford: Oxford University Press, 2007), pp. 328–29.

13 Ezra Pound, *The Cantos of Ezra Pound* (New York: New Directions, 1996), p. 61.

14 Ezra Pound, *Literary Essays of Ezra Pound*, T. S. Eliot (ed.) (New York: New Directions, 1968), p. 3.

15 Randolph Bourne, "The War and Intellectuals," *War and Intellectuals: Collected Essays, 1915–1919* (Indianapolis: Hackett, 1999), p. 11.

16 John Dewey, "No Matter What Happens–Stay Out," *Common Sense* (March 1939). Reprinted in *John Dewey: The Later Works, 1925–1953*, vol. 14, Jo Ann Boydston (ed.) (Carbondale: Southern Illinois University Press, 1988), p. 364. For Dewey's position on American neutrality, see also the following pieces collected in the same volume: "Higher Learning and War," *Bulletin of the American Association of University Professors* 25 (December 1939); "Creative Democracy–The Task Before Us"; "The Meaning of the Term: Liberalism."

17 For more details from Sherwood's life, see Harriet Alonso, *Robert E. Sherwood: The Playwright in Peace and War* (Amherst: University of Massachusetts Press, 2007).

18 Robert Sherwood, *Idiot's Delight* (New York: Charles Scribner's Sons, 1936), p. 34.

19 Sidney Howard White, *Sidney Howard* (Boston: Twayne Publishers, 1977), pp. 20–25.

20 Sidney Howard, "Our Professional Patriots," *The New Republic*, August 20, 1924, 346.

21 Sidney Howard, *The Ghost of Yankee Doodle: A Tragedy* (New York: Charles Scribner's Sons, 1938).

22 Ronald Steel, *Walter Lippmann and the American Century* (Boston: Little, Brown, 1980), p. 366.

23 Maxwell Anderson, "By Way of Preface: The Theatre as Religion," *The New York Times*, October 26, 1941, v, xi.

24 On the evolution of Anderson's stance on war, see Arthur T. Tees, "Maxwell Anderson's Changing Attitude toward War," *North Dakota Quarterly* 48 (1980): 5–11.

25 Maxwell Anderson, "By Way of Preface: The Theatre as Religion," *The New York Times*, October 26, 1941, xi, x2; "Theatre as Religion," *The New York Times*, November 2, 1941, x3.

26 For Dreiser's isolationism during the prewar years, see Theodore Dreiser, *America Is Worth Saving* (New York: Modern Age Books, 1941), an angry and bitter compendium of all the currently popular arguments against internationalism.

27 For the flag salute case, see *Minersville School Dist. v. Gobitis*, 310 U.S. 586 (1940).

28 For a comprehensive list of federal and states statutes curtailing freedom of speech, see Zechariah Chafee, *Free Speech in the United States* (Cambridge, MA: Harvard University Press, 1941), pp. 573–97.

29 Dalton Trumbo, *The Remarkable Andrew: Being the Chronicle of a Literal Man* (Philadelphia: J. B. Lippincott, 1941), p. 241.

30 Among examples worthy of mention are Phillip Davidson, *Propaganda and the American Revolution, 1763–1783* (Chapel Hill: University of North Carolina Press, 1941) and John C. Miller, *Sam Adams, Pioneer in Propaganda* (Boston: Little, Brown, 1936).

31 Martha Gellhorn, *A Stricken Field* (New York: Duell, Sloan and Pearce, 1940), pp. 282, 288, 296.

32 Gellhorn, "Portrait of a Lady," *The Heart of Another* (New York: Charles Scribner's Son, 1941).

33 Maxwell Anderson, *Dramatist in America: Letters of Maxwell Anderson, 1912–1958*, Laurence G. Avery (ed.) (Chapel Hill: University of North Carolina Press, 1977), p. 117.

34 Untitled document, undated, Playwrights Company Records, Box 3, Folder "Candle in the Wind," New York Public Library.

35 Obituary, *Time*, August 31, 1942, 81.

36 Alice Duer Miller, "The White Cliffs," *Life*, March 31, 1941, 80–88, 90.

37 Alice Duer Miller, *The White Cliffs* (New York: Coward-MacCann, 1940), p. 44. This anti-British passage was cut from the *Life* version.

38 Samuel Rosenman, *Working with Roosevelt* (New York: Harper, 1952), p. 260.

39 Franklin D. Roosevelt, *The Public Papers and Addresses of Franklin D. Roosevelt, 1940*, vol. 9 (New York: Macmillan, 1941), p. 199.

40 Lewis Mumford, *Men Must Act* (New York: Harcourt, Brace, 1939), pp. 103–04.

41 Archibald MacLeish, *Three Short Plays* (New York: Dramatists Play Service, 1964), p. 39.

42 My analysis here draws on a comparable analysis of *Fall of the City* in Neil Verma, *Theater of the Mind: Imagination, Aesthetics, and American Radio Drama* (Chicago: University of Chicago Press, 2012), pp. 49–56.

43 Cedric Larson, "The Council for Democracy," *The Public Opinion Quarterly* 6 (1942): 284–90; Carl Friedrich Papers, Council for Democracy, 1940–1942, Box 1–Box 11, Pusey Library, Harvard University.

44 Stephen Vincent Bénet, *Nightmare at Noon* (New York: Council for Democracy, 1940), p. 7.

45 Stephen Vincent Bénet, "Listen to the People," *Life*, July 7, 1941, 90–96.

46 Allen Tate, "Tension in Poetry," *Southern Review* 4 (1938), 105.

47 Millay's husband, Eugen Jan Boissevain, had his family in Holland, and a stream of letters from them kept Millay and Eugen appraised of their ordeals. Millay sought to put together some writing out of these letters so as to publicize the plight of Europeans living in German-occupied territories. See "A Dutch Family in Wartime," Edna St. Vincent Millay Papers, Box 2, Folder 2, Library of Congress.

48 Nancy Milford, *Savage Beauty: The Life of Edna St. Vincent Millay* (New York: Random House, 2001), p. 435.

49 Edna St. Vincent Millay, "There Are No Islands, Any More," (New York: Harper & Brothers, 1940), pp. 5, 10.

50 Gellhorn to Charles Scribner, May 17, 1940, Charles Scribner's Sons Papers, Box 1, Folder "Hemingway, Martha Gellhorn," Firestone Library, Princeton University.

51 Clare Boothe, *Margin for Error* (New York: Random House, 1940), p. 119.

52 Robert Adrey, *Thunder Rock* (New York: Dramatists Play Service Inc., 1941), p. 62.

53 Undated typescript of a speech MacLeish gave at the dinner given in honor of Edward R. Murrow on December 2, 1941, Archibald MacLeish Papers, Box 46, Library of Congress.

54 Robert Sherwood, *There Shall Be No Night* (New York: Charles Scribner's Sons, 1940), pp. 10, 17.

55 Sherwood, *There Shall Be No Night*, p. 148.

56 See Peter Butenhuis, "Prelude to War: The Interventionist Propaganda of Archibald MacLeish, Robert E. Sherwood, and John Steinbeck," *Canadian Review of American Studies* 21 (1996): 1–30; Barry B. Witham, "*There Shall Be No Night* and the Politics of Isolation," *Theatre Symposium* 9 (2001), 120; Ikka Joki and Roger D. Sell, "Robert E. Sherwood and the Finnish Winter War: Drama, Propaganda and Context 50 Years Ago," *American Studies in Scandinavia* 21 (1989): 51–68; Albert Wertheim, *Staging the War: American Drama and World War II* (Bloomington: Indiana University Press), pp. 22–25.

NOTES TO CHAPTER 2

1 Detailed accounts of key events during the war can be found in George W. Baer, *The Coming of the Italian-Ethiopian War* (Cambridge, MA: Harvard University Press, 1967); Angelo Del Boca, *The Ethiopian War, 1935–1941* (Chicago: University of Chicago Press, 1969). On the U.S. policy during the war, see Brice Harris, *The United States and the Italo-Ethiopian Crisis* (Stanford: Stanford University Press, 1964).

2 Robin D. G. Kelly, "'But a Local Phase of a World Problem': Black History's Global Vision, 1883–1950," *Journal of American History* 86 (1999), 1066. For black antifacism in Britain and its empire, see S. K. B. Asante, "The Italo-Ethiopian Conflict: A Case Study in British West African Response to Crisis Diplomacy in the 1930s," *The Journal of African History*, 15 (1974): 291–302; Cedric J. Robinson, "The African Diaspora and the Italo-Ethiopian Crisis," *Race and Class* 27 (1985): 51–65.

3 For the U.S. government's policy during the war, see Wayne S. Cole, *Roosevelt and the Isolationists, 1932–35* (Lincoln: University of Nebraska Press, 1983), pp. 180–82.

4 For more details, see testimonies by Elmer Rice and Hallie Flanagan (head of the Federal Theater Project). Elmer Rice, *Minority Report: An Autobiography* (Simon and Schuster: New York, 1963), p. 357; Hallie Flanagan, *Arena* (New York: Duell, Sloan and Pearce, 1940), pp. 65–67.

5 For positive views of Fascist Italy, see John Patrick Diggins, *Mussolini and Fascism: A View From America* (Princeton: Princeton University Press, 1972), pp. 302–06; Thomas Guglielmo, *White on Arrival: Italians, Race, Color, and Power in Chicago, 1890–1945* (New York: Oxford University Press, 2003), pp. 117–22.

6 Ian Mugridge, *The View from Xanadu: William Randolph Hearst and United States Foreign Policy* (Montreal: McGill-Queen's University Press, 1995), p. 194.

7 Richard Wright, *Native Son* (New York: Harper, 1966 [1940]), pp. 109–10.

8 James Baldwin, "Many Thousands Gone," in *Notes of a Native Son* (Boston: Beacon, 1955), p. 42.

9 Harvard Sitkoff, *A New Deal for Blacks: The Emergence of Civil Rights as a National Issue: The Depression Decade*, 30th Anniversary Edition (New York: Oxford University Press, 2009), p. 202.

10 Nancy J. Weiss, *Farewell to the Party of Lincoln: Black Politics in the Age of FDR* (Princeton: Princeton University Press, 1983), p. 48.

11 Richard Wright, *12 Million Black Voices* (New York: Basic Books, 2008 [1941]), p. 123, 124, 114.

12 James H. Meriwether, *Proudly We Can Be Africans: Black Americans and Africa, 1935–1961* (Chapel Hill: University of North Carolina Press, 2002), pp. 11–22.

13 Meriwether, *Proudly We Can Be Africans*, p. 42.

14 Duke Ellington, *Duke Ellington Reader*, Mark Tucker (ed.) (New York: Oxford University Press, 1995), p. 47.

15 W. E. B. Du Bois, "Forum of Fact and Opinion," *The Pittsburgh Courier*, June 6, 1936, A1. See also Du Bois, *Dusk of Dawn: An Essay Toward an Autobiography of a Race Concept* (New York: Harcourt, Brace, 1940), p. 310; Brenda Gayle Plummer, *Rising Wind: Black Americans and U.S. Foreign Affairs, 1935–1960* (Chapel Hill: University of North Carolina Press, 1996), pp. 24–36.

16 The emergence of this global-mindedness among Afro-Americans is the main story of Penny M. Von Eschen, *Race Against Empire: Black Americans and Anticolonialism, 1937–1957* (Ithaca: Cornell University Press, 1997).

17 Du Bois, "Forum of Fact and Opinion," *The Pittsburgh Courier*, April 25, 1936, A1, A2.

18 George Padmore, "Ethiopia and World Politics," *The Crisis*, May 1935, 138–39.

19 Ralph J. Bunche, "French and British Imperialism in West Africa," *The Journal of Negro History* 21 (1936), 31. For Bunche, however, blacks in America and colonials in Africa and Asia shared the same destiny to the extent that both groups were victims of the capitalist system. He regarded "race" as fundamentally a language of justification to explain away what was actually the subjugation of relatively powerless groups by the state acting consciously and unconsciously at the behest of capital. On his Marxist-Leninist approach to international politics, see his *A World View of Race* (Washington, DC: The Associates in Negro Folk Education, 1936), pp. 23–29.

20 W. E. B. Du Bois, "Inter-Racial Implications of the Ethiopian Crisis: A Negro View," *Foreign Affairs* 14 (1935), 92, 89.

21 Langston Hughes, "Air Raid Over Harlem," *New Theatre and Film* 3 (1936), 19.

22 Joseph Harris, *African-American Reactions to War in Ethiopia* (Baton Rouge: Louisiana State University Press, 1944), pp. 39, 41; William Scott, *The Sons of Sheba's Race: African-Americans and the Italo-Ethiopian War, 1935–1941* (Bloomington: Indiana University Press, 1993), p. 66.

23 See John Cullen Gruesser, *Black on Black: Twentieth-Century African American Writing about Africa* (Lexington: University Press of Kentucky, 2000); Eric Sundquist, *To Wake the Nations: Race in the Making of American Literature* (Cambridge, MA: Harvard University Press, 1993), pp. 540–80; George Shepperson, "Ethiopianism and African Nationalism," *Phylon* 14 (1953): 9–18; Wilson Moses, "The Poetics of Ethiopianism: W. E. B. Du Bois and Literary Black Nationalism," *American Literature* 47 (1975): 411–26; *The Wings of Ethiopia: Studies in African-American Life and Letters* (Ames: Iowa State University, 1990).

24 Schuyler, *Black No More* (New York: Macaulay, 1931), p. 92.

25 For Schuyler's early years, see Oscar R. Williams, *George S. Schuyler: Portrait of a Black Conservative* (Knoxville: University of Tennessee Press, 2007). Schuyler tells the story of the bootblack incident in his column, "Aframerica Today: Tulsa-Little Chicago," *The Pittsburgh Courier*, March 13, 1926, 14.

26 Schuyler, "Views and Reviews," *The Pittsburgh Courier*, November 23, 1935, 10.

27 George Schuyler, *Black and Conservative* (New Rochelle: Arlington House, 1966), p. 102.
28 Schuyler, "Views and Reviews," *The Pittsburgh Courier*, December 7, 1935, 10.
29 Schuyler, "An Open Letter to Arthur Brisbane," *The Pittsburgh Courier*, December 14, 1935, 1.
30 Schuyler, "Views and Reviews," *The Pittsburgh Courier*, June 8, 1940, 6.
31 Schuyler, "Views and Reviews," *The Pittsburgh Courier*, May 25, 1935, 12.
32 Schuyler, "The Rise of the Black Internationale," *The Crisis*, August 1938, 277.
33 Schuyler, "'European War Will Free Colored World'–Schuyler," *The Pittsburgh Courier*, September 2, 1939, 1.
34 Schuyler, "Views and Reviews," *The Pittsburgh Courier*, September 13, 1940, 6.
35 George Schuyler, *Black Empire* (Boston: Northeastern University Press, 1991), p. 46.
36 Schuyler, *Black Empire*, pp. 133, 129.
37 George Schuyler, "The Ethiopian Murder Mystery: A Story of Love and International Intrigue," in Robert A. Hill ed., *Ethiopian Stories* (Boston: Northeastern University Press, 1994), p. 122.
38 Quoted in "Foreword," John A. Williams, *Black Empire* (Boston: Northeastern University Press, 1991), p. 56.
39 Schuyler, "Views and Reviews," *The Pittsburgh Courier*, February 23, 1935, 10.
40 Schuyler, "Views and Reviews," *The Pittsburgh Courier*, May 29, 1937, 10.
41 "Schuyler-McKay Debate Aroused Wide Attention," *The Pittsburgh Courier*, May 29, 1937, 7.
42 Schuyler, "Views and Reviews," *The Pittsburgh Courier*, November 6, 1937, 10.
43 Schuyler, "Views and Reviews," *The Pittsburgh Courier*, April 11, 1936, 12.
44 W. E. B. Du Bois, "Forum of Fact and Opinion," *The Pittsburgh Courier*, May 1, 1937.
45 Schuyler, *Black and Conservative*, p. 121.
46 Schuyler, *Black and Conservative*, p. 146. See also "The Phantom American Negro," *Freeman*, April 23, 1951, 457–59.
47 Schuyler, "Views and Reviews," *The Pittsburgh Courier*, August 3, 1935, 10. See also his attack on the party's alleged maltreatment of George Padmore, "Views and Reviews," *The Pittsburgh Courier*, August 25, 1934, 10.
48 Schuyler, "Views and Reviews," *The Pittsburgh Courier*, April 11, 1936, 12.
49 Williams, *George S. Schuyler*, pp. 38, 69, 88–89.
50 See Schuyler's testimony, quoted in Robert A. Hill and R. Kent Rasmussen, "Afterword," *Black Empire* (Boston: Northeastern University Press, 1991), p. 260: "I have been greatly amused by the public enthusiasm for 'The Black Internationale,' which is hokum and hack work of the purest vein. I deliberately set out to crowd as much race chauvinism and sheer improbability into it as my fertile imagination could conjure. The result vindicates my low opinion of the human race." Most critics accept Schuyler's testimony. See Alexander M. Bain, "*Shocks Americana!*: George Schuyler Serializes Black Internationalism," *American Literary History* 19 (2007), 938–39; Etsuko Taketani, "Colored Empires of the 1930s: Black Internationalism, the U.S.

Black Press, and George Samuel Schuyler," *American Literature* 82 (2010), 140; John Gruesser, *Black on Black*, pp. 104–19. The lone dissenting opinion is voiced by Mark Christian, who sees no irony in these stories. See *Black Fascisms: African American Literature and Culture Between the Wars* (Charlottesville: University of Virginia Press, 2007), p. 72.

51 I am here following a powerful point made by Schuyler's most perceptive reader, Jeffrey S. Ferguson. See *The Sage of Sugar Hill: George S. Schuyler and the Harlem Renaissance* (New Haven: Yale University Press, 2005), pp. 47–62.

52 Kenneth Burke, *Attitudes Toward History* (Berkeley: University of California Press, 1984 [1937]), p. 55.

NOTES TO CHAPTER 3

1 W. H. Auden, "Spain," *Selected Poems*, Edward Mendelson (ed.) (New York: Vintage, 1989), 53.

2 Alan Calmer (ed.), *Salud!: Poems, Stories and Sketches of Spain by American Writers* (New York: International Publishers, 1938), p. 37.

3 Robert Dallek, *Franklin D. Roosevelt and American Foreign Policy, 1932–1945* (New York: Oxford University Press, 1979), pp. 126–27.

4 The international repercussions of the Spanish Civil War have been studied by a number of historians. Allen Guttmann's *The Wound in the Heart: America and the Spanish Civil War* (New York: Free Press, 1962) remains the most comprehensive treatment of the U.S. reaction to the war. For a reconstruction of poets' reaction, see Cary Nelson, *Revolutionary Memory: Recovering the Poetry of the American Left* (New York: Routledge, 2001), 181–243. For the American churches' reactions to the war (unlike Catholics, Protestants overwhelmingly supported the republican government, though most were hostile to Communism), see Lord Ralph Roy, *Communism and the Churches* (New York: Harcourt, Brace, 1960), pp. 110–22. For additional information regarding other Western democracies, I largely relied on Frederick R. Benson, *Writers in Arms: The Literary Impact of the Spanish Civil War* (New York: NYU Press, 1967) and Larry Ceplair, *Under the Shadow of War* (New York: Columbia University Press, 1987). For England, see Samuel Lynn Hynes, *The Auden Generation: Literature and Politics in England in the 1930s* (Princeton: Princeton University Press, 1982), pp. 242–95; James K. Hopkins, *Into the Heart of the Fire: The British in the Spanish Civil War* (Palo Alto: Stanford University Press, 1998).

5 Alfred Kazin, *Starting Out in the Thirties* (Boston: Little, Brown, 1962), pp. 82–83.

6 This is reflected in letters of volunteer fighters in Spain. See *Madrid 1937: Letters of the Abraham Lincoln Brigade from the Spanish Civil War*, Cary Nelson and Jefferson Hendricks (eds.) (New York: Routledge, 1996), pp. 32, 34, 38, 45, 309, 312, 325, 330.

7 The list of the respondents can be read as a who's who of major literary players in the late 1930s. To list some of the most illustrious: Herbert Agar, Sherwood Anderson, Maxwell Anderson, Brooks Atkinson, Stephen Vincent Benét, Louis

Bromfield, Pearl S. Buck, Van Wyck Brooks, Kenneth Burke, Robert
M. Coates, Theodore Dreiser, Edna Ferber, Dorothy Canfield Fisher, Daniel
Fuchs, Dashiell Hammett, Robert Herrick, Ernest Hemingway, James Wel-
don Johnson, Alfred Kazin, Alfred Kreymborg, Alain Locke, Edgar Lee
Masters, Marianne Moore, Kathleen Norris, Clifford Odets, Katherine Ann
Porter, Edwin Seaver, Upton Sinclair, John Steinbeck, Thornton Wilder,
William Carlos Williams.

8 *Writers Take Sides: Letters about the War in Spain from 418 American Authors*
(New York: The League of American Writers, 1938), pp. 44, 23, 56, 66–67.

9 Robert S. Thornberry, "Writers Take Sides, Stalinists Take Control: The
Second International Congress for the Defense of Culture," *The Historian* 62
(2000), 592.

10 Edwin Rolfe, "Elegy for Our Dead," *Salud!*, p. 13.

11 Thus, Ellery Sedgwick, pro-Franco editor of *Atlantic Monthly*, wrote: "If they
[the Soviets] could get a Red Spain, they could get all to the south of us.
They've already got Mexico"; Quoted in Michael E. Chapman, "Pro-Franco
Anti-Communism: Ellery Sedgwick and the *Atlantic Monthly*," *Journal of
Contemporary History* 41 (2006), 649.

12 The phrase "innocents and stooges" is from Eugene Lyons's anti-Communist
classic, *The Red Decade: The Stalinist Penetration of America* (Indianapolis:
Bobs Merrill, 1941), p. 17.

13 For a vivid anecdote, see Bernard Knox, "Premature Anti-fascist," *Antioch
Review* 57 (1999): 147–48. On the charge of discrimination during and after
World War II, which has been made by veterans of the Abraham Lincoln
Brigade, see John Gerassi, *The Premature Antifascists: North American Volun-
teers in the Spanish Civil War, 1936–1939, An Oral History* (New York: Praeger,
1986), pp. 159–233; Peter Carroll, *The Odyssey of the Abraham Lincoln Brigade:
Americans in the Spanish Civil War* (Stanford: Stanford University Press, 1994),
pp. 250–64.

14 For the tribulations of the Lincoln veterans during the McCarthy era, see Cecil
Eby, *Between the Bullet and the Lie: American Volunteers in the Spanish Civil
War* (New York: Holt, Reinhart, Winston, 1969), pp. 315–19. Some commen-
tators on the right have disputed the U.S. government's alleged discrimin-
ations against "premature antifascists." For the controversy, see Bernard Knox,
"The Spanish Tragedy," *New York Review of Books*, March 26, 1987, 21–28;
Harvey Klehr and John Haynes, "The Myth of 'Premature Anti-Fascism,'"
New Criterion, September 2002, 19–26.

15 See Whittaker Chambers, *Witness* (Washington, DC: Regnery Publishing,
1980 [1952]), p. 458. The official induction of the Franco government into
the West in the new war against global Communism did not come about as
swiftly as some Cold Warriors wished, due mainly to Harry S. Truman's
disapproval of autocracy (see Robert L. Beisner, *Dean Acheson: A Life in the
Cold War* [Oxford: Oxford University Press, 2006], pp. 382–87), but the
public outlook on fascism in Spain grew positive steadily after World
War II. The end of the Cold War only revivified this script, for some of the

Soviet archives that momentarily opened to Western scholars in the early 1990s, new evidence garnered from the FBI files under the Freedom of Information Act, and the declassified Venona Project decrypts conferred additional documentary respectability on some of the hair-raising misdeeds alleged by the detractors of the left's romance with Communism. For the VENONA decrypts, see John Earl Haynes and Harvey Klehr, *Venona: Decoding Soviet Espionage in America* (New Haven: Yale University Press 1999), but beware of the authors' penchant for sweeping generalizations built on guilt by association. For a reconsideration of the Soviet role in the Spanish Civil War using the VENONA decrypts and Soviet archives, see Herbert Romerstein, *Heroic Victims: Stalin's Foreign Legion in the Spanish Civil War* (Washington, DC: Council for the Defense of Freedom, 1994); *Spain Betrayed: The Soviet Union in the Spanish Civil War*, Ronald Radosh, Mary R. Habeck, and Grigory Sevostianov (eds.) (New Haven: Yale University Press, 2001). My caveat regarding *Venona* applies to the latter work as well. For a criticism of the right's exploitation of Soviet archives, see Helen Graham, "Spain Betrayed? The New Historical McCarthyism," *Science and Society* 68 (2004): 364–69.

16 For the activities of Contemporary Historians, Inc., see Folder "Contemporary Historians, Inc.," Box 51, Archibald MacLeish Papers, Library of Congress. For Hemingway's financial contribution, see Herman Shumlin to Ralph Ingersoll, undated (the same folder). The weight of evidence today makes it seem highly plausible that, unbeknownst to himself, "Argot" (the Soviet code name for Hemingway) was marked by the Comintern as a particularly valuable prize for its public diplomacy campaigns. See William Braasch Watson, "Joris Ivens and the Communists: Bringing Hemingway into the Spanish War," *Hemingway Review* 10 (1990): 2–18; Hans Schoots, *Living Dangerously: A Biography of Joris Ivens*, trans. David Colmer (Amsterdam: Amsterdam University Press, 2000); Allen Weinstein and Alexander Vassiliev, *The Haunted Wood* (New York: Vintage, 2000), p. 273.

17 Cary Nelson, "Hemingway, the American Left, and the Soviet Union: Some Forgotten Episodes," *Hemingway Review* 14 (1994), 42.

18 *Ernest Hemingway: Selected Letters*, Carlos Baker (ed.) (New York: Scribner's, 1981), p. 480.

19 Matthew J. Bruccoli, ed., *The Only Thing That Counts: The Ernest Hemingway/Maxwell Perkins Correspondence, 1925–1947* (New York: Scribner's, 1996), p. 278.

20 Alan M. Wald, *Trinity of Passion: The Literary Left and the Antifascist Crusade* (Chapel Hill: University of North Carolina Press, 2007), p. 13.

21 Ernest Hemingway, "Fascism Is a Lie," *The New Masses*, June 22, 1937, 4.

22 Ernest Hemingway, *For Whom the Bell Tolls* (New York: Scribner's, 2003), pp. 248, 230. All further references are to this edition and will be cited parenthetically.

23 Hemingway's gesture toward objective coverage here unwittingly confirms that the ping-pong reporting may create a semblance of neutrality but cannot

guarantee "objectivity." In sending the chapter containing this episode to Max
Perkins, Hemingway flourished his brave commitment to "truth" and threw
in, for good measure, a few scornful words for ideologically inflexible writers
like Alvah Bessie: "Don't let the ideology boys that have to claim we never
killed anybody see that chapter . . . It is as bad to have a ring in your brain that
people lead you around by as to have a ring in your nose" (Bruccoli, *The Only
Thing*, 278). And yet, the particularly repellent aspect of the so-called Ronda
massacre (the allegation that a prorepublican mob threw Franco sympathizers
off the cliff), which Pilar's account accepts and embellishes, never occurred,
most likely having been fabricated by Franco's propaganda campaign. See
Ramon Buckley, "Revolution in Ronda: The Facts in Hemingway's *For Whom
the Bell Tolls*," *Hemingway Review* 17 (1997): 49–57.

24 For an analysis of the propaganda along this line in the Nationalist-controlled
area, see Xosé-Manoel Núñez Seixas, "Nations in Arms against the Invader:
On Nationalist Discourses during the Spanish Civil War," in Chris Ealham
and Michael Richards (eds.), *The Splintering of Spain: Cultural History and the
Spanish Civil War, 1936–1939* (Cambridge: Cambridge University Press, 2005),
pp. 55–60.

25 "Walbridge Abner Field," in Oliver Wendell Holmes, *Speeches* (Boston: Little,
Brown, 1900), p. 81. See also his address, "The Soldier's Faith," pp. 56–66.

26 Dwight MacDonald, "Reading from Left to Right," *Partisan Review*, January–
February 1941, 25.

27 Robert Van Gelder, "Ernest Hemingway Talks of Work and War," *The New
York Times Book Review*, August 11, 1940, 2.

28 Among the more than 2,300 books listed in the book inventory Hemingway
compiled in 1940, 131 titles pertain to military history and espionage, including
Carl von Clausewitz's classic, *On War*. See Michael S. Reynolds, *Hemingway's
Reading, 1910–1940: An Inventory* (Princeton: Princeton University Press, 1981).

29 Carlos Baker, *Hemingway: The Writer as Artist* (Princeton: Princeton University Press, 1952), pp. 252–53; Allen Guttmann, *The Wound in the Heart*,
pp. 167–95; Allen Josephs, *For Whom The Bell Tolls: Ernest Hemingway's
Undiscovered Country* (New York: Twayne, 1994), pp. 95–96.

30 Martha Gellhorn to Charles Scribner, August 23, 1940, Charles Scribner's
Sons Record, Hemingway Series 4, Box 1, Folder "Hemingway, Martha
Gellhorn," Firestone Library, Princeton Library.

31 Hemingway to Perkins, telegram, September 9, 1940, Charles Scribner's Sons
Record, Hemingway Series 1, Box 4, Folder 22.

32 Bruccoli (ed.), *The Only Thing*, p. 288.

33 Ernest Hemingway, introduction, *Men at War* (New York: Random House,
1979), xiv.

34 Hemingway, *Selected Letters*, p. 482.

35 Hemingway, *Selected Letters*, p. 309.

36 Hemingway, *Selected Letters*, p. 468.

37 Hemingway, *Selected Letters*, p. 479.

38 Bruccoli (ed.), *The Only Thing*, p. 281.

39 See Alvah Bessie, "For Whom the Bell Tolls," *The New Masses*, November 5, 1940, 25–29. For the reactions of the veterans of the Abraham Lincoln Brigade to the novel, see Carroll, *The Odyssey*, pp. 235–40.

40 Edmund Wilson, "Return of Ernest Hemingway," *The New Republic*, October 28, 1940, 591.

41 Lionel Trilling, "An American in Spain," *Partisan Review*, January–February 1941, 64.

42 Baker, *Hemingway*, pp. 240, 245.

43 See Michael J. B. Allen, "The Unspanish War in *For Whom the Bell Tolls*," *Contemporary Literature* 13 (1972), 204; David Sanders, "Ernest Hemingway's Spanish Civil War Experience," *American Quarterly* 12 (1960), 134; Richard Hovey, *Hemingway: The Inward Terrain* (Seattle: University of Washington Press 1968), pp. 153, 170; William Watson, "Hemingway's Attacks on the Soviets and the Communists in *For Whom the Bell Tolls*," *North Dakota Quarterly* 60 (1992), 117–18. See also Richard Slotkin's explication of how the novel Americanizes the Spanish Civil War. Richard Slotkin, *Gunfighter Nation: The Myth of the Frontier in Twentieth-Century America* (New York: Macmillan, 1993), pp. 315–18.

44 The composition of republican forces in this major counterattack, on which the novel is based, bears testimony to the emerging communist hegemony within the republican army. Of the three divisions deployed for this offensive, two were commanded by Communists: José María Galán and General Walter. Also, the 14th International Brigade, under French Communist Jules Dumont, fought with Walter's division. See Hugh Thomas, *The Spanish Civil War*, 3rd ed. (London: Harper, 1977), pp. 688–89; Anthony Beevor, *The Spanish Civil War* (Harmondsworth: Penguin, 1982), p. 195. Hemingway's character Golz (the "*Général Soviétique*") is drawn from Walter, who was particularly notorious for his ideological and disciplinarian fanaticism. When one division retreated during the Segovia offensive, he ordered the "machine-gunning of those who pulled back, executions on the spot, and the beating of stragglers"; Anthony Beevor, "The Callous Betrayal of Anti-Franco Forces," *London Times*, May 24, 2006, 19.

45 On the change in the manner of salutation within the ranks of Lincolns after the Barcelona insurrection, see Eby, *Between the Bullet and the Lie*, pp. 25, 119.

46 On SIM, see Graham, *The Spanish Republic*, pp. 375–78. Jordan's safe conduct bears a curious resemblance to the safe conduct Hemingway carried when he visited the fronts. A photographic reproduction of Hemingway's safe conduct can be found in William Braasch Watson, "Investigating Hemingway: The Story," *North Dakota Quarterly* 59 (1991), 55. Watson misses this correspondence between Jordan and Hemingway, but his essay is noteworthy in that he is the only scholar who has so far attempted to demonstrate by using circumstantial as well as documentary evidence, including this safe conduct, that Hemingway participated in a guerrilla campaign behind the enemy lines. See also Watson's sequel, "Investigating Hemingway: The Trip," *North Dakota Quarterly* 60 (1992): 79–95.

47 Stanley Payne, "Americans in Spain," *New York Sun*, April 11, 2005, arts and letters section, 18.

48 My reading agrees with Dwight Macdonald's early review. See MacDonald, "Reading from Left to Right," 24–33.

49 Benson, *Writers in Arms*, pp. 169–85.

50 George Orwell, *Homage to Catalonia* (San Diego: Harcourt, 1952), pp. 150–79.

51 See Hemingway, *Selected Letters*, pp. 463–64; David C. Duke, *Distant Obligations: Modern American Writers and Foreign Causes* (New York: Oxford University Press, 1983), pp. 165–97; Stephen Koch, *The Breaking Point: Hemingway, Dos Passos, and the Murder of José Robles* (New York: Counterpoint, 2005).

52 Hemingway later changed "In Paris" to "In Paris, we say" during the galley reading. It is likely that by the summer of 1940 Hemingway had second thoughts about the Party explanation for Nin's disappearance.

53 Historians have traditionally attributed the arrest and murder of Andreu Nin to the Soviet agents in Spain. See Thomas, *The Spanish Civil War*, pp. 701–09; Beevor, *The Spanish Civil War*, pp. 193–94. Recently, Helen Graham has suggested a more nuanced scenario that plays down the centrality of Soviet involvement in the Barcelona May Day (*The Spanish Republic*, pp. 289, 296).

54 Walter Krivitsky, *In Stalin's Secret Service: An Exposé of Russia's Secret Policies by the Former Chief of the Soviet Intelligence in Western Europe* (New York: Harper, 1939), pp. 110–11.

55 Hemingway, *Selected Letters*, p. 465.

56 David Sanders, "Ernest Hemingway's Spanish Civil War Experience," *American Quarterly* 12 (1960), 141, 143; Stephen Cooper, *The Politics of Ernest Hemingway* (Ann Arbor: UMI Research Press, 1987), p. 104.

57 Hemingway, *Selected Letters*, p. 513.

58 Ernest Hemingway, "Series 1.1. Manuscripts: Published Novels," Ernest Hemingway Personal Papers, Box 8, Folder 83, John F. Kennedy Presidential Library.

59 Scott Donaldson and Allen Josephs have noticed the change Hemingway made to the dialogue between Jordan and Maria, but they both erroneously assume that Hemingway himself offered to make this change. See Scott Donaldson, *By Force of Will: The Life and Art of Ernest Hemingway* (New York: Viking, 1977), p. 118; Josephs, *For Whom the Bell Tolls*, p. 82.

60 Gellhorn to Charles Scribner, August 20, 1940, Charles Scribner's Sons Record, Hemingway Files 4, Box 1, Folder "Hemingway, Martha Gellhorn."

61 Geoffrey Roberts, *Stalin's War: From World War to Cold War, 1939–1953* (New Haven: Yale University Press, 2006), pp. 30–35.

62 On this scholastic debate among anti-Stalinists, see Judy Kutulas, *The Long War: The Intellectual People's Front and Anti-Stalinism, 1930–1940* (Durham: Duke University Press, 1995); Alan M. Wald, *The New York Intellectuals: The Rise and Decline of the Anti-Stalinist Left from the 1930s to the 1980s* (Chapel Hill: University of North Carolina Press, 1987), pp. 187–92.

63 On the CPUSA's reaction, see Maurice Isserman, *Which Side Were You On? The American Communist Party During the Second World War* (Urbana: University of Illinois Press, 1993), pp. 32–102; Harvey Klehr, *The Heyday of American Communism: The Depression Decade* (New York: Basic Books, 1984), chapter 20.

64 Payne, *The Spanish Civil War*, pp. 137–38. The British policy was partly dictated by a domino theory, the fear that the Popular Front government in Madrid portended a Bolshevization of Western Europe. See Douglas Little, "Red Scare, 1936: Anti-Bolshevism and the Origins of British Non-Intervention in the Spanish Civil War," *Journal of Contemporary History* 23 (1988), 291–93, 304.

65 Frank A. Warren, *Liberals and Communism: The "Red Decade" Revisited* (Bloomington: Indiana University Press, 1966), p. 132.

66 A typical and illuminating enunciation of these claims is the PCE's December 1936 manifesto on the Civil War. See Geoffrey Roberts, "Soviet Foreign Policy and the Spanish Civil War," in *Spain in an International Context*, Christian Leitz and David J. Dunthorn (eds.), (New York: Berghahn Books, 1999), p. 94.

67 See Peter Carroll, "Ernest Hemingway, Screenwriter: New Letters on *For Whom the Bell Tolls*," *Antioch Review* 53 (1995), 267, 270, 277–79.

68 Quoted in Harriet Hyman Alonso, *Robert E. Sherwood: The Playwright in Peace and War* (Amherst: University of Massachusetts Press, 2007), p. 189.

NOTES TO CHAPTER 4

1 David Holbrook Culbert, *News for Everyman: Radio and Foreign Affairs in Thirties America* (Westport: Greenwood Press, 1976), p. 76. For the birth of radio foreign news, see also Gerd Horten, *Radio Goes to War: The Cultural Politics of Propaganda During World War II* (Berkeley: University of California Press 2003); David Goodman, *Radio's Civic Ambition: American Broadcasting and Democracy in the 1930s* (New York: Oxford University Press, 2011).

2 Elmer Rice, *Minority Report: An Autobiography* (New York: Simon and Schuster, 1963), p. 380.

3 Quoted in John Mason Brown, *The Worlds of Robert E. Sherwood: Mirror to His Times* (New York: Harper and Row, 1962), p. 384.

4 Harriet Alonso, *Robert E. Sherwood: The Playwright in Peace and War* (Amherst: University of Massachusetts Press, 2007), p. 191.

5 R. Baird Shuman, "Shifting Pacifism of Robert E. Sherwood," *South Atlantic Quarterly* 65 (1966), 383.

6 Untitled document, undated, Playwrights' Producing Company, Press Department Records, 1930s–1960, Box 3, New York Public Library.

7 Mason, *The Worlds of Robert E. Sherwood*, p. 378.

8 "Hitler Is Denounced at Drama Benefits," *The New York Times*, November 21, 1938, 4.

9 Quoted in Alfred S. Shivers, *The Life of Maxwell Anderson* (New York: Stein and Day, 1983), p. 182.

10 See Laurence G. Avery (ed.), *Dramatist in America: Letters of Maxwell Anderson, 1912–1958* (Chapel Hill: University of North Carolina Press, 1977), pp. 298, 302. On Anderson's libertarianism, see also Vincent Wall, "Maxwell Anderson: The Last Anarchist," *The Sewanee Review* 49 (1941), 339.

11 "Speech for Abe Lincoln Benefit," Robert Sherwood Papers, Folder 2183, Houghton Library, Harvard University.

12 Robert Sherwood, *There Shall Be No Night* (New York: Charles Scribner's Sons, 1940), p. xxv.

13 Sherwood to Wilbur Lewis, October 13, 1939, Sherwood Papers, Folder 1056.

14 Untitled document, undated, Playwrights' Producing Company, Press Department Records, 1930s–1960, Box 3. Emphasis added.

15 See for instance Sherwood to MacLeish, May 24, 1940, Sherwood Papers, Folder 1348.

16 Sherwood to Harry Hopkins, December 12, 1939, Sherwood Papers, Folder 1232. The premier was attended by many Washington dignitaries including the Finnish minister, Hjalmar Procope, the British Ambassador Lord Lothian, Henry Wallace, Cordell Hull, and the Navy Secretary Edison. See *Washington Post*, January 14, 1940, S2; *The New York Times*, January 23, 1940, 23.

17 Sherwood to Roosevelt, January 25, 1940, Sherwood Papers, Folder 1468.

18 Sherwood to Raymond Massey, January 24, 1940, Sherwood Papers, Folder 1361.

19 Sherwood to White, December 11, 1939, Sherwood Papers, Folder 1621.

20 Barry Witham, "There Shall Be No Night and the Politics of Isolationism," *Theatre Symposium: A Journal of the Southeastern Theatre Conference* 9 (2001), 124; Ikka Joki and Roger D. Sell, "Robert E. Sherwood and the Finnish Winter War: Drama, Propaganda and Context 50 Years Ago," *American Studies in Scandinavia* 21 (1989), 52; Albert Wertheim, *Staging the War: American Drama and World War II* (Bloomington: Indiana University Press, 2004), pp. 22–25.

21 Mark Lincoln Chadwin, *The Hawks of World War II* (Chapel Hill: University of North Carolina Press, 1968), pp. 38, 64, 113.

22 Folder "Stop Hitler Now!" The Committee to Defend America by Aiding Allies Records, Mudd Library, Princeton University; Walter Johnson, *The Battle against Isolation* (Chicago: University of Chicago Press, 1944), pp. 85–88; *The New York Times*, June 10, 1940, 36.

23 John DeWitt McKee, *William Allen White: Maverick on Main Street* (Westport: Greenwood Press, 1975), p. 183.

24 Franklin D. Roosevelt, *F.D.R.: His Personal Letters, 1928–1945* (New York: Duell, Sloan and Pearce, 1950), p. 968.

25 White to Sherwood, December 27, 1939, William Allen White Papers, Box 321, Library of Congress.

26 White to Roosevelt, December 22, 1939, White Papers, Box 320.

27 Richard Steele, "Preparing the Public for War: Efforts to Establish a National Propaganda Agency, 1940–41," *The American Historical Review* 75 (1970), 1642.

28 Sherwood, *Roosevelt and Hopkins: An Intimate History* (New York: Harper, 1948), p. 184; Samuel I. Rosenman, *Working with Roosevelt* (New York: Harper, 1952), p. 232.

29 In 1940 and 1941 Roosevelt made reference to Lincoln at least on the following occasions (it is important to note that his cabinet members and other pro-war associates were at the same time drawing the Lincoln-Roosevelt parallel in their own public addresses): on June 5, 1940, in his three-hour discussion with the leaders of a left-leaning youth organization, Roosevelt, in a rare flash of frankness, acknowledged that domestic programs of social reform sometimes conflicted with national defense programs and likened his dilemma to Lincoln's predicament (citing Carl Sandburg's new biography). See Kenneth S. Davis, *FDR: Into the Storm, 1937–1940* (New York: Random House, 1993), p. 565. Carl Sandburg was mentioned here because of his four-volume *Abraham Lincoln: The War Years*, which had been just published in 1939 to critical acclaim. Sherwood drew his Lincoln largely from Sandburg's earlier volume *Abraham Lincoln: The Prairie Years* (1926). In a short address he gave on October 23, 1940, Roosevelt at some length quoted from Lincoln's 1864 address at a Sanitary Fair in which Lincoln contrasted two definitions of "liberty" by using a homely metaphor of the "wolf's dictionary." See Roosevelt, *Public Papers and Addresses of Franklin D. Roosevelt* (New York: Random House, 1941), vol. 9, p. 484. On October 28, 1940, Roosevelt quoted from the 1860 Cooper Union Address Lincoln's warning against "'appeasers' of that troubled time." See *Public Papers*, vol.9, p. 498. On April 25, 1941, Roosevelt attempted a brutal comparison between Charles Lindbergh and Copperheads. See Wayne S. Cole, *Charles A Lindbergh and the Battle against American Intervention in World War II* (New York: Harcourt Brace Janovitch, 1974), pp. 130–31. At the press conferences on June 5, 1940 and August 19, 1941, Roosevelt asked reporters if they had read Carl Sandburg's Lincoln biography. For the August 19 conference he prepared an excerpt from the biography and read Lincoln's criticism of those northerners who deluded themselves into believing that the North was not at war with the South. After reading the excerpt, the president commented thus: "That is rather an interesting parallel. Lincoln's belief that this country hadn't yet waked up to the fact that they had a war to win, and Lincoln saw what had been going on. Well, there are quite a lot of things for us to think about in this—in this day and age." See Roosevelt, *Complete Presidential Press Conferences of Franklin D. Roosevelt*, vol. 17 (New York: Da Capo Press, 1972), pp. 91–93. For other references, see the March 17, 1941 address (*Public Papers*, vol. 10, p. 75); the March 29, 1941 address (*Public Papers*, vol. 10, p. 87); the June 19, 1941 address (*Public Papers*, vol. 10, p. 226); the November 6, 1941 address (*Public Papers*, vol. 10, p. 475).

30 Roosevelt, *Complete Presidential Press Conferences*, pp. 91–93.

31 Waldo Frank, "Our Guilt in Fascism," *The New Republic*, May 5, 1940, 608.

32 Mumford to Roosevelt, undated, Lewis Mumford Papers, Box 81, Folder 6119, Rare Book and Manuscript Library, the University of Pennsylvania.

33 Anne Morrow Lindbergh, *The Wave of the Future* (New York: Harcourt, Brace, 1940), p. 18.
34 Olive M. Buggie to Anne Morrow Lindbergh, October 10, 1940, Box 5, Charles and Anne Morrow Lindbergh Papers, Firestone Library, Princeton University.
35 Quoted in Frederick W. Marks, *Wind over Sand: The Diplomacy of Franklin Roosevelt* (Athens: University of Georgia Press, 1988), p. 164.
36 Untitled document, MacLeish Papers, Box 49, Folder "Addresses: Speeches Prepared for Others," Library of Congress.
37 Niebuhr to Mumford, November 14, Mumford Papers, 1940, Box 49, Folder 3609.
38 John Melvin, "Lincoln Myth," *Partisan Review*, May–June 1941, 249, 250.
39 Bernard DeVoto, "Father Abraham," *Harper's Magazine*, March 1940, 333–36.
40 Nancy J. Weiss, *Farewell to the Party of Lincoln: Black Politics in the Age of FDR* (Princeton: Princeton University Press, 1983), pp. 224–25.
41 For a typical example, see Theodore Dreiser, *America Is Worth Saving* (New York: Modern Age Books, 1941), pp. 59–145, 184–224.
42 On the utilization of the Lincoln mythology in general for a host of political purposes by various presidents in the twentieth century, see Barry Schwartz, *Abraham Lincoln and the Forge of National Memory* (Chicago: University of Chicago Press, 2000), chapters 5, 6, 7; Merrill D. Peterson, *Lincoln in American Memory* (New York: Oxford University Press, 1994), chapters, 4, 5, 6; Brook Thomas, "Thomas Dixon's *A Man of the People*: How Lincoln Saved the Union by Cracking Down on Civil Liberties," *Law and Literature* 20 (2008): 1–20. For an overview of the Lincoln legend in the American dramatic literature, see Scott R. Irelan, "Goon, Warrior, Communitarian, and Mythos," *Theatre History Studies* 28 (2008): 49–63. On the Lincoln legend's utility for Roosevelt's foreign policy, see Peterson, *Lincoln in American Memory*, pp. 319–23; Barry Schwartz, "Memory as a Cultural System: Abraham Lincoln in World War II," *American Sociological Review* 61 (1996): 914; Roanld D. Rietveld, "Franklin D. Roosevelt's Abraham Lincoln," in *Franklin D. Roosevelt and Abraham Lincoln*, Williamd D. Pederson and Frank J. Williams (eds.) (Armonk: M. E. Sharpe, 2003), pp. 32–50. On Sherwood's contribution in particular, see Malcolm Goldstein, *The Political Stage: American Drama and the Theater of the Great Depression* (New York: Oxford University Press, 1974), p. 399; R. Baird Shuman, *Robert E. Sherwood* (New York: Twayne, 1964), p. 86; Alfred Haworth Jones, *Roosevelt's Image Brokers: Poets, Playwrights, and the Use of the Lincoln Symbol* (Port Washington: Kennikat, 1974), pp. 38–50; Walter J. Meserve, *Robert E. Sherwood: Reluctant Moralist* (New York: Pegasus, 1970), pp. 144, 159–60. For an analysis focusing on the domestic implications of the Lincoln-Roosevelt analogy, see Scott R. Irelan, "The Shine of Egalitarian Morality: Staging a Connective Aesthetic in Robert Sherwood's *Abe Lincoln in Illinois*," *Journal of American Drama and Theatre* 20 (2008): 75–88.

43 Sherwood to White, December 11, 1939, Sherwood Papers, Folder 1621.
44 Robert Sherwood, *Abe Lincoln in Illinois* (New York: Charles Scribner's Sons, 1939). All subsequent references are to this edition and noted parenthetically in the text.
45 Robert Sherwood, "Afterword," in *Abe Lincoln in Illinois*, pp. 222–23.
46 Numerous factors combined to sharpen the sectional conflict, and the literature on how relative values should be apportioned has long since reached awesome proportions. Some historians have focused on ideological origins of sectionalism, such as free soil ideology in the North (Eric Foner, *Free Soil, Free Labor, Free Men: The Ideology of the Republican Party before the Civil War* [New York: Oxford University Press, 1995], pp. 11–39) and a new nationalism in the South (John McCardell, *The Idea of a Southern Nation: Southern Nationalists and Southern Nationalism, 1830–1860* [New York: Norton, 1979], pp. 3–4). Others have tried to explain the exacerbation of sectionalism in economic terms, as an inevitable result of the clash between industrial capitalism and agrarianism (Charles A. and Mary Beard, *The Rise of American Civilization*, [New York: Macmillan, 1927], vol. 2, pp. 36–40, 53–54; Barrington Moore Jr., *Social Origins of Dictatorship and Democracy: Lord and Peasant in the Making of the Modern World* [Boston: Beacon Press, 1966], chapter 3) or between two dissentient regimes of property rights (James L. Huston, "Property Rights in Slavery and the Coming of the Civil War," *The Journal of Southern History* 65 (1999): 251–52. Political historians, on the other hand, have stressed the collapse of the second American party system, arguing that political expediency, rather than moral or ideological convictions, ultimately motivated the politicians to inject slavery issues into national politics (Michael Holt, *The Fate of Their Country: Politicians, Slavery Extension, and the Coming of the Civil War* [New York: Hill and Wang, 2004], pp. 13, 100, 103, 124). For the immediate purposes of this chapter, it is enough to say that of all these competing narratives of the Civil War's genesis Sherwood chose to highlight the slim area of agreement: the question of the slavery extension into the West was the most crucial factor (Michael Morrison, *Slavery and the American West: The Eclipse of Manifest Destiny and the Coming of the Civil War* [Chapel Hill: University of North Carolina, 1997], pp. 4–6).
47 David M. Potter, *The Impending Crisis, 1848–1861* (New York: Harper and Row, 1976), p. 48.
48 Quoted in Eric Foner, "Politics, Ideology, and the Origins of the American Civil War" in *A Nation Divided: Problems and Issues of the Civil War and Reconstruction*, George M. Frederickson (ed.) (Minneapolis: Burgess Pub. Co., 1975), p. 22.
49 The conversion scene is inspired by chapter 91 of Sandburg's biography, in which the narrator digresses from Lincoln's life as a young lawyer in the 1830s and glances forward to the republic's rapid westward expansion taking place during the 1850s. Carl Sandburg, *Abraham Lincoln: The Prairie Years* (New York: Harcourt, Brace, 1926), pp. 289–98.

50 Don E. Fehrenbacher, *The Dred Scott Case: Its Significance in American Law and Politics* (New York: Oxford University Press, 1978), p. 437.

51 Abraham Lincoln, *Speeches and Writings, 1832–1858*, Don E. Fehrenbacher (ed.) (New York: Library of America, 1984), p. 515.

52 Lincoln's seemingly gradualist position vis-à-vis the question of emancipation during the first years of the Civil War militates against the absolutist posturing of Sherwood's Lincoln. Nonetheless, as LaWanda Cox and Allen Guelzo have demonstrated, Lincoln's pragmatism should not be exaggerated to such an extent as to obscure the ultimate goal of general emancipation, which Lincoln consistently took steps to realize, despite his occasionally appearing to subordinate emancipation to political and military ends (LaWanda Cox, *Lincoln and Black Freedom: A Study in Presidential Leadership* [Columbia: University of South Carolina Press, 1981], p. 6; Allen C. Guelzo, *Lincoln's Emancipation Proclamation: The End of Slavery in America* [New York: Simon and Schuster, 2004], p. 4). Whether intended or not, Sherwood's portraiture of Lincoln embellished but barely distorted the radicalism of the original figure.

53 The idealized physicality evoked in the prairie scene is not essentially different from what Myra Jehlen has termed "American incarnation," the imbedding of democratic ideals in the physically experienced quality of the continent. See Myra Jehlen, *American Incarnation: The Individual, the Nation, and the Continent* (Cambridge, MA: Harvard University Press, 1986), pp. 1–21.

54 See Lunabelle Wedlock, *The Reaction of Negro Publications and Organizations to German Anti-Semitism* (Washington, DC: Howard University Graduate School, 1942), pp. 91–115; Harvard Sitkoff, *A New Deal For Blacks: The Emergence of Civil Rights as a National Issue: The Depression Decade*, 30th anniversary edition (New York: Oxford University Press, 2009), pp. 226–44. On how actually Southern racists and the National Socialists viewed each other, see Johnpeter Horst Grill and Robert L. Jenkins, "The Nazis and the American South in the 1930s: A Mirror Image?" *The Journal of Southern History* 58 (1992): 667–94.

55 Sherwood, *Roosevelt and Hopkins*, pp. 756–57. On the dilemma that the administration faced, see also Alexander DeConde, "The South and Isolationism," *The Journal of Southern History* 24 (1958), 340–42.

56 Charles A. Beard, *The Devil Theory of War: An Inquiry into the Nature of History and the Possibility of Keeping Out of War* (New York: The Vanguard Press, 1936), p. 120.

57 Lincoln, *Speeches and Writings, 1832–1858*, p. 426.

58 Don E. Fehrenbacher, "The Origins and Purpose of Lincoln's 'House-Divided' Speech," *The Mississippi Valley Historical Review* 46 (1960), 624.

59 Guelzo, *Lincoln's Emancipation Proclamation*, p. 24.

60 For literary critics, this spatial vision of Cartesian uniformity may recall Phillip Fisher's "democratic social space" thesis. See Philip Fisher, "Democratic Social Space: Whitman, Melville, and the Promise of American Transparency," *Representations* 24 (1988): 60–101.

61 Stephen Douglas, "First Lincoln-Douglas Debate, Ottawa, Illinois," in *Abraham Lincoln: Speeches and Writings, 1832–1858*, p. 507.

62 Harry Jaffa, *Crisis of the House Divided: An Interpretation of the Issues in the Lincoln-Douglas Debates* (Garden City: Doubleday, 1959), p. 100.

63 Lincoln, *Speeches and Writings, 1832–1858*, p. 427.

64 Thomas B. Bonner, "Civil War Historians and the 'Needless War' Doctrine," *Journal of the History of Ideas* 17 (1956), 197–203.

65 Michael Steiner, "Regionalism in the Great Depression," *Geographical Review* 73 (1983), 430–32.

66 Marian J. Morton, "'My Dear, I Don't Give a Damn': Scarlett O'Hara and the Great Depression," *Frontiers: A Journal of Women Studies* 5 (1980), 52.

67 Don E. Fehrenbacher, *The Changing Image of Lincoln in American Historiography* (Oxford: Oxford University Press, 1968), p. 17.

68 Quoted in Betty L. Fladeland, "Revisionists vs. Abolitionists: The Historiographical Cold War of the 1930s and 1940s," *Journal of the Early Republic* 6 (1986), 15.

69 Theodore Strauss, *The New York Times*, October 30, 1938, sec. 9, 3.

70 "Stimson's Address," *The New York Times*, June 12, 1941, 18.

71 David Brion Davis, *The Slave Power Conspiracy and the Paranoid Style* (Baton Rouge: Louisiana State University Press, 1969), pp. 72–74.

72 For Roosevelt's fear of rumored Nazi infiltrations into Latin America, see Donald C. Watt, *Succeeding John Bull* (New York: Cambridge University Press, 1984), pp. 91, 94; Stanley E. Hilton, *Hitler's Secret War in South America* (Baton Rouge: Louisiana State University Press, 1981), pp. 192–96; James Bratzel and Leslie B. Rout, "FDR and the 'Secret Map'," *The Wilson Quarterly* 9 (1985), 168.

73 Robert Sherwood, "Front Line is in Our Hearts," *Ladies' Home Journal*, August 1941, 104.

74 This is essentially a decoction of William Appleman Williams's "Open Door Theory." See *The Tragedy of American Diplomacy* (New York: Norton, 1959). Despite himself, Williams gave the erroneous impression that this fear was rational-economic, but actually it was ideological due to its origination in the national tradition. See also Colin Dueck, *Reluctant Crusaders: Power, Culture, and Change in American Grand Strategy* (Princeton: Princeton University Press, 2006), pp. 21–26; Christopher Layne, *The Peace of Illusions: American Grand Strategy from 1940 to the Present* (Ithaca: Cornell University Press, 2006), pp. 30–33.

75 Roosevelt, *The Public Papers*, vol. 10, p. 477.

76 James Burnham, *The Machiavellians: Defenders of Freedom* (Chicago: Henry Regnery Company, 1963), pp. 26–30.

77 Irwin F. Gellman, *Secret Affairs: Franklin Roosevelt, Cordell Hull, and Sumner Welles* (Baltimore: The Johns Hopkins University Press, 1995), p. 252. On issues related to the Monroe Doctrine and hemispheric defense, see John A. Logan, *No Transfer: An American Security Principle* (New Haven: Yale University Press, 1961); Warren Kimball, *The Juggler: Franklin Roosevelt as Wartime Statesman* (Princeton: Princeton University Press, 1994), pp. 107–26;

Phillip C. Jessup, "The Monroe Doctrine in 1940," *The American Journal of International Law* 34 (1940), 704–11.

78 So on April 25, 1940, Adolf Berle recorded a discussion he had with Under Secretary of State Sumner Welles: "Defense is one thing if you are going to defend the Philippines and, let us say, the Dutch East Indies. If you are going to begin at Hawaii, that is something else. It is one thing if you think you wish to defend in Europe; a second thing if you envisage it as a defense of the Atlantic line." *Navigating the Rapids, 1918–1971: From the Papers of Adolf A. Berle*, Beatrice Bishop Berle and Travis Jacobs (ed.) (New York: Harcourt Brace Jovanovich, 1973), p. 307.

79 Quoted in Zarefsky *Lincoln, Douglas, and Slavery*, p. 177.

80 Sherwood reworked Lincoln's September 11, 1858 speech at Edwardsville. The original continues: "Our defense is in the preservation of the spirit which prizes liberty as the heritage of all men, in all lands, every where. Destroy this spirit, and you have planted the seeds of despotism around your own doors. Familiarize yourselves with the chains of bondage, and you are preparing your own limbs to wear them. Accustomed to trample on the rights of those around you, you have lost the genius of your own independence, and become the fit subjects of the first cunning tyrant who rises." Lincoln, *Speeches and Writings, 1832–1858*, p. 584. Note Lincoln's language of universality ("all men, in all lands, every where") as well as his solicitude for the liberty of those who trample on others' liberty.

81 For a view that Thomas Jefferson originally understood "liberty" as a "natural right," see Michael P. Zuckert, *The Natural Rights Republic: Studies in the Foundation of the American Political Tradition* (Notre Dame: University of Notre Dame Press, 1996), pp. 81–83.

82 See Isaiah Berlin, "Two Concepts of Liberty," in *Four Essays on Liberty* (New York: Oxford University Press, 1969), pp. 166–217.

83 John Stuart Mill, *On Liberty* (Indianapolis: Hackett, 1978), p. 9.

84 For Locke's identification of freedom with biological life: "This *Freedom* from Absolute, Arbitrary Power, is so necessary to, and closely joined with a Man's Preservation, that he cannot part with it, but by what forfeits his Preservation and Life together." *Two Treatises of Government*, Peter Laslett (ed.) (New York: Cambridge University Press, 1988), p. 284.

85 Locke, *Two Treatises*, p. 287.

86 As Anders Stephanson points out, the demonization of America's enemy as a slave power predated the Civil War and later resurfaced during the Cold War, with the Soviets now cast as the Asiatic slave power. See "Liberty or Death: The Cold War as US Ideology," in *Reviewing the Cold War: Approaches, Interpretations, Theory*, Odd Arne Westad (ed.) (London: Frank Cass, 2000), pp. 81–100.

87 On liberalism's expansionist tendency, see Jeremi Suri *Power and Protest: Global Revolution and the Rise of Détente* (Cambridge, MA: Harvard University Press, 2003), pp. 131–32; Michael C. Desch, "America's Liberal Illiberalism: The Ideological Origins of Overreaction in U.S. Foreign Policy," *International Security* 32 (2007–8): 7–43.

NOTES TO CHAPTER 5

1 Franklin D. Roosevelt, *The Public Papers and Addresses of Franklin D. Roosevelt* (New York: MacMillan, 1941), vol. 8, p. 463.
2 Roosevelt, *The Public Papers*, vol. 8, p. 462.
3 Sarah E. Igo, *The Averaged American: Surveys, Citizens, and the Making of a Mass Public* (Cambridge, MA: Harvard University Press, 2007), pp. 103–48.
4 Fortune Survey October 1939 (released on September 21). See Hodgins to Roosevelt, September 18, 1939, Presidential Personal File, Container 18, Folder 1820, FDR Library and Museum.
5 Bruce Cook, *Dalton Trumbo* (New York: Scribner's, 1977), pp. 26–29, 32, 39–40, 48, 51, 54–57, 77–78, 86–89, 91–92, 121–22.
6 Dalton Trumbo, *Johnny Got His Gun* (New York: Citadel Press, 2007), p. 122. All subsequent references are to this edition and will be cited parenthetically.
7 Editorial Department, J. B. Lippincott Company to Dalton Trumbo, September 18, 1939, Dalton Trumbo Papers, Box 1, Folder 7, Wisconsin Historical Society.
8 Alice Reily to Dalton Trumbo, September 13, 1939, Trumbo Papers, Box 1, Folder 7.
9 Editorial Department, J. B. Lippincott Company to Elsie McKeogh, April 14, 1939, Trumbo Papers, Box 1, Folder 7. Bound galley copies were also mailed to other major participants in the war debate, including H. L. Mencken (isolationist), William Allen White (interventionist), and Dorothy Thompson (interventionist). Borah died two months after his defeat in the congressional battle over the revision of the Neutrality Act.
10 Trumbo to McKeogh, undated (c. August 1938), Trumbo Papers, Box 1, Folder 6.
11 Trumbo to McKeogh, undated, Trumbo Papers, Box 1, Folder 6.
12 Trumbo to McKeogh, October 12, 1938, Trumbo Papers, Box 1, Folder 7.
13 Trumbo to McKeogh, February 20, 1939, Trumbo Papers, Box 1, Folder 7.
14 McKeogh to Trumbo, February 27, 1939, Trumbo Papers, Box 1, Folder 7.
15 Bertram Lippincott to McKeogh, March 10, 1939, Trumbo Papers, Box 1, Folder 7.
16 Editorial Department, J. B. Lippincott to McKeogh, April 19, 1939, Trumbo Papers, Box 1, Folder 7.
17 Eventually, *The Daily Worker* serialized *Johnny* from March 17 through April 27, 1940. The CPUSA was in the middle of the "Yanks Are Not Coming" phase (due to the Soviet-German Pact), and so the novel's pacifist message suited Moscow's foreign policy platform perfectly. The notices on its pages touted this new feature thus: "Johnny was one of many courageous young Americans out of whose bodies Wall Street built a barricade behind which they guarded their profits. His story, as told by Dalton Trumbo, is already acclaimed as a masterpiece of anti-war literature. Every page of 'Johnny Got His Gun' is a passionate indictment of imperialist war." *The Daily Worker*, March 16, 1940, 3. Note the phrase "imperialist war," a Stalinist appellation for

the new European war until June 1941. This serialization would later give credence to a speculation that *Johnny Got His Gun* was originally conceived of as a communist propaganda, but a more detailed and nuanced account I offer here shows that the propaganda utility for the Soviet foreign policy was discovered by both Trumbo and the CPUSA only retroactively.

18 Francis Henshaw to Trumbo, September 30, 1939, Trumbo Papers, Box 1, Folder 8.

19 The critical role the Great War played in the birth of propaganda and public relations was recognized by diverse commentators. Lasswell, *Democracy through Public Opinion* (Menasha: George Banta Publishing Co., 1941), p. 76. For the modernization of American advertising during the interwar years, see Roland Marchand, *Advertising the American Dream: Making Way for Modernity, 1920–1940* (Berkeley: University of California Press, 1985). On the founders of public relations during the interwar years, such as Ivy Lee and Edward Bernays, see Stuart Ewen, *PR!: A Social History of Spin* (New York: Basic Books, 1996), chapters 4 and 8. On the cross-pollination of talents between the PR industry and wartime propaganda, see Stephen Vaughn, *Holding Fast the Inner Line: Democracy, Nationalism, and the Committee on Public Information* (Chapel Hill: University of North Carolina Press, 1980), chap. 8.

20 Lasswell, *Democracy through Public Opinion*, p. 40.

21 Reinhold Niebuhr, "Editorials," *Radical Religion*, Fall 1939, 8.

22 Harold Lavin and James Wechsler, *War Propaganda and the United States* (New Haven: Yale University Press, 1940), p. vii.

23 John Dewey, "The Basic Values and Loyalties of Democracy," *American Teacher* 25 (May 1941), reprinted in *John Dewey: The Later Works, 1925–1953*, Jo Ann Boydston (ed.) (Carbondale: Southern Illinois University Press, 1988), p. 275.

24 Edna St. Vincent Millay, untitled document, n.d., Edna St. Vincent Millay Papers, Box 116, Library of Congress.

25 Roosevelt, *The Public Papers*, vol. 9, p. 487. See also MacLeish Papers, Box 49, Folder "Addresses: Speeches Prepared for Others," Library of Congress.

26 David Riesman, "Government Education for Democracy," *The Public Opinion Quarterly* 5 (1941), 198.

27 T. S. Eliot, *The Idea of a Christian Society* (New York: Harcourt, Brace, 1940), p. 17.

28 See Thurman Arnold, *The Symbols of Government* (New Haven: Yale University Press, 1935), pp. 232, 253; Stuart Chase, *The Tyranny of Words* (New York: Harcourt, Brace, 1938), pp. 53–55, 58–72; S. I. Hayakawa, *Language in Action* (New York: Harcourt, Brace, 1941), pp. 32, 137–39, 146, 217. Arnold expanded his thesis in another widely discussed book, *The Folklore of Capitalism* (New Haven: Yale University Press, 1937). Chase and Hayakaway were mainly influenced by Alfred Korzibski, I. A. Richards, and C. K. Ogden, but they were also familiar with Arnold's work.

29 A number of historians have written of this general propaganda fatigue and the challenges it posed to the U.S. government. See Brett Gary, *The Nervous*

Liberals: Propaganda Anxieties from World War I to the Cold War (New York: Columbia University Press, 1999); J. Michael Sproule, *Propaganda and Democracy: The American Experience of Media and Mass Persuasion* (Cambridge: Cambridge University Press, 1997); Ellen Herman, *The Romance of American Psychology: Political Culture in the Age of Experts* (Berkeley: University of California Press, 1995); Richard W. Steele, *Propaganda in an Open Society: The Roosevelt Administration and the Media, 1933–1941* (Westport: Greenwood Press, 1985); "The Great Debate: Roosevelt, the Media, and the Coming of the War, 1940–1941," *The Journal of American History* 71 (1984): 69–92; Igo, *The Averaged American.*

30 Langston Hughes, "Comment on War," *The Crisis*, June, 1940, 190.

31 In the following few paragraphs I recapitulate main themes and critical points of emphasis in the controversy over art's relation to propaganda. For more details on the personalities involved and its shifting contexts, see the following works: Walter Rideout, *The Radical Novel in the United States, 1900–1954: Some Interrelations of Literature and Society* (Cambridge, MA: Harvard University Press, 1956), chapters 6–9; Daniel Aaron, *Writers on the Left: Episodes in American Literary Communism* (New York: Harcourt, Brace, 1961), part 2 and part 3; James F. Murphy, *The Proletarian Moment: The Controversy over Leftism in Literature* (Urbana: University of Illinois Press, 1991); Barbara Foley, *Radical Representations: Politics and Form in U.S. Proletarian Fiction, 1929–1941* (Durham: Duke University Press, 1993).

32 Karl Marx, "The Civil War in France," in *The First International and After: Political Wirings*, vol. 3, David Fernbach (ed.) (Harmondsworth: Penguin, 1974), p. 213.

33 This view, which justified the use of art as a weapon in class struggle, not on the basis of its direct agitational efficacy but on the basis of its epistemological utility, was given the clearest formulation in Georg Lukács's influential essay, "Propaganda or Partisanship?" *Partisan Review*, April–May, 1934, 37, 40, 44–46.

34 Lasswell, who embraced Freudianism more fervently than any other social scientists of his generation, concluded after conducting exhaustive content analysis of propaganda materials used by the Allied Powers and the Central Powers during the Great War that the success in wartime propaganda depended on three factors: "traditional prejudices, objective connections between nations, and the changing level of popular irritability." See Harold Lasswell, *Propaganda Technique in the World War* (New York: A. A. Knopf, 1927), p. 192. Bernays concurred: "Mental habits create stereotypes just as physical habits create certain definite reflex actions. These stereotypes or reflex images are a great aid to the public relations counsel in his work." See Edward Bernays, *Crystallizing Public Opinion* (New York: Boni and Liveright, 1923), p. 162 (also, 98, 102, 161).

35 Sheryl Kaskowitz, *God Bless America: The Surprising History of an Iconic Song* (New York: Oxford University Press, 2013), p. 16.

36 Susan Schweick, *A Gulf So Deeply Cut* (Madison: University of Wisconsin Press, 1991), chapters 1–5.

37 On these "revisionist" historians, see Warren Cohen's *The American Revisionists: The Lessons of Intervention in World War I* (Chicago: University of Chicago Press, 1967).

38 Hadley Cantril (ed.), *Public Opinion, 1935–1946* (Princeton: Princeton University Press, 1951), p. 202.

39 For a more comprehensive list, see Philip E. Hager and Desmond Taylor (eds.), *The Novels of World War I: An Annotated Bibliography* (New York: Garland, 1981). Not all of these novels painted a grim portrait of war and heroism. To generalize, there was a significant correlation between the degree of "realism" and the educational level of the implied readership. Between the modernist literature of disenchantment and protest and the ordinary middle-class readers yawned a vast chasm of incomprehension. The latter would have found a much more recognizable self-portrait in, for instance, Claude Wheeler of Willa Cather's Pulitzer Prize–winning *One of Ours* (1922). On this divergence in the treatment of the last war between modernist and popular literatures, see David M. Kennedy, *Over Here: The First World War and American Society* (Oxford: Oxford University Press, 1980), pp. 229–30.

40 Ernest Hemingway, "Note on the Next War: A Serious Topical Letter," *Esquire*, September 1935. Reprinted in *By-Line: Ernest Hemingway*, William White (ed.) (New York: Charles Scribner's Sons, 1967), p. 206.

41 Charles A. Beard, "How to Stay Out of War," *Forum*, February 1937, 90.

42 Editorial, "Mr. Mumford and the Liberals," *The New Republic*, April 28, 1940, 562.

NOTES TO CHAPTER 6

1 *Johnny Got His Gun* has been neglected by literary scholars, and what little scholarship we have fixates on the representation of body and violence. See, for example, Tim Blackmore, "Lazarus Machine: Body Politics in Dalton Trumbo's *Johnny Got His Gun*," *Mosaic: A Journal of the Interdisciplinary Study of Literature* 33 (2000): 1–18. Leonard Kriegel rightly classifies *Johnny* as a psychological novel, comparing the novel's "successful use of the mind of a basket case as its point of view" to "Faulkner's use of the mind of the idiot Benjy as the point of view for the opining section of *The Sound and the Fury*." "Dalton Trumbo's 'Johnny Got His Gun'" in *Proletarian Writers of the Thirties*, David Madden (ed.) (Carbondale: Southern Illinois University Press, 1968), p. 107.

2 A canonical definition of "psychological realism" or "psychological novel" is hard to come by, although the roster of its most illustrious practitioners seems fairly established: Stendhal, Flaubert, Eliot, James, Joyce, Woolf, Musil, and Faulker. Most accounts tell a story of the "inward turning" (Leon Edel) or "inward turn" (Eric Kahler), a narrative of increasing refinement of a battery of techniques for achieving a greater verisimilitude in the presentation of the mind's operations and workings, which calumniates in the Joycean revolution in the early 1920s. See Leon Edel, *The Psychological Novel 1900–1950* (New York:

Lippincott, 1955); Erich Kahler, *The Inward Turn of Narrative* (Princeton: Princeton University Press, 1973).

3 Nicholas Dames tells us that despite her pivotal role in the evolution of this tradition, George Eliot, when she joined "psychological" and the "novel" in the mid-nineteenth century, mocked the feminization and domestication of the characters in psychological realism: "men are judged almost entirely on 'carpet consideration.'" See his "'The Withering of the Individual': Psychology in the Victorian Novel," in *A Concise Companion to the Victorian Novel*, Francis O'Gorman (ed.) (London: Blackwell, 2005), p. 91.

4 My taxonomy closely follows Cohn and Palmer. They agree on the basic tripartite structure of the taxonomy but part company on terminology. I borrow "psycho-narration" and "quoted (internal) monologue" from Cohn and "free indirect thought" from Palmer. Alan Palmer, *Fictional Minds* (Lincoln: University of Nebraska Press, 2004); Dorrit Cohn, *Transparent Minds: Narrative Modes for Presenting Consciousness in Fiction* (Princeton: Princeton University Press, 1978).

5 Ezra Pound, *ABC of Reading* (New York: New Direction, 1960 [1934]), p. 88.

6 The standard work on the "sacralization" of culture in the closing decades of the nineteenth century is Lawrence W. Levine's massively documented *Highbrow / Lowbrow: The Emergence of Cultural Hierarchy in America* (Cambridge, MA: Harvard University Press, 1988). The big story of the 1930s, the maturation of the middlebrow culture, should not be confused with a re-profanation of culture. The popularization of culture that disquieted the elite and assisted the rise of new cultural workers like Dalton Trumbo undid the old cultural hierarchy by building up a new regime of universal accessibility. The rapid increase in governmental expenditures (federal, state, and municipal) on education during the first third of the new century bears witness to the spread of basic cultural literacy. In 1902, the total expenditure was \$282m, \$565m in 1913, \$2,490m in 1929, and \$2,372m in 1937. See table X, Alvin H. Hansen, *Fiscal Policy and Business Cycle* (New York: W. W. Norton, 1941), p. 121. On the "second industrial revolution" and its consequences (mechanization, the rise in productivity and wages, the reduction in working hours), see Robert H. Zieger, *The CIO, 1935–1955* (Chapel Hill: University of North Carolina Press, 1995), pp. 6–11. In the historic U.S. Steel-SWOC settlement of 1937, the working class finally attained the symbolic milestone: the forty-hour week and time and a half for overtime (Zieger, *The CIO*, p. 59). On the rise of the consumer culture in the 1920s and 1930s side by side with the professionalization of advertising, see Roland Marchant, *Advertising the American Dream: Making Way for Modernity, 1920–1940* (Berkeley: University of California Press, 1985).

7 The seminal distillation of this thesis can be found in Warren I. Susman, *Culture as History: The Transformation of American Society in the Twentieth Century* (New York: Pantheon Books, 1974), chapter 11. The Susman thesis has been influential, and many subsequent scholarly works on American culture during the Great Depression have extended it by using a variety of sources. Among the most ambitious of these works is Michael Denning's *The Cultural*

Front: The Laboring of American Culture in the Twentieth Century (London: Verso, 1997), which seeks to interpret the Popular Front literally, as a wholly new type of people's culture that was born in the mid-1930s. On the importance of the concept of "the people" for the depression-era culture, see also Jane De Hart Mathews, "Arts and the People: The New Deal Quest for a Cultural Democracy," *The Journal of American History* 62 (1975): 316–39.

8 The metaphor of "prostitution" recurs in the testimonies left by modernists who sought refuge in Hollywood during the depression decade. Baudelaire's storied fondness for prostitutes notwithstanding, modernists' general antipathy makes sense, as long as one recognizes an economic logic underlying it, as pointed out by Robert Michels in the 1930s: "Prostitutes stand in contradiction to the character of bohemia" because they value, unlike bohemians, time and money. See his essay, "On the Sociology of Bohemia and Its Connection to the Intellectual Proletariat," *Catalyst* 15 (1983), 11.

9 For consideration of this often neglected group of collaborators in the system, see Richard Fine, *West of Eden: Writers in Hollywood, 1928–1940* (Washington DC: Smithsonian Institution Press, 1993); Richard Corliss, *Talking Pictures: Screenwriters in American Cinema* (New York: Overlook, 1974); Thomas A. Dardis, *Some Time in the Sun* (New York: Scribner's, 1976); Ian Hamilton, *Writers in Hollywood, 1915–1951* (New York: Caroll and Graf, 1991). Corliss's chapter on Dalton Trumbo offers an astute examination of his style.

10 Raymond Chandler, "Writers in Hollywood," *The Atlantic*, November, 1945, 51.

11 *F. Scott Fitzgerald: A Life in Letters*, Matthew J. Bruccoli (ed.) (New York: Scribner's, 1994), p. 294.

12 F. Scott Fitzgerald, *The Pat Hobby Stories* (New York: Scribner's, 1995), p. 22.

13 Margaret Brenman-Gibson, *Clifford Odets: American Playwright* (New York: Atheneum, 1981), p. 421.

14 Ben Hecht, *A Child of the Century* (New York: Simon and Schuster, 1954), p. 471.

15 Trumbo to Elsie Mckeogh, March 23, 1940, Trumbo Papers, Box 7.

16 Memo "General, Re: Dalton Trumbo," February 15, 1941, Trumbo Papers, Box 7.

17 Dalton Trumbo, "Stepchild of the Muses," *The North American Review*, December 1933, 560.

18 Dalton Trumbo, "The Fall of Hollywood," *The North American Review*, August 1933, 140, 147.

19 See Janice Radway, "The Book-of-the-Month Club and the General Reader: On the Uses of 'Serious' Fiction," *Critical Inquiry* 14 (1988): 516–38; "The Scandal of the Middlebrow: The Book-of-the-Month Club, Class Fracture, and Cultural Authority," *The South Atlantic Quarterly* 89 (1990): 703–36. Joan Shelley Rubin also discusses the birth of the middlebrow in the 1920s in *Making of Middlebrow Culture* (Chapel Hill: University of North Carolina Press, 1992). Victoria Grieve reconstructs how in the late 1930s the avant-garde and abstract art came to be associated with American freedom as representational paintings catering to the nationalized masses were demonized as a

totalitarian form of art in *The Federal Art Project and the Creation of Middle-brow Culture* (Urbana: University of Illinois Press, 2009), pp. 163–80.

20 I borrow the phrase "Eliotic Trotskyite" from T. J. Clark, "Clement Greenberg's Theory of Art," *Critical Inquiry* 9 (1982), 148. Clark does not define this felicitous moniker, but as I take it, it is meant to evoke a peculiar combination of conservative modernism in aesthetics and reckless utopianism in politics.

21 Dwight Macdonald, "Kulturbolschewismus Is Here," *Partisan Review*, November–December 1941, 451.

22 On the death of the bourgeoisie, the decomposition of the ethos of buccaneering capitalism, and the rise of state capitalism, see Joseph Schumpeter, *Capitalism, Socialism and Democracy* (New York: Harper, 1975 [1942]), pp. 121–62. Schumpeter was no doubt influenced by one of the most widely discussed books in economics and business history in the 1930s: Adolf A. Berle and Gardiner C. Means, *The Modern Corporation and Private Property* (New York: Harcourt, Brace, 1932). See especially Book 4, Chapters 3–4. Among other notable books that popularized the same themes were Peter F. Drucker, *The End of Economic Man: The Origins of Totalitarianism* (New York: John Day, 1939), Edward Chamberlin, *The Theory of Monopolistic Competition* (Cambridge, MA: Harvard University Press, 1933), Arthur Burns, *Decline of Competition: A Study of the Evolution of American Industry* (New York: McGraw-Hill, 1936), Caroline F. Ware and Gardiner Means, *The Modern Economy in Action* (New York: Harcourt, Brace, 1936), Mordecai Ezekiel, *Jobs for All through Industrial Expansion* (New York: Knopf, 1939), and James Burnham, *The Managerial Revolution* (New York: John Day, 1941). Around the same time, a related notion of "state capitalism" also gained traction with leftist émigré social scientists including Friedrich Pollock, Herbert Marcuse, Max Horkheimer, Franz Neumann, and Otto Kirchheimer. See Friedrich Pollock, "State Capitalism: Its Possibilities and Limitations," *Studies in Philosophy and Social Science* 9 (1941): 200–55. Harold Lasswell characteristically scripted the bleakest scenario for the ongoing merger of the state and business in his two prewar articles: "The Garrison State versus the Civilian State," *China Quarterly* 2 (1937): 643–49; "The Garrison State," *The American Journal of Sociology* 46 (1941): 455–68.

23 T. J. Clark, *Image of the People: Gustave Courbet and the 1848 Revolution* (Berkeley: University of California Press, 1973), p. 34.

24 By "bohemia" is meant here a combination of ideas such as "aestheticism," "love of art for art's sake," and the "avant-garde" that rationalized the life style, aesthetic tastes, and political attitudes of alienated artists and writers during the belle epoch, roughly from the turn of the nineteenth century to the Great War. See George S. Snyderman and William Josephs, "Bohemia: The Underworld of Art," *Social Forces* 18 (1939): 187–99. For an extensive treatment of bohemians in the U.S. context during this period, see Christine Stansell's *American Moderns: Bohemian New York and the Creation of a New Century* (New York: Metropolitan, 2000). Jack Selzer reconstructs the post–Great War bohemian scene in New York by using Kenneth Burke's career as a

synecdoche in *Kenneth Burke in Greenwich Village: Conversing with the Moderns, 1915–1931* (Madison: University of Wisconsin Press, 1996). The vintage of the term itself is older and, as critics agree, goes back to a pre-1848 Paris. See Mary Gluck, "Theorizing the Cultural Roots of the Bohemian Artist," *MODERNISM / modernity* 7 (2000): 351–78.

25 Kenneth Burke, *Counter-Point* (Los Altos, CA: Hermes, 1953 [1931]), p. 119.

26 A homogeneous national culture of consumption really took off in the 1920s. On the working class's increasing access to this national-popular culture, see Lizabeth Cohen, *Making a New Deal: Industrial Workers in Chicago, 1919–1939* (New York: Cambridge University Press, 1990), chapter 3.

27 Dwight Macdonald, "Kulturbolschewismus Is Here," *Partisan Review*, November–December 1941, 451.

28 Walter Benjamin's now-famous essay, "The Work of Art in the Age of Its Technological Reproducibility," appeared in 1936 in the *Zeitschrift für Sozial-forschung*, published by the *Institut für Sozialforschung*, which was then based at Columbia University. There is little evidence that this piece was read and discussed by Benjamin's confreres in the United States, although it would influence the highly negative evaluation of U.S. popular culture–especially music–developed by Adorno, who read a draft and criticized Benjamin's optimistic hope for the revolutionary potential of mechanized art.

29 Robert Warshow, "The Legacy of the 30's," in *The Immediate Experience: Movies, Comics, Theatre, and Other Aspects of Popular Culture* (Cambridge, MA: Harvard University Press, 2001), pp. 4–5.

30 On the Marxists' antipathy (both Stalinists and anti-Stalinists) toward popular culture in the 1930s, see Paul R. Gorman, *Left Intellectuals and Popular Culture in Twentieth-Century America* (Chapel Hill: University of North Carolina Press, 1996), chapters 5 and 6.

31 Daniel Fuchs gives a puzzled but sympathetic reminiscence of his own experience at "sneak previews" from a scenarist's vantage point in "Writing for the Movies," *Commentary*, February 1962, 107–08.

32 Terminology of course varied, but these were all standard arguments shared by these critics. For the clearest articulations of these views, see Theodor W. Adorno, "On Popular Music" (1941); "The Radio Symphony" (1941); "On the Fetish Character in Music and the Regression of Listening" (1938); all in *Essays on Music*, Richard Leppert (ed.) (Berkeley: University of California Press, 2002). Clement Greenberg, "The Avant-Garde and Kitsch," *Partisan Review*, September 1939, 34–49. Heta Hertzog, "On Borrowed Experience: An Analysis of Listening to Daytime Sketches," *Studies in Philosophy and Social Science* 9 (1941): 65–95. The two most intellectualized variants of mass culture critique in the late 1930s, one by the émigré scholars associated with the Institute for Social Research and the other by the New York Intellectuals, are strikingly similar, but there was little cross-pollination of ideas between the two groups. See Thomas Wheatland, *The Frankfurt School in Exile* (Minneapolis: University of Minnesota Press, 2009), pp. 173–75.

33 Greenberg, "The Avant-Garde and Kitsch," 47; James Burnham, "The Theory of the Managerial Revolution," *Partisan Review*, May–June 1941, 192–98.

34 Thus, the aesthetic conservatism of the Soviet cinema that came after the glorious revolutionary experimentalism of the 1920s struck Dwight Macdonald as "Americanization." Incidentally, for Macdonald too, the reactionary character of socialist realism in the Soviet cinema was evident in its generic impurity, its appropriation of "literary-theatrical" conventions at the expense of purely cinematic techniques like montage and the use of real locations and amateur actors. Dwight Macdonald, "The Soviet Cinema: 1930–1938–Part II," *Partisan Review*, August–September 1938, 57; "The Soviet Cinema: 1930–1938– Part I," *Partisan Review*, July 1938, 37.

35 The avant-garde was defined by Clement Greenberg as a collection of impulses toward purity and against the "confusion of the arts." Speaking of the development in fine arts, he wrote in 1940, "the history of avant-garde painting is that of a progressive surrender to the resistance of its medium." He left no doubt what the archenemy of the avant-garde was: kitsch or mass culture, which acted as an agent of miscegenation among distinct fields of artistic activities. Its prime exemplifier was obviously motion picture. Popular novels and short stories were routinely bought, "treated," and "adapted" for screen (the industry referred to these narrative raw materials as "property"). That confused the distinctions among genres and mediums. Again it is vitally important to note here that a new breed of cultural workers like Dalton Trumbo at once facilitated and cashed in on this new confusion of the arts, which in turn made possible the production of illusions on industrial scale. See Clement Greenberg, "Toward a Newer Laocoon," *Partisan Review*, July–August 1940, 297–310. The quotations are from pages 296, 304, and 307.

36 Kenneth Burke, *Permanence and Change: An Anatomy of Purpose* (New York: New Republic, 1935), p. 65.

37 On Lenin's assault on ultra-left sectarianism and his insistence that the revolutionary party must burrow itself within the existing cultural apparatus trusted by the lower middle class, see "Left-Wing Communism: An Infantile Disorder," *Collected Works*, vol. 31, (Moscow: Progress Publishers, 1964), pp. 17–118.

38 *Aesthetics and Politics*, Ronald Taylor (ed.) (London: NLB, 1977), pp. 124–25.

39 Dwight Macdonald and Clement Greenberg, "Ten Propositions on the War," *Partisan Review*, July–August, 1941, 278.

40 Trumbo, "Stepchild of the Muses," 560.

41 Marion Meade, *Dorothy Parker: What Fresh Hell Is This* (New York: Penguin, 1989), p. 277.

42 Max Horkheimer and Theodor W. Adorno, *Dialectic of Enlightenment*, trans. Edmund Jephcott (Stanford: Stanford University Press, 2002), p. 132. Most of the fragments in this book were written during the war, between 1942 and 1947, when both authors lived in Southern California.

43 This distinction is the one Bertolt Brecht made in an essay he wrote before he moved to the United States, "The Popular and the Realistic" (1937). Toward the

end of the essay, in which he addressed "the popular" and "the realistic," two hotly contested concepts in leftist literary circles in the mid-1930s, Brecht wrote rather mystifyingly without much elaboration: "Besides *being popular* there is such a thing as *becoming popular*." *Brecht on Theatre: The Development of an Aesthetic*, John Willett (ed.) (New York: Hill and Wang, 1964), pp. 107–15.

NOTES TO CHAPTER 7

1 By "hegemony" I do not imply that the United States aimed to control China formally or informally. Rather, as Walter Lafeber observes, the United States had a definite idea (the "Open Door") about *how* China should be modernized, and Japan's neocolonial approach clashed with it in a way that left little room for compromise and negotiation. See Walter Lafeber, *The Clash: U.S.-Japanese Relations Throughout History* (New York: Norton, 1997), p. 161.

2 This is not a place to engage with the existing literature of tremendous proportions addressing whether or not during the final negotiation over the oil embargo in the fall of 1941 the United States anticipated a Japanese attack on U.S. territories. My view is that the U.S. officials were aware of the possibility that Japan might lash out in one direction or another, but very few if any expected that Japan would attack the navy base in Hawaii. Of all the existing theories, this view most closely follows Marc Trachtenberg's. See Marc Trachtenberg, *The Craft of International History: A Guide to Method* (Princeton: Princeton University Press, 2006), chapter 4.

3 See Harold Isaacs's study of China as it appeared in the American mind in the 1930s, *American Images of China and India* (New York: John Day, 1958), pp. 168–69.

4 Due to their enormous circulations and the proprietor's connection with China, the coverage by Henry Luce's *Time* and *Life* (and, to a lesser extent, *Fortune*) has been subjected to close scrutiny. T. Christopher Jespersen and Patricia Neils view Luce's support for the Nationalists as firm and strong enough to bias his publications' coverage of the Sino-Japanese War in favor of the Chinese. See T. Christopher Jespersen, *American Images of China, 1931–1949* (Palo Alto: Stanford University Press, 1996), pp. 11–43; Patricia Neils, *China Images in Life and Times of Henry Luce* (Lanham: Rowman & Littlefield, 1990). Alan Brinkley's recent biography takes a more nuanced view, recognizing the relative autonomy of the editorial lines of his magazines from Luce's personal conviction and at the same time pointing out that Luce himself did not begin to devote himself to Far Eastern affairs until relatively late, around mid-1941. Alan Brinkley, *The Publisher: Henry Luce and His American Century* (New York: Knopf, 2010), pp. 241–43, 273.

5 For the activities of UCR, see Jespersen, *American Images of China*, chapter 3 and Robert Herzstein, *Henry R. Luce: A Political Portrait of the Man Who Created the American Century* (New York: Scribner's, 1994), chapter 19. For the activities of the American Committee for Non-Participation, see my discussion later in the chapter and Donald J. Friedman, *The Road from Isolation: The*

Campaign of the American Committee for Non-Participation in Japanese Aggression, 1938–1941 (Cambridge, MA: East Asian Research Center, Harvard University, 1968).

6 On these pro-Chinese lobby groups' influence on the government policy and public opinion, see two contemporary studies: John W. Masland, "Missionary Influence Upon American Far Eastern Policy," *Pacific Historical Review* 10 (1941): 279–96; William E. Daugherty, "China's Official Publicity in the United States," *Public Opinion Quarterly* 6 (1942): 70–86.

7 *Public Opinion, 1935–1946*, Hadley Cantril (ed.) (Princeton: Princeton University Press, 1951), pp. 265, 1081.

8 Letter, Ernest Hemingway to Henry Morgenthau, July 30, 1941, Hemingway Papers, JFK Museum and Library.

9 Warren I. Cohen, *America's Response to China: A History of Sino-American Relations*, 4th edition (New York: Columbia University Press, 2010), pp. 117–25.

10 Smedley was in China for much of the 1930s, first as a Comintern agent and then after a falling-out with Moscow, as a freelance journalist. Her books on the war and revolution in China include *Chinese Destinies: Sketches of Present-Day China* (1933), *China's Red Army Marches* (1934), and *China Fights Back: An American Woman with the Eight Route Army* (1938). The best source on her activities in China is Ruth Price, *The Lives of Agnes Smedley* (Oxford: Oxford University Press, 2005). Snow's international bestseller, *Red Star over China* (1938, American edition), introduced what was then obscure guerrilla armies led by Chinese communist leaders such as Mao Zedong, Zhou Enlai, and Lin Biao to the West. Its coverage treated the Communists as reformers and antifascists and helped spread a positive view of Chinese Communism among U.S. intellectuals. For details regarding the writing and reception of the book, see S. Bernard Thomas, *Season of High Adventure: Edgar Snow in China* (Berkeley: University of California Press, 1996), chapters 9 and 10. On Teddy White's career in China before Pearl Harbor and his relationship with his boss Henry Luce, see Thomas Griffith, *Harry and Teddy: The Turbulent Friendship of Press Lord Henry R. Luce and His Favorite Reporter, Theodore H. White* (New York: Random House, 1995), pp. 3–45.

11 On this excitement that infected many reporters in China in 1938–1939, see Stephen R. MacKinnon and Oris Friesen, *China Reporting: An Oral History of American Journalism in the 1930s and 1940s* (Berkeley: University of California Press, 1987), pp. 37–47.

12 *The Good Earth* was the number one bestseller two years in a row, in 1931 and 1932. See Alice Payne Hackett, *60 Years of Best Sellers, 1895–1955* (New York: R. R. Bowker Co., 1956), pp. 111, 113.

13 *Public Opinion, 1935–1946*, Hadley Cantril (ed.) (Princeton: Princeton University Press, 1951), p. 49.

14 See, for instance: Buck to Emma Edmunds White, November 3, 1939, Emma Edmunds White Collections, Randolph-Macon College; Buck to Harry B. Price, November 8, 1939, American Committee for Non-Participation in

Japanese Aggression in China Records, Box 1, Folder "Buck, Miss Pearl," Littauer Library, Harvard University; Pearl Buck, "Women and War," *Ladies' Home Journal*, May 1940, 94.

15 Buck, "Women and War," *Ladies' Home Journal*, May 1940, 94–96; "Japan Loses the War," *Reader's Digest*, August 1938, 38–41.

16 Peter Conn, *Pearl S. Buck: A Cultural Biography* (Cambridge: Cambridge University Press, 1996), p. 173.

17 "Warning to Free Nations," *Asia*, March 1941, 161; "Harlem Seen as a Symbol," *The New York Times*, November 15, 1941, 16; Buck to Franklin Roosevelt, January 10, 1941, Presidential Personal File 7339, FDR Library and Museum; Buck to Franklin Roosevelt, May 4, 1942, Presidential Personal File 7339; Pearl Buck, "Speaking of Liberty" sound recording, November 6, 1941, Recorded Sound Reference Center, Library of Congress.

18 The Mercury Theatre of the Air, "The Patriot," Milo Ryan Phonoarchive. The National Archives, College Park.

19 Wayne Cole, *Roosevelt and the Isolationists, 1932–45* (Lincoln: University of Nebraska Press, 1983), p. 241.

20 Editorial, "Blood Money," *Collier's*, October 7, 1939, 181.

21 Buck to Maxine McBride, April 14, 1939, ACNPJAC Records, Box 1, Folder "Buck, Miss Pearl."

22 "Speech–Stop Arming Japan Rally," ACNPJAC Records, Box 1, Folder "Buck, Miss Pearl."

23 Cole, *Roosevelt and the Isolationists*, p. 349.

24 Price to Mrs. Richard Walsh [Pearl Buck], October 14, 1939, ACNPJAC Records, Box 1, Folder "Buck, Miss Pearl."

25 Price to Mrs. Richard Walsh, October 23, 1939, ACNPJAC Records, Box 1, Folder "Buck, Miss Pearl."

26 Buck to Harry B. Price, October 25, 1939, ACNPJAC Records, Box 1, Folder "Buck, Miss Pearl."

27 Price to Mrs. Richard Walsh, October, 28, 1939, ACNPJAC Records, Box 1, Folder "Buck, Miss Pearl."

28 Buck to Emma Edmunds White, November 3, 1939, Emma Edmunds White Collections, Randolph-Macon College.

29 Buck to Price, November 8, 1939, ACNPJAC Records, Box 1, Folder "Buck, Miss Pearl."

30 Buck to Greene, November 8, 1939, ACNPJAC Records, Box 1, Folder "Buck, Miss Pearl."

31 To cite but a few representative essays: "Japan Loses the War," *Reader's Digest*, August 1938; "America's Gunpowder Women," *Harper's Magazine*, July 1939; "People in Pain," *Reader's Digest*, November 1941; "Women and War," *Ladies' Home Journal*, May 1940; "Warning to Free Nations: A Comment," *Asia* 41 (1941); "The Future of the White Man in the Far East," *Foreign Affairs*, October 1940.

32 Pearl S. Buck. Untitled handwritten manuscript, W. Aubrey and Corrier Funai Chenault Collection, Folder 17, Randolph-Macon College.

33 Friedman, *The Road from Isolation*, p. 95.

34 Pearl S. Buck, "Flight into China," unpublished typescript, Pearl S. Buck Collection, Box 1, Folder 12, Butler Library, Columbia University. Act one, scene one, pp. 4–5. Hereafter "Act-Scene-Page #."

35 Buck added Mollie to the play at a fairly late phase in the composition of the play in order, according to her own testimony, to underscore the symbolic meaning of the choice Reinhart faces: "This letter is just to say that when you talk about the play to other producers, please say that I am going to develop a little more the character of Reinhardt, and make sharper the fact that he faces a choice, whether to merge himself into another people or to continue his separate existence as a Jew. I think I shall introduce another rather young modern Chinese woman to make sharper this choice, not so much as a major character but as a contrast between what he has and what he may want." Pearl Buck to David Lloyd, November 28, 1938, David Lloyd Files, Box 22, Folder 5, Firestone Library, Princeton University.

36 Pearl S. Buck, "Flight into China," 3–1–18.

37 Bernard Wasserstein, *Secret War in Shanghai: An Untold Story of Espionage, Intrigue, and Treason in World War II* (Boston: Houghton Mifflin, 1999), pp. 4–5; Christian Henriot, *Shanghai, 1927–1937: Municipal Power, Locality, and Modernization* (Berkeley: University of California Press, 1993), pp. 155–60.

38 Between 1933 and 1941, some 20,000 Jewish refuges from Europe arrived in Shanghai. Wasserstein, *Secret War*, p. 140.

39 This chain of inferences is not overdrawn. In her letter to her agent, Buck wrote in 1939 that Jews "must give up being Jews as quickly as possible. . . . They have no country and they must belong wherever they happen to be. And they must lose their very blood as quickly as they can. Only thus can there cease to be persecution of the Jews." Buck to David Llyod, February 24, 1939, David Lloyd Files, Box 15, Folder 5.

40 Interview, Nora Sterling Collections, Box 6, Folder 19.

41 On the positive, romanticized, and progressive image of China as a reflection of America's democratic values, see Karen J. Leong, *The China Mystique: Pearl S. Buck, Anna May Wong, Mayling Soong, and the Transformation of American Orientalism* (Berkeley: University of California Press, 2005), chapter 1.

42 The most notable examples are: "Tiger! Tiger!" *Cosmopolitan*, April 1938; "Golden Flower," *Women's Home Companion*, March 1940; "The Face of Gold," *The Saturday Evening Post*, August 24, 1940; "There Was No Peace," *Colliers*, November 2, 1940; "Iron," *Los Angeles Times*, December 22 and 29, 1940; "China Sky," *Collier's*, ten installments from February 1, 1940 through April 5, 1941.

43 Buck to Roosevelt, January 10, 1941, Presidential Personal File 7339, FDR Library and Museum.

44 Pearl S. Buck, "Harlem Seen as a Symbol," *The New York Times*, November 15, 1941, 16

45 During the war, Buck and her allies launched a campaign to repeal the Chinese Exclusion Act (Chinese immigrants' citizenship eligibility was quickly

becoming a thorny issue, an embarrassment for both the United States and China, America's official ally). See Scott Wong, *Americans First: Chinese Americans and the Second World War* (Cambridge, MA: Harvard University Press, 2005); Frederick Riggs, *Pressures on Congress: A Study of the Repeal of Chinese Exclusion* (New York: Oxford University Press, 1950). As part of this campaign, Buck developed what Richard So has called the "fiction of natural democracy," an argument that the Chinese were "by nature" democratic, deserving of U.S. citizenship. My argument here strengthens So's claim that for Buck this theory was a deeply felt one, not an opportunistic stratagem to give Congress an excuse to repeal the Act. See Richard Jean So, "Fictions of Natural Democracy: Pearl Buck, *The Good Earth*, and the Asian American Subject," *Representations* 112 (2010): 87–111. Colleen Lye, on the other hand, offers a much more critical interpretation of Buck's attribution of natural predilections for democratic values to the Chinese peasantry. Buck's characterization of the Chinese as agrarian, egalitarian, freedom-loving democrats, uncompromised by the corruption of the Nationalists, indifferent to Communist doctrines, and fiercely anti-Japanese, Lye maintains, largely mirrored the ideologically most acceptable role the United States fantasized for itself to play in East Asia from the late 1930s through World War II. See Colleen Lye, *America's Asia: Racial Form and American Literature, 1893–1945* (Princeton: Princeton University Press, 2005), chapter 5.

46 Pearl S. Buck to Roosevelt, September 29, 1939, Presidential Personal File 7339, FDR Library and Museum.

47 Akira Iriye, *The Origins of the Second World War in Asia and the Pacific* (London: Longman, 1987), p. 91.

48 Stephen R. MacKinnon and Oris Friesen, *China Reporting*, p. 15.

NOTES TO CHAPTER 8

1 Sherwood to White, May 19, 1940, Robert Sherwood Papers, Folder 1321, Houghton Library, Harvard University.

2 Harold Ickes, *The Secret Diary of Harold L. Ickes* (New York: Simon and Schuster, 1954), vol. 3, pp. 188–89.

3 *Ernest Hemingway: Selected Letters*, Carlos Baker (ed.) (New York: Scribner's, 1981), p. 506. Hemingway to Perkins, June 26, 1940, Hemingway Series I, Box 4, Firestone Library, Princeton University.

4 Buck to an unknown recipient, May 2, 1940, Nora Sterling Collection, Box 6, Folder 19, Randolph-Macon University.

5 Pound to Buck, January 31, 1940, Ezra Pound Papers, Box 6, Folder 273, Beinecke Library, Yale University.

6 Ezra Pound, "Letter from Rapallo: In War Appear Responsibilities," *The Japan Times and Mail* (July 22, 1940), reprinted in *Ezra Pound and Japan: Letters and Essays*, Sanehide Kodama (ed.) (Redding Ridge: Black Swan Books, 1987), pp. 173, 174.

7 The Almanac Singers, "The Ballad of October 16th" (1941). The bill passed on September 25, and the title of this song refers to the day when it was announced that 16 million men had registered for the first peacetime draft. *The Songs That Fought the War: Popular Music and the Home Front, 1939–1945*, John Bush Jones (ed.) (Waltham: Brandeis University Press, 2006), p. 61.

8 On the changing meaning of liberalism, see Alan Brinkley, *The End of Reform: New Deal Liberalism in Recession and War* (New York: Vintage, 1996), pp. 8–11.

9 John Dewey, *Liberalism and Social Action* (New York: G. P. Putnam's Sons, 1935), p. 21.

10 Reinhold Niebuhr, "Leaves from the Notebook of a War-bound American," *The Christian Century*, October 25, 1939, 1298.

11 Anne O'Hare McCormick, "Europe," *The New York Times*, October 30, 1939, 16.

12 "Roosevelt Joins Nation in Prayers For Peace Today," *Washington Post*, September 9, 1940, 1.

13 "Presidents Warns on Need for Unity," *The New York Times*, July 9, 1941, 21.

14 "Sermon preached in the Madison Avenue Presbyterian Church on Jan. 14, 1940," Henry Sloane Coffin Papers, Box 10, Folder 10:150, Union Theological Seminary.

15 Adolf Berle, *Navigating the Rapids* (New York: Harcourt Brace Javanovich, 1973), p. 279.

16 Myron C. Taylor (ed.), *Wartime Correspondence between President Roosevelt and Pope Pius XII* (New York: Macmillan, 1947), p. 19. For Roosevelt's possible motives behind the Myron Mission, see John S. Conway, "Pope Pius XII and the Myron Taylor Mission," in David Woolner and Richard Kurial (ed.), *FDR, the Vatican, and the Roman Catholic Church in America, 1933–1945* (New York: Palgrave, 2003), pp. 143–52.

17 A reasonably comprehensive study of these Catholic intellectuals has yet to be written, although in his study *The Crisis of Democratic Theory: Scientific Naturalism and the Problem of Value*, Edward A. Purcell, Jr. provides rough outlines (see especially chapter 3). For more details, I refer my readers to essays by these thinkers in scholarly journals, including law reviews published by the law schools of major Catholic colleges such as Notre Dame, Georgetown, and Fordham, the annual proceedings of the American Catholic Philosophical Association, *The Thomist*, and *The Review of Politics*. See also Yves Simon, *Nature and Functions of Authority* (Milwaukee: Marquette University Press, 1940) and Jacques Maritain, *Scholasticism and Politics* (New York: Macmillan, 1940). We ought to evaluate carefully the interest and influence of this episode, bearing in mind the still very much precarious social position of Catholic intellectuals at that time. Useful historical contexts are provided in Philip Gleason, "Pluralism, Democracy, and Catholicism in the Era of World War II," *The Review of Politics* 49 (1987): 208–30; Zachary R. Calo, "The Indispensable Basis of Democracy: American Catholicism, the Church-State Debate, and the Soul of American Liberalism, 1920–1929," *Virginia Law Review* 91 (2005): 1037–73. On the relationship of the two French exiles, Simon and

Maritain, with Charles de Gaulle during the war, see John Hellman, "The Anti-Democratic Impulse in Catholicism: Jacques Maritain, Yves Simon, and Charles de Gaulle during World War II," *Journal of Church and State* 33 (1991): 453–71.

18 Lippmann's attempt to ground democracy on the bedrock of the natural law was given the most systematic exposition in his last major work *Essays in the Public Philosophy* (1954), but his interest in Catholicism and the "higher law" went back to the late 1930s. See *The Good Society* (New York: Little, Brown, 1937), chapter 15. Main themes developed in *Essays* can be detected germinating in the keynote speech he gave at the annual meeting of the American Catholic Philosophical Association in 1941. See "Man's Image of Man," *Proceedings of the Seventeenth Annual Meeting of the American Catholic Philosophical Association* (1941): 66–75. John Patrick Diggins traces the evolution of Lippmann's political philosophy, from his pragmatism during the 1920s to his embrace of the natural law at the height of the Cold War, in his essay "From Pragmatism to Natural Law: Lippmann's Quest for the Foundations of Legitimacy," *Political Theory* 19 (1991): 519–38. The most prolific, prolix, and pugnaciously antiliberal of all neo-Thomists, Adler was at the forefront of the religious counterattack on the decadence of liberal democracy. His important writings from this period include: Mortimer Adler, "God and the Professors," Gail Kennedy (ed.) *Pragmatism and American Culture* (Boston: Heath, 1950): 67–76; "The Demonstration of Democracy," *Proceedings of the Fifteenth Annual Meeting of the American Catholic Philosophical Association* (1939): 122–65; "Parties and the Common Good," *The Review of Politics* 1 (1939): 51–83; "A Dialectic of Morals," *The Review of Politics* 3 (1941): 3–41; "A Dialectic of Morals II," *The Review of Politics* 3 (1941): 188–224; "A Dialectic of Morals III," *The Review of Politics* 3 (1941): 350–94; Adler and Walter Farrell, "The Theory of Democracy," *The Thomist* 3 (1941): 397–449.

19 Jacques Maritain, *Scholasticism and Politics* (New York: Macmillan, 1940), pp. 109–10, 98; Paul Kennedy, "The Principles of Democracy," *Proceedings of the Fifteenth Annual Meeting of the American Catholic Philosophical Association* (1939), 169; Yves Simon, "Liberty and Authority," *Proceedings of the Sixteenth Annual Meeting of the American Catholic Philosophical Association* (1940): 86–114; "Thomism and Democracy," *Conference on Science, Philosophy and Religion in their Relation to the Democratic Way of Life* (1941; an unpublished proceeding of the conference; Andover Theological Library, Harvard University); *Nature and Functions of Authority* (Milwaukee: Marquette University Press, 1940), p. 18; John A. Ryan and Francis J. Boland, *Catholic Principles of Politics* (New York: Macmillan, 1940), p. 5.

20 Donald Meyer, *The Protestant Search for Political Realism, 1919–1941* (Middletown: Wesleyan University Press, 1988) remains by far the best treatment of the evolution of Protestant realism. Writings by protestant realists from the prewar years on which my synopsis here draws include: Henry P. Van Dusen, "Irresponsible Idealism," *Christian Century*, July 24, 1940, 925; John C.

Bennett, "Not a Holy War," *Christian Century*, October 8, 1941, 1244 and *Christian Realism* (New York: Charles Scribner's Sons, 1941); H. Richard Niebuhr, "The Christian Church in the World's Crisis," *Christianity and Society*, summer 1940, 11; Reinhold Niebuhr, *Christianity and Power Politics* (New York: Charles Scribner's Sons, 1940) and *The Europe's Catastrophe* (London: Nisbet, 1940); Henry Sloan Coffin, "Evangelism and the Present Crisis," *The Presbyterian Tribune*, December 1940, 6. On Van Dusen's prewar political activities, the best account is Dean K. Thompson, "World War II, Interventionism, and Henry Pitney Van Dusen," *Journal of Presbyterian History* 55 (1977): 327–45. On the development of the discourse of "responsibility" by these realists after World War II, see Mark Edwards, "'God Has Chosen Us': Re-Membering Christian Realism, Rescuing Christendom, and the Contest of Responsibilities during the Cold War," *Diplomatic History* 33 (2009): 67–93. On Reinhold Niebuhr's gradual de-radicalization on political economy and his waxing hawkishness on foreign policy, see William H. Becker, "Reinhold Niebuhr: From Marx to Roosevelt," *Historian* 35 (1973): 539–50.

21 The quotations of Mussolini, Goebbels, and Stalin are from John D. Lewis, "The Element of Democracy," *The American Political Science Review*, 34 (1940), 469; Robert MacIver, *Leviathan and the People* (Baton Rouge: Louisiana State University Press, 1939), pp. 142–44.

22 Thurman Arnold, *The Folklore of Capitalism* (New Haven: Yale University Press, 1937), p. 40. In the same vein, Charles Merriam observed in 1941: "[T]he symbolisms of democracy, the attitudes of popular rule, and the demands of popular welfare are by this time so deeply ingrained in the modern mind that they cannot safely be challenged, even by those who hold in their hands weapons that seem to be irresistible for the moment." *What Is Democracy?* (Chicago: University of Chicago Press, 1941), p. 8.

23 Major works by émigré thinkers diagnosing the causes of the collapse of the nineteenth-century liberalism that were published or began to be written during the prewar years include: Karl Loewenstein, *The Balance between Legislative and Executive Power: A Study in Comparative Constitutional Law* (Chicago: University of Chicago Press, 1938); Karl Loewenstein, *Hitler's Germany: The Nazi Background to War* (New York: Macmillan, 1939); Karl Polanyi, *The Great Transformation* (New York: Rinehart, 1944); Joseph Schumpeter, *Capitalism, Socialism, and Democracy* (New York: Harper, 1942); Franz Neumann, *Behemoth: The Structure and Practice of National Socialism* (New York: Oxford University Press, 1942); Emil Lederer, *State of the Masses: The Threat of the Classless Society* (New York: Norton, 1940); Peter Drucker, *The End of Economic Man: A Study of the New Totalitarianism* (New York: John Day, 1939); Erich Fromm, *Escape from Freedom* (New York: Rinehart, 1941); Friedrich Pollock, "State Capitalism: Its Possibilities and Limitations," *Studies in Philosophy and Social Science* 9 (1941): 200–255.

24 Edmund Wilson, "The Omelet of A. MacLeish," *New Yorker*, January 14, 1939, 23.

25 Archibald MacLeish, "Sentiments for a Dedication," *The Nation*, February 13, 1929, 194.
26 On intellectuals and artists working within Luce's media empire, see Robert Vanderlan, *Intellectuals Incorporated: Politics, Art, and Ideas Inside Henry Luce's Media Empire* (Philadelphia: University of Pennsylvania Press, 2010); Michael Augspurger, *An Economy of Abundant Beauty: Fortune Magazine and Depression America* (Ithaca: Cornell University Press, 2004).
27 See Scott Donaldson, *Archibald MacLeish: An American Life* (Boston: Houghton Mifflin, 1992), pp. 298, 320–346.
28 The Broadway producer Herman Shumlin served as president, but MacLeish, as vice-president of the company, played the most instrumental role in raising funds for Ivens's movies. Financial contributors to this venture company included Henry Luce and Ralph Ingersoll of Time Inc., Lillian Hellman, Hemingway, and Dos Passos. See MacLeish Papers, Box 51, Folder "Contemporary Historians Inc." See also Michael Reynolds, *Hemingway: The 30s* (New York: W. W. Norton, 1997), p. 259; Townsend Ludington, *John Dos Passos: A Twentieth-Century Odyssey* (New York: Dutton, 1980), p. 363; Scott Donaldson, *Archibald MacLeish*, p. 264.
29 Archibald MacLeish, "Ars Poetica," *Poetry* 28 (1926), pp. 126, 27.
30 Archibald MacLeish, "Public Speech and Private Speech in Poetry," *The Yale Review*, March 1938, 541, 544, 543, 545.
31 Archibald MacLeish, "Poetry and the Public World," *The Atlantic Monthly*, June 1938, 826, 830.
32 Archibald MacLeish, "The Irresponsibles," *The Nation*, May 18, 1940, 622.
33 MacLeish, "The Irresponsibles," 622.
34 Archibald MacLeish, "Post-war Writers and Pre-war Readers," *The New Republic*, June 10, 1940, 789.
35 I drew on contents of MacLeish Papers, Box 37, Folder "Post-war Writers and Pre-war Readers," Library of Congress.
36 MacLeish, "Post-war Writers," 790.
37 "Topics of the Times," *The New York Times*, May 26, 1940, E8.
38 Sherwood to MacLeish, May 24, 1940, Sherwood Papers, Folder 1348.
39 See *Congressional Record Appendix* (the 77th Congress), 13441–44.
40 Perry to MacLeish, June 5, 1940. A duplicate in Box 6, Thomas Verner Smith Papers, the University of Chicago. On Perry's anti-appeasement activities, see American Defense-Harvard Group Papers, Pusey Library, Harvard University.
41 Bernard DeVoto to Archibald MacLeish, July 21, 1940, MacLeish Papers, Box 6.
42 See "War Writers on Democracy," *Life*, June 24, 1940, 8, 12.
43 "War Writers on Democracy," 15.
44 Dalton Trumbo, *The Remarkable Andrew: Being the Chronicle of a Literal Man* (Philadelphia: J. B. Lippincott, 1941), p. 309.
45 Other critical responses include: Edmund Wilson, "Archibald MacLeish and the 'Word'," *The New Republic*, July 1, 1940, 31; Burton Rascoe, "The

Tough-Muscle Boys of Literature," *The American Mercury*, November 1940, 369–373; Dwight MacDonald, "Reading from Left to Right," *Partisan Review*, January–February 1941, 24–32. For sympathetic reactions, see Roy Helton, "The Inner Threat: Our Own Softness," *Harper's*, September 1940, 337–43; Mortimer J. Adler, "This Pre-War Generation," *Harper's*, October 1940, 524–34.

46 Archibald MacLeish, "Of the Librarian's Profession," *The Atlantic Monthly*, June 1940, 788.

47 MacLeish to Felix Frankfurter, May 2, 1940, MacLeish Papers, Box 2. See also Ickes, *The Secret Diary*, vol. 3, pp. 198–99.

48 Donaldson, *Archibald MacLeish*, p. 341.

49 Ickes, *The Secret Diaries*, vol. 3, p. 199.

50 William Langer and Sarell Gleason, *The Challenge to Isolation* (New York: Council on Foreign Relations, 1952), p. 764; Ickes, *The Secret Diaries*, vol. 3, pp. 292–93.

51 For circumstances surrounding Patterson's promotion, see John Morton Blum, *From the Morgenthau Diaries*, vol. 1 (Boston: Houghton Mifflin, 1959), pp. 197–99. For Lovett, see H. H. Arnold, *Global Mission* (New York: Harper, 1949), pp. 195–96.

52 For Acheson's role in this campaign, see Mark Chadwin, *The Hawks of World War II* (Chapel Hill: University of North Carolina Press, 1968), pp. 58–59. See also his letter to the *Times*, "No Legal Bar Seen to Transfer of Destroyers," *The New York Times*, August 11, 1940, 8E. As assistant secretary of war, he would play an instrumental role in radicalizing, at the stage of implementation, Hull's and Roosevelt's more cautious policy toward Japan. See Jonathan Utley, *Going to War with Japan, 1937–1941* (Knoxville: University of Tennessee Press, 1985), pp. 151–56; Irvine Anderson: *The Standard-Vacuum Oil Company and United States East Asian Policy, 1933–1941* (Princeton: Princeton University Press, 1975), pp. 171–88.

53 For Cohen's role in facilitating the destroyer-for-base deal, see William Lasser, *Benjamin V. Cohen: Architect of the New Deal* (New Haven: Yale University Press, 2002), pp. 216–31; Franklin D. Roosevelt, *F.D.R.: His Personal Letters, 1928–1945* (New York: Duell, Sloan and Pearce, 1950), pp. 1048–49; Ickes, *The Secret Diaries*, vol. 3, pp. 270–71.

54 Randall Jarrell's trenchant criticism, "Poetry in a Dry Season," *Partisan Review*, March–April, 1940, 165.

55 Ickes, *The Secret Diaries*, vol. 3, p. 209.

56 See Robert E. Herzstein, *Henry R. Luce: A Political Portrait of the Man Who Created the American Century* (New York: Scribner's, 1994), pp. 1–23.

57 Ickes, *The Secret Diaries*, vol. 3, pp. 282, 289. Circumstances surrounding this abortive effort to establish a propaganda bureau remain murky. In his July 30 letter to Harry Hopkins, Robert Sherwood wrote: "You may know that I am working very hard with the group that includes Archie MacLeish, John Steinbeck, Henry Luce, and others for a Bureau of Propaganda for American Democracy, an attempt to expedite the psychological and spiritual

mobilization of the people. I believe this organization has the President's sympathetic interest. I certainly hope it will have and deserve yours." It appears certain that there was a concerted effort among the aforementioned writers to establish a sort of information clearing house for various interventionist organizations. Sherwood to Harry Hopkins, July 30, 1940, Sherwood Papers, Folder 1232.

58 Charles Peters, *Five Days in Philadelphia* (New York: Public Affairs, 2005), pp. 154–73.

59 *The New York Times*, August 1, 1940, 3. MacLeish to Herbert Agar, August 21, 1940, MacLeish Papers, Box 1 (Agar, an editor of *Louisville Courier-Journal*, was also connected to the Century Group). See also Ickes, *The Secret Diaries*, vol. 3, p. 292; Chadwin, *The Hawks of World War II*, p. 105.

60 Roosevelt asked Frankfurter to draft a memorandum setting forth plausible rationales that would justify Roosevelt's candidacy for an unprecedented third term. Frankfurter asked MacLeish to prepare a second memorandum. Roosevelt ended up lifting large portions from the MacLeish memorandum in his acceptance speech. See *Roosevelt and Frankfurter: Their Correspondence, 1928–1945*, Max Freedman (ed.) (Boston: Little Brown and Company, 1967), pp. 531–35.

61 Frank to Mumford, undated, Mumford Papers, Box 20, Folder 1678, the University of Pennsylvania.

62 Mumford to Bruce Bliven, February 19, 1940, Mumford Papers, Box 81, Folder 6063.

63 Editorial, "Mr. Mumford and the Liberals," *The New Republic*, April 28, 1940, 562.

64 Lewis Mumford, "Call to Arms," *The New Republic*, May 18, 1938, 42.

65 Donald L. Miller, *Lewis Mumford: A Life* (New York: Weidenfeld and Nicholson, 1989), 403–04.

66 Mumford to the American Artists Congress, April 14, 1940, Mumford Papers, Box 73, Folder 5622.

67 Mumford to Wright, May 31, 1941, Mumford Papers, Box 83, Folder 6267.

68 Lewis Mumford, *Men Must Act* (New York: Harcourt, Brace, 1939), p. 95.

69 Mumford, *Men Must Act*, pp. 101, 103.

70 Here Mumford was echoing a consensus among informed observers of foreign affairs after the Munich Crisis. On the Munich's impact on America's strategic thinking and the emergent understanding of air power as an instrument of international blackmailing, see Michael Sherry, *The Rise of American Air Power: The Creation of Armageddon* (New Haven: Yale University Press, 1987), pp. 70–115.

71 Mumford, *Men Must Act*, pp. 105, 125–26.

72 Mumford, *Men Must Act*, pp. 116–17.

73 "A Brief Outline of Hell," Mumford Papers, Box 152, Folder 7323.

74 Mumford to Luce, February 4, 1940, Mumford Papers, Box 75, Folder 5805.

75 Mumford to Frank, September 14, 1940, Waldo Frank Papers, Box 19, Folder "Mumford, Lewis 1936–40," the University of Pennsylvania.

76 Mumford, "The Corruption of Liberalism," *The New Republic*, April 29, 1940, 569.

77 Mumford, "The Corruption of Liberalism," 570.

78 Mumford, "The Corruption of Liberalism," 572.

79 Niebuhr to Ursula Niebuhr, October 2, 1939, Reinhold Niebuhr Papers, Box 59, Folder 2, Library of Congress. See also Reinhold Niebuhr, *The Europe's Catastrophe* (London: Nisbet, 1940), p. 22.

80 Mumford to Frank, February 2, 1940, Frank Papers, Box 19, Folder "Mumford, Lewis 1936–40."

81 Mumford to Frank, April 16, 1940, Frank Papers, Box 19, Folder "Mumford, Lewis 1936–1940."

82 Mumford to Frank, May 20, 1940, Frank Papers, Box 19, Folder "Mumford, Lewis 1936–1940."

83 Niebuhr to Mumford, July 6, 1940, Mumford Papers, Box 49, Folder 3609.

84 Mumford to Frank, July 21, 1940, Frank Papers, Box 19, Folder "Mumford, Lewis 1936–1940."

85 *The Van Wyck Brooks-Lewis Mumford Letters*, Robert E. Spiller (ed.) (New York: E. P. Dutton, 1970), p. 185.

86 Mumford to Frank, July 26, 1940, Frank Papers, Box 19, Folder "Mumford, Lewis 1936–1940."

87 Mumford, *Faith for Living* (New York: Harcourt, Brace, 1940), p. 203.

88 Mumford, *Faith for Living*, p. 200.

89 Mumford, *Faith for Living*, p. 200.

90 Mumford, *Faith for Living*, p. 208.

91 Mumford, "The Corruption of Liberalism," 570.

NOTES TO CHAPTER 9

1 Waldo Frank, *Our America* (New York: Boni and Liveright, 1919), pp. 13–77, 222–32.

2 On Frank's reputation during the Jazz Age, see Gorham Munson, *The Awakening Twenties: A Memoir-History of a Literary Period* (Baton Rouge: Louisiana State University Press, 1985), pp. 54–69.

3 Frank to Lewis Mumford, undated (mid-February?), Mumford Papers, Box 20, Folder 1678.

4 Waldo Frank, *Chart for Rough Waters* (New York: Doubleday, 1940), pp. 23, 20, 7, 152.

5 Frank, *Chart for Rough Waters*, p. 121. Emphasis in the original.

6 "There is no. . .," Baker (ed.), *Hemingway; Selected Letters* (New York: Scribner's, 1981), p. 155. "writes a language. . .," Hemingway, *Death in the Afternoon* (New York: Scribner's, 1967[1932]), p. 53. Here Hemngway was self-servingly slandering Frank's book on Spanish culture, *Virgin Spain* (1926).

7 Frank, *Chart for Rough Waters*, p. 127.

8 Frank, *Chart for Rough Waters*, p. 105.

9 Frank, *Chart for Rough Waters*, p. 34.

10 John Dewey, "No Matter What Happens–Stay Out," *Common Sense* (March 1939), reprinted in *John Dewey: The Later Works, 1925–1953*, vol. 14, Jo Ann Boydston (ed.) (Carbondale: Southern Illinois University Press, 1988), p. 364. For Dewey's position on America's role during the last war, see, for instance, "America in the World," *The Nation*, March 14, 1918, 287; "In a Time of National Hesitation," *The Seven Arts*, March 1917, 5–7.

11 Mumford, *Faith for Living* (New York: Harcourt, Brace, 1940), pp. 184–85.

12 Frank, *Chart for Rough Waters*, p. 155.

13 Frank, *Chart for Rough Waters*, p. 165.

14 Frank, "Our Guilt in Fascism," *The New Republic*, May 6, 1940, 608.

15 See Richard Overy's discussion of the discourse of decline in interwar Britain, *The Twilight Years: The Paradox of Britain Between the Wars* (New York: Viking, 2009), pp. 9–49. Toynbee's influence on American intellectuals is hard to assess. The first three volumes of his monumental *A Study of History*, which dealt with the genesis-to-growth part of civilizations, came out in 1934, and coincidentally or not, the next three volumes dealing with the breakdown and disintegration of civilizations appeared in 1939. These latter three volumes obviously resonated with the academics on both sides of the Atlantic now faced with the breakdown of the West. On the American side, these volumes were widely reviewed by the most respected figures of various disciplines, including Charles A. Beard (history), Robert K. Merton (sociology), Pitirim A. Sorokin (sociology), John U. Nef (economic history), and George Catlin (political philosophy).

16 Karl Polanyi, *The Great Transformation: The Political and Economic Origins of Our Time* (New York: Beacon, 1957 [1944]), p. 3. Polanyi completed this book while on a Rockefeller fellowship at Bennington College in 1941–1943, a position he secured through Peter Drucker's good offices.

17 Carl Becker, *Modern Democracy* (New Haven: Yale University Press, 1941), p. 99.

18 Pitirim A. Sorokin, *The Crisis of Our Age: The Social and Cultural Outlook* (New York: E. P. Dutton, 1941), pp. 311–14.

19 T. S. Eliot, *The Idea of a Christian Society* (New York: Harcourt, Brace, 1940), p. 58.

20 T. S. Eliot, *After Strange Good: A Primer of Modern Heresy* (New York: Harcourt, Brace, 1934), p. 12.

21 Eliot, *The Idea*, p. 16.

22 T. S. Eliot, "Truth and Propaganda," (a letter to the editor) *The New England Weekly*, September 14, 1939, 291.

23 Reinhold Niebuhr, *The Nature and Destiny of Man, volume 1, Human Nature* (New York: Charles Scribner's Sons, 1941), pp. 93–122, 208–14.

24 Niebuhr, *The Nature and Destiny of Man*, pp. 18–25.

25 Mumford, "The Corruption of Liberalism," *The New Republic*, April 29, 1940, 568.

26 This is the one view to which Niebuhr took exception in his otherwise favorable review of MacLeish's collected essays. See Reinhold Niebuhr, "Essays by MacLeish," *The Nation*, April 26, 1941, 506.

27 MacLeish, "Post-War Writers and Pre-War Readers," *The New Republic*, June 10, 1940 790.
28 James T. Farrell, "The Cultural Front," *Partisan Review*, July–August 1941, 311–13.
29 Frank, *Chart for Rough Waters*, pp. 70, 72, 100, 160, 164.
30 Frank, *Chart for Rough Waters*, p. 100.
31 Mumford, *Faith for Living*, p. 129.
32 Niebuhr, *The Nature and Destiny of Man: Human Nature*, p. 110.
33 Robert Spliller (ed.), *The Van Wyck Brooks-Lewis Mumford Letters* (New York: Dutton, 1970), p. 37.
34 On Dewey's influence on Niebuhr, see Daniel F. Rice, *Reinhold Niebuhr and John Dewey: An American Odyssey* (Albany: SUNY Press, 1993). See also June Bingham, *Courage to Change: An Introduction to the Life and Thought of Reinhold Niebuhr* (Lanham: University Press of America, 1961), pp. 225–35.
35 Warhawks' attack on pragmatism and science took place against the backdrop of broader overlapping debates over science's significance for democracy among human scientists, social scientists, and natural scientists in the thirties. For an overview, see Andrew Jewett, *Science, Democracy, and the American University: From the Civil War to the Cold War* (Cambridge: Cambridge University Press, 2012), chapters 9 and 10.
36 John Dewey, *Freedom and Culture* (New York: G. P. Putnam, 1939), p. 145.
37 MacLeish, "The Irresponsibles," *Nation*, May 18, 1940 622.
38 Merriam to Dewey, October 11, 1940, Charles Merriam Papers, Box 47, Folder 7, the University of Chicago.
39 Dewey, *Freedom and Culture*, p. 153.
40 Dewey, *Freedom and Culture*, p. 147.
41 Dewey, *Freedom and Culture*, p. 153.
42 John Dewey, "Higher Learning and War," *Bulletin of the American Association of University Professors* 25 (December 1939). Reprinted in *The Later Works*, p. 274.
43 John Dewey, "Creative Democracy–The Task Before Us." Reprinted in *The Later Works*, p. 227.
44 Dewey, *Freedom and Culture*, pp. 123, 124, 125.
45 Mumford, *Faith for Living*, p. 231.
46 Sidney Hook, "Metaphysics, War, and Intellectuals," *The Menorah Journal*, August 1940, 327–37. See also his attacks on the "medievalism" of responsible liberalism: "The Counter-Reformation in American Education," *The Antioch Review* 1 (1941): 109–16; "Academic Freedom and 'The Trojan Horse' in American Education," *Bulletin of the American Association of University Professors*, 25 (1939): 550–55; "The New Medievalism," *The New Republic*, October 28, 1940, 602–06.
47 See Frank Knight, "Ethics and Economic Reform I: The Ethics of Liberalism," *Economica* 6 (1939), 5; "Ethics and Economic Reform II: Idealism and Marxism," *Economica* 6 (1939), 314; "Democracy: Its Politico-Economic Structure," *The Journal of Negro Education* 10 (1941), 323; T. V. Smith, "The Tragic Realm of Truth," *Proceedings and Addresses of the American Philosophical Association* 9 (1935), 115–18; "Philosophy and Democracy," *Ethics* 47 (1937),

414–18, 421–22, 424–25; "The Democratic Process," *The Public Opinion Quarterly* 2 (1938), 15–16; *The Democratic Way of Life* (Chicago: University of Chicago Press, 1939), pp. 263, 268; *The Legislative Way of Life* (Chicago: Chicago University Press, 1940), pp. 26–28; Pendleton Herring, "A Prescription for Modern Democracy," *Annals of the American Academy of Political and Social Science* 180 (1935), 138; *Politics of Democracy* (New York: Norton, 1940), pp. 102–03, 106, 111–12, 176, 247–48, 261, 257; *Presidential Leadership: The Political Relations of Congress and the Chief Executive* (New York: Farrar and Rinehart, 1940), p. 117; Felix S. Cohen, "The Relativity of Philosophical Systems and the Method of Systematic Relativism," *The Journal of Philosophy* 36 (1939): 57–72; Zechariah Chafee, *Free Speech in the United States* (Cambridge, MA: Harvard University Press, 1941), p. 526; Robert McIver, *Leviathan and the People* (Baton Rouge: Louisiana State University Press, 1939), p. 49; Carl Friedrich, "Democracy and Dissent," *The Political Quarterly*, 10 (1939), 577; *Constitutional Government and Democracy: Theory and Practice in Europe and America* (Boston: Little, Brown, 1941), pp. 441–42; Harold Lasswell, *Democracy through Public Opinion* (Menasha: George Banta Publishing Co., 1941), p. 96; Ralph Barton Perry, *Shall Not Perish from the Earth* (New York: The Vanguard Press, 1940), p. 133.

48 Frank, *Chart for Rough Waters*, p. 126.
49 Eliot, *The Idea*, p. 65.
50 Frank, *Chart for Rough Waters*, p. 159.
51 Untitled document, undated, Mumford Papers, Box 152, Folder 7333.
52 MacLeish, "Irresponsibles," 618.
53 MacLeish to Auden, October 19, 1939; June 21, 1940. MacLeish Papers, Box 1. Auden was not directly acquainted with Niebuhr at this time. Niebuhr would publish a collection of essays under the title *Christianity and Power Politics* in August 1940, and Auden would review it for *The Nation*. This became the beginning of their lifelong friendship. See an unpublished memoir by Ursula Niebuhr, "Memories of Wystan in the Nineteen Forties," Niebuhr Papers, Box 34, Folder "Auden, W. H."
54 W. H. Auden, "Romantic or Free?" *Smith Alumnae Quarterly* (August 1940), reprinted in Edward Mendelson (ed.), *Complete Works of W. H. Auden*, vol. 2, (Princeton: Princeton University Press, 1988), p. 64.
55 Auden, "Romantic or Free?" pp. 64, 67, 68, 69.
56 Mumford to Osmond K. Frankel, November 16, 1940, Mumford Papers, Folder 5626, Box 73.
57 MacLeish, "The Librarian and the Democratic Process," *American Library Association Bulletin*, July 1940, 388.
58 MacLeish, "Post-War Writers and Pre-War Readers," 790.
59 Mumford, *Faith for Living*, pp. 194–95, 195, 191, 195–96.
60 A classic formulation of this view is found in Walter Lippmann, *The Phantom Public* (New York: Harcourt, Brace, 1925). See also Dewey's critical rejoinder, *Public and Its Problems* (New York: Henry Holt and Company, 1927). In the late 1930s, Schumpeter developed an even more cynical version. Joseph

Schumpeter, *Capitalism, Socialism and Democracy* (New York: HarperCollins, 1976 [1942]), pp. 269–83.

61 "What distinguishes these fascist nations is their metaphysical purpose." Mumford, *Faith for Living*, p. 197.

NOTES TO EPILOGUE

1 The speech, which was originally drafted by Adolf Berle at State, eventually went through seven revisions, with input from Robert Sherwood and Sam Rosenman. The famous "four freedoms" appeared in the fourth draft, but at this point the universalizing modifier "everywhere in the world" was appended only to the first two freedoms: freedom of speech and freedom of worship. In the fifth draft, however, Roosevelt added "everywhere in the world" and "anywhere in the world" after the third and fourth freedoms: freedom from want and freedom from fear. See Master Speech File, Box 58, File 1353, FDR Library and Museum. At one point, Harry Hopkins, who would later administer the Lend-Lease program, raised a question: "That [everywhere in the world] covers an awful lot of territory, Mr. President. I don't know how interested Americans are going to be in the people of Java." According to Rosenman, Roosevelt replied: "I'm afraid they'll have to be some day, Harry. The world is getting so small that even the people in Java are getting to be our neighbors now." See Samuel Rosenman, *Working with Roosevelt* (New York: Harper, 1952), pp. 263–64.

2 The single most useful source for this phase of Pound's career is Tim Redman's *Ezra Pound and Italian Fascism* (Cambridge: Cambridge University Press, 2009).

3 Pound to Mencken, October 27, 1939; October 31, 1939. Pound Papers, Box 37, File 1421, Beinecke Library, Yale University. "I take it my surviving auditors...," typescript, undated (June 1941 from internal evidence), Box 131, File 5523.

4 Pound to Lothrop Stoddard, November 17, 1939, Pound Papers, Box 23, File 1017.

5 Ickes to Pound, April 16, 1940, Pound Papers, Box 24, File 1035.

6 Mencken to Pound, November 13, 1939, Pound Papers, Box 37, File 1421.

7 Buck to Pound, February 23, 1940, Pound Papers, Box 6, File 273.

8 This British violation of U.S. neutrality and the freedom of high seas infuriated Pound as he saw Roosevelt's tepid protest as evidence of his sympathies for the Anglo-Jewish alliance. Transcript of Short Wave Broadcast, October 13, 1941, Records of the Foreign Broadcast Intelligence Service (hereafter RFBIS), Box 508, National Archives, College Park.

9 Transcript of Short Wave Broadcast, July 17, 1941, RFBIS, Box 503.

10 The quote is from Pound's broadcast on May 19, 1941. Cited in a report, Baltimore, July 11, 1945. FBI File on Ezra Pound [Microform]. Wilmington: Scholarly Resources, 2001.

11 Based on recordings RFBIS, RG 262, National Archives, College Park.

12 "Pound Assails Nicholas Murray Butler," "Daily Variety Seen by Ezra Pound," "Interventionists Seek Stock Profits," Records of the Central Intelligence Agency, Foreign Broadcast Information Service Daily Reports, 1941–1959, Box 1, 2, 3, National Archives.

13 Transcript of Short Wave Broadcast, September 29, 1941, RFBIS, Box 507.

14 "Lindbergh Sees a 'Plot' for War," *The New York Times*, September 12, 1941, 2; Wayne S. Cole, *Charles A. Lindbergh and the Battle Against American Intervention in World War II* (New York: Harcourt, Brace, 1974), pp. 173–76.

15 On the link between isolationism and anti-Semitism, see Edward S. Shapiro, "The Approach of War: Congressional Isolationism and Anti-Semitism, 1939–1941," *American Jewish History* 74 (1984): 45–64.

16 Pound to Taft, April 8, 1940; Pound to Tinkham, November 2, 1939; Pound to Nye, undated (1936?); Pound to Wheeler, June 18, 1940, July 19, 1940; Pound to Voohris, September 13, 1939, October 24, 1939, November 2, 1939; Pound to Wallace, July 19, 1940. All in Pound Papers. Pound's correspondence with William Borah is collected in Sarah C. Holmes (ed.), *The Correspondence of Ezra Pound and Senator William Borah* (Urbana: University of Illinois Press, 2001).

17 For Pound's championing of Wilsonian internationalism during and after the Great War, see "This Super-Neutrality," *The New Age*, October 21, 1915, 595; "Provincialism the Enemy-I," *The New Age*, July 12, 1917, 244; "The Revolt of Intelligence-V," *The New Age*, January 8, 1920, 153–54; "The Revolt of Intelligence-VI," *The New Age*, January 15, 1920, 176–77; "The Revolt of Intelligence-III," *The New Age*, December 18, 1919, 106.

18 Ezra Pound, *The Cantos of Ezra Pound* (New York: New Directions, 1970), pp. 420, 350, 410, 415. See also a stanza counseling against foreign embroilment on page 377 and Pound's choice of the Chinese character 中 ("middle," "neutral," "center") to translate "balance" on page 413.

19 Transcript of Short Wave Broadcast, July 7, 1941, RFBIS, Box 502.

20 Transcript of Short Wave Broadcast, May 22, 1941, RFBIS, Box 502.

21 Pound, *The Cantos of Ezra Pound*, p. 818.

22 John Connelly, "Nazis and Slavs: From Racial Theory to Racist Practice," *Central European History* 32 (1999), 33.

23 The association of the Jew with cosmopolitanism had a long history in German conservatism. The young Hegel on Abraham: "With his herds Abraham wandered hither and thither over a boundless territory without bringing parts of it any nearer to him by cultivating and improving them. Had he done so, he would have become attached to them and might have adopted them as parts of *his* world. . . . He was a stranger on earth, a stranger to the soil and to men alike. Among men he always was and remained a foreigner, yet not so far removed from them and independent of them that he needed to know nothing of them whatever, to have nothing whatever to do with them." G. W. F. Hegel, *The Early Theological Writings*, trans. T. M. Knox (Chicago: University of Chicago Press, 1967), p. 186. More than a century later, in his 1922 *Das Dritte Reich*, Moeller van den Bruck wrote of Marx thus:

"as a Jew he was a stranger in Europe and nevertheless mingled in the affairs of the European peoples. ... As a Jew he had no fatherland." Quoted in Fritz Stern, *Politics of Cultural Despair: A Study in the Rise of the Germanic Ideology* (Berkeley: University of California Press, 1961), p. 257.

24 Ezra Pound, *Gaudier-Brzeska: A Memoir* (New York: New Directions, 1970), p. 83, 113–14, 117; *Literary Essays of Ezra Pound*, T. S. Eliot (ed.) (New York: New Directions, 1968), pp. 7, 11–12, 21, 371, 434; *ABC of Reading* (New York: New Directions, 1934), p. 33; *Guide to Kulchur* (New York: New Directions, 1938), p. 127.

25 *Gaudier-Brzeska*, pp. 86, 121; *Literary Essays*, pp. 5, 77, 205, 401, 403; *Selected Prose, 1909–1965*, William Cookson (ed.) (New York: New Directions, 1973), p. 33; *Guide to Kulchur*, pp. 48–49.

26 *Gaudier-Brzeska*, p. 115; *Literary Essays*, pp. 411–12; *ABC of Reading*, pp. 19–22; *Selected Prose*, pp. 28–29, 41–42.

27 *Literary Essays*, pp. 50, 56; *ABC of Reading*, pp. 32, 36, 44, 64, 77–78, 97.

28 *Gaudier-Brzeska*, pp. 84–85, 91; *Literary Essays*, pp. 45, 54, 86, 92, 267, 406; *ABC of Reading*, pp. 2, 6–27, 29–30, 56; *Selected Prose*, pp. 30–31, 86; *Guide to Kulchur*, pp. 16–17, 28, 97–101, 107–08.

29 *ABC of Reading*, pp. 25, 48, 194.

30 Transcript of Short Wave Broadcast. December 7, 1941, RFBIS, Box 511.

31 Alan Brinkley, *The Publisher: Henry Luce and His American Century* (New York: Knopf, 2010), pp. 265–66.

32 Henry Luce, "The American Century," *Life*, February 17, 1941, 61, 62; Clare Boothe, *Margin for Error* (New York: Random House, 1940), p. xi.

33 Luce, "The American Century," 65, 63.

34 For a trenchant critique of the fallacy of cynical motivation in general and the doctrine of the "economic interpretation" in particular, see Frank Knight, "Ethics and the Economic Interpretation," *The Quarterly Journal of Economics* 36 (1922): 454–81. The dramatic expansion of America's world commitment before and during World War II has been interpreted from an "economic" vantage point. See William A. Williams, *The Tragedy of American Diplomacy* (Cleveland: The World Publishing, 1959), pp. 162–228; Patrick J. Hearden (Williams's doctoral student), *Roosevelt Confronts Hitler: America's Entry into World War II* (DeKalb: Northern Illinois University Press, 1987). "Economic" interests did matter during the prewar years, but it is important to remember that these "interests" or "economic" considerations are not data. They are often cultural aspirations in disguise and hence are not ulterior to anything. See Kenneth Burke, *Change and Permanence* (New York: New Republic, Inc., 1935), pp. 28–29; *Attitudes Toward History* (New York: Editorial Publications, Inc., 1937), pp. 336–38.

Bibliography

PRIMARY SOURCES

Archival Collections

American Committee for Non-Participation in Japanese Aggression in China Records. Littaur Library. Harvard University.

Archibald MacLeish Papers. Manuscript Division. Library of Congress.

Business Files of Charles Scribner. Archives of Charles Scribner's Sons. Firestone Library. Princeton University.

Carl Friedrich Papers. Pusey Library. Harvard University.

Charles A. and Anne Morrow Lindbergh Papers. Firestone Library. Princeton University.

Charles Merriam Papers. The University of Chicago.

Committee to Defend America by Aiding the Allies Records. Mudd Library. Princeton University.

Dalton Trumbo Papers. Wisconsin Historical Society.

David Lloyd Agency Files of Pearl S. Buck Collection. Firestone Library. Princeton University.

Edna St. Vincent Millay Papers. Manuscript Division. Library of Congress.

Emma Edmunds White Collection. Randolph-Macon Women's College.

Ernest Hemingway Collection. The John F. Kennedy Library and Museum.

Ezra Pound Papers. Beinecke Library. Yale University.

Fight for Freedom Committee Records. Mudd Library. Princeton University.

Hemingway Files. Archives of Charles Scribner's Sons. Firestone Library. Princeton University.

Henry Sloane Coffin Papers. Union Theological Seminary.

Lewis Mumford Papers. Rare Book and Manuscript Library. The University of Pennsylvania.

Maxwell Anderson. Interview. Oral History Research Office. Butler Library. Columbia University.

Milo Ryan Phonoarchive. The National Archives. College Park.

Nora Sterling Collection. Randolph-Macon College.

Pearl S. Buck Collection. Butler Library. Columbia University.

Playwrights' Producing Company Press Records. The New York Public Library.

Presidential Personal File. The Franklin D. Roosevelt Library and Museum.

Ralph Barton Perry Papers. Pusey Library. Harvard University.
Records of the Foreign Broadcast Intelligence Service. National Archives. College Park.
Reinhold Niebuhr Papers. Manuscript Division. Library of Congress.
Robert E. Sherwood Papers. Houghton Library. Harvard University.
Thomas Vernor Smith Papers. The University of Chicago.
W. Aubrey and Corrier Funai Chenault Collection. Randolph-Macon College.
Waldo Frank Papers. Rare Book and Manuscript Library. The University of Pennsylvania.
William Allen White Papers. Manuscript Division. Library of Congress.

Books and Articles

Adler, Mortimer J. "The Demonstration of Democracy." *Proceedings of the Fifteenth Annual Meeting of the American Catholic Philosophical Association* (1939): 122–65.
    "A Dialectic of Morals." *The Review of Politics* 3 (1941): 3–41.
    "A Dialectic of Morals II." *The Review of Politics* 3 (1941): 188–224.
    "A Dialectic of Morals III." *The Review of Politics* 3 (1941): 350–94.
    "God and the Professors." Edited by Gail Kennedy. *Pragmatism and American Culture*. Boston: Heath, 1950, 67–76.
    "Parties and the Common Good." *The Review of Politics* 1 (1939): 51–83.
    "This Pre-War Generation." *Harper's Magazine*, October 1940, 524–34.
Adler, Mortimer and Walter Farrell. "The Theory of Democracy." *The Thomist* 3 (1941): 397–449.
Adorno, Theodore. *Aesthetics and Politics*. Edited by Ronald Taylor. London: NLB, 1977.
    Dialectic of Enlightenment. Translated by Edmund Jephcott. Stanford: Stanford University Press, 2002.
    Essays on Music. Edited by Richard Leppert. Berkeley: University of California Press, 2002.
Adrey, Robert. *Thunder Rock*. New York: Dramatists Play Service Inc., 1941.
Anderson, Maxwell. "By Way of Preface: The Theatre as Religion." *The New York Times*, October 26, 1941, v–ff.
    Candle in the Wind: A Play in Three Acts. Washington, DC: Anderson House, 1941.
    Dramatist in America: Letters of Maxwell Anderson, 1912–1958. Edited by Laurence G. Avery. Chapel Hill: University of North Carolina Press, 1977.
    "Theatre as Religion." *The New York Times*, November 2, 1941, x3.
Arnold, H. H. *Global Mission*. New York: Harper, 1949.
Arnold, Thurman. *The Folklore of Capitalism*. New Haven: Yale University Press, 1937.
    The Symbols of Government. New Haven: Yale University Press, 1935.
Auden, W. H. *Complete Works of W. H. Auden*. Princeton: Princeton University Press, 1988.

Selected Poems, Edited by Edward Mendelson. New York: Vintage, 1989.

Beard, Charles A. *The Devil Theory of War: An Inquiry into the Nature of History and the Possibility of Keeping out of War*. New York: The Vanguard Press, 1936.

"How to Stay out of War." *Forum*, February 1937, 90.

Beard, Charles A. and Mary Beard. *The Rise of American Civilization*. New York: Macmillan, 1927.

Beard, Charles Austin and George Howard Edward Smith. *The Open Door at Home*. New York: Macmillan, 1934.

Becker, Carl. *Modern Democracy*. New Haven: Yale University Press, 1941.

Bénet, Stephen Vincent. "Listen to the People." *Life*, July 7, 1941, 90–96.

Nightmare at Noon. New York: Council for Democracy, 1940.

Benjamin, Walter. "The Work of Art in the Age of Its Technological Reproducibility." In *Selected Writings*, vol. 3., 1935–1938. Cambridge, MA: Harvard University Press, 2003, 101–40.

Bennett, John C. *Christian Realism*. New York: Charles Scribner's Sons, 1941.

"Not a Holy War." *Christian Century*, October 8, 1941, 1244.

Bergreen, Laurence. *As Thousands Cheer: The Life of Irving Berlin*. New York: Da Capo Press, 1996.

Berle, Adolf A. *Navigating the Rapids, 1918–1971: From the Papers of Adolf A. Berle*. Edited by Beatrice Bishop Berle and Travis Jacobs. New York: Harcourt, Brace, and Jovanovich, 1973.

Berle, Adolf A. and Gardiner C. Means, *The Modern Corporation and Private Property*. New York: Harcourt, Brace, 1932.

Bernays, Edward. *Crystallizing Public Opinion*. New York: Boni and Liveright, 1923.

Bessie, Alvah. "For Whom the Bell Tolls." *The New Masses*, November 5 1940, 25–29.

Boland, Francis J. and John A. Ryan. *Catholic Principles of Politics*. New York: Macmillan, 1940.

Boothe, Clare. *Margin for Error*. New York: Random House, 1940.

Bourne, Randolph. *War and Intellectuals: Collected Essays, 1915–1919*. Indianapolis: Hackett, 1999.

Brecht, Bertolt. *Brecht on Theatre: The Development of an Aesthetic*. Edited by John Willett. New York: Hill and Wang, 1964.

Brooks, Van Wyck. *The Van Wyck Brooks-Lewis Mumford Letters*. Edited by Robert E. Spiller. New York: E. P. Dutton, 1970.

Buck, Pearl S. "America's Gunpowder Women." *Harper's Magazine*, July 1939, 126–35.

"China Sky." *Collier's*, ten installments from February 1, 1940 through April 5, 1941.

"The Face of Gold," *The Saturday Evening Post*, August 24, 1940, 16ff.

"The Future of the White Man in the Far East." *Foreign Affairs: An American Quarterly Review* 19 (1940): 22–33.

"Golden Flower." *Women's Home Companion*, March 1940, 26ff.

"Harlem Seen as a Symbol." *The New York Times*, November 15, 1941, 16.

"Iron," *Los Angeles Times*, December 22 and 29, 1940, H8ff.

"Japan Loses the War." *Reader's Digest*, August 1938, 38–41.

The Patriot. New York: John Day, 1939.

"There Was No Peace," *Colliers*, November 2, 1940, 9ff.

"Warning to Free Nations: A Comment." *Asia*, May 1941, 161.

"Women and War." *Ladies' Home Journal*, May 1940, 94–97.

Bunche, Ralph J. "French and British Imperialism in West Africa." *The Journal of Negro History* 21 (1936): 31–46.

A World View of Race. Washington, DC: The Associates in Negro Folk Education, 1936.

Burke, Kenneth. *Attitudes Toward History*. Berkeley: University of California Press, 1984 [1937].

Counter-Point. Los Altos: Hermes, 1953 [1931].

Permanence and Change: An Anatomy of Purpose. New York: New Republic, 1935.

Burnham, James. "The Theory of the Managerial Revolution." *Partisan Review*, May–June 1941, 192–98.

Burns, Arthur. *Decline of Competition: A Study of the Evolution of American Industry*. New York: McGraw-Hill, 1936.

Cantril, Hadley, ed. *Public Opinion, 1935–1946*. Princeton: Princeton University Press, 1951.

Chafee, Zechariah. *Free Speech in the United States*. Cambridge, MA: Harvard University Press, 1941.

Chamberlin, Edward. *The Theory of Monopolistic Competition*. Cambridge, MA: Harvard University Press, 1933.

Chambers, Whittaker. *Witness*. Washington, DC: Regnery Publishing, 1980 [1952].

Chandler, Raymond. "Writers in Hollywood." *The Atlantic*, November 1945, 50–54.

Chase, Stuart. *The Tyranny of Words*. New York: Harcourt, Brace, 1938.

Coffin, Henry Sloan. "Evangelism and the Present Crisis." *The Presbyterian Tribune*, December 1940, 6.

Cohen, Felix S. "The Relativity of Philosophical Systems and the Method of Systematic Relativism." *The Journal of Philosophy* 36 (1939): 57–72

Cowley, Malcolm. "A Farewell to the 1930s." *The New Republic*, November 8, 1939, 42–43.

The Long Voyage: Selected Letters of Malcolm Cowley, 1915–1987. Edited by Hans Bak. Cambridge, MA: Harvard University Press, 2014.

"Shipwreck." *The New Republic*, September 9, 1940, 357.

Devoto, Bernard. "Father Abraham." *Harper's Magazine*, March 1940, 333–36.

Dewey, John. *Freedom and Culture*. New York: G. P. Putnam, 1939.

John Dewey: The Later Works, 1925–1953. Edited by Jo Ann Boydston. Vol. 14. Carbondale: Southern Illinois University Press, 1988.

Liberalism and Social Action. New York: G. P. Putnam's Sons, 1935.

Public and Its Problems. New York: Henry Holt and Company, 1927.

Dreiser, Theodore. *America Is Worth Saving.* New York: Modern Age Books, 1941.

Drucker, Peter F. *The End of Economic Man: The Origins of Totalitarianism.* New York: John Day, 1939.

Du Bois, W. E. B. *Dusk of Dawn: An Essay Toward an Autobiography of a Race Concept.* New York: Harcourt, Brace, 1940.

"Forum of Fact and Opinion." *The Pittsburgh Courier,* June 6, 1936, A1.

"Forum of Fact and Opinion." *The Pittsburgh Courier,* April 25, 1936, A1–A2.

"Forum of Fact and Opinion." *The Pittsburgh Courier,* May 1, 1937, A1.

"Inter-Racial Implications of the Ethiopian Crisis: A Negro View." *Foreign Affairs* 14 (1935): 82–92.

Eliot, T. S. *After Strange Good: A Primer of Modern Heresy.* New York: Harcourt, Brace, 1934.

The Idea of a Christian Society. New York: Harcourt, Brace, 1940.

"Truth and Propaganda." *The New English Weekly,* September 14, 1939, 291.

Ellington, Duke. *Duke Ellington Reader.* Edited by Mark Tucker. New York: Oxford University Press, 1995.

Farrell, James T. "The Cultural Front." *Partisan Review,* July–August 1941, 311–13.

Fitzgerald, F. Scott. *F. Scott Fitzgerald: A Life in Letters.* Edited by Matthew J. Bruccoli. New York: Scribner's, 1994.

The Pat Hobby Stories. New York: Scribers, 1995.

Flanagan, Hallie. *Arena.* New York: Duell, Sloan and Pearce, 1940.

Frank, Waldo. *Chart for Rough Waters.* New York: Doubleday, 1940.

Our America. New York: Boni and Liveright, 1919.

"Our Guilt in Fascism." *The Nation,* May 5, 1940, 607–09.

Frankfurter, Felix. *Roosevelt and Frankfurter: Their Correspondence, 1928–1945.* Edited by Max Freedman. Boston: Little, Brown and Company, 1967.

Friedrich, Carl. *Constitutional Government and Democracy: Theory and Practice in Europe and America.* Boston: Little, Brown, 1941.

"Democracy and Dissent." *The Political Quarterly* 10 (1939): 571–82.

Fuchs, Daniel. "Writing for the Movies." *Commentary,* February 1962, 107–08.

Gelder, Robert Van. "Ernest Hemingway Talks of Work and War." *The New York Times Book Review,* August 11, 1940, 2.

Gellhorn, Martha. *The Heart of Another.* New York: Charles Scribner's Son, 1941.

A Stricken Field. New York: Duell, 1940.

Greenberg, Clement. "Avant-Garde and Kitsch." *Partisan Review,* Fall 1939, 34–41.

"Toward a Newer Laocoon," *Partisan Review.* July–August 1940, 297–310.

Greenberg, Clement and Dwight Macdonald. "Ten Propositions on the War." *Partisan Review,* July–August 1941, 278.

Hayakawa, S. I. *Language in Action.* New York: Harcourt, Brace, 1941.

Hecht, Ben. *A Child of the Century.* New York: Simon and Schuster, 1954.

Hecht, Ben and Charles MacArthur. *Fun To Be Free.* New York: Dramatists Play Service, 1941.

Helton, Roy. "The Inner Threat: Our Own Softness." *Harper's Magazine,* September 1940, 337–43.

Hemingway, Ernest. *By-Line: Ernest Hemingway.* Edited by William White. New York: Charles Scribner's Sons, 1967.

Death in the Afternoon. New York: Scribner's, 1967 [1932].

"Ernest Hemingway, Screenwriter: New Letters on *For Whom the Bell Tolls.*" *Antioch Review* 53 (1995): 261–83.

Ernest Hemingway, Selected Letters, 1917–1961. Edited by Carlos Baker. New York: Charles Scribner's Sons, 1981.

"Fascism Is a Lie." *The New Masses,* June 22, 1937, 4.

A Farewell to Arms. New York: Charles Scribner's Sons, 2003 [1929].

For Whom the Bell Tolls. New York: Charles Scribner's Sons, 1940.

"Introduction." *Men at War.* Edited by Ernest Hemingway. New York: Bramhall House, 1979.

The Only Thing That Counts: The Ernest Hemingway/Maxwell Perkins Correspondence, 1925–1947. Edited by Matthew J. Bruccoli. New York: Scribner's, 1996.

Herring, Pendleton. *Politics of Democracy.* New York: Norton, 1940.

"A Prescription for Modern Democracy." *Annals of the American Academy of Political and Social Science* 180 (1935): 138–48.

Presidential Leadership: The Political Relations of Congress and the Chief Executive. New York: Farrar and Rinehart, 1940.

Hertzog, Heta. "On Borrowed Experience: An Analysis of Listening to Daytime Sketches." *Studies in Philosophy and Social Research* 9 (1941): 65–95.

Hook, Sidney. "Academic Freedom and 'The Trojan Horse' in American Education." *Bulletin of the American Association of University Professors* 25 (1939): 550–55.

"The Counter-Reformation in American Education." *The Antioch Review* 1 (1941): 109–16.

"Metaphysics, War, and Intellectuals." *The Menorah Journal,* August 1940, 327–37.

"The New Medievalism." *The New Republic,* October 28, 1940, 602–06.

Howard, Sidney. *The Ghost of Yankee Doodle: A Tragedy.* New York: Scribner's Sons, 1938.

"Our Professional Patriots." *The New Republic,* August 20, 1924, 346–52.

Hughes, Langston. "Air Raid Over Harlem." *New Theatre and Film* 3 (1936): 19.

"Call of Ethiopia." *Opportunity,* September 1935, 276.

"Comment on War." *The Crisis,* June 1940, 190.

Ickes, Harold. *The Secret Diary of Harold L. Ickes.* New York: Simon and Schuster, 1954.

Jarrell, Randall. "Poetry in a Dry Season." *Partisan Review,* March–April 1940, 165–66.

Jessup, Phillip C. "The Monroe Doctrine in 1940." *The American Journal of International Law* 34 (1940): 704–11.

Josephs, William and George S. Snyderman. "Bohemia: The Underworld of Art." *Social Forces* 18 (1939): 187–99.

Josephson, Matthew. *Infidel in the Temple: A Memoir of the Nineteen-Thirties.* New York: Alfred Knopf, 1967.

Kennedy, Paul. "The Principles of Democracy." *Proceedings of the Fifteenth Annual Meeting of the American Catholic Philosophical Association* (1939): 166–75.

Knight, Frank. "Democracy: Its Politico-Economic Structure." *The Journal of Negro Education* 10 (1941): 318–32.

"Ethics and the Economic Interpretation." *The Quarterly Journal of Economics* 36 (1922): 454–81.

"Ethics and Economic Reform I: The Ethics of Liberalism." *Economica* 6 (1939): 1–29.

"Ethics and Economic Reform II: Idealism and Marxism." *Economica* 6 (1939): 398–422.

Krivitsky, Walter. *In Stalin's Secret Service: An Exposé of Russia's Secret Policies by the Former Chief of the Soviet Intelligence in Western Europe.* New York: Harper, 1939.

Larson, Cedric. "The Council for Democracy." *The Public Opinion Quarterly* 6 (1942): 284–90.

Lasswell, Harold. *Democracy through Public Opinion.* Menasha: George Banta Publishing Co., 1941.

"The Garrison State." *The American Journal of Sociology* 46 (1941): 455–68.

"The Garrison State versus the Civilian State." *China Quarterly* 2 (1937): 643–49.

Propaganda Technique in the World War. New York: A. A. Knopf, 1927.

Lavin, Harold and James Wechsler. *War Propaganda and the United States.* New Haven: Yale University Press, 1940.

Lenin, Vladimir. "Left-Wing Communism: An Infantile Disorder." *Collected Works*, vol. 31. Moscow: Progress Publishers, 1964, 17–118.

Lewis, John D. "The Element of Democracy." *The American Political Science Review* 34 (1940): 469–80.

Lindbergh, Anne Morrow. *The Wave of the Future.* New York: Harcourt, Brace, 1940.

Lippmann, Walter. *The Good Society.* New York: Little, Brown, 1937.

"Man's Image of Man." *Proceedings of the Seventeenth Annual Meeting of the American Catholic Philosophical Association* (1941): 66–75.

The Phantom Public. New York: Harcourt, Brace, 1925.

Luce, Henry R. "The American Century." *Life*, February 17, 1941, 61–65.

Lukács, Georg. "Propaganda or Partisanship?" *Partisan Review*, April–May, 1934, 37ff.

Lyons, Eugene. *The Red Decade: The Stalinist Penetration of America.* Indianapolis: Bobs Merrill, 1941.

Macdonald, Dwight. "Kulturbolschewismus Is Here." *Partisan Review*, November–December 1941, 442–51.

"Reading from Left to Right." *Partisan Review*, January–February 1941, 24–32.

"The Soviet Cinema: 1930–1938 – Part I." *Partisan Review*, July 1938, 37–50.

"The Soviet Cinema: 1930–1938 – Part II." *Partisan Review*, August–September 1938, 35–62.

MacLeish, Archibald. "The American Writers and the New World." *The Yale Review* 31 (1941): 61–76.

"Ars Poetica." *Poetry* 28 (1926), 27.

"Irresponsibles." *The Nation*, May 18, 1940, 18–23.

"Liberalism and the Anti-fascist Front." *Survey Graphic* 28 (1939): 321–23.

"The Librarian and the Democratic Process." *American Library Association Bulletin* (1940): 385–88.

"Libraries in the Contemporary Crisis." *Library Journal* 64 (1939): 879–82.

"Obligation of Libraries in a Democracy." *Wilson Library Bulletin* 14 (1940): 560–61.

"Of the Librarian's Profession." *The Atlantic Monthly*, June 1940, 786–90.

"Poetry and the Public World." *The Atlantic Monthly*, June 1938, 823–30.

"Post-War Writers and Pre-War Readers." *The New Republic*, June 10, 1940, 789–91.

"Public Speech and Private Speech in Poetry." *The Yale Review*, March 1938, 536–47.

"Sentiments for a Dedication." *The Nation*, February 13, 1929, 194.

Three Short Plays. New York: Dramatists Play Service Inc., 1964.

A Time To Speak: The Selected Prose of Archibald MacLeish. Boston: Houghton Mifflin, 1941.

Maritain, Jacques. *Scholasticism and Politics*. New York: Macmillan, 1940.

McIver, Robert. *Leviathan and the People*. Baton Rouge: Louisiana State University Press, 1939.

Means, Gardiner and Caroline F. Ware. *The Modern Economy in Action*. New York: Harcourt, Brace, 1936.

Melvin, John. "Lincoln Myth." *Partisan Review*, May–June 1941, 249–50.

Merriam, Charles. *What Is Democracy?* Chicago: University of Chicago Press, 1941.

Millay, Edna St. Vincent. *"There Are No Islands, Any More": Lines Written in Passion and in Deep Concern for England, France and My Own Country*. New York: Harper and Brothers, 1940.

Miller, Alice Duer. "The White Cliffs." *Life*, March 31, 1941, 80–92.

The White Cliffs. New York: Coward-MacCann, 1940.

Morgenthau, Henry. *From the Morgenthau Diaries*. Edited by John Morton Blum. Boston: Houghton Mifflin, 1959.

Mumford, Lewis. "Call to Arms." *The New Republic*, May 18, 1938, 39–42.

"The Corruption of Liberalism." *The New Republic*, April 29, 1940, 568–73.

Faith for Living. New York: Harcourt, Brace, 1940.

Men Must Act. New York: Harcourt, Brace, 1939.

Niebuhr, Reinhold. *Christianity and Power Politics*. New York: Charles Scribner's Sons, 1940.

"The Crisis." *Christianity and Crisis*, February 10, 1941, 1–3.

"Editorials." *Radical Religion*, Fall 1939, 1–11.

"Essays by MacLeish." *The Nation*, April 26, 1941, 506.

The Europe's Catastrophe. London: Nisbet, 1940.

"Leaves from the Notebook of a War-Bound American." *The Christian Century*, October 25, 1939, 1298–99.

The Nature and Destiny of Man: Human Nature. New York: Charles Scribner's Sons, 1941.

Niebuhr, H. Richard. "The Christian Church in the World's Crisis." *Christianity and Society*, Summer 1940, 11.

Orwell, George. *Homage to Catalonia*. San Diego: Harcourt Brace Jovanovich, 1952 [1938].

Padmore, George. "Ethiopia and World Politics." *The Crisis*, May 1935, 138ff.

Perry, Ralph Barton. *Shall Not Perish from the Earth*. New York: The Vanguard Press, 1940.

Polanyi, Karl. *The Great Transformation: The Political and Economic Origins of Our Time*. New York: Beacon, 1957 [1944].

Pollock, Friedrich. "State Capitalism: Its Possibilities and Limitations." *Studies in Philosophy and Social Science* 9 (1941): 200–55.

Pound, Ezra. *ABC of Reading*. New York: New Direction, 1960 [1934].

The Cantos of Ezra Pound. New York: New Directions, 1996.

The Correspondence of Ezra Pound and Senator William Borah. Urbana: University of Illinois Press, 2001.

Ezra Pound and Japan: Letters and Essays. Edited by Sanehide Kodama. Redding Ridge: Black Swan Books, 1987.

FBI File on Ezra Pound [Microform]. Wilmington: Scholarly Resources, 2001.

Gaudier-Brzeska: A Memoir. New York: New Directions, 1970.

Guide to Kulchur. New York: New Directions, 1970.

Literary Essays of Ezra Pound. Edited by T. S. Eliot. New York: New Directions, 1968.

"Provincialism the Enemy – I." *The New Age*, July 12, 1917, 244.

"The Revolt of Intelligence – III." *The New Age*, December 18, 1919, 106.

"The Revolt of Intelligence – V." *The New Age*, January 8, 1920, 153–54.

"The Revolt of Intelligence – VI." *The New Age*, January 15, 1920, 176–77.

The Selected Poems of Ezra Pound. New York: New Directions, 1957.

Selected Prose, 1909–1965. Edited by William Cookson. New York: New Directions, 1973.

"This Super-Neutrality." *The New Age*, October 21, 1915, 595.

Rascoe, Burton. "The Tough-Muscle Boys of Literature." *The American Mercury*, November 1940, 369–73.

Rice, Elmer. *Flight to the West: A Play in Seven Scenes*. New York: Coward-MacCann, 1941.

Minority Report. New York: Simon and Schuster, 1963.

Riesman, David. "Government Education for Democracy." *The Public Opinion Quarterly* 5 (1941): 195–209.

Roosevelt, Franklin D. *Complete Presidential Press Conferences of Franklin D. Roosevelt*. Vol. 17. New York: Da Capo Press, 1972.

F.D.R.: His Personal Letters, 1925–1945. Edited by Elliot Roosevelt. Vol. 2. New York: Duell, Sloan and Pearce, 1950.

The Public Papers and Addresses of Franklin D. Roosevelt. Vols. 8, 9, 10. Edited by Samuel I. Rosenman. New York: MacMillan, 1939–42.

Wartime Correspondence between President Roosevelt and Pope Pius XII. Edited by Myron C. Taylor. New York: MacMillan, 1947.

Sandburg, Carl. *Abraham Lincoln: The Prairie Years*. New York: Harcourt, Brace, 1926.

Schumpeter, Joseph. *Capitalism, Socialism and Democracy*. New York: Harper, 1975 [1942].

Schuyler, George. "Aframerica Today: Tulsa-Little Chicago." *The Pittsburgh Courier*, March 13, 1926, 14.

Black and Conservative. New Rochelle: Arlington House, 1966.

Black Empire. Boston: Northeastern University Press, 1991.

Black No More. New York: Macaulay, 1931.

Ethiopian Stories. Edited by Robert A. Hill. Boston: Northeastern University Press, 1994.

"'European War Will Free Colored World' – Schuyler." *The Pittsburgh Courier*, September 2, 1939, 1.

"An Open Letter to Arthur Brisbane." *The Pittsburgh Courier*, December 14, 1935, 1.

"The Phantom American Negro." *Freeman*, April 23, 1951, 457–59.

"The Rise of the Black Internationale." *The Crisis*, August 1938, 277.

"Views and Reviews." *The Pittsburgh Courier*, August 25, 1934, 10.

"Views and Reviews." *The Pittsburgh Courier*, February 23, 1935, 10.

"Views and Reviews." *The Pittsburgh Courier*, August 3, 1935, 10.

"Views and Reviews." *The Pittsburgh Courier*, November 23, 1935, 10.

"Views and Reviews." *The Pittsburgh Courier*, December 7, 1935, 10.

"Views and Reviews." *The Pittsburgh Courier*, April 11, 1936, 12.

"Views and Reviews." *The Pittsburgh Courier*, April 11, 1936, 12.

"Views and Reviews." *The Pittsburgh Courier*, May 29, 1937, 10.

"Views and Reviews." *The Pittsburgh Courier*, November 6, 1937, 10.

"Views and Reviews." *The Pittsburgh Courier*, June 8, 1940, 6.

"Views and Reviews." *The Pittsburgh Courier*, September 13, 1940, 6.

Sherwood, Robert. *Abe Lincoln in Illinois: A Play in Twelve Scenes*. New York: Charles Scribner's Sons, 1939.

"Front Line Is in Our Hearts." *Ladies' Home Journal*, August 1941, 104.

Idiot's Delight. New York: Charles Scribner's Sons, 1936.

Roosevelt and Hopkins: An Intimate Story. New York: Harper, 1948.

There Shall Be No Night. New York: Charles Scribner's Sons, 1940.

Simon, Yves. "Liberty and Authority." *Proceedings of the Sixteenth Annual Meeting of the American Catholic Philosophical Association* (1940): 86–114.

Nature and Functions of Authority. Milwaukee: Marquette University Press, 1940.

"Thomism and Democracy." *Conference on Science, Philosophy and Religion in their Relation to the Democratic Way of Life* (1941; an unpublished proceeding of the conference; Andover Theological Library, Harvard University)

Smith, T. V. "The Democratic Process." *The Public Opinion Quarterly* 2 (1938), 15–20.

The Democratic Way of Life. Chicago: University of Chicago Press, 1939.

The Legislative Way of Life. Chicago: University of Chicago Press, 1940.

"Philosophy and Democracy," *Ethics* 47 (1937): 413–27.

"The Tragic Realm of Truth." *Proceedings and Addresses of the American Philosophical Association* 9 (1935): 111–25.

Sorokin, PitIrim A. *The Crisis of Our Age: The Social and Cultural Outlook.* New York: E. P. Dutton, 1941.

Stevens, Wallace. *Wallace Stevens: Collected Poetry and Prose.* Edited by Frank Kermode and Joan Richardson. New York: The Library of America, 1997.

Tate, Allen. "Tension in Poetry." *Southern Review* 4 (1938): 101–15.

Trilling, Lionel. "An American in Spain." *Partisan Review*, January–February 1941, 63–67.

Trumbo, Dalton. "The Fall of Hollywood." *The North American Review*, August 1933, 140–147

Johnny Got His Gun. New York: Citadel Press, 2007 [1939].

The Remarkable Andrew: Being the Chronicle of a Literal Man. Philadelphia: J. B. Lippincott, 1941.

"Stepchild of the Muses." *The North American Review*, December 1933, 559–566.

Van Dusen, Henry P. "Irresponsible Idealism." *Christian Century*, July 24, 1940, 925.

Various. Editorial, "Mr. Mumford and the Liberals." *The New Republic*, April 28, 1940, 562.

Obituary. *Time*, August 31, 1942, 81.

Salud!: Poems, Stories and Sketches of Spain by American Writers. Edited by Alan Calmer. New York: International Publishers, 1938.

"War Writers on Democracy." *Life*, June 24, 1940, 8ff.

"The Week." *The New Republic*, September 13, 1939, 141–43.

Writers Take Sides: Letters About the War in Spain from 418 American Authors. New York: The League of American Writers, 1938.

Warshow, Robert. *The Immediate Experience: Movies, Comics, Theatre, and Other Aspects of Popular Culture.* Cambridge, MA: Harvard University Press, 2001.

Wilson, Edmund. "The Omelet of A. MacLeish." *New Yorker*, January 14, 1939, 23.

"Return of Ernest Hemingway." *The New Republic*, October 28, 1940, 591–92.

Wright, Richard. *12 Million Black Voices.* New York: Basic Books, 2008 [1941].

Native Son. New York: Harper, 1966 [1940].

"Not My People's War." *The New Masses* June 17, 1941, 8–12.

"US Negroes Greet You." *The Daily Worker*, September 1, 1941, 7.

SECONDARY SOURCES

Aaron, Daniel. *Writers on the Left: Episodes in American Literary Communism.* New York: Harcourt, Brace, 1961.

Adler, Les K. and Thomas G. Paterson. "Red Fascism: The Merger of Nazi Germany and Soviet Russia in the American Image of Totalitarianism." *The American Historical Review* 75 (1970): 1046–64.

Adorno, Theodore and Max Horkheimer. *Dialectic of Enlightenment: Philosophical Fragments.* Translated by Edmund Jephcott. Stanford: Stanford University Press, 2002.

Allen, Michael J. B. "The Unspanish War in *For Whom the Bell Tolls.*" *Contemporary Literature* 13 (1972): 204–12.

Alonso, Harriet. *Robert E. Sherwood: The Playwright in Peace and War.* Amherst: University of Massachusetts Press, 2007.

Alpers, Benjamin. *Dictators, Democracy, and American Public Culture: Envisioning the Totalitarian Enemy, 1920s–1950s.* Chapel Hill: University of North Carolina Press, 2003.

Anderson, Irvine. *The Standard-Vacuum Oil Company and United States East Asian Policy, 1933–1941.* Princeton: Princeton University Press, 1977.

Asante, S. K. B. "The Italo-Ethiopian Conflict: A Case Study in British West African Response to Crisis Diplomacy in the 1930s." *The Journal of African History* 15 (1974): 291–302.

Augspurger, Michael. *An Economy of Abundant Beauty: Fortune Magazine and Depression America.* Ithaca: Cornell University Press, 2004.

Bain, Alexander M. "*Shocks Americana!*: George Schuyler Serializes Black Internationalism." *American Literary History* 19 (2007): 937–63.

Baker, Carlos. *Hemingway: The Writer as Artist.* Princeton: Princeton University Press, 1952.

Baldwin, James. *Notes of a Native Son.* Boston: Beacon, 1955.

Becker, William H. "Reinhold Niebuhr: From Marx to Roosevelt." *Historian* 35 (1973): 539–50.

Beevor, Anthony. "The Callous Betrayal of Anti-Franco Forces." *London Times*, May 24, 2006, 19.

  The Spanish Civil War. Harmondsworth: Penguin, 1982.

Beisner, Robert L. *Dean Acheson: A Life in the Cold War.* Oxford: Oxford University Press, 2006.

Bensel, Richard. *Sectionalism and American Political Development, 1880–1980.* Madison: University of Wisconsin Press, 1984.

Benson, Frederick R. *Writers in Arms: The Literary Impact of the Spanish Civil War.* New York: New York University Press, 1967.

Benson, Jackson. *John Steinbeck, Writer.* New York: Viking, 1984.

Berlin, Isaiah. *Four Essays on Liberty.* Oxford: Oxford University Press, 1969.

Bingham, June. *Courage to Change: An Introduction to the Life and Thought of Reinhold Niebuhr.* Lanham: University Press of America, 1961.

Birdwell, Michael E. *Celluloid Soldiers: The Warner Bros. Campaign against Nazism*. New York: New York University Press, 1999.

Blackmore, Tim. "Lazarus Machine: Body Politics in Dalton Trumbo's *Johnny Got His Gun*." *Mosaic: A Journal of the Interdisciplinary Study of Literature* 33 (2000): 1–18.

Bonner, Thomas B. "Civil War Historians and the 'Needless War' Doctrine." *Journal of the History of Ideas* 17 (1956): 193–216.

Bratzel, John F. and Leslie B. Rout. "FDR and the 'Secret Map'." *The Wilson Quarterly* 9 (1985): 167–73.

Brenman-Gibson, Margaret. *Clifford Odets: American Playwright*. New York: Atheneum, 1981.

Brinkley, Alan. *The End of Reform: New Deal Liberalism in Recession and War*. New York: Vintage, 1996.

The Publisher: Henry Luce and His American Century. New York: Knopf, 2010.

Brown, John Mason. *The Ordeal of a Playwright: Robert Sherwood and the Challenge of War*. New York: Harper and Row, 1970.

The Worlds of Robert E. Sherwood: Mirror to His Times. New York: Harper and Row, 1962.

Buckley, Ramon. "Revolution in Ronda: The Facts in Hemingway's *For Whom the Bell Tolls*." *Hemingway Review* 17 (1997): 49–57.

Burnham, James. *The Machiavellians: Defenders of Freedom*. Chicago: Henry Regnery Company, 1963.

The Managerial Revolution. New York: John Day, 1941.

Butenhuis, Peter and Barry Witham. "Prelude to War: The Interventionist Propaganda of Archibald Macleish, Robert E. Sherwood, and John Steinbeck." *Canadian Review of American Studies* 21 (1996): 1–30.

Calo, Zachary R. "The Indispensable Basis of Democracy: American Catholicism, the Church-State Debate, and the Soul of American Liberalism, 1920–1929." *Virginia Law Review* 91 (2005): 1037–73.

Carr, Virginia. *Dos Passos: A Life*. Garden City: Doubleday, 1984.

Carroll, Peter. *The Odyssey of the Abraham Lincoln Brigade: Americans in the Spanish Civil War*. Stanford: Stanford University Press, 1994.

Ceplair, Larry. *Under the Shadow of War: Fascism, Anti-Fascism, and Marxists, 1918–1939*. New York: Columbia University Press, 1987.

Chadwin, Mark Lincoln. *The Hawks of World War II*. Chapel Hill: University of North Carolina Press, 1968.

Chapman, Michael E. "Pro-Franco Anti-Communism: Ellery Sedgwick and the *Atlantic Monthly*." *Journal of Contemporary History* 41 (2006): 641–62.

Christian, Mark. *Black Fascisms: African American Literature and Culture between the Wars*. Charlottesville: University of Virginia Press, 2007.

Clark, T. J. "Clement Greenberg's Theory of Art." *Critical Inquiry* 9 (1982): 139–56.

Image of the People: Gustave Courbet and the 1848 Revolution. Berkeley: University of California Press, 1973.

Clausewitz, Carl von. *On War.* Translated by Michael Howard and Peter Paret. Princeton: Princeton University Press, 1976.

Cohen, Lizabeth. *Making a New Deal: Industrial Workers in Chicago, 1919–1939.* New York: Cambridge University Press, 1990.

Cohen, Warren. *The American Revisionists: The Lessons of Intervention in World War I.* Chicago: University of Chicago Press, 1967.

   America's Response to China: A History of Sino-American Relations. Fourth edition. New York: Columbia University Press, 2010.

Cohn, Dorrit. *Transparent Minds: Narrative Modes for Presenting Consciousness in Fiction.* Princeton: Princeton University Press, 1978.

Cole, Wayne S. *Charles A. Lindbergh and the Battle against American Intervention in World War II.* New York: Harcourt Brace Jovanovich, 1974.

   Roosevelt and the Isolationists, 1932–45. Lincoln: University of Nebraska Press, 1983.

Conn, Peter. *Pearl S. Buck: A Cultural Biography.* Cambridge: Cambridge University Press, 1996.

Connelly, John. "Nazis and Slavs: From Racial Theory to Racist Practice." *Central European History* 32 (1999): 1–33.

Cook, Bruce. *Dalton Trumbo.* New York: Scribner's, 1977.

Cooper, Stephen. *The Politics of Ernest Hemingway.* Ann Arbor: UMI Research Press, 1987.

Corliss, Richard. *Talking Pictures: Screenwriters in American Cinema.* New York: Overlook, 1974.

Cox, LaWanda. *Lincoln and Black Freedom: A Study in Presidential Leadership.* Columbia: University of South Carolina Press, 1981.

Culbert, David Holbrook. *News for Everyman: Radio and Foreign Affairs in Thirties America.* Westport: Greenwood Press, 1976.

Dallek, Robert. *Franklin D. Roosevelt and American Foreign Policy, 1932–1945.* Oxford: Oxford University Press, 1979.

Dames, Nicholas. "'The Withering of the Individual': Psychology in the Victorian Novel." *A Concise Companion to the Victorian Novel.* Edited by Francis O'Gorman. London: Blackwell, 2005, 91–112.

Dardis, Thomas A. *Some Time in the Sun.* New York: Scribner's, 1976.

Daugherty, William E. "China's Official Publicity in the United States." *Public Opinion Quarterly* 6 (1942): 70–86.

Davis, David Brion. *The Slave Power Conspiracy and the Paranoid Style.* Baton Rouge: Louisiana State University Press, 1969.

Davis, Kenneth S. *FDR: Into the Storm, 1937–1940.* New York: Random House, 1993.

DeConde, Alexander. "The South and Isolationism." *The Journal of Southern History* 24 (1958) 332–46.

Denning, Michael. *The Cultural Front: The Laboring of American Culture in the Twentieth Century.* London: Verso, 1997.

Desch, Michael C. "America's Liberal Illiberalism: The Ideological Origins of Overreaction in U.S. Foreign Policy." *International Security* 32 (2007–2008): 7–43.

Diggins, John Patrick. "From Pragmatism to Natural Law: Lippmann's Quest for the Foundations of Legitimacy." *Political Theory* 19 (1991): 519–38.

  Mussolini and Fascism: A View From America. Princeton: Princeton University Press, 1972.

Doenecke, Justus D. *Storm on the Horizon: The Challenge to American Intervention, 1939–1941.* Lanham: Rowman and Littlefield, 2000.

Donaldson, Scott. *Archibald MacLeish: An American Life.* Boston: Houghton Mifflin, 1992.

  By Force of Will: The Life and Art of Ernest Hemingway. New York: Viking, 1977.

Dueck, Colin. *Reluctant Crusaders: Power, Culture, and Change in American Grand Strategy.* Princeton: Princeton University Press, 2006.

Duke, David C. *Distant Obligations: Modern American Writers and Foreign Causes.* Oxford: Oxford University Press, 1983.

Eby, Cecil. *Between the Bullet and the Lie: American Volunteers in the Spanish Civil War.* New York: Holt, Reinhart, Winston, 1969.

Edel, Leon. *The Psychological Novel 1900–1950.* New York: Lippincott, 1955.

Edwards, Mark. "'God Has Chosen Us': Re-Membering Christian Realism, Rescuing Christendom, and the Contest of Responsibilities during the Cold War." *Diplomatic History* 33 (2009): 67–93.

Ewen, Stuart. *PR!: A Social History of Spin.* New York: Basic Books, 1996.

Fehrenbacher, Don E. *The Changing Image of Lincoln in American Historiography.* Oxford: Oxford University Press, 1968.

  The Dred Scott Case: Its Significance in American Law and Politics. Oxford: Oxford University Press, 1978.

  "The Origins and Purpose of Lincoln's 'House Divided' Speech." *The Mississippi Valley Historical Review* 46 (1960): 615–43.

Ferguson, Jeffrey S. *The Sage of Sugar Hill: George S. Schuyler and the Harlem Renaissance.* New Haven: Yale University Press, 2005.

Filreis, Alan. *Modernism from Right to Left: Wallace Stevens, the Thirties, and Literary Radicalism.* Cambridge: Cambridge University Press, 1994.

Fine, Richard. *West of Eden: Writers in Hollywood, 1928–1940.* Washington, DC: Smithsonian Institution Press, 1993.

Fisher, Phillip. "Democratic Social Space: Whitman, Melville, and the Promise of American Transparency." *Representations* 24 (1988): 60–101.

Fladeland, Betty L. "Revisionists vs. Abolitionists: The Historiographical Cold War of the 1930s and 1940s." *Journal of the Early Republic* 6 (1986): 1–21.

Foley, Barbara. *Radical Representations: Politics and Form in U.S. Proletarian Fiction, 1929–1941.* Durham: Duke University Press, 1993.

Foner, Eric. *Free Soil, Free Labor, Free Men: The Ideology of the Republican Party before the Civil War.* New York: Oxford University Press, 1995.

  "Politics, Ideology, and the Origins of the American Civil War." *A Nation Divided: Problems and Issues of the Civil War and Reconstruction.* Edited by George M. Frederickson. Minneapolis: Burgess Pub. Co., 1975, 15–34.

Franklin, Richard. *Sectionalism and American Political Development, 1880–1980*. Madison: University of Wisconsin Press, 1984.

Freehling, William W. *The Road to Disunion: Secessionist at Bay, 1776–1854*. Vol. 1. Oxford: Oxford University Press, 1990.

Friedman, Donald J. *The Road from Isolation: The Campaign of the American Committee for Non-Participation in Japanese Aggression, 1938–1941*. Cambridge, MA: East Asian Research Center, Harvard University, 1968.

Friesen, Oris. *China Reporting: An Oral History of American Journalism in the 1930s and 1940s*. Berkeley: University of California Press, 1987.

Gary, Brett. *The Nervous Liberals: Propaganda Anxieties from World War I to the Cold War*. New York: Columbia University Press, 1999.

Gellman, Irwin F. *Secret Affairs: Franklin Roosevelt, Cordell Hull, and Sumner Welles*. Baltimore: Johns Hopkins University Press, 1995.

Gerassi, John. *The Premature Antifascists: North American Volunteers in the Spanish Civil War, 1936–1939, an Oral History*. New York: Praeger, 1986.

Gleason, Abbott. *Totalitarianism: The Inner History of the Cold War*. Oxford: Oxford University Press, 1995.

Gleason, Philip. "Pluralism, Democracy, and Catholicism in the Era of World War II." *The Review of Politics* 49 (1987): 208–30.

Gluck, Mary. "Theorizing the Cultural Roots of the Bohemian Artist." *MODERNISM / modernity* 7 (2000): 351–78.

Goldstein, Malcolm. *The Political Stage: American Drama and Theater of the Great Depression*. Oxford: Oxford University Press, 1974.

Goodman, David. *Radio's Civic Ambition: American Broadcasting and Democracy in the 1930s*. New York: Oxford University Press, 2011.

Gorman, Paul R. *Left Intellectuals and Popular Culture in Twentieth-Century America*. Chapel Hill: University of North Carolina Press, 1996.

Graham, Helen. "Spain Betrayed? The New Historical McCarthyism." *Science and Society* 68 (2004): 364–69.

   The Spanish Republic at War, 1936–1939. Cambridge: Cambridge University Press, 2002.

Grassmuck, George L. *Sectional Biases in Congress on Foreign Policy*. Baltimore: Johns Hopkins University Press, 1951.

Grieve, Victoria. *The Federal Art Project and the Creation of Middlebrow Culture*. Urbana: University of Illinois Press, 2009.

Griffith, Thomas. *Harry and Teddy: The Turbulent Friendship of Press Lord Henry R. Luce and His Favorite Reporter, Theodore H. White*. New York: Random House, 1995.

Gruesser, John Cullen. *Black on Black: Twentieth-Century African American Writing about Africa*. Lexington: University Press of Kentucky, 2000.

Guelzo, Allen C. *Lincoln's Emancipation Proclamation: The End of Slavery in America*. New York: Simon and Schuster, 2004.

Guglielmo, Thomas. *White on Arrival: Italians, Race, Color, and Power in Chicago, 1890–1945*. New York: Oxford University Press, 2003.

Guttmann, Allen. *The Wound in the Heart: America and the Spanish Civil War*. New York: The Free Press, 1962.

Habeck, Mary R., Ronald Radosh, and Grigory Sevostianov, eds. *Spain Betrayed: The Soviet Union in the Spanish Civil War*. New Haven: Yale University Press, 2001.

Hackett, Alice Payne. *60 Years of Best Sellers, 1895–1955*. New York: R. R. Bowker Co., 1956.

Hager, Philip E. and Desmond Taylor eds. *The Novels of World War I: An Annotated Bibliography*. New York: Garland, 1981.

Hamilton, Ian. *Writers in Hollywood, 1915–1951*. New York: Caroll and Graf, 1991.

Hansen, Alvin H. *Fiscal Policy and Business Cycle*. New York: W. W. Norton, 1941.

Harris, Joseph. *African-American Reactions to War in Ethiopia*. Baton Rouge: Louisiana State University Press, 1994.

Haynes, John and Klehr Harvey. "The Myth of 'Premature Anti-Fascism'." *The New Criterion*. September 2002, 19–26.

 Venona: Decoding Soviet Espionage in America. New Haven: Yale University Press 1999.

Hearden, Patrick J. *Roosevelt Confronts Hitler: America's Entry into World War II*. Dekalb: Northan Illinois University Press, 1987.

Hegel, G. W. F. *The Early Theological Writings*. Translated by T. M. Knox. Chicago: University of Chicago Press, 1948.

Heinrichs, Waldo H. *Threshold of War: Franklin D. Roosevelt and American Entry into World War II*. Oxford: Oxford University Press, 1988.

Hellman, John. "The Anti-Democratic Impulse in Catholicism: Jacques Maritain, Yves Simon, and Charles de Gaulle during World War II." *Journal of Church and State* 33 (1991): 453–71.

Hendricks, Jefferson and Cary Nelson, eds. *Madrid 1937: Letters of the Abraham Lincoln Brigade from the Spanish Civil War*. New York: Routledge, 1996.

Henrikson, Alan K. "The Map as an 'Idea': The Role of Cartographic Imagery During the Second World War." *The American Cartographer* 2 (1975): 19–53.

Henriot, Christian. *Shanghai, 1927–1937: Municipal Power, Locality, and Modernization*. Berkeley: University of California Press, 1993.

Herman, Ellen. *The Romance of American Psychology: Political Culture in the Age of Experts*. Berkeley: University of California Press, 1995.

Herzstein, Robert Edwin. *Henry R. Luce: A Political Portrait of the Man Who Created the American Century*. New York: Charles Scribner's Sons, 1994.

Hill, Robert A. and R. Kent Rasmussen. "Afterword." *Black Empire*. Boston: Northeastern University Press, 1991, 25–324.

Hilton, Stanley E. *Hitler's Secret War in South America*. Baton Rouge: Louisiana State University Press, 1981.

Holmes, Oliver Wendell. *Speeches*. Boston: Little, Brown, 1900.

Holt, Michael. *The Fate of Their Country: Politicians, Slavery Extension, and the Coming of the Civil War*. New York: Hill and Wang, 2004.

The Political Crisis of the 1850s. New York: W. W. Norton, 1983.

Hopkins, James K. *Into the Heart of the Fire: The British in the Spanish Civil War.* Stanford: Stanford University Press, 1998.

Horst, Johnpeter and Robert L. Jenkins. "The Nazis and the American South in the 1930s: A Mirror Image?" *The Journal of Southern History* 58 (1992): 667–94.

Horten, Gerd. *Radio Goes to War: The Cultural Politics of Propaganda During World War II.* Berkeley: University of California Press, 2003.

Hovey, Richard. *Hemingway: The Inward Terrain.* Seattle: University of Washington Press, 1968.

Huston, James L. "Property Rights in Slavery and the Coming of the Civil War." *The Journal of Southern History* 65 (1999): 249–86.

Hutner, Gordon. *What America Read: Taste, Class, and the Novel, 1920–1960.* Chapel Hill: University of North Carolina Press, 2009.

Hynes, Samuel. *The Auden Generation: Literature and Politics in England in the 1930s.* London: The Bodley Head, 1976.

Hynes, Samuel Lynn. *The Auden Generation: Literature and Politics in England in the 1930s.* Princeton: Princeton University Press, 1982.

Igo, Sarah E. *The Averaged American: Surveys, Citizens, and the Making of a Mass Public.* Cambridge, MA: Harvard University Press, 2007.

Irelan, Scott R. "Goon, Warrior, Communitarian, and Mythos." *Theatre History Studies* 28 (2008): 49–63.

"The Shine of Egalitarian Morality: Staging a Connective Aesthetic in Robert Sherwood's *Abe Lincoln in Illinois.*" *Journal of American Drama and Theatre* 20 (2008): 75–88.

Iriye, Akira. *The Globalizing of America, 1913–1945.* Vol. 3, *The Cambridge History of American Foreign Relations.* Cambridge: Cambridge University Press, 1993.

The Origins of the Second World War in Asia and the Pacific. London: Longman, 1987.

Isaacs, Harold. *American Images of China and India.* New York: John Day, 1958.

Isserman, Maurice. *Which Side Were You On? The American Communist Party during the Second World War.* Middletown: Wesleyan University Press, 1982.

Jaffa, Harry. *Crisis of the House Divided: An Interpretation of the Issues in the Lincoln-Douglas Debates.* Garden City: Doubleday, 1959.

Jehlen, Myra. *American Incarnation: The Individual, the Nation, and the Continent.* Cambridge, MA: Harvard University Press, 1986.

Jespersen, Christopher. *American Images of China, 1931–1949.* Palo Alto: Stanford University Press, 1996.

Jewett, Andrew. *Science, Democracy, and the American University: From the Civil War to the Cold War.* Cambridge: Cambridge University Press, 2012.

Johnson, Walter. *The Battle against Isolation.* Chicago: University of Chicago Press, 1944.

Joki, Ikka and Roger D. Sell. "Robert E. Sherwood and the Finnish Winter War." *American Studies in Scandinavia* 21 (1989): 51–69.

Jonas, Manfred. *Isolationism in America, 1935–1941*. Ithaca: Cornell University Press, 1966.

Jones, Alfred Haworth. *Roosevelt's Image Brokers: Poets, Playwrights, and the Use of the Lincoln Symbol*. Port Washington: Kennikat, 1974.

Jones, John Bush. *The Songs That Fought the War: Popular Music and the Home Front*. Waltham: Brandeis University Press, 2006.

Josephs, Allen. *For Whom the Bell Tolls: Ernest Hemingway's Undiscovered Country*. New York: Twayne, 1994.

Kahler, Erich. *The Inward Turn of Narrative*. Princeton: Princeton University Press, 1973.

Kaskowitz, Sheryl. *God Bless America: The Surprising History of an Iconic Song*. New York: Oxford University Press, 2013.

Kelly, Robin D. G. "'But a Local Phase of a World Problem': Black History's Global Vision, 1883–1950." *Journal of American History* 86 (1999): 1045–77.

Kennedy, David M. *Over Here: The First World War and American Society*. Oxford: Oxford University Press, 1980.

Kiernan, Victor. *America, the New Imperialism*. London: Zed Press, 1978.

Kimball, Warren F. *The Juggler: Franklin Roosevelt as Wartime Statesman*. Princeton: Princeton University Press, 1991.

Klehr, Harvey. *The Heyday of American Communism: The Depression Decade*. New York: Basic Books, 1984.

Knox, Bernard. "Premature Anti-fascist." *Antioch Review* 57 (1999): 147–48.

  "'Spanish Tragedy': An Exchange." *The New York Review of Books*, March 26, 1987, 21–28.

Koch, Stephen. *The Breaking Point: Hemingway, Dos Passos, and the Murder of José Robles*. New York: Counter Point, 2005.

Kriegel, Leonard. "Dalton Trumbo's 'Johnny Got His Gun'." *Proletarian Writers of the Thirties*. Edited by David Madden. Carbondale: Southern Illinois University Press, 1968, 106–113.

Kutulas, Judy. *The Long War: The Intellectual People's Front and Anti-Stalinism, 1930–1940*. Durham: Duke University Press, 1995.

Lafeber, Walter. *The Clash: U.S.-Japanese Relations Throughout History*. New York: Norton, 1997.

Langer, William L. and Everett S. Gleason. *The Challenge to Isolation: The World Crisis of 1937–1940 and American Foreign Policy*. New York: Harper and Row, 1952.

Lasser, William. *Benjamin V. Cohen: Architect of the New Deal*. New Haven: Yale University Press, 2002.

Layne, Christopher. *Peace of Illusions: American Grand Strategy from 1940 to the Present*. Ithaca: Cornell University Press, 2006.

Leong, Karen J. *The China Mystique: Pearl S. Buck, Anna May Wong, Mayling Soong, and the Transformation of American Orientalism*. Berkeley: University of California Press, 2005.

Levine, Lawrence W. *Highbrow / Lowbrow: The Emergence of Cultural Hierarchy in America*. Cambridge, MA: Harvard University Press, 1988.

Lifka, Thomas E. *The Concept of "Totalitarianism" and American Foreign Policy, 1938–1939*. New York: Garland, 1988.

Lincoln, Abraham. *Abraham Lincoln: Speeches and Writings, 1832–1858*. Edited by Don E. Fehrenbacher. New York: Library of America, 1984.

Little, Douglas. "Red Scare, 1936: Anti-Bolshevism and the Origins of British Non-Intervention in the Spanish Civil War." *Journal of Contemporary History* 23 (1988): 291–311.

Locke, John. *Two Treatises of Government*. Edited by Peter Laslett. Cambridge: Cambridge University Press, 1988.

Logan, John A. *No Transfer: An American Security Principle*. New Haven: Yale University Press, 1961.

Ludington, Townsend. *John Dos Passos: A Twentieth-Century Odyssey*. New York: Dutton, 1980.

Lye, Colleen. *America's Asia: Racial Form and American Literature, 1893–1945*. Princeton: Princeton University Press, 2005.

Maddux, Thomas. "Red Fascism, Brown Bolshevism: The American Image of Totalitarianism in the 1930s." *Historian* 40 (1977): 85–103.

Marchand, Roland. *Advertising the American Dream: Making Way for Modernity, 1920–1940*. Berkeley: University of California Press, 1985.

Marks, Frederick W. *Wind Over Sand: The Diplomacy of Franklin Roosevelt*. Athens: University of Georgia Press, 1988.

Marx, Karl. "The Civil War in France." *The First International and After: Political Writings*, vol. 3. Edited by David Fernbach. Harmondsworth: Penguin, 1974, 187–268.

Masland, John W. "Missionary Influence Upon American Far Eastern Policy." *Pacific Historical Review* 10 (1941): 279–96.

Mathews, Jane De Hart. "Arts and the People: The New Deal Quest for a Cultural Democracy." *The Journal of American History* 62 (1975): 316–39.

McCardell, John. *The Idea of a Southern Nation: Southern Nationalists and Southern Nationalism, 1830–1860*. New York: Norton, 1979.

McKee, John DeWitt. *William Allen White: Maverick on Main Street*. Westport: Greenwood Press, 1975.

Meade, Marion. *Dorothy Parker: What Fresh Hell Is This*. New York: Penguin, 1989.

Meriwether, James H. *Proudly We Can Be Africans: Black Americans and Africa, 1935–1961*. Chapel Hill: University of North Carolina Press, 2002.

Meserve, Walter J. *Robert E. Sherwood: Reluctant Moralist*. New York: Pegasus, 1970.

Meyer, Donald. *The Protestant Search for Political Realism, 1919–1941*. Middletown: Wesleyan University Press, 1988.

Michels, Robert. "On the Sociology of Bohemia and Its Connection to the Intellectual Proletariat." *Catalyst* 15 (1983): 5–25.

Milford, Nancy. *Savage Beauty: The Life of Edna St. Vincent Millay*. New York: Random House, 2001.

Mill, John Stuart. *On Liberty*. Indianapolis: Hackett, 1978.

Miller, Donald L. *Lewis Mumford: A Life*. New York: Weindenfeld and Nicholson, 1989.

Moody, A. David. *Ezra Pound: Poet*. Oxford: Oxford University Press, 2007.

Moore Jr., Barrington. *Social Origins of Dictatorship and Democracy: Lord and Peasant in the making of the Modern World*. Boston: Beacon Press, 1966.

Morrison, Michael. *Slavery and the American West: The Eclipse of Manifest Destiny and the Coming of the Civil War*. Chapel Hill: University of North Carolina, 1997.

Morton, Marian J. "'My Dear, I Don't Give a Damn': Scarlett O'Hara and the Great Depression." *Frontiers: A Journal of Women Studies* 5 (1980): 52–56.

Moses, Wilson. "The Poetics of Ethiopianism: W. E. B. Du Bois and Literary Black Nationalism." *American Literature* 47 (1975): 411–26.

   The Wings of Ethiopia: Studies in African-American Life and Letters. Ames: Iowa State University, 1990.

Mugridge, Ian. *The View from Xanadu: William Randolph Hearst and United States Foreign Policy*. Montreal: McGill-Queen's University Press, 1995.

Munson, Gorham. *The Awakening Twenties: A Memoir-History of a Literary Period*. Baton Rouge: Louisiana State University Press, 1985.

Murphy, James F. *The Proletarian Moment: The Controversy over Leftism in Literature*. Urbana: University of Illinois Press, 1991.

Neils, Patricia. *China Images in Life and Times of Henry Luce*. Lanham: Rowman & Littlefield, 1990.

Nelson, Cary. "Hemingway, the American Left, and the Soviet Union: Some Forgotten Episodes." *Hemingway Review* 14 (1994): 36–45.

   Revolutionary Memory: Recovering the Poetry of the American Left. New York: Routledge, 2001.

Osgood, Robert Endicott. *Ideals and Self-Interest in America's Foreign Relations*. Chicago: University of Chicago Press, 1953.

Overy, Ricahrd. *The Twilight Years: The Paradox of Britain Between the Wars*. New York: Viking, 2009.

Palmer, Alan. *Fictional Minds*. Lincoln: University of Nebraska Press, 2004.

Payne, Stanley G. "Americans in Spain." *New York Sun*. April 11, 2005, arts and letters section, 18.

   The Spanish Civil War, the Soviet Union and Communism. New Haven: Yale University Press, 2004.

Peters, Charles. *Five Days in Philadelphia*. New York: Public Affairs, 2005.

Peterson, Merrill D. *Lincoln in American Memory*. Oxford: Oxford University Press, 1994.

Plummer, Brenda Gayle. *Rising Wind: Black Americans and U.S. Foreign Affairs, 1935–1960*. Chapel Hill: University of North Carolina Press, 1996.

Potter, David M. *The Impending Crisis, 1848–1861*. New York: Harper and Row, 1976.

Price, Ruth. *The Lives of Agnes Smedley*. Oxford: Oxford University Press, 2005.

Purcell, Edward A. *The Crisis of Democratic Theory*. Lexington: University Press of Kentucky, 1973.

Radosh, Ronald. "'Spanish Tragedy': An Exchange." *The New York Review of Books*, March 26, 1987, 21–28.

Radway, Janice. "The Book-of-the-Month Club and the General Reader: On the Uses of 'Serious' Fiction." *Critical Inquiry* 14 (1988): 516–38.

"The Scandal of the Middlebrow: The Book-of-the-Month Club, Class Fracture, and Cultural Authority." *The South Atlantic Quarterly* 89 (1990): 703–36.

Redman, Tim. *Ezra Pound and Italian Fascism.* Cambridge: Cambridge University Press, 2009.

Reynolds, David. *From Munich to Pearl Harbor.* Chicago: Ivan R. Dee, 2001.

Reynolds, Michael. *Hemingway's Reading 1910–1940: An Inventory.* Princeton: Princeton University Press, 1981.

Hemingway: The 30s. New York: W. W. Norton, 1997.

Rice, Daniel F. *Reinhold Niebuhr and John Dewey: An American Odyssey.* Albany: SUNY Press, 1993.

Richard, David and Kurial Woolner, eds. *FDR, the Vatican and the Roman Catholic Church in America, 1933–1945.* New York: Palgrave, 2003.

Rideout, Walter. *The Radical Novel in the United States, 1900–1954: Some Interrelations of literature and Society.* Cambridge, MA: Harvard University Press, 1956.

Rieselbach, Leroy N. *The Roots of Isolationism: Congressional Voting and Presidential Leadership in Foreign Policy.* Indianapolis: The Bobbs-Merrill Company, 1966.

Rietveld, Ronald D. "Franklin D. Roosevelt's Abraham Lincoln." *Franklin D. Roosevelt and Abraham Lincoln.* Edited by Williamd D. Pederson. Armonk: M. E. Sharpe, 2003, 10–60.

Riggs, Frederick. *Pressures on Congress: A Study of the Repeal of Chinese Exclusion.* New York: Oxford University Press, 1950.

Roberts, Geoffrey. "Soviet Foreign Policy and the Spanish Civil War." *Spain in an International Context.* Edited by Christian Leitz and David J. Dunthorn. New York: Berghahn Books, 1999, 81–103.

Stalin's Wars: From World War to Cold War, 1939–1953. New Haven: Yale University Press, 2006.

Robinson, Cedric J. "The African Diaspora and the Italo-Ethiopian Crisis." *Race and Class* 27 (1985): 51–65.

Rochester, Stuart I. *American Liberal Disillusionment.* University Park: Pennsylvania State University Press, 1977.

Romerstein, Herbert. *Heroic Victims: Stalin's Foreign Legion in the Spanish Civil War.* Washington, DC: Council for the Defense of Freedom, 1994.

Rosenman, Samuel I. *Working with Roosevelt.* New York: Harper and Brothers, 1952.

Rowley, Hazel. *Richard Wright: The Life and Times.* New York: Henry Holt, 2001.

Roy, Lord Ralph. *Communism and the Churches.* New York: Harcourt, Brace, 1960.

Rubin, Joan Shelley. *Making of Middlebrow Culture.* Chapel Hill: University of North Carolina Press, 1992.

Sanders, David. "Ernest Hemingway's Spanish Civil War Experience." *American Quarterly* 12 (1960): 133–43.

Schlesinger Jr., Arthur. "Back to the Womb?: Isolationism's Renewed Threat." *Foreign Affairs* 74 (1995): 2–8.

Schoots, Hans. *Living Dangerously: A Biography of Joris Ivens*. Translated by David Colmer. Amsterdam: Amsterdam University Press, 2000.

Schwartz, Barry. "Memory as a Cultural System: Abraham Lincoln in World War II." *American Sociological Review* 61 (1996): 908–27.

Schweick, Susan. *A Gulf So Deeply Cut*. Madison: University of Wisconsin Press, 1991.

Scott, William. *The Sons of Sheba's Race: African-Americans and the Italo-Ethiopian War, 1935–1941*. Bloomington: Indiana University Press, 1993.

Seixas, Xosé-Manoel Núñez. "Nations in Arms Against the Invader: On Nationalist Discourses During the Spanish Civil War." *The Splintering of Spain: Cultural History and the Spanish Civil War, 1936–1939*. Edited by Chris Ealham and Michael Richards. Cambridge: Cambridge University Press, 2005, 45–67.

Selzer, Jack. *Kenneth Burke in Greenwich Village: Conversing with the Moderns, 1915–1931*. Madison: University of Wisconsin Press, 1996.

Shapiro, Edward S. "The Approach of War: Congressional Isolationism and Anti-Semitism." *American Jewish History* 74 (1984): 45–64.

Shepperson, George. "Ethiopianism and African Nationalism." *Phylon* 14 (1953): 9–18.

Shivers, Alfred S. *The Life of Maxwell Anderson*. New York: Stein and Day, 1983.

Shuman, R. Baird. *Robert E. Sherwood*. New York: Twayne, 1964.

"Shifting Pacifism of Robert E. Sherwood." *South Atlantic Quarterly* 65 (1966): 382–89.

Sitkoff, Harvard. *A New Deal for Blacks: The Emergence of Civil Rights as a National Issue: The Depression Decade*. 30th Anniversary Edition. New York: Oxford University Press, 2009.

Slotkin, Richard. *Gunfighter Nation: The Myth of the Frontier in Twentieth-Century America*. New York: HarperPerennial, 1993.

Smith, Tony. *America's Mission: The United States and the Worldwide Struggle for Democracy in the Twentieth Century*. Princeton: Princeton University Press, 1994.

Snyder, Jack. *Myths of Empire: Domestic Politics and International Ambition*. Ithaca: Cornell University Press, 1991.

So, Richard Jean. "Fictions of Natural Democracy: Pearl Buck, *The Good Earth*, and the Asian American Subject." *Representations* 112 (2010): 87–111.

Sproule, J. Michael. *Propaganda and Democracy: The American Experience of Media and Mass Persuasion*. Cambridge: Cambridge University Press, 1997.

Stansell, Christine. *American Moderns: Bohemian New York and the Creation of a New Century*. New York: Metropolitan, 2000.

Steel, Ronald. *Walter Lippmann and the American Century*. Boston: Little, Brown, 1980.

Steele, Ronald. "The Great Debate: Roosevelt, the Media, and the Coming of the War, 1940–1941." *The Journal of American History* 71 (1984): 69–92.

Propaganda in an Open Society: The Roosevelt Administration and the Media, 1933–1941. Westport: Greenwood Press, 1985.

Steiner, Michael. "Regionalism in the Great Depression." *Geographical Review* 73 (1983), 430–46.

Stephanson, Anders. "Liberty or Death: The Cold War as US Ideology." *Reviewing the Cold War: Approaches, Interpretations, Theory*. Edited by Odd Arne Westad. London: Frank Cass, 2000, 81–100.

Stern, Fritz. *Politics of Cultural Despair: A Study in the Rise of the Germanic Ideology*. Berkeley: University of California Press, 1961.

Sundquist, Eric. *To Wake the Nations: Race in the Making of American Literature*. Cambridge, MA: Harvard University Press, 1993.

Suri, Jeremi. *Power and Protest: Global Revolution and the Rise of Détente*. Cambridge, MA: Harvard University Press, 2003.

Susman, Warren I. *Culture as History: The Transformation of American Society in the Twentieth Century*. New York: Pantheon Books, 1974.

Tees, Arthur T. "Maxwell Anderson's Changing Attitude toward War." *North Dakota Quarterly* 48 (1980): 5–11.

Thomas, Brook. "Thomas Dixon's *A Man of the People*: How Lincoln Saved the Union by Cracking Down on Civil Liberties." *Law and Literature* 20 (2008): 1–20.

Thomas, Hugh. *The Spanish Civil War*. Third edition. London: Hamish Hamilton, 1977.

Thomas, S. Bernard. *Season of High Adventure: Edgar Snow in China*. Berkeley: University of California Press, 1996.

Thompson, Dean K. "World War II, Interventionism, and Henry Pitney Van Dusen," *Journal of Presbyterian History* 55 (1977): 327–45.

Thornberry, Robert S. "Writers Take Sides, Stalinists Take Control: The Second International Congress for the Defense of Culture." *The Historian* 62 (2000): 589–606.

Trachtenberg, Marc. *The Craft of International History: A Guide to Method*. Princeton: Princeton University Press, 2006.

Tuathail, Gearóid Ó. *Critical Geopolitics: The Politics of Writing Global Space*. Minneapolis: University of Minnesota Press, 1996.

Utley, Jonathan. *Going to War with Japan, 1937–1941*. Knoxville: University of Tennessee Press, 1985.

Vanderlan, Robert. *Intellectuals Incorporated: Politics, Art, and Ideas Inside Henry Luce's Media Empire*. Philadelphia: University of Pennsylvania Press, 2010.

Vassiliev, Alexander and Allen Weinstein. *The Haunted Wood*. New York: Vintage, 2000.

Vaughn, Stephen. *Holding Fast the Inner Lines: Democracy, Nationalism, and the Committee on Public Information*. Chapel Hill: University of North Carolina Press, 1980.

Verma, Neil. *Theater of the Mind: Imagination, Aesthetics, and American Radio Drama*. Chicago: University of Chicago Press, 2012.

Von Eschen, Penny M. *Race against Empire: Black Americans and Anticolonialism, 1937–1957*. Ithaca: Cornell University Press, 1997.

Wald, Alan M. *The New York Intellectuals: The Rise and Decline of the Anti-Stalinist Left from the 1930s to the 1980s*. Chapel Hill: University of North Carolina Press, 1987.

  Trinity of Passion: The Literary Left and the Antifascist Crusade. Chapel Hill: University of North Carolina Press, 2007.

Wall, Vincent. "Maxwell Anderson: The Last Anarchist." *The Sewanee Review* 49 (1941): 339–69.

Walter, Johnson. *The Battle against Isolation*. Chicago: University of Chicago Press, 1944.

Warren, Frank A. *Liberals and Communism: The "Red Decade" Revisited*. Bloomington: Indiana University Press, 1966.

Wasserstein, Bernard. *Secret War in Shanghai: An Untold Story of Espionage, Intrigue, and Treason in World War II*. Boston: Houghton Mifflin, 1999.

Watson, William Braasch. "Hemingway's Attacks on the Soviets and the Communists in *For Whom the Bell Tolls*." *North Dakota Quarterly* 60 (1992): 117–18.

  "Investigating Hemingway: The Story." *North Dakota Quarterly* 59 (1991): 79–95.

  "Investigating Hemingway: The Trip." *North Dakota Quarterly* 60 (1992): 1–27.

  "Joris Ivens and the Communists: Bringing Hemingway into the Spanish War." *The Hemingway Review* 10 (1990): 2–18.

Watt, Donald C. *Succeeding John Bull*. Cambridge: Cambridge University Press, 1984.

Wedlock, Lunabelle. *The Reaction of Negro Publications and Organizations to German Anti-Semitism*. Washington, DC: Graduate School, Howard University, 1942.

Weiss, Nancy J. *Farewell to the Party of Lincoln: Black Politics in the Age of FDR*. Princeton: Princeton University Press, 1983.

Wertheim, Albert. *Staging the War: American Drama and World War II*. Bloomington: Indiana University Press, 2004.

Wheatland, Thomas. *The Frankfurt School In Exile*. Minneapolis: University of Minnesota Press, 2009.

White, Sidney. *Sidney Howard*. Boston: Twayne Publishers, 1977.

Williams, Oscar R. *George S. Schuyler: Portrait of a Black Conservative*. Knoxville: University of Tennessee Press, 2007.

Williams, William Appleman. *Tragedy of American Diplomacy*. Cleveland: World Publishing Co., 1959.

Witham, Barry. "There Shall Be No Night and the Politics of Isolationism." *Theatre Symposium: A Journal of the Southeastern Theatre Conference* 9 (2001): 116–25.

Wong, Scott. *Americans First: Chinese Americans and the Second World War*. Cambridge, MA: Harvard University Press, 2005.

Zarefsky, David. *Lincoln, Douglas, and Slavery: In the Crucible of Public Debate*. Chicago: University of Chicago Press, 1990.

Zieger, Robert H. *The CIO, 1935–1955*. Chapel Hill: The University of North Carolina Press, 1995.

Zuckert, Michael P. *The Natural Rights Republic: Studies in the Foundation of the American Political Tradition*. Notre Dame: University of Notre Dame Press, 1996.

Index